The Healer

1066

THE HEALER

By

John Wright

Copyright 2018

ISBN-13: 9781439200643

To Neil

To Bessie,

Mother mine.

May it entertain and inform

John Wright

In Appreciation

No storyteller is the total creator of his tale. I am indebted to Dr. Chris Lewis, editor of the Victoria County of Sussex and reader in history at the Institute of Historical Research, University of London. It was his thesis on the Norman governance on the Welsh frontier that gave me the place in time to put my two protagonists. Dr. Lewis also did English translations into Welsh and Norman; Prof. Frederick Suppe of Ball State University, Indiana, for his background on Welsh warrior lords and family life; John Clark, curator at the Museum of London for an insight into the cleverness of William the Conqueror; book cover designers Leanne Wright and Robi Walters of London, UK and Jim Algie, my reporter desk mate at the Owen Sound Sun Times daily for more than 20 years who did the first edit and made literary suggestions that improved the novel.

And most important of all, to my wife Elaine who encouraged me to keep going handed me in the end the first manuscript of The Healer. It is a most emotional moment for an author's first attempt.

8

HISTORIC NOTE:

Two wealthy magi arrive from the Islamic far East in 1067 bearing a force more powerful than the swords or longbows of Dark Age England.

Riennes de Montford and Haralde Longshield, kidnapped from Normandy and Wales as children and sold into Silk Road slavery, return home some 12 years later. Trained in Islamic sciences, de Montford is a physician and surgeon and Longshield a mathematician in geometry and algebra.

In my three novels, The Healer, Knight Haralde and The Welsh Lords, I create a medieval world where their efforts to impart scientific knowledsge to improve the lot of their own people fails miserably because their own people cannot read or write. Here peasants in all of England are prisoners of the land and their jailers are brutes who exploit them under a system called feudalism.

In reality my novels are a prelude to a revelation 30 years later when kings and knights return from The Crusades raving about the Islamic scientific advances in medicines, mathematics, astronomy, mechanical engineering and architecture let alone the spices travelling down the Silk Road.

Though a medieval tale, my two protagonists represent a small flickering light in the darkness of Europe at that time. Such begins the enlightenment of the Italian Renaissance from such sources as the small cadre of Islamic scholars called the Faylasufs, the findings of which are later studied by Copernicus and Galileo Galilei.

And thus in modern times today is the revolution in the Western World of all branches of science.

11

Chapter One

An island is an environment in perfect balance with nature,
and so is a fine sailing vessel.

Haralde fell to one knee and drove hand and horny calloused fingers into the gravel of the sand bar where he stood on the shores of the Thames River. Through the mist upstream was London, heartland city of his long dreamed of native Britannia.

He lifted to his feet, spread his legs and stood large. Taller than most of the men of this land, his frame carried a heavy set of muscle. With his yellow hair closed-cropped, his chin clean shaved and his green-eyed aspect, he had the look of a foreigner. The crinkled skin of his face bespoke of more southern climes.

Holding out his arm, the smooth gravel pebbles streamed out of his hand like cheap coins. In truth, it was the first physical touch of his native land after more than 10 years of exiled bondage.

"Angloterre and home!" he choked, almost sobbing before the other man who stood with him. Haralde struggled to keep control of his emotions. "Begins now our new life, do thee believe?" he asked, commemorating the moment in the Welsh tongue of his homeland.

Haralde Longshield was 20 years old but had the look of an older, experienced man, a survivor of many ordeals that had tested and shaped him; a warrior's stamina and endurance.

"My dear, with all my heart," said his companion stepping forward and clapping a hand on the shoulder of his friend and brother, "though I suspect this beginning will be but more weary steps down another road. An ending is what I would prefer of all our travails."

His companion, Riennes de Montford, younger by a year, stood as tall though his body when he moved was lithe, of a natural liquid grace suggesting a soul of quieter refinement. He too was clean-shaved with close-cropped black hair and sharp blue eyes.

Their visages were cadaverous; high sharp eye bones and hollowed cheeks, which bespoke of some hunger and of a physical trial that had stressed the strength of their bodies.

In truth, they had just completed a hardship voyage from the other side of the known world. Though tired, their eyes shone with joy, of successful completion of an arduous travel.

The profile of the two merged, arms around each other's shoulders, signifying a deep personal moment.

A shout made them turn and look across the river.

A large Viking ship in the river worshipped its tethered anchor. Some 25 seamen stood in iron silhouette on the ship's thwarts and watched as Haralde and Riennes stepped out of a large leather *curragh* onto the Britannia shore.

The crew had longed for this special moment. They had furled the ship's single great sail. The vessel's high dragon head bow had been cut away. The sea boat had a tiller attached to a centre stern rudder. The Chinois marine contrivance was a superior steering replacement over the Viking single side *steorboard* oar.

A small cabin had been built aft of the mast. The bow carried a bowsprit, rigged with a small sail to enable the vessel to pass better through the eye of the wind when tacking. No fighting wooden shields carbuncled her freeboards. The profile was that of a large, well equipped Viking trading vessel, not a raiding ship.

The men crowding the side of the ship lifted their arms and saluted in a rough, male chorus, understanding deeply the achievement of the two ashore. For them all it meant they had reached safe harbour, a dream sought for years.

Haralde cupped a hand to visor his eyes under the lip of his woolen capuchin cowl. He looked across the misty river to the line of sailors, their hands fisted skyward.

"Why do they do that?"

Riennes, he who saw what other men could not see, turned and looked at the large, sea-going commerce hull.

"They bless us my brother," said Riennes the Norman. "They are happy for our dream and thankful it has led them to what they too dream as a safe place. We have honoured them again by keeping our promise of a final safe harbor."

"Aye yes," understood Haralde. "We tried so hard some weeks ago. They thought we had found it in your homeland. Remember Dives?"

The mention of that river welled up sharp images that flooded into the mind of Riennes, of excitement at first, then misery. They had sailed up the Norman coast in the face of a spring storm to turn up river and to celebrate the return of Riennes to his family estate.

* * *

"PIG TURDS! STOAT-SHIT! BOTH OF YOU AWAY BEFORE YOU STAIN THE BOARDS OF MY BRIDGE!"

A helmeted man loomed over them from the rampart above and shouted out a foulness. Riennes and Haralde could not make him out from under his war helmet and chain mail but it was obvious the man acted the lord of this stone bastion. Beside him were other armed men, family members warning them both away.

"I AM RIENNES DE MONTFORD, SON OF RAOUL DE MONTFORD AND THIS IS MY MANORIAL ESTATE!" Riennes shouted back more forcefully to the man on the wall. There were many more looking down on he and Haralde, some holding pennant banners that flapped in the wind. "WHERE IS MY FATHER?"

After 10 years, Riennes had returned home as if from the dead but instead of a joyous reception, a disappointment, nay a growing dread his dreams of a reunion with his family were being torn apart.

Weeks ago they had dropped anchor at the mouth of The Dives, a Norman river into Riennes's heartland. There, the two had stepped onto a beach and Riennes had performed the same ritual, his knees beach-moist in his native sea gravel almost at the same spot where Viking slavers had boarded and kidnapped him off a storm-tossed boat as a nine-year-old.

His shipmates standing on the gunnels of their ship had run it deliberately up onto a small tidal sand bar and had shouted their salute and joy to his homecoming, believing they also had reached safety and the end of their voyage.

Haralde and Riennes had bought horses. They asked farmers and serfs along the roads the way to the de Montford stone fortress. The poor warned them to be careful. Wars, brigands, pestilence and poverty had scarred the land clear of anything familiar.

Now sitting astride their horses on the wooden moat bridge, a dread pulled him low as he realized a stranger now denied him entry to his own manor, and in a way, to a resumption of his lost childhood.

"WHERE IS MY MOTHER? MY FATHER? MY SISTER?

"DEAD! CARRIED AWAY IN SACKS. THEY STUNK OF THE BLACK POX!"

Riennes almost sobbed at the abruptness of that reply. Haralde leaned over and touched him. "LET ME IN THEN," he shouted back. "GREET ME THAT I MAY SEE MY FAMILY HALLS AGAIN!"

"AAHH! BE AWAY!" The helmet head turned to another helmet. That man stepped up and leveled a crossbow.

Haralde yelled and they turned away from each other as a *quarrel* clicked from the bow. The feathered bolt struck the bridge between them.

As they pulled away, the great doors of the de Montford castle rumbled open and inside they saw a confusion of many armed men mounting horses. Three bolted through the doors ahead of the armed host, one a younger version of the ugly helmet above. Two sword companions accompanied him.

Rather than being hacked from behind as they fled, Riennes and Haralde turned and met the rush of the three. Riennes engaged the interloper youth while Haralde rushed by to challenge the other two.

The youth swung clumsily his broadsword of Baltic iron. It clanged against the harder Chinese steel of Riennes's short, curved blade, a weapon mated to the violence of infighting. Riennes slipped under the heavy sword to inflict only a wounding to the body. Riennes turned and left the youth bowed over, blood on the saddle.

Haralde was into the first of the two lesser. The first screamed from his sword hand almost severed from his wrist. The last sword tried to haul his mount around but Haralde and his horse smashed into the beast and sent the fighter tumbling into the filthy moat water.

An angry Riennes fled the fight with his brother, forced away from his own house. The Norman lord, his family and his sword men harassed close behind, determined to kill any heirs or challengers to the former de Montford lands. The pursuit faltered when Riennes and Haralde contrived an ambush. Experts ahorse with short horned bows, they felled and seriously wounded the Norman lord and a cousin with two bamboo arrows.

In their headlong dash back to the coast and the safety of their sailor companions, the two discovered in roadside talks with serfs and farm folk a Norman Duchy that was full of impoverished sons of Norman families and roaming horse soldiers seeking their own land and booty.

Rootless and with very few allegiances, these land- hungry victims of primogeniture had joined the bastard Duke William of Normandy in a sea invasion of Saxon Britannia. Normandy, they learned, was a dangerous place of ruthless barons and viscomtes who viciously indulged in grabbing ownerships of various manors and lands.

On the coast, Riennes fell into a depression. That reclaiming his birthright after all these years was not going to come about after voyaging half way round the world imprisoned his spirit. Huddled on the deck in the corner of their vessel, his shipmates stepped around him quietly, undone, confused.

Haralde stayed with him, urged him to believe this was not the end of his reclaiming home and hearth. When Riennes slept, he prowled amongst the sheltered fishing hovels at the river mouth in search of information and the name of the family occupying his brother's property and rights. As he did, he also searched for the prospect of more coin. Haralde's penchant for victuals and trade led him to the merchant Broulet. Local fishermen described him as an honest broker. Through Broulet, Haralde learned the superior wine of the Bordeau was much in demand by Saxon merchants.

A late winter storm had raged up and down the canalem, cutting Britannia from mainland trade, Broulet said. There was a thirsty market over there if the captain of that fine Viking trader was bold enough to take his ship through the sea rage, the trader had said, whispering the code name of his Saxon merchant counterpart. Like all merchants, Broulet indulged in gossip, rumours and for a few coins let slip tidbits of information that brightened Haralde's ambitions.

When Heimr creaked and tilted slightly, Riennes sensed Haralde come aboard. Haralde hit the boards with a thump, came over to his brother and tilted Riennes's head back in both hands, the better to command his attention. What he beheld was a face haggard, with darkened eyes slovenly of their attention to his surroundings.

This was not like his brother. He leaned over and kissed his brother's forehead. Some of the crew turned away, some in respect for the affection shown between their leaders, some repulsed by this male intimacy.

Haralde did not like what he saw; Riennes, who had come so way away, only to have his dream of home sour. "This be not like thee brother. Listen to me! I have been told a good thing. Did thee not tell me your uncle's first name was Gilbert and your aunt, Hilga?"

"Yes," answered Riennes.

"My merchant friend here says they are in Britannia with Duke William, and that William has won a great battle and now has gained an English Crown." Haralde continued: "Gilbert has his family there with William and now is a trusted one of the king."

Riennes spirits stirred. "My father and my uncle loved one another. Our families are close. If this be true, then indeed in the Creator's hands we must place ourselves and speed through this blasted storm to your Saxon kingdom."

"Yes. I have left coin in the pocket of our local merchant. He will be our ears here into any future plotting of the family occupying your inheritance. Any crack in that citadel, any stumbling by them will have us rushing in to reclaim your fortunes. Yea, but it would seem the road back to your estate now leads through the front gate of my Welsh stockade," suggested Haralde.

The effects of Haralde's story were like a dose of one of Riennes's medicants. Riennes stirred, then rose. He rubbed his eyes and gazed into the earnest face of his brother. Then he moved. He began pushing Haralde across the deck, urging him to get "this ship off its knees or keelson or whatever it is called and out upon those waves".

They hefted aboard wine barrels and lashed them onto the open deck. Unbeknownst to the wine trader Broulet, the hull beneath was crammed with a king's treasure in silks, spices, peppers, fragrances, gold, silver, gems, carpets and golden objects, cargoes from the east in such demand in Europe that Broulet would have given all the money he possessed to buy even a small share.

Now the two stood on the bar in the Thames tidal estuary with the sun burning through a curtain of white mist.

A new beginning? Or will we face another hostile family? thought Riennes. *Only upon the sea and aboard our ship have we been safe. Pray this Britannia will be our haven also.*

Their deportment was strange, dressed as they were in foreign raiments. Therefore, they had covered themselves in dark woolen capuchins cinched at the waist with silver belts, the hoods pulled up over their heads. The cloaks concealed leather cuirasses with pure silver rings that acted as a kind of chain mail. The pommels of those curved, wicked-looking swords sheathed on their backs poked up behind their hoods.

They stood in silence for a moment, two exhausted travelers who had just reached the end of a quest across thousands of miles from the other side of the world.

"Methinks brother, we had better get ashore," suggested Riennes, glancing down at a rising tide squishing up through the shale wetting his ship sandals. "I am experiencing English baptismal. A welcome ashore it should be, not a drowning. "

"Grab hold," shouted Haralde bunching the material of his brother's capuchin.

Riennes complied and they splashed through clay and muck onto a solid beach, shared laughter shattering the river peace as one stumbled.

Then they turned and looked to their vessel emerging from the mist dissipating over the river. Their shipmates dropped back down into their vessel, smoke from the mast shack curling upwards indicating a meal. Beyond their vessel, the hulls of small fishing boats waited at anchor to go upstream on the rising tide, mere undefined smudges in the fog. From the shore, it was obvious their vessel and others were in a pool anchorage, waiting to move upstream to London.

"We are not alone," observed Riennes, turning to Haralde. "Thee knew to drop anchor here with these others."

"Yea brother; as directed by our Norman merchant friend with whom we are in league. He instructed me how to enter this river, where to anchor with other vessels and to make contact with his brethren merchant who, I suspect, is right now in his counting house near that wharf straight ahead of us."

The two made their way up onto a path that lead to the wharf. They cautiously approached a strong wooden palisade higher than their heads with a solid wooden warehouse inside. The whole complex was backed against a deciduous forest of such a density the likes of which they had not seen thus in their travels.

They knocked upon a slatted door and yelled their presence. Someone approached from inside.

A wooden portal slid open. A pair of eyes examined them, first staring straight ahead at their chests, then crawling up their bodies to look at their shadowed faces, then down over their cloak sea and sandals..

The eyes widened in alarm, then disappeared. The portal was about to slam shut when Haralde whispered: "At your favour, we are here on the permit of merchant Broulet."

The eyes glared for a moment, then the portal slammed shut. Inside, a muffled voice said: "Sirrahs, wait one moment."

As they waited, Riennes poked Haralde as he leaned over his shoulder. "It is thee again. He did not like the cut of thee. Every time we get into these situations, it is thee they object to." He assumed a long-suffering tone. "So many doors shut against me. Thee are such a burden on me sometimes."

"Belay that. It is thee who is a weight on my discomfort. Will I again have to explain thee to everyone? I do not know how many times in these matters someone later whispers in my ear that my character would be held in greater regard if thee were not of my company."

Riennes grinned. From long days held in chains in the dark hold of ships, under the burning sun of open slave markets, of stumbling in the sand tied to slave ropes or pulling harness leads of bawling camels amidst a dusty raucous caravan, laughter had been their spiritual sustenance. A lightness of spirits helped chain the terror within.

Riennes heard a bump inside and the shuffle of many feet. Then, the door creaked open.

"Enter, sirrahs."

Riennes and Haralde ducked under a low door and into a sunlit stable square before a warehouse. They stopped inside a loose circle of small men, some pointing crossbows carelessly, some badly hefting short, stabbing swords.

Haralde and Riennes slid instantly back-to-back, hands moving slowly to the pommels of the swords peeking over their shoulders.

Haralde carefully flexed muscular shoulders, green eyes scanning the cross bowmen: his immediate concern. His mind rehearsed the moves to take out the two nearest men holding those weapons if they so much as lifted one towards them.

"Who are you? Are you raiders off that big Viking ship? And what do you know of Broulet?" demanded a bearded older man dressed in a coarse wool robe. The merchant peeked over the shoulder of his armed retainers.

"Who are thee?" Haralde asked in return, knowing the man was the one they sought. He asked to gain time to ascertain whether he and his brother were in any danger.

"First, to me young man," demanded the older man.

"I am Haralde Longshield, son of Stoerm Longshield, Thegn of Neury and Wym, newly arrived from the sea in that Viking ship in the river, bound for my home in the Welsh mountains," Haralde replied. "And I find this welcome of yours not to my liking."

"And I am Riennes de Montford, son of Count Raoul de Montford, a Norman Breton, yes, but no Viking."

The old man stared perplexed, digesting what they had said.

He scratched into a round red beard, then: "Thousaytru??"

Haralde and Riennes were apt linguists, having to learn many languages and a number of dialects to survive, but their Saxon was rough. Haralde was having some difficulty understanding the merchant. They kept asking him to repeat certain words as they sought to pick up the inflections and the syntax.

"Oh. I understand. Thee are asking if we speak the truth," concluded Haralde.

"I think I understand what you just said. But your Saxon is coarse lad. What is this thee you speak of? And you sirrah, I have lived and carried on business in Normandy. I cannot place your accent. Your clothing is foreign. Men of these lands you may be but I suspect you have been away for a time." The old man eyed them closely. "That on the river is not a Viking sea raider, is it? That is a knorr cargo ship. It is no dragon boat. Bulkier than most I grant you, but a sound, sea goer nonetheless. By its draught, it carries much cargo."

"Thee are right sirrah," agreed Haralde. "We have come from very far away and to reach our island home, needed a vessel like her to escape onto the open sea." Then: "Are thee Jhon, Master of the House of Muck?"

Broulet had instructed Haralde to use that title. Jhon was just a small trader of London's burgher community but a comer nonetheless. Muck used the title to endow himself with importance.

Riennes who listened closely to all men's hearts, heard ambition in this man's speech; a desire to one day have his own successful trading house. He listened to the old man's tone and inflections and heard neither malice nor deceit, only ambition. He and Haralde were safely where they were supposed to be.

"I am Jhon of Muck," said the merchant, waiving away his servants. They lowered their weapons and slowly returned to their various mercantile chores, watching over their master as they did so.

"Come with me," he said finally, and with a curl of a finger led them up a small stair, through a heavy door with a raised bar for locking security and into a large room with an open window overlooking the river.

Haralde and Riennes squatted on two stools as directed by their host. Haralde looked past open shutters at a good view of the water, at their vessel and at others at anchor on the river. Their new trading partner in Normandy had described this view to them.

Haralde glanced at Riennes whose nod was barely susceptible. This was obviously a very careful man.

He is also a man who does not bathe, thought Riennes who became aware of the closeness of the room and an offensive, cloying bouquet of body odor. It was as the same when they came off the clean, sweet sea and disembarked in Normandy. Very quickly, it became apparent to both that their countrymen, contrary to their own life in the eastern deserts, lacked in basic cleanliness.

Riennes dropped his head as to appear in deep thought, but was in fact searching for cleaner air closer to the room's floor. He glanced sideways and struck Haralde's eyes turned briefly sideways back at him. *Thee too? Yes. Me too.* As always, they thought and reacted alike.

The smell wafted up memories; the body odor of slaves packed into small rooms sleeping tightly together, of bodies, of soldiers coming into barracks at night, and the musk of fellow hands coming in from the fields they had all worked together, only water enough to slake thirsts.

Yet they were taught to use rags to wipe each other down, remembered Haralde. They scrubbed down with a shirt, sand, dirt, anything, even of the wasteful spilling on to rags of drinking water if it could be spared.

Later, Sena the physician taught them cleanliness led to good hygiene which all evidence the Egyptian had discovered promoted continued good health.

Muck appraised these two young men, so tall in stature they seemed to inhabit one quarter of his counting room. *My lord, there is something here of great import. And maybe of profit,* he thought.

"You have something other to tell me?" the old man let slip casually, one eye hooked up under a red bush eyebrow. From a sideways glance, he watched their response.

Riennes asked Muck to repeat the question. They were listening closely to Muck, trying to pick up the inflections of the Saxon tongue.

"Yes. Thee are a secret partner with another in canalem trading," answered Haralde. "Thee have three secret words between thee, none of which I am to speak out loud." Haralde whispered the words. It was a code between the traders, signaling these two young men now were to be trusted in any commerce dealings.

"How is my friend? His health is good?" asked Muck, his body posture more relaxed. "Is his beard growing any whiter?"

Haralde smiled. "I will have to watch thee in our dealings Master Muck. He has no beard as thee know. He is a younger man than thee."

Muck's head bobbed gently up and down. "We are of one accord then. Broulet is indeed a younger man than me. His wife is Mathille. He has two children. His harbour wharf buildings on The Dives River are like mine here. Young men, how can I be of service?"

Haralde nodded. "Sirrah, we have a ship loaded with wine from the Bordeau area. Master Broulet said thee would advise us on the markets in London, how the transactions would take place and that your fee would be reasonable or more to the point, negotiable."

Riennes sat quietly and watched Haralde quickly transform himself from warrior, adventurer and sailor to that of mathematical merchant trader. He marveled at his brother's grasp of the ship's exact Norman wine manifest, how he negotiated for no cost in the unloading, ("we will unload it ourselves"), the storage costs in Muck's warehouse and the greater return for the ship if the wine was sold quickly.

Haralde plumbed Muck's expectation of his share of the Bordeux sale to London wine merchants he knew. As plotted between Riennes and he, there was to be no mention to Muck of the Oporto wines hidden deeper in the hull.

Haralde knew from Broulet about the rising wine prices in the London market. Riennes saw Muck's eyes widen more than once over Haralde's acumen.

The old man sized up Haralde as a trader not to trifle with. Muck's commercial activities included buying wines through his merchant partner or through other merchants in Norman cities. He sold English wool for export to the cloth makers in the Low Countries, fish and fur to Broulet across the waters.

Right now his wine supply was deplete due to months of storms that reduced the wine trade to a trickle. He must negotiate for this cargo quickly and rush it through the night upriver to a thirsting London. His list of inns, alehouses and the houses of the wealthy would return him a fine price for this Bordeux wine.

Haralde haggled briefly over Muck's price. He gave in some but only after negotiating the right to store some of the ship's general cargo in one of his warehouse rooms, to tie their ship to his wharf for a few days and to grant his ship and their crew the need to camp in a grove immediately behind his trading building. As part of the transaction, the respite included water and food. When Haralde brought out an abacus, started clicking the beads, and came up with Muck's secret figure bottom line, the old trader's eyes seized on the instrument.

"What the devil is that machine that just picked apiece my mind," demanded Muck, instantly grasping the advantage of the device's calculating speed.

Haralde smiled, explained it was a tool used by traders in great empires Muck had never heard of.

Without even a signal between them, but on hearing their vessel could tie up, Riennes stood up, excused himself from Muck's presence. He left the room and moved quickly downstairs, across the stable yard where the workmen turned to watch him. He headed for the wharf.

He noted the buildings and dock structure were of rough-hewn wood, but sturdy in nature and well maintained. With more men it could withstand an attack by sea raiders if need be.

Muck obviously was tight with money, but spent where it was essential.

The Norman liked what he saw. Muck's employed seemed loyal to his determinations. In the stables three heavy horses murmured at him, the moist jewels of their eyes glinted out of the half light in the dark inside as they watched him pass. Lined up neatly in the yard were single-wheeled dray carts for hauling trade.

Riennes sat down at the wharf's end and looked through dissipating mist.

Riennes was a tall young male who should have been in the final stages of his youth, but who hardship and adversity had prematured into an early experienced man. By nature he was introspective, an observer of the curiosities and cruelties of life, both of which he beheld in a kind of neutral appraisal. His chief struggle was of depression. Worse, he had to contend with growing waves of strange emotions in advance of certain personal events.

Many cultures had a word for this curse. Riennes was *fey*, a prescient. Still young, he struggled to understand not only the meaning of these sharp, quick rushes of energy but also strong, accompanying images. He could not comprehend why he was the repository of these visitations. Often these flash visions influenced which direction he and Haralde took in times of peril. Many a time acting on these had saved them from injury, even death.

His more physical interests were in healing, in those things that rendered relief and happiness to the sick and injured. Thus, restoratives such as potions, unguents, plants and liquids he carried in a leather bag. Also secreted away were bundled surgical tools. That it was possible to reverse some injuries of life and bring balm to others was something in which he took great joy. He avoided pain, injury, hurt, even battle if he could.

If goaded out of his calmness, he was cold and calculating in physical action. That reserve, that control over anger rendered him deadly in hand-to-hand conflict. Their 10 years together had been full of such violence. He had become an expert at it.

Haralde was his opposite: an outgoing roisterer who physically barged his way through life, but only under the control of his intelligence and cunning.

For Riennes, Haralde had a way of balancing adversity by containing it in the exact centre of his own life forces. From the day the two first met, tumbled together as children into the bilge of a raiding slaver Viking ship, Haralde had used that as a shield to protect he and Riennes. In the midst of adversity, Haralde always maintained an inner balance. His brother seemed to negate tension and strife, to break them up as if nothing. Haralde could take even menial resources available to them and hammer them into something that protected them. The result would be a new idea or a new direction. *Out of nothing, something* was Haralde's philosophy.

If Haralde did have one weakness, it was the heat of battle. His great physical strength would get his blood up and the flames of that forge would roar out of control. So intense Haralde became in battle that he risked falling into a yellow funk, drained from drawing so deeply on his physical reserves. The blood in his body took a time to cool afterwards. Often Riennes had to step in to stabilize Haralde's spirits.

Riennes's interest in healing first sprung from Haralde's body. Forced was he to pull spent arrows out of his brother's fleshy parts and sew up many bleeding slash wounds. Stemming the leakage of wounds to the body he had learned from the teachings of Azat, the Persian bone mender and wound healer.

However, surgery, the unheard of cutting into the body, he had come to master after years of tutelage under the great Yaqub ibn Sena. Little known in the Franklands and Britannia, Sena was a great Egyptian physician who attempted things even his own culture forbid as the violation of the body sacred.

The sun was getting higher and he was hot. He undid the belt holding bamboo scabbard and curved sword and laid it across his knees, keeping it in arms reach as was taught by their arms masters, nay beaten into him and Haralde as youths.

He pulled off his capuchin and stripped off his leather cuirasse. He pulled out a small flute pipe and played. Matching the mood of the river, he composed a lilting haunting Indus *rasa* to its moving waters. The bells in each note floated across the silent currents to the crewmen aboard ship. A bump aboard was an immediate response.

Someone shouted, feet thumped along boards. Amont, their captain, bounded up onto the gunnels, hand visored his eyes toward Riennes, then waved. Their Mahamad/Christian (he practised both) captain was not wearing his rag *keffie*h. Instead, he wore a Frankish woolen cowl with ear flaps to keep his head warm from these cold northern climes against which he nattered constantly.

Someone shouted, pulled lines and a great block squeaked. Up went the great sail and the vessel called *Heimr* bestirred herself.

She ponderously slid forward, then someone shouted: "Up and Down!", the vessel's rope tightened directly over its anchor. Heimr neatly plucked her hook off the bottom. As she turned towards the wharf, long sweeps slid out both sides and the crew leaned on their oars driving her on a finer course shoreward.

Heimr meant going home in old Norse. She was aptly named. The 25 crewmen aboard now hastened towards shore, dreaming of this day as the final end of their voyaging, safe at the end of the greatest journey of their lives; safe and free; stepping from one island onto another.

Riennes put his pipe away, feeling weak from an emotional dread washing downriver from London. A tension, a conflict was imposing itself upon their enterprise. He was not alarmed. Yea, but this warning tested him.

Safe, he wondered. *Is this isle safe like Heimr? Is this isle our green haven, as was the sea our blue home aboard?* "Pray it is so here. We can go no further," he murmured aloud.

"Ren, we are here." Haralde appeared beside him looking riverward at the approaching Norse vessel, his eyes bright with achievement. "Muck says to land our crew and baggage in the clearing behind his warehouse. There is a stream there, wood, and he will supply meats, cheese, bread and a keg of ale after we unload his wine and our cargo. We are going to cut our wolf loose tonight. It is time. We have a beachhead unto our dreams."

"The cost of all these considerations, did thee offer him some *baksheesh?* asked Riennes.

"No bribe was called for. I gave him the abacus, straight gift. He wanted it very much."

Heimr growled against the wharf and the dock's sudden swaying beneath almost knocked them off their feet. There was coarse shouting from the boat and lines flew through the air. Riennes and Haralde ran up and down hauling and looping spring, fore and aft lines around pilings, pulling taut until they warped the boat snug against the wood.

Amont was the first to jump ship, thump across the boards and grab Riennes. "Are we to stay? Is this permanent?"

Their ship's captain was dark, wiry and short with a thin black wire beard around his mouth ending in a barb at the chin. He barely reached Riennes's jaw. So small in stature, yet he had a presence about him, a strength of command. Men discovered swiftly who held sway over them aboard his vessel. In their long final voyage, there were times Amont overruled decisions even he and Haralde, owners of the longship, wanted to make. Inevitably, Amont's was the correct one. They learned early they had picked a right seaman to take them across the Middle Sea and out into the Sea of the North.

Emotional by nature, Amont hugged Riennes who said: "Yes. We are steadfast. We have sold the cargo, and just as final, we have a place where we can throw down our dunnage, swallow some ale and wine, get our land legs and piss the salt out of our bodies."

"And women. Will there be warm women in this accursed cold place? I need to give them something else out of my body," demanded the former fisherman, slave and Saracen pirate.

Riennes pushed him away. "Yes, and I can feel it is a very hard thing thee are demanding," he joked, looking down at his captain's loins as he extracted himself.

"And as thee are, what would thee do my captain? Thee have been asea too long. Thee probably have forgotten what to do with it, where to put it.

"I would teach her what to do with it, eh?" Amont crackled and slapped him on the back. "Just like thee. Everyone knows your reputation for fucking beautiful women. The crew passes nights with stories of your many women. Thee taught each of them how, eh? For me, a great lover and piercer of women, I need no advice. It would be a joy to teach them how Amont likes it."

Another crew member, Raenulf the Norseman, loomed up; long blond hair but with a rusty moustache and beard: the image of a terrible North Sea Viking. There were times over the voyage when Raenulf would come rolling across the deck in a pitching sea towards Riennes. Riennes would suddenly shudder from the nightmares of his frightening Viking childhood abduction, and of rough treatment at the hands of such men who sold him and Haralde into the even rougher hands of Arab slave masters. Riennes knew Raenulf was not one of the Norse raiders who scoured the North Sea coasts killing for loot and slaves. Raenulf was a Rus, an energetic trader whose Viking ship plowed southward down the rivers Volga and Dnieper towards the wondrous markets of Byzantium and Baghdad to trade north goods for Saracen silver. No matter, he was still a Viking, albeit a mercantile one. No doubt he had sold fair slaves in his time.

"Are we lashing up here for just overnight or are we moving on. Is this it? Have we arrived?" boomed the big man who dreamed constantly of disappearing back north into some misty fjord, finding his former hearth and home and never to launch mercenary expeditions again.

"Enough have I! It is farming for me," he told his fellows who also echoed their deep sentiment. They just all wanted to go home.

Raenulf was the ship's first owner and master. If he could, he would have been their captain as he was an experienced seaman before he was boarded, carried away and forced to be a mercenary in Byzantium's foreign armies. In the voyage since Antioch, he had attempted to reassert command over his ship.

However, the shorter, darker, and wily Amont had somehow imposed his will over Raenulf. It was hard to believe it could happen, but Riennes and Haralde had watched in wonder as it slowly unfolded.

They, as owners, let Amont work his will over the Norseman. He was a better navigator than Raenulf, having piloted Arab dhows in the Indian Ocean, off Jerusalem's shore and fished in small shallots around the islands off the Lombard Peninsula. Raenulf finally begrudged Amont his place. It was Amont's ability to keep them away from the dangers of slaver pirates and sea-roving Saracens that impressed all. He dared to run to the open sea lanes into fog and deep water storms. Most seamen trembled at the thought of losing sight of land for long. This had impressed Raenulf enough that he bowed to Amont's role of leader.

Riennes and Haralde knew the secret of Amont's navigation successes. One night, Riennes had awakened for a midnight piss overboard. While still in the dark shade of the great sail, his eyes fell upon the stooped back of Amont by the centre board tiller. In the weak light of a candle under a glass, Amont dangled on a gold chain a dolphin medallion that always swam north. It cast a shadow on the wall beside him. That shadow never wavered. Amont would occasionally peer forward the bow. The tiller moved rarely in his hand and when it did, but only a nudge. That medallion was somehow pointing their way home.

He told Haralde what he had seen. Haralde gathered him close and told him the medallion was a gift to Amont from a Chinois castaway and his family after they had been thrown on an island in the Indian Ocean following a storm that had sunk their ship. The castaway was a dignitary of the faraway Chinois imperial court.

Amont fled those waters after being accused of being a pirate. He travelled overland to The Middle Sea. The magic in the black -colored dolphin brought the Arab success as a trader until he was captured by Saracen pirates and sold into slavery.

Haralde joined their fellowship, gently bumped Raenulf, threw his arm around the substantial shoulders of his friend and shipmate and shouted: "We are here to stay."

"Indeed," exclaimed the big Norseman, "and what do you want done?"

Having finished the ship's mooring, the rest of their boat fellows joined them. The crew jostled Haralde and Riennes and slapped them on the backs and a great "Hurrah!" went up from the crew when they learned they indeed had arrived. They would sleep on the ground of what for many was home, the green isle England.

Of their original crew of 35, 10 had left the boat in Normandy, taken their small share of the cargo and headed to their various homelands amidst the Franks. Of the remaining 25, ten were Picts, Scots, Celts, Saxons – and five of those were Orkney Islanders in haste to home to swear their allegiances again to their respective landlord Jarls. The remaining were Hibernians, Danes and Norse.

They all huddled together as Haralde with Raenulf knew best the lay of the goods within Heimr and the planned order of the cargo unloading.

"First we unload all the Bordeau to the warehouse space where Master Muck indicates. He has paid us a healthy price," ordered Haralde. "Then we unload our own goods in a warehouse room Muck's servant will indicate. About our cargo, protect our interests. Cover everything thee can and keep them away from curious eyes. After our efforts, our pockets will jingle tonight over wine and ale in a clearing set aside behind his warehouse here. Let us at it."

Roughhousing, they broke up and headed for the vessel. Haralde grabbed Raenulf aside. "After the unloading of the wine, thee begin on our cargo. I want thee and thee alone to take special care of the Sharp-Toothed One. Make sure that after the first of our displacement takes place, wrap the heavy brass Chinois shooting tube in oil cloth, lay it on top, then bury it under the remaining bulk of our cargo. We want no eyes to see this mysterious weapon until we so determine the time."

"It shall be done as you wish Lord Haralde," said the Norseman as he headed for the vessel to direct the others.

Haralde's brow wrinkled in puzzlement over the sudden formality between shipmate and friend. For almost a year they had lived in harmony, sacrificed religious beliefs, culture and character to achieve a superb balance in such a small space. Now, Raenulf addressed him formally. Then, Haralde recognized it signaled a change in their relationship. He was saying you are home. Assume the mantle of your family's station.

For the next hour, they worked hard. Haralde and Riennes joined in, hoisted barrels and carried bundles. The crew formed a gang to screen the Sharp-Toothed One to its hiding place before Muck came out to watch the unloading.

The merchant's sharp eyes were unable to discern what private cargo was going into his building. He grew increasingly suspicious when he could make no sense of it, other than the fact everything was wrapped and there was a lot of it. The actions of these foreign men cloaked the cargo in secrecy. His merchant's instincts told him the value of each of its parts may be greater than the cargo's total sum. It reeked of profit.

Riennes, feeling suddenly tired, dropped out and walked back into a clearing where already some of his shipmates were stacking their personal things along with food and cooking ware. Amont had the ship's great sail brought off the vessel. A long bough was passed under, then all lofted up into the trees. The sun shone through the swathes of red and white woven cloth strips of their sail roof, lending a festive air to the activity below. Even as it went up over the clearing, trestle tables and benches were set up under it.

He sat under a tree as one of Muck's men bumped a barrel of ale onto a table. He heard whinnying and the rumble of heavy horse's hoofs as two black Frisian fighting horses bought in Normandy thundered off the wharf and onto Britannic soil.

Haralde had trundled the big beasts off the boat with the coarse verbal blessings of Amont who was glad to see the disappearing rumps of those manure dropping, deck-soiling beasts.

Riennes jumped up as Haralde handed him the reins of his mount. Shipmates drew taut a piece of seal rope between the trunks of trees. Haralde and Riennes tied their spirited animals to the line, provided grain and water, petted and stroked them into a quiet, then walked away.

Haralde opened a box, pulled out a clay bottle, splashed the contents into wooden bowls and handed one to his brother.

"Bordeau. The aqua vita of your homeland. I bless thee my dear with my life," toasted Haralde with a big smile. "As was your word, thee brought me home."

"Bless thee brother and your pledge. Thee brought me home," Riennes returned the toast. The two bumped cups. "*Inshallah,*" toasted Haralde. "*Inshallah,*" returned Riennes.

He sipped but did not drink deep the draught as did his brother.

Around them shipmates filled cups and bowls with their strong liquid libations. They drank and saluted their liberty, then strangely, dispersed to sit quietly on benches, under trees or just cross-legged on the ground.

Haralde drank deep, then looked down at his wine with some misgivings. "Cloudy. Muddy taste. Your clansmen need more work on fermenting," he joked with Riennes. Haralde looked up at the sail and around the clearing at his men, at the equipment of their travels and the memories of it all washed over him and he was content.

Riennes looked upon Haralde and marveled at how his brother had fallen in love with the sea; a landsman who had suddenly discovered a different freedom on the tossing, open deep sea fields so different from open land fields.

Haralde had told him he had found the profound silence of ocean waves conducive to the refreshment of his mind and constitution. Indeed, there he could truly think and ruminate on their future.

Riennes saw him again, walking on the tossing deck six paces from the mast angling to a backstay where he would catch his balance, then turn and back to the mast. His head would be down and he would be deep in thought. He would do this for an hour, then his head would jerk up and with glee, he would seek out Riennes's attention across the deck and exclaim not about their present problems, but on something unrelated, like agriculture.

"Do you know that on the slopes of the Mother Mountains they build terrace after terrace and there they deposit the wastes of their animals, and of themselves, and that the fields are rotated every second year, while the crops of the others are switched every year.

"Is that not clever? I think on our rocky, Welsh mountain sides, we could do the same, increase yields. Can thee imagine Riennes?"

"I think your observations are delightful my dear, something to try when thee get home." Riennes would wonder how the embrace of the green sea over a field slave, a horse fighter and a lord of his lands could be so absolute.

Haralde observed the faraway look in his brother's eyes. *He is on the sea again.* Haralde recalled Riennes shouting at a monstrous fish surfacing and blowing explosive out his head in a high foul mist, and his brother, exclaiming his wonder, shouting to Amont to bring the ship about so that all could be witness to this great god creature. Down below the boards he would go, scrabble through his pack and come up with a piece of charcoal and white papyrus and sketch, scratch, sketch.

He could see it was not the machinery of pushing a boat over the water that was a wonder to his brother, but rather of the deep sea well and the creatures down under.

Riennes would shout down the ship of some sea creature surfacing and demand of Amont or Raenulf that they relate to him what they knew about these beasts. Riennes had a deep wonder of how natural things happened: how a fish could breathe water, how a bird could work the wind, or how when a milkweed burst, it blessed a butterfly.

A silence settled on the clearing. Heads dropped as a deep fatigue struck their company. They were tired, deeply tired, not just from the last hour's labour but also from the escape from foreign enslavement and the long voyage. For the first time, they did not have to be afraid. For the first time, they could release their fear.

Free they were from servitude and abuse. They were exhausted, but they were home. They were individuals again.

Haralde looked around and understood. He too wanted to lay down his soul and breath.

"Thee do not drink," noted Haralde. "Are thee tired?"

"No," answered Riennes as he bowed his head. "I am feeling undone."

"It is upon thee?" Haralde asked of Riennes's affliction.

"Yes. It comes down the river."

"From London?"

"Yes. There is a conflict. A tension. We are to be tried."

"Is it bad?"

Riennes looked at a fire someone from the House of Muck was setting in the central clearing. "I do not know!" He turned and looked into his brother's face. "It will be as before. A storm which we must weather." He set his cup down. He rarely drank when this dark befell him. These emotions mixed him up as it was. "We must hope my uncle Gilbert is here in your London. My uncle can convince all I am his nephew. He will patron us through our troubles."

Haralde formed a fist and lightly bumped his brother on the top of his head. "I am glad. Now, put your black curse to rest. Stop trying to protect us, at least for this little while. Turn your affections to us, your shipmates. Rejoice in their freedom."

"Aye brother," affirmed Riennes. "Come, let us salute them. We owe them much."

Separately, they went through the ranks, joking, bumping their drinks together, rousing, toasting the health of each and lifting spirits. Riennes was sparing in his sipping but expansive in his affections.

The ale and the wine began to flow. Their fellows shook off their lethargy and began to roust out their hopes and long-suppressed dreams. Shouts of: "When I get home. . . ," and, "I am going to buy. . . ," echoed under the huge canopy of the sail and trees.

The drinking, shouting, and planning went on for a few hours. The day ended and the fire became more central to the community of their spirits. The shadows darkened. Some began to stagger a bit on the way to the ale keg.

Neither Haralde nor Riennes saw any reason to put a clamp on it. No wine drinking was ever allowed aboard; such was the disciplined agreed upon in the initial escape. Now, these men who had been asea so long needed to get roaring drunk. The two knew it would not take much drink for them to collapse in a stupor and hug the earth because this crew now was exhausted. The brothers would watch over them through the night.

Then a shout went up as merchant Muck and his retainers pulled up into the light of the clearing on horse-drawn drays loaded with the Frank wine.

Muck pulled Haralde and Riennes aside. "I am on my way to sell my wine to my London buyers. I shall be pulling wagons and selling wine throughout the night. By dawn, I will bear heavy coin," he said. "Here. It is my first payment to you. I have miscalculated and come up short. I am much burdened. Here is my note for the difference. I will be here in the morning with the balance," he said offering the two a small bag of some heft.

Haralde and Riennes looked at each other, then Riennes nodded to his brother.

Haralde turned to Muck. "Thine gift of the ale and wine and this resting place in the clearing signal to my brother and I a good heart. Disturb not yourself. Trust grows within us for the House of Muck."

Muck's eyes twinkled at the House joke, but he also marked the comment as a promise of the future in his mind.

"There is no doubt within us we will settle all in the morning. Agreed?" posed Haralde.

Muck smiled, nodded his head and handed over the bag of coin. "I am off to make my living. Trade here is controlled by William's pack of avarice, high-strung dogs. I am but a lowly mongrel who must move quickly through the gutter of night to capture his morsel. Tomorrow we will talk," said the trader hauling body bulk back up onto the cart. He waved as his booming drays full of sloshing barrels melted into the dark.

Riennes kicked an empty ale keg upright and Haralde plunked a stool in front of it as the keg was set down beside him. Every arm stopped heaving drink to lips and every voice went silent as Haralde's hand went into the bag and they heard the 'tinkle' of coin.

"Ronan, Kearns, Jerome," shouted Haralde, calling forward the Hibernians of their crew. They had expressed a wish to leave early and find their way home immediately.

The three who had been sold as youths on the Dublin slave market brought forth leather pouches into which Haralde poured a stream of coin. While Heimr had been anchored in the river, the three had shouted at a small passing fishing boat where onboard they had heard their native Gaelic spoken. The helmsman, father of three fishing sons, gladly agreed to weigh anchor and take the three home with them with the tide the next day on promise of payment for their passage

"We give thee a greater part of the share of our total cargo because we do not know at this moment what the final return will be so that you head home with fat purses. Are thee content?" asked Haralde who rose and approached them.

"We are!" said the three who jingled their leather purses with big creasing smiles.

In good cheer, their fellows raised cups and wished their Irish mates fair winds home.

"Good," answered Haralde who along with Riennes embraced them as fellows, the kind of free men found only on ships.

On it went with the others who wanted solid wealth poured into their hands before they all fell under the stupor of drink.

When the Norseman made to step forward also to claim coin, Amont kicked the giant in the knee to quiet him: "Be still you bugger. You will not quit my grasp just yet. Delay and more will be given you."

Riennes stepped up to all the faces pink with fire and drink. "Be that agreeable to all?"

In good cheer, their fellows raised cups and wished all a quick journey home.

Haralde's eyes went around the crowd of men, then stopped as Amont's eyes locked with his.

Amont then nodded, as if reading Haralde's thoughts, saying in effect: *You and Riennes, I and Raenulf, will settle the greater largess later.* Good enough, mused Haralde to himself. He had plans for Amont, and Raenulf.

Riennes and he had been taught to think beyond the present. Thoughts led to plans and plans led to preparations for the future. "Sit quiet in the day, be contemplative," Sena had taught them. Sena was a member of a scientific movement called *The Faylasufs* which believed al-Lah was pure reason and thus a pure thinking man could find and measure God on earth. He taught them not to abdicate one's will to al-Lah as many Mahamads did. Through many afternoon philosophical discussions, Sena had enlightened the power of their unleavened intellect. It did not matter they were Christians, that they also took instructions from a Nestorian Christian priest. "Same God," Sena had taught them. "Just a different path of enlightenment. Room has al-Lah for all his creatures."

A captive like them, but now a renowned physician in the Khan's court, he had taught them the art of quiet primary reasoning. "Not only understand a thought, but thee must break it into pieces. Only by tearing it apart and examining its primary components will thee understand the why of it, the how of it and where it will take thee. What made up that thought will tell thee the forces of life that are playing upon thee at that moment. When thee can do that, the dread of life will pass away and thee will be masters of your mind and thus of your every day circumstances."

One day the two broke down and wept. They told him all they ever dreamed about was escaping and going home. Sena had smiled, and told them if they would open up their minds to him, he would show them the pathway to their freedom.

One central thought that grew was independence through knowledge and wealth. Sena encouraged them to nurture that idea, that it would get them on the road home. "Honour, duty, service – think about these things and they will lead thee home," Sena taught. "Honour thyself and those things thee hold dear; fulfill your duty to a lord or king or a beggar and serve to protect the most high and the most low."

Honour, duty, service - it resonated deeply with Haralde. It became his code, his principa. He applied it to everything as he grew up, even to the accumulation of wealth. The mechanics of trade they learned in the deserts and on the steppes of Asia where they served their king, the Gher Khan, ruler of the 10 walled cities of the Kush.

When they gained favor as young men, they were elevated to high rank. Quietly Haralde engaged in trade on his and Riennes's behalf. He relished creating something out of nothing. He liked taking emotions and information and forging them into knowledge, loyal friends, new acquaintances, purchases, private wealth and security.

He sought security outside the glow of the Khan's good graces. Their personal wealth grew along the Silk Road and over the Spice Route Sea. He tucked that wealth away in little desert holdings guarded by merchants paid annual commissions. They had lost some of it.

They anticipated that. However, out of the land of the Seljuk, the Persians and Mahamad tribes of Asia, they had carried away much of it. It now was stored in Muck's warehouse. As well, they had hid some in secret places in the Caliphate Cordoba of al-Andalus along the north shore of the Middle Sea.

Muck described how he carried on trade across the canalem. Now, it had been interrupted of late by the Norman occupation.

Haralde was very much interested in all Muck's telling of the situation in this land. He needed to know what lay ahead for Riennes and he. They were to soon mount their horses and begin their trek to find the long mountain trails that led to Wales and home.

However, an idea niggled away at him. He wanted to establish a trading partnership here with Muck before they left.

Haralde knew with the support of Muck and his cohorts, trade could be founded and wealth secured here. He would talk to Amont and Raenulf later because he needed their skills.

Honour, duty, service. A similar credo had guided Haralde through his youth.

As a boy, he remembered the great sword in his father's main hall that governed his family's conduct in Wales. It bore one word: Honour. His own two other principles would follow later, seared upon him in the forge of his short violent life to manhood.

He sighed over this code. He had struggled to conform to it. Often he had failed, and memories of those failures welled up inside him.

Riennes sat down directly in front of him and their eyes locked. Riennes said silently into Haralde's eyes: honour, duty and service yet will you do it.

Haralde Longshield, son of a Saxon Welsh lord, walked early in the morning through a misty clearing in the greenery of his home land and marveled at the color and smell and moist lushness of this place in late spring.

Just eight months ago he was sitting in the heat and sand of the brown, burnt land near Jerusalem in Outremer, smelling his own body sweat and scraping away layers of bugs biting and sucking at the moist corners of his mouth and eyes.

Shortly after, he was on the great blue sea, storm tossed, wind scoured and wave battered, fearing the sight of any sail lest it be Turk or pirates in chase to enslave them all again.

Now, he was walking his kinland; a soft place smelling of wild things, of moss, and dew and rich black earth and deliciously stinking peat bogs and marshlands of the nearby estuary. His legs vanished beneath his waist when he stepped down into a low bog hole full of puffing mist. Standing under a big oak, he leaned against it, looked up into the green arbor and marveled at the swollen tree's arms holding up that massive green. All simply overwhelmed him.

They had trees in the desert and the mountains but nothing like these. He had thrown off his warrior's clothes and now wore loose leggings and a green silk shirt with no sleeves, muscular arms free to enjoy the cool of the early morn. He walked alone, trailing his hands through spring flowers and over bushes and rocks. He tried so hard to remember it all, to use the scents and sights to provoke his childhood memories. He broke a branch, smelled, then tasted the rich sharp sap. Then he picked up a wooden stave and bent it in an arc over his head feeling the strength and resilience of it.

In a hidden adjacent fog, Riennes of a Frankish magnate family and owner of extensive Norman lands and orchards, bent over, plucked some leaves and berries, squeezed the juices and carefully tasted them.

He pulled the roots of some ground-hugging plants and wondered if they would have certain medicinal qualities. He stuffed samples into a small bag he carried.

He wore a blue shirt of comfortable silk to match his eyes and the soft true sky above him. As he walked, he examined bugs and listened to the songs of various birds, cataloguing everything. If only he could spend months in such luscious surroundings. The joy of discovery was upon him and he felt the first warm waves of wonder welling up in him. In fact, he was happier now than at any time he could remember in his life. His constant sadness dissipated somewhat in the joy of it all.

He was smiling as he came around a great knurled trunk of an elm and bumped into Haralde who was shuffling backwards looking up.

Aaaah!" whispered Riennes, dropping his bundle and sliding out his cutting kandos which greeted his two hands with accustomed familiarity. The slightly curved and exceedingly sharp sword sang as it came clear of the self-made leather and bamboo scabbard.

Haralde turned to face Riennes with his kandos already straight out and pointing at him.

He cursed his brother: "Begone from my sight you donkey shit!"

"Get thee from my presence or I will condescend to cut your balls away!" threatened Riennes.

They initiated the opening gambit gracefully. There was a 'ting' and 'sing' as the two swords touched ever so lightly.

The two stepped slightly around each other, sometimes each under the other's arms, swords singing as pure as silver in a deadly ballet. In no time, they were across to the other side of the clearing, slashing and cutting, parrying and thrusting.

Riennes turned and exposed a defenceless back and Haralde, seeing an opportunity, slashed his sword down as if to cleave Riennes through skull to genitals, only to be deflected sideways by Riennes's blade, which Riennes had brought over his head in a smooth defensive move. With the miss, Haralde turned half away knowing his brother's counter would swiftly follow; a move that would surely sting the blade in his hand. It did not. Instead, Riennes's kandos whispered across Haralde's throat. The air from that pass he felt on his skin. *Damn!* Instead of force, Riennes had used the touch of air. *He always fools me.*

The two practised the non-lethal art of air's breath. It was the martial teachings of their master, Taigen, a Manchura monk whose name meant tranquility. The monk had instructed them in the singular discipline of killing but not killing. Only the blades were to almost touch each other in offensive and defensive moves. Upon the sacred body of one's opponent, the blade was forbidden to touch even the skin. Get past your opponent's defenses yes, but the cut must be no more than a breath of air passing over the victim.

The blade must stop a breath of air away from the skin. It was the real object of the ritual; to practice the killing thrust but to do so only to the air around each other. Kill, yes if you must, protect yourself, yes, but the greater honour to you is mercy. Life is sacred; preserve that sanctity.

Taigen's teachings dictated their every move as they worked against each other. If the blade of one was to touch the skin of the other even lightly, both would end the ritual immediately, recognizing the offending one was not of his best that day, that there might be a mental distraction corrupting the exercise.

The long, sharp, single-edged steel blades were mated only to the hands of Riennes and Haralde, fitted each to their mental outlook and physical stature. No one else would be able to wield them and expect to get the most out of their deadly nature. If Haralde and Riennes were to switch weapons, they would be unable to perfect air's breath.

The weapons moved so fast in their hands that at times the steel became almost invisible. Of the two, Riennes was the finer practitioner of the form. Even as they fought, something inside analyzed each move, suggested improvements. Haralde was brasher, more aggressive, wanting conclusion. For him, the effort must produce a quick result; for Riennes, latent perfection was the goal.

The two danced and pirouetted around the clearing, fighting up a sweat. The action heated their bodies until the alcohol, food and the frustrations of the affairs of their world leaked out and beaded into a moist slick over muscles. There was the sound of the swords and the "uhhh" of exertion. They grunted, but breathed easily. Then, on the bank of the Thames where the marshland hid a small gravel beach by a clear pool of water, the action stopped as suddenly as it began.

The two bowed, slid their blades slowly, reverently, into the scabbards behind their backs, then laughed the laughter of two lost boys now found. They stripped their clothes off and ran naked down the bank to plunge into the water in a spray of silver.

Haralde plunged in and dug up soft river bottom. Riennes attempted to follow, only to be stopped by a ball of muck which blackened his face. He fell back into the water, to come up with a ball of his own that he hurled at Haralde and the lucky missile turned Haralde's yellow hair into the black of Riennes's.

When the laughing and rousting slowly ended, they climbed out and lay on a grassy patch in the sun. For awhile they sat quiet to dry in the day's growing warmth.

Then: "Shall I tell thee something most secret, most disturbing Ren? Something that must remain only between us?" asked Haralde.

"My dear. It shall be a thing private between us," Riennes whispered softly, as if to keep it away even from the trees leaning over them.

"I feel much disturbed Ren. I feel disjointed, like my parts, my arms, my legs, my head, my soul, my heart, they are adrift from each other. I feel I am becoming unhinged, that nothing fits. I have not felt this way for a long time. Home are we in this wonderful place, as rich a place as I have never seen. Yet, I feel estranged."

"I am feeling much as thee." Riennes was silent for a moment, then he went on. "I think it has to do with us having lived in another place in time, what was then our home. Now we are back at our other home. It is that our real house is unfamiliar to us. We are not connected yet. Let us sit quiet a moment and dwell on this."

"Pray, I think thee are right."

Riennes walked over and sat under a small hanging tree, crossed his legs and sat immobile. Haralde crossed to the other side of the clearing and found himself a place to sit cross-legged, and for a quiet time the sound of birds, of insects, of a soughing wind and whispering leaves flowed softly over them.

From the teachings of both their Arab healers, philosophers and their monk master, the two cleansed their minds, examined their thoughts and prepared for the conflicts they knew awaited.

In the clearing under the great sail, last night's smoke and the morning's mist mingled. The Irish were gone. Haralde and Riennes said goodbye to a few more who were leaving within hours.

The two then departed by plan.

Riennes vaulted over the high thwarts of Heimr and dropped down onto the deck to find the big Norse gathering loops of line binding himself in a body rope vest. Amont was sitting in his usual station in the stern. His dark eyes watched Riennes drag the big sea Norseman towards him in what was obviously to be a brethren's conference.

Riennes faced them both and with a growing smile, said: "Thee did not join in last night's celebrations. And thee did not partake of your share of the wine monies. What is amiss?"

Amont glanced at Raenulf who nodded.

Amont bestirred himself. Before his very eyes, Riennes watched his small friend grow upwards, outwards to become that captain of Heimr he knew so well.

"I wish none of it. I wish instead this vessel as my reward," he said in his control voice. "And if the vessel were to be mine, I would convince my second here not to go home to farming but to join me in sailing and trading, something we both know best. We feel we not only carried out our promise to get thee home but that we bore the greater responsibility for your lives in doing so."

Riennes was silent for a moment, then said: "We all agreed to share all wine cargoes equally."

"Raenulf and I bore an extra burden, one that could not be shared by thee, by the others, by our command of the vessel. We carried the responsibility for your lives, your safety, and for the deliverance of your great wealth wrapped in those bundles and bales and chests stowed below but now in yon warehouse. And Raenulf and I agreed to protect it. What we ask is no great thing of Lord Riennes and Haralde. Thee have yours, thee are secure. We have nothing. For us, the sea is everything. It is our home, our livelihood, our soul."

Amont paused, then resumed. "It is as written in the greatest book in the world: 'Verily, in the creation of the heavens and of the earth and the succession of night and day and in the ships that speed through the sea' . . . ."

" . . . . 'with what is useful to man," finished Riennes, "and in the waters which God sends down from the sky giving life thereby to the earth after it has been lifeless, and causing all manner of living creatures to multiply thereon, and in the change of the winds and the clouds that run their appointed courses between sky and earth: there are messages indeed for a people who use their reason."

Startled, Amont said: "Thee know the voice of al-Lah?"

Riennes rose. "I have memorized some of the *ayats* of Mahamad's Qur'an. This is a favorite of mine."

Amont was deflated. What control as captain he thought he could cast over his sponsor was lost him. He thought he knew men and most especially this crew.

After almost a year at sea, the realization that Riennes had managed to hide something of his character from his captain shook somewhat his resolve for the boat.

What happened next destroyed it.

Mustering his command voice, one Riennes used often in leading his company of Gher Khan's one hundred Turkic horse warriors into a fight, he said: "Thee cannot have the vessel and thee must not expect such a thing. Haralde and I have long-term plans for it. There is something of our new homeland whereupon Heimr will play a role. We have further voyaging planned."

Amont's voice was but a mouse compared to this wolf. Amont's inner voice warned to take heed, that this young lord and his brother were deeper personages than he had assessed.

"However my friends," continued Riennes, the steel coming out of his voice and his hands coming to rest on both their shoulders, "thee can own part of it."

"What means this?" asked Raenulf who had just witnessed the putting in place of his captain, something he had tried but failed to do in this voyage. As well, their plan to float this request by the two young lords and to head north over the open sea to his Dane land had now gone aground.

Amont shook his head: "No! Thee refuse us, we who sea roved for thee. Then, thee ask us for money. We have no wealth to buy into her. Nor will I share command of her."

"Nor will thee. Hear us," said Riennes sitting them both down. He outlined Haralde's observation of how little trade was being carried out, how it was controlled by a family pack of greedy men and how basic the goods were between England, the Frankish lands across the canalem, the Low Country and Ireland. There was not the volume and sophistication of trade here as found in the East along The Silk Road and around the Roman Middle Sea.

Yet, there was opportunity here, one that could bring security to each of them. So, they would form their own pack of traders. Amont would be captain and ship cargo around these northern waters. The little captain would own one quarter interest in the vessel and in any cargo he and Haralde shipped out. He and Haralde would fund cargoes Raenulf and Amont saw value; more if Amont found his own cargo. The cabal would provide the captain a house in London or along the river. If the enterprise proved successful, Amont would command his own ship or ships.

"Raenulf, this enterprise involves thee if your heart was here, but thee are bound to your hearth in the Norseland."

"Yea, but your offer is tempting my lord," pondered the big sea man scratching into his red beard. "I might delay if I could return home with chests of gold and gifts. I like your words."

Riennes turned to Amont again. "My captain, thee will return one day to your heartland home, but thee cannot go as a beggar. Thee will one day sail into the port of your soul but it must be in your own ship bearing your own wealth."

Riennes dropped his voice to a beguiling, soothing, convincing drone "Come join our enterprise, both of thee. Thee know us. Thee will command all things maritime. Muck will handle all things mercantile. Money will be what Haralde and I must contribute to support both. The mantle of this enterprise fits us all well."

Defeated in his demand, Amont dropped his head and stared at the deck. Then, he shifted his fate and his future as he always did when the winds went around suddenly and blew upon his ship of life from another quarter. Change course or flounder.

A white smile creased his dark brown sea face. He swung and faced Riennes.

"It is a good offer," he said and up came his wiry arm. Riennes and he shook, each grasping almost under elbows.

Riennes grimaced as he did the same with Raenulf, suffering the Viking's powerful grip.

"However, there are two conditions that must be met," added Amont.

Taken aback, Riennes warned: "Mark thee Amont, we will not suffer any sudden unreasonable whims in this partnership."

"Nay, my lord. It is simple. We are without money by not accepting our share of the wine sale . . . ."

"Thee shall have it, thee and Raenulf . . . ."

"Ah, good. And more to our joint enterprise, Raenulf and I have been over the vessel since the cargo has been off loaded and we have found she is taking on water. Planking is sprung. Toredo worms have been at her. We need to careen her somewhere to scrape her bottom, replank and recaulk."

Riennes shrugged. "I know naught of ship problems. This is your command so yours to solve. Come. Let us join Haralde and Master Muck. We must now forge the tools that strike at our common problems, and shape our future."

"Agreed, but give us pause for one moment my lord," said Amont. "I need a word with my friend here to fathom his intent. We will join thee, Haralde and Master Muck in the blink of a camel's eye."

Riennes looked at Raenulf, then Amont and suspected something else was in the wind, but acquiesced. "Done! In a moment then join us in Muck's upstairs room."

Then he was away across the deck and over the freeboard like a sea breath. Amont was reminded of the lightness and firmness of Riennes's physical movements; no wasted motion. *How is it that I did not see that in his intellect?*

Raenulf turned to Amont. "I said I will stay, but it will be for a short time, or, if I know of a cargo we could propose that will afford us a good return in my homeland. And there you will find the wood, iron works and the best, right boatmen to properly careen and repair her,"

"That is a good idea. We will explore that, but right now I want a word with thee, to caution thee. Let us from now on husband our thoughts, information and feelings. Keep them to ourselves and away from sirrahs Riennes and Haralde, at least until we are more sure of ourselves in this enterprise of theirs."

The blond Viking put a finger and thumb into his beard and twisted some into a course wool knot.

"By the gods, I do not understand you at times. Why, if we have just agreed to join them."

"That young Riennes, he can be a danger to us. One should be guarded around him. I did not see it before. And I now suspect Lord Haralde the same."

"Then let us back out of their accord."

"No, no. These are dangerous times. Best let dangerous men lead us. To be a lesser in the middle of a pack of these wolves, well therein lay our best protection. Just do not let one bite thee."

"Such a tale cannot be true. Only a *jongleur* conjures up such tales, exaggerates it in songs to entertain the rich in the great halls of the kings of the known world."

Muck stood up and walked around shaking his head in disbelief, stopping to glance at Haralde as if to catch the young man out; a smirk here or a secret smile there that hid a joke or some mischief. Then surely, a falsehood it would be.

They were sitting in Muck's upstairs counting room. Muck had drawn a table over to the open window overlooking the Thames to take advantage of the light. A candle in a holder sat unlit in the middle of the table. The penurious, pinch-penny nature of Haralde's trader heart appreciated such economy. Candles were expensive and not to be wasted.

The young Welsh traveler had just finished telling Muck his life story.

"And yet I look at you, your strange clothes, your foreign ways and rough speech and I must concede, as you have been honest with me in our dealings so far, that it must be true, that you are upstanding."

Muck stood over Haralde and after asking politely, fingered the young man's green silk shirt. Then he fingered his own drab brown heavy woolen jerkin.

"Silk. In my lifetime, I have had only a small kerchief of this exquisite cloth. Beautiful! Do you know young man you are wearing a small fortune on your back?"

Muck sat down and Haralde was again enclosed in the same air of body odor the merchant carried about him.

"A four-legged animal as big as a house with a nose so long he drags it on the ground?"

"An elephant. And an orange horse with a neck so long he cannot reach the ground but grazes on the grass of the trees. To be found nowhere else in the world but in the Mahamad lands south of those we passed through," asserted Haralde.

"By the true heart of St. Hilga, the world then is a wondrous place. Oh, to be a young man, to travel and have my mind open by the mysteries beyond the far horizon. And here am I an old stick grubbing out my days in this little river world," snorted Muck.

Haralde's eyes dropped to the small chest Muck had banged down on the floor beside them. How his ears picked up the tink of coin even inside a wooden box was always a source of joy to him. "May I say your grubbing seems to give thee such heartfelt returns."

"Ah!" snorted Muck who burst into laughter and placed it onto the table. "As so agreed, the final payment for the wine." Muck opened the chest, pulled out some leather bags of coin and pushed two to Haralde, then closed it and put it away under lock in a heavy box. "Your arrival here was well timed. Not only is the canalem a maelstrom interrupting shipments of Frankish wine here but London's thirst is great."

The stair door opened slightly and Riennes was silently before them. His appearance was so sudden he startled the old merchant.

"God's truth lad. Do not do that to an old heart," admonished Muck. "Knock or make some noise when you come into a man's home. A mouse could not have been as quiet."

Riennes apologized and heartedly wished the merchant a good morn as he sat down. He laid his scabbard on the floor at his feet as Haralde had done.

Riennes said to Haralde: "They have agreed to join us; but a moment they will be here."

"Wonderful. This is good. Master Muck, our captain and his mate will be here whereupon we wish to make a proposal to thee, to enter upon a joint enterprise that we hope will intrigue thee. Secretly, we wish to partner with thee on something that will stand us all well, rich cargoes and bags of coin."

Feet thumped up the stairs, a knock on the door followed. Riennes ushered Amont and Raenulf in and introduced them again to the elder merchant who welcomed them and bade them sit on extra stools.

They gathered round the table as if conspirators plotting to bring down some royal house.

Haralde said: "This is our company Master Muck, solid, honest, an able band of men. They have held together under adversity, and then by a loyalty that I vouch for will endure for what we have to propose."

Haralde described to Muck an idea, one where Muck would operate a new trading business out of his river location. Rather than running his business solely on waiting to make first contact with ships coming up the river or chartering ships to take goods down, he would buy and ship trade goods on the Heimr.

Amont and Raenulf with their skills of hauling long distances on the open sea would work with him in rounding up goods and getting them to such trading partners across the channel as his friend Broulet. With Raenulf 's knowledge of the Norse lands and Amont's along the southern shores of al-Andalusia and into the warm Roman sea, his business would have access to more markets with greater diversity of goods, create more demand and thus attract more customers to his house.

"And Riennes and I . . . .," Haralde stopped. He looked down at Riennes's hand grasping his arm.

Haralde looked around to find Muck looking down. Hooded, closed was his countenance.

A short time into Haralde's proposal, Riennes had felt Muck stiffen, and then cease listening. The old merchant's attention had slipped away and was entrenched behind a defensive mental disinterest.

Riennes looked around the room, and then partially understood. First, the setting was wrong. Surrounded by three big young men and a small, bearded, swarthy, foreign-looking seafarer, all people Muck did not know two days ago, he was feeling beset.

Of course. By nature an elder merchant like Muck would be reserve, conservative, guarded about his business, considered Riennes.

"Master Muck, we apologize," said Riennes. "We have done this wrong. It would have been better if we had taken the time to get to know each other before launching into this. Sirrah, thee feel we piggy back onto your business, do thee not? Thee think we ask thee to invest your money in our business. And thee do not even know us."

Muck sat up, looked around and sighed with relief. "Yes young lord. Many have come to me with invitations to join my business with theirs. I have been successful because I have avoided empty schemers. I believe you are fine young men, but you know nothing of trade here."

Haralde, moving into Riennes's lead, also apologized.

For a brief moment of memory, a time, space, color and smell washed over him. The light and smoke of perfumed lamps cast a golden sheen across the blue waters of a marble pool. The light shimmered on the face of trader and caravan organizer Hammid who sat on satin pillows across from him sucking on a water pipe. Beside him sat the Turkish spice merchant Bashir and the Cathayan Li-Muyin, owner of many houses of silk. All sat together in their rich and brightly-colored silk or cotton raiments. Behind, the young women of Haralde's pavilion moved in and out of the shadows serving green tea and *bhang* wine. Hammid, a Muslim, drank the tea while his other two guests sipped the wine. The heat of summer was upon the city of Baktra below but Haralde's pavilion was up on the upper steppes of the Pamir Mountains and his partners in trade had stopped in their travels to enjoy the cooler temperatures.

For two years, these three had enjoyed the gold and gems Haralde had bestowed upon them for transporting and warehousing their wealth near the shores of the Middle Sea. Now, they were warning him their enterprise must end because the long caravans and sea routes for moving silk and spices and hard wealth like gold, rubies and emeralds were being interrupted by great collapsing empires, pirates and armies in civil wars crashing one against the other. The power of the Seljuq Turks would soon overwhelm Gher Khans little empire.

"Whole tribes are at the throat of tribes. The times are corrupting our plans. I told thee that one day such times would befall us and our partnership must dissolve," said Hammid. "We must withdraw into our estates. Thee did refuse to believe we would fade away one day and start again some other place in time. I told thee in the beginning our enterprise was momentary, that all things change." The other two nodded in agreement. "Thee are young and therefore brash. These things thee must accept. Let us seek our fortunes in another time."

The soft vision of that last secret circle of rich foreign men saying goodbye faded into the huddling of their conspiratorial five around a rough wooden table in a dim odorous room on the banks of the Thames River.

Haralde took in the rough, dark brown woolen jerkin of Jhon Muck. "Master Muck," said Haralde. "We do not wish to enter into business with thee. We wish in fact to offer thee the chance to enter into business with us. This would be separate from your own here. With your knowledge of local trade, we wish thee would lead us. The risk and any loss would be all ours. The gain, if any, thee would share in."

Riennes smiled to himself. Haralde was again taking bits and pieces and twisting them together to make something desirable, of something out of nothing.

"Go on young man. I give you my interest, but mind you, at this point nothing more," Muck said with caution.

"Have thee ever heard of a *karum*. No I did not think so," Haralde creaked back on his stool and gathered them all in his eyes to better watch their expressions. "It is an ancient eastern way of carrying out transactions and arranging trade without paying actual coin."

Haralde explained that in the land of the Nestorian Christians between the Roman Sea and the gates of Chinois far to the east, silk and spices, horses, gold, gems, sandalwood, incense, unguents and slaves were traded across vast deserts and mountain by merchants and moneylenders of various tongues, cultures and races. Through common secret symbols, merchants use chits of credit and debits to restore some actual coin. Later, maybe once a year, maybe two years they meet to balance the transactions.

"But how do you buy and sell? You do need money sometimes to . . . . ," pondered Muck.

"Well, for example, I leave a small chest of silver with Broulet in Normandy," said Haralde explaining, "and I come here from there with a chit of credit which I present to thee. I use it to debit from your chest of silver and thee add a certain surcharge for that so I can go about my business. Thee eventually will meet or send that chit to the Norman merchant in Normandy either for cash or to put on account for thee. One day thee might go to the Norman and settle accounts with him. Each time the original investment is paid up to the chest with an added surcharge, it grows. Also, thee yourself may know of a good transaction but are short of cash. Thee use our coin to buy a cargo. Thee eventually return the original investment to the chest with the added charge."

Amont stroked the black barb on his chin. He had himself borrowed money from a karum. It had worked out fine. He understood Haralde and more.

Muck's eyes flashed with fascination. "And with this karum, no brigand, no pirate, no King's tax man can rob us of all our coin. The money never travels on drays or ships or on one's person."

"And the king's tax collectors will have a hard time assessing how much thee are worth. And if thee are taxed or robbed, remember some of your wealth is elsewheres. Thee have money on account across England and the canalem. It gives thee time to recover. Thee can draw on one's credit and recover after such dire times," explained Haralde. "Like a game of chess, there are so many other combinations."

It sounded complicated but Muck grasped its underlying simplicity. The abacus. That's how to keep track of it all. *That is why Sirrah Haralde made a gift of it to me.*

"This karum. How do you hold the pieces together?" asked Amont.

"Trust. Greed. That is the secret web that binds us together successfully. If one cheats, word flies like wildfire to the others and his loss of reputation will doom him to poverty. The transgressor will lose the money he has on account elsewhere. Without it, nothing works. Except greed and fear. The others visit that upon the scoundrel later. Together, we become wealthy or at least secure."

Conversation died. In that space of quiet, Amont hummed a little tune of contemplation and tapped his cheek and barb. Then: "You would hazard your money in these times? I think the dangers of these days will tear the web apart."

"My captain, thee know better than to say that," jumped in Haralde. "Riennes and I placed our lives, our fortune and the dream of home in your hands. The loyalty of thee, Raenulf and our ship, it was the best investment we ever made. Now let us make some money out of that loyalty. Like bees to honey, let trust and greed bind us to the sweet security of more coin sticking within the folds of our heavy purses."

Raenulf smacked hands on his knees and roared with laughter. "Lord Haralde. I think it is your tongue that is sweet and sticky. But you have caught this bee in your honey bag. I am for it."

Amont cackled and bobbed his head up and down a couple of times. "A fool I would be not to have a ship under me and to grow heavy with coin. Confusion spawns danger but it is in times of such disarray running men make money."

Muck blushed. He was truly infected with the good feelings these men had for each other. Always, he followed his instincts.

Those instincts now drove him to these men and the bosom of Haralde's proposal.

"You have presented yourself well young men. I have watched you from aside. I have preyed upon your discourse, each with the other, your regard for each other, and your respect for your leaders. I had hoped to pick away the flesh to find some greedy hearts or pull apart the bones of your enterprise to uncover some putrefaction. I have found none," said Muck. "Your company is sound. In fact, I am taken aback at the sight of two such young fighting men involving themselves in trade," said Muck. "Today, here in this country, warrior soldiers think only of violence and brutalizing. And then they go rob someone to pay for their bloodletting. They can't even read. But you four, you are much ahead of everyone here in the pursuit of a better life."

Then his voice became very serious. "But before I agree and before we think to assemble this karum, mark me well. You may want to change your mind. Amont said the times are too dangerous. He speaks the truth. This land, your homeland, is a place now of much cruelty and death Lord Haralde. We Saxons are a conquered, brutalized people.

"Any wealth any of us possessed has been swept up by William, the bastard Norman duke. (Muck glanced nervously at Riennes but continued with his narrative), now crowned King here. He has stolen away even our language. Only the Norman tongue is spoken by those of position. A Saxon word dare not go beyond an Anglo's hearth."

With the afternoon sun sparkling on the river, the five scraped their stools closer as Muck unraveled a tale about kings and princes of the church, coronations and falling crowns battles and crashing armies, scepters and swords and history rising and falling. They were told when Britannia's King Edward the Confessor died, an argument arose over who would be the next king.

The Witan Gemot, England's wise council of the archbishops of Canterbury and York, bishops, earls, abbots and powerful thegns chose Lord Harold Godwinson of Wessex to succeed Edward. That inflamed Duke William in his Norman bastion. William claimed Edward had promised and publicly named him his heir and that Harold had promised to honour the old king's wish. While Harold was crowned, William brought together his warriors, organized an army of kin, warlords and freebooters from across the former Viking Duchy. He conspired with an abbot named Lanfranc who gained the ear of the Roman pope. The pope blessed William's claim. Other ambitious leaders across the sea saw England as a gem ready to be seized. King Haralde Hardrada of Norway, sensing affairs were timely for him also to strike, launched a Viking fleet and landed near York. Saxon's new King Harold marched north, killed Hardrada and drove the Norse army away. Thus ended the last Viking dream of another King Cnut over all England.

However, history played cruel with King Harold. Exhausted, his army suffering from heavy losses, Harold had to return quickly south to engage William who had landed with a large army. In a great battle near Hastings, King Harold fell mort, some say from an arrow in the eye, some say under a host of charging Norman horse fighters, and William was crowned King in London.

"What followed was the sweeping away of all Saxon high born, lords, ladies, lands, holdings, herds, fields and fiefdoms," lamented Muck. "Not an earldom, not a shire, not a village but will have a Norman master or a favorite of the plunderer king in the year to come."

Muck was silent, then quietly he warned: "These Normans know naught of trade as we do. Their daily pursuit is to find money to outfit themselves in fine clothes, buy the best of armour, swords and those heavy fighting horses, those destriers. A merchant today follows a hazardous trade. They and the church demand all your coinage, tax you if they can but by God outright steal it on a grand scale if they must."

"That is why you leave in the night, to do business with your buyers when most of the king's men are home abed." guessed Haralde.

"Ah, yes, or unbeknownst those same tax men got besotted in some night tavern on my wine after looking for it and me all day."

The four conspirators grinned over Muck's joke on his tormenters.

"Are thee with us then Master Muck?" asked Riennes.

"Yes, but that is the easy part. Now, how are you going to fund our karum?"

They all looked to Haralde. Riennes watched as a lightness, a mirth passed over Haralde's face.

"Like you Jhon Muck, we will get the money from the king and his subjects," answered the young man.

"How?" asked the merchant.

"Press us no more. Let us say they will pay handsome sums for what we have, that which is safely in your storeroom."

Muck boomed his fist on the table. "Why you young foxes! That is why a condition of the Bordeau wine sale hinged on free warehouse rent for the rest of your cargo. That is where the greater value lay."

"Yes," beamed Haralde enjoying the coup for his goods. "However, if thee feel we have unduly tricked thee, gladly we will pay a small rental fee if and when we sell those goods."

"No, no. The deal was fairly struck man between man. It stands," laughed the merchant. "You are a step ahead sir. Now more than ever, I am glad to be in this with you."

The five gathered closer around the table and for the next few hours they worked on the details of their enterprise. In the late afternoon, they filed down the stairs and into the sunlit work yard. Amont and Raenulf took their wine money back to the vessel. Muck asked Riennes and Haralde to tarry a moment.

When alone, the merchant turned to them. "I must warn you both to look to your affection one for the other with deeper resolve. You are a Saxon Lord Haralde. Lord Riennes, you are a Norman. That meant nothing to either while you struggled for years to get home. Now, you will find home a place not of your liking where Saxon is set against Norman. You both are about to be sorely tested when you go on to London."

The two young men looked at each other, then both nodded their understanding. "Thee are a wise man Master Muck. I have observed thee but for a short time but I know your heart is good and thee mean us kind," answered Riennes. "The intent of your words we will take seriously."

"Now I must get about my first business," ended Muck. "These lazy helpers of mine will sleep away my profits if I am not watchful."

Haralde and Riennes moved off quietly and headed for the clearing to see to their dark horses.

As they fed and watered the two blacks, Haralde mused on Muck's words. "What Master Muck said, is that why it has come upon thee my brother?"

Riennes stopped brushing his mount, then: "I do not know," he said of the depression that weighed on him. "I will have to think on his words. We are strangers here in this place we call home. There are forces afoot we must guard against."

As Riennes said these words, he observed a look of concern fall across his dear friend's face. He paused a moment, then leaned over and stiff-armed Haralde's shoulder so firmly he rocked his brother off balance. "So to stay on my good side, step carefully around me and use not hurtful words about me to strangers, especially if she is beautiful of form. If she has a less attractive sister, t'would be well between us if thee take the ugly one."

"S'truth I have to take the better looking one off your hands all the time before thee disappoint her," smiled Haralde as he flung a handful of hay into Riennes's face.

"Thousayfals."

They worked a moment longer on their animals, then Haralde asked: "Is it London? I know thee felt concern before we had our talk with Muck. It is not because we are Norman and Saxon, is it?" He looked at his friend. "Ren. I think it is London."

"Yes. It must be that thee are right."

Haralde leaned his cheek against the warm flanks of his horse. He eyes went pensive. "For me, it is the road after London. I fear the pathway to the frontier land of the March from whence I am sprung. I carry a memory of someone saying, maybe it was my mother, maybe it was my father, that the Welsh are wilder than the beasts of the forests. Mother, father, are thee still alive? I fear they may not be."

Chapter Two

So many life roads to take; only one will choose you.

Haralde slipped a Mongol leather boot into the stirrup and lifted bodily into the saddle.

Riennes rose quickly beside him on his own big dark horse. Then he grunted and swung grumbling back out of his saddle down to the ground.

"Brother?" asked Haralde leaning over curious to observe Riennes

"Too long. Stirrups need adjusting." he answered. Under his breath he grumbled to himself: "Too long at sea and too long away from horse."

Unbeknownst to both as Riennes swung back up, the stirrup was new to England. The Moors introduced it when masses of their fighting horseman swept into the southern duchies of the Franks a few hundred years earlier. Up until then, wars were fought by foot soldiers overcoming foes with shield walls and spears. The medieval western world adopted the stirruped horse and it proved to be the decisive tactic that won William victory over King Harold's foot soldiers.

Stirrup and better saddles created a horse nobility for northern men of bigger stature and of brutish mentality. The politics of brutality and the economics of a horse culture resulted in a dark system of enslavement– feudalism.

Haralde and Riennes were expert desert, small horse warriors. However, instead of spears, they were trained to fight with the short, horned composite bow, to ride swiftly by their enemy and to shoot rapidly from a distance.

They could in one swift motion bend their bow back over their knee in full gallop and string it tight. Their skill in rapid but accurate shooting as taught them as youths by desert horsemen was unmatched anywhere else in the world.

"I fear if we have to ride this rocking beast all day to this London of yours, I will likely be sore of thigh and ass," started Riennes. "If that happens, I shall demand a certain personage be ready to rub with great gentleness salve upon those nether regions. And I will also demand he be sympathetic for having inflicted such discomfort upon my person."

"Now Ren. You bitch like a braying ass."

"For your own sake, pray not a sore one in the end."

About to reply, Haralde's mouth slowly closed again. He had been hit clever. "Ho, ho, ha, ha!" Haralde's deep belly laugh washed over them both. Whenever Riennes struck him funny, Haralde' enjoyment of his brother's wit would go on for minutes. If it were particularly good, Haralde would roll it around for hours inside his mirthfulness. Even later, Riennes would sometimes hear him ruminate intimate over the joke, then would follow barely within hearing a soft rumble of enjoyment.

They touched their knees to their two mounts and moved forward, again picking their own pathway, their own adventure along the road of the day. They left Muck's yard in the early morning, eager to see the countryside and reach London in good time to seek out their future in the city of Haralde's dreams. For days they had sat working together, hammering out their company.

Muck's sharp trading acumen was subjected to a shock when Haralde and Riennes supplied just a small portion of the company's capital - a small chest of Byzantium gold. "My God! Our success is assured!" the master trader had exclaimed.

Then they swore an oath that their's would be a brotherhood of burghers based on trust in each other, that it could not work any other way. If one so ever betrayed that trust, their fortune would be forfeit and their character taken down in the community of their own interests.

Then Haralde and Riennes did something that underscored what they meant by 'character taken down'.

"We have joined together as we are all men of varied parts and may I add, abilities," Haralde had said leading them all out of Muck's trading buildings into the open area where they were camped. Haralde pulled out a copper pence with a hole in it and pinned it to a tree trunk with a wooden peg. Riennes went to one of the two-wheeled drays which held all of their personal property and pulled out two bows.

Haralde joined Riennes at the far end of the clearing. Riennes handed him one of the short Eastern horn bows recurved at each of its ends just before it joined the end bone nock whereupon the bowstring was strung. It was a three-foot desert warrior's bow; a wooden core with strips of buffalo horn glued over the outside. Once an arrow was released, the horn material urged the bow to return to its restful form. The outer curve was bound with animal gut to give it even more force. The inside belly was kept moist with oils and fats to encourage an ease of the pull back into the tension D-form of a bow loaded with arrow.

The two men loosed dark-feathered bamboo shafts. There was a disturbance in the clearing air. Everyone heard a series of solid wood thuds into the tree's bole. Instantly, the trunk bristled with feathers around the brown coin.

Some like Muck walked over and examined the results; six bamboo arrows clustered tight to the coin with some arrowheads nicking off pieces of the copper's outer circumference. Whatever, it was deadly shooting said the company's mental consensus. The message of those six foreign arrows around that coin was undisputable.

"We will protect our enterprise against any thief who thinks to rob us," a severe Haralde spoke as he and Riennes pulled out the six arrows and stuffed them into their belts at their waist.

Deadly. Yes, and for us as well? thought Amont who glanced thence to Raenulf.

Raenulf caught his eye and remembered what the captain had said of these two earlier: best let dangerous men lead us. *Just do not let one bite you.*

Nonetheless, the demonstration fortified the Dane. He would delay going home. Making coin with a group of men who would filch it from others, through action if need be, warmed his basic raider nature just fine.

Thus, Amont and Raenulf along with their remaining crew and a pilot supplied by Muck slipped Heimr from the wharf the day before to catch a rising tide. Muck instructed them to drop an anchor in the pool below the bridge to London, then in the evening to strike down their mast and slip under that bridge. At the end of the western wall of the city in the mouth of the Holborn River, they were to drop anchor and to disappear amongst the many marshy islands and to hide from the eyes of king's men.

They were to wait until they saw a lantern shoreward. At that signal, they were to slip in and tie up under a building overhang, Muck's wharf revetment outside the city.

In that cargo were gifts to King William from the Khan, or whoever was the English king at the time of their homecoming To present them to the king, Haralde and Riennes had to get inside the city, locate Riennes's uncle and come under the sponsorship of a powerful Norman noble family. This would grant their enterprise immediate protection.

"Harry, watch for any flags or family insignia's in our travels today. My uncle's is a red castellate on a green mount. I remember. It was the stamp of his character to have it flutter whenever he travelled formally."

Muck had recommended that to slip into London unnoticed, both needed to dress in local clothing; dun-colored jerkins with leggings and leather footwear.
However. Haralde over ruled Muck, suggesting they enter London dressed as important men, thus would a Norman common hesitate to encumber their progress into the city. They lashed their kandos in bamboo scabbards under saddles partially hidden under riding blankets.

"The city and environs are full of king's men, soldiers and their vassals who are overbearing and full of bombast," Muck had warned. He said the king was in Normandy putting down a rebellion and rumored he might return any day and they were to be at hand to greet him. "They will pick at anyone they feel is not appropriate and should be upbraided. Take care. These are dangerous men."

Both marveled at the heavy forests as they trotted along. Being desert and mountain horsemen, the huge forests, trees and brushes seemed to hem them in. At first they felt crowded, somewhat threatened by all this cover. Used to the opens, it was easier to spot an enemy and gain time to prepare. They feared an ambuscade here. They had left bows, quivers and small shields back onboard. They had decided to travel and then enter London with only the short kandos for protection.

As the morning warmed, they began to relax. Haralde enjoyed the sudden bark of delight from Riennes as they flushed small animals along the way or watched wild fowl exploded upward out of the flora before them.

Shortly they broke out of the forest cover and into farmland. The path they were on went on its way close to the river while a more travelled road appeared on their left.

"Which way?" Haralde asked.

"Your adventure. You choose brother."

They entered onto the more travelled road. Haralde wanted eagerly to see populace, life, traffic, to take the measure of his people.

As they clip clopped along, they marveled over this new richer land. Mud was everywhere; under their horses' hooves on the road, by the wayside and in the fields that became ever more cultivated as they moved inward. Dry earth was not a thing of this place; instead a rich, moist, muck. There was a tang in the air, so rich, redolent in their nostrils. So foreign but so invigorating.

Riennes took out his flute pipe and peeped them along the road. The notes chimed about the rhythm of life. The times were light, alive. Like the river, he felt the surge of the earth and whistled in joy over its richness, to the fecund opulence of it. Then, he broke off suddenly, not able to wrestle down the turmoil upon his spirits.

"I'm sorry brother."

"Thee cannot hold it from you?"

"No."

"Lean on me. I am sorry it is upon thee. But that now is past. Thee have warned us. We are ready. I will take the burden now," said Haralde as he leaned over the space between them, a hand onto his brother's shoulders.

"Find in your own way and your own time the road west of London. Get us home, and it will absolve your depression. It will be no more than a thing to sport about."

The land was so rich. Green and true and tender was this north sea land. They stopped and looked at a little Roman carved stone beside the road. It was a *montjoie,* to mark a distance to London.

On a rise, they looked down upon a farmer wrestling a plow and horse in a May field. He clucked and rippled his reins. Another farmer up ahead wore dirty, drab clothes. He moved while flinging seeds from a sack across his chest. With a steady rhythm, his arms salted the earth with seed. Flocks of birds followed, swooping down into the furrows, preying upon the pellets freely offered them. Behind, the plowman followed riding a horse that dragged a device weighed down by a rock that closed the furrow to protect their labour.

Haralde stood up stiff in stirrups, absorbed totally with what he saw. Agriculture and animal husbandry was a chief interest of his and he took in the farmer's every effort. In the Gher's hierachery, Haralde was elevated to horse master, an expert in breeding excellent blood stock.

"Ho there sir. What seed is that thee fling so freely."

The farmer stopped in his labor. Haralde observed deep caution, nay almost fear in the man's eyes. Finally: "Barley, peas, oats and seeds go into the earth here my lord," he answered quietly.

"Ah," observed Haralde and called the peasant over. He questioned the man, now obviously in a state of agitation, about farming practices hereabouts. Haralde's quiet tone and his obvious interest quieted the man who answered more readily.

He was absorbed in the farmer's discourse of how the fields were rotated every three years, one to lie fallow, the other two for planting.

Riennes shouted: "Harry!" Riennes waved from the top of a nearby hillock, nodding ahead.

The walls of London loomed through a smoke haze. Haralde rode up and took all in. The true reality of his young life drifted out of the dream vision ahead. There before him was the central city of his father and his mother. He had never seen it as a youth, only through tales of his parents.

Ahead was a Saxon town. Its Roman walls had been restored, such as they had seen with other Roman cities around the Middle Sea. The city village spread across two major hills. Many smokes drifted upwards behind the walls.

There were men and horses everywhere, most in encampments on this side of the river but west of some royal buildings. There were nags, working heavy horses, field horses and warrior mounts. Some rode their destriers, the kind they saw in the fight before Riennes's Montford estate in Normandy. These were king's forces, summoned it seemed to be on hand for some purpose.

Riennes looked at the armed activity. The road was clear to a wide wooden bridge a mile ahead of them. The bridge over the river was wide. They could see a stream of traffic moving across it, two wagons passing each other easily over The Thames River.

"There are soldiers at that gate," observed Haralde. "With all this activity, how to get past them all without being noticed and halted. We have to get ourselves and the cargo aboard Heimr unnoticed past the king's men and into London." He turned to Riennes, raised his eyebrows and made an inquiring funny face.

Riennes kicked a foot out of a stirrup, crossed his leg before him and studied the ground and activity ahead for a while. Then a memory flooded over him of similar circumstance, of when they were children and faced the sudden terror of separation. Riennes solved that by losing himself in the milieu of a big busy caravan.

Finally: "No. Not unnoticed. Noticed. Really noticed. We will become as they. We will fit in. We have done this before. We will not try to sneak past. Let us be part of the very tumult, such we did after the Tarzig slave market when we were sold apart, remember?"

"I do." Haralde smiled, partially over the memory and partially over Riennes's ability to come up with quick solutions to difficult enterprises.

They were babes still. Boys. Slavers sold Haralde on the Turkish market to a caravanser as a piece of goods to be sold far to the east and Riennes south to a rich merchant family in Egypt. Torn apart, they bawled. That night Riennes, before manacled in an iron shackle, bolted out a narrow open door and ran through the night crying for his friend and brother and fearful he was going to die because he did not know if he was running in the right direction under the desert moon. He caught up with the Haralde caravan that morning. He exposed himself daily over the next week under the legs of the braying camels and openly moved around in the general noise and tumult of a caravan. Too busy, everyone thought he was part of the mass movement eastward. Haralde fed him out of his small food and water allotment. Sometimes through charming a drover's wife, he was fed bits of her family sustenance. No one noticed the extra slave. Weeks later under Haralde's constant confirmations, his master scratched his barb. He searched his memory, plumbed the depth of his shrewdness and his confusion over how he had acquired this additional valuable property.

Riennes slung his foot back into the stirrup. "We have newly arrived from Normandy with an important message for my uncle Gilbert. We are tired, exhausted, in much haste and will not suffer the impediment of a lowly gate guard."

"It will work if your uncle is in these environs," suggested Haralde.

"Will not matter. I suspect the de Montford family name as one amongst the powerful of Normandy will influence against any interference," suggested Riennes.

"You lead then."

"No. It is your road. Your dream."

"Can not get there without thee. Always is and always will be."

"Aaaah! You have a way of tiring a man right out," sighed Riennes.

"When we get back to your Normandy and walk your road and through your gate, I will remind thee said this."

They nudged their beasts forward and moved towards the southern end of London's big bridge. A few peasants appeared on the road with animals and foodstuffs for sale in the big city. Those they approached quickly scuttled off to one side to make room for them to pass, avoiding any eye contact with them as they did. Their actions were those of men on a special purpose.

A little man and a little family appeared just ahead of them and he did not give way. There was agitation and the raising of voices. A small woman shielded a little boy behind her while at the same time she clung hesitantly to her husband. The man, fear in his eyes, shrugged her off and stepped out into the middle of the road.

"Please my lords, can you help us?"

The man was trembling. He was in near panic but desperation pricked him on.

Haralde and Riennes pulled up, looked into the foliage behind the family suspecting an ambuscade, then down at the man who had taken off his rag cap.

"What ails thee sirrah?" asked Haralde.

"Lords. Help us. My wife and son, we are starving," pleaded the man. "We have been without food for almost a week." "Then go home," said Riennes. "Thee look like a farmer to me. Can thee not grow food for yourselves anymore?"

"Lords. We can but we were driven from our homes and farms as were our neighbors. The king drove us off our land, took our belongings, our animals. Please sir, a coin, any coin. Food. We need food."

"Why would the king do that?" Haralde asked joining in.

"We were told he had set our forest lands aside as a deer forest, for the royal family and friends to hunt in," answered the farmer. "We were driven out. We have been on the road for weeks, begging, looking for a place of our own."

"There is none?"

"Only under trees and bushes. Please, just one coin. We need to buy food now. Strike me down, whip me if you must, but please leave a coin in the dirt for your pleasure."

Riennes looked at Haralde, then dug into his side bag and pulled out some copper coins. He leaned down and offered it.

"Belay that a moment brother," said Haralde, interrupting with a hand on Riennes's arm.

"He asked us for help Haralde." Such direct appeals demanded, they believed, an immediate and positive response. They had adopted this way early in their kidnapped days. Once, when they too were starving and had to beg and were afforded a gentle and positive response. The kindness had struck their young psyches so deeply, they vowed always to return in kind.

"Aye, but coin will only quiet their bellies once. He and his family need it daily if they are to survive," answered Haralde. "Give me a piece of that charcoal and some papyrus on which thee are always sketching things."

Riennes complied by digging into his small travel bag, then watched as Haralde scratched a symbol down on the scrap. He showed it to Riennes who immediately recognized a symbol of their new company.

"Here. Give him this and your coins."

Riennes handed both down to the man whose fear turned to surprise.

"What is your name sir?" asked Riennes.

"Wilf my lord. And this is my son Wilbert and my wife Emah."

Haralde looked upon the wife and boy. Her eyes were full of terror and desperation. Silently they pleaded for mercy. It was a look all too familiar. As soldiers, they had to harden their hearts to it when their commanders or the Khan ordered a city populace put to the sword. It was a life they had led. Only through a suggestion whispered by Haralde into the Khan's ear at a quiet time was he able to end the barbarity. Imprison the populace, he had posit. By selling them on the slave markets of neighboring city states Gher Khan would realize substantial subsidies to the royal coffers. It was so ordered.

"My name is Haralde and my friend Riennes. Remember those names. Madame. Take your man and your son and go into London," said Haralde enfolding the woman into the solution. He narrowed down on the man. "Master Wilf, buy some food and make your way outside the walls to the western end of the city. Look for a Viking trading ship with its mast down and an odd-looking squat captain of swarthy aspect in charge. His vessel will be warped tonight to a dock under an overhang. Give him this linen. Tell him two men gave thee this and it is your warrant to help unload the boat. Thee may have to work well into the night but for your efforts, thee are to be paid another coin.

"Wife, thee will cook your remaining food for the captain, crew and yourselves at the end of the loading. Then, thee are to sleep aboard the vessel tonight, to awake to any new employment your captain may put thee to, for which he will pay thee in coin again if thee are loyal to his demands. Do thee understand?"

"Aye my lord. Western corner of London, Viking ship, no mast. Foreign-looking' captain. Present this. Work through the night."

"Aah! A bright man. Good for thee," said Riennes smiling down at the family. "Thee must knowWilf, we are king's men. But no harm will come to thee at our hands. Go about this secretly but with an honest heart and good things may happen."

"Thank you my lords. Thank you. You are a light to us on this our darkest day," bobbed Wilf shuffling back into the embrace of his family.

"Tell me. Why did thee stop us? Many went before us," questioned Haralde.

"It was Emah my lords. She said there was something in your faces as you came down the road. I acted. She was afraid, but I acted," the farmer answered.

Riennes looked at Haralde who nodded back.

"Thee do us honor wife," said Riennes, and Haralde bowed to her for both of them.

"Master Wilf, Emah, Wilbert, cleave to each other in these unsettled times. Your partnership is the strong bond that will see thee through," instructed Riennes.

"We are off. If luck is with all of us, likely we will see each other again either tonight or on the morrow," said Haralde, pulling his big black back to the road ahead, Riennes right behind.

As they pulled away, they heard: "God bless your good hearts." Emah immediately clapped a hand over her mouth for seemingly to be so bold.

The two urged their mounts to a trot and then a gallop. They shouted the form of their opening gambit to each other as they rushed the gate. They approached the people on the bridge, thundered up onto the wooden apron and pushed against the crowd ahead.

The bridge was wide. Carts rumbled side by side. The crowd shouted and parted before mounted men moving in haste amongst them.

As they thundered toward the gate, Haralde quickly cast his eyes downstream. There were a few ships of Viking cut anchored in the pool below, but he was relieved to see no Heimr. Upstream, he saw the old Roman quayside and wharves broken and decayed. Some vessels were pulled to pilings with planking on the top to aid in offloading. He could not see their vessel. He hoped that bode well.

As they approached the gate, he saw some fishing shallops pulled onto the gravel shore before London. The tide was out.

Ahead two soldiers stepped out dressed in breeches and leather jerkins over which they wore *hacquetons*. The hacquetons also protected them from a slight sword attack. They stood before Billingsgate, the bridge entrance into the city, and attempted to cross spears to halt their progress.

"Stand away or we will ride thee down," shouted Riennes coming up to them. "Stand aside for important king's business."

Riennes's authoritative rush upon the soldiers prompted them to jump back. However, a mounted soldier wearing a chain mail hauberk from his head to below his belt with a metal cone-shaped helm on his head brought his horse before them and shouted: "Hold!"

Riennes and Haralde slowed their horses but kept moving against the guard, forcing him to make a quick decision."

"My name is Riennes de Montford. My companion and I have newly arrived from Normandy. With the king still in the duchy, I bring dispatch to Gilbert de Montford. Is he here?" demanded Riennes, using his command voice with its inflection of irritated impatience by one used to being obeyed instantly.

The mounted guard's resolve suddenly began to melt away.

"Hurry man! I have not the time to tarry," Riennes's horse pressed back that of the mounted guard.

"My lord! He is encamped back across the bridge. However, he most likely at this moment is at the Great Hall at Westminster Abbey west of the city wall," replied the horseman giving way.

Riennes surged past him and Haralde bumped him as he passed. Like a ship's bow, the guard fell away as a wave before their urgency. His confusion was flotsam in the wake of their purpose as they passed into the city.

London under the new reign of William was still a Saxon city. Haralde pointed out to Riennes places where the city's occupants had fortified the ancient walls. The remains of Roman walls such as these they had seen repeatedly in the east.

However, inside they saw not a city but a collection of villages; Saxons built mainly wood, thatch and mud-daubed wattled homes. Many cities the two had invaded and conquered had mighty stone edifices, buildings and even brick and tiled homes. Some had palaces with fountains and administration complexes with stables and guards that humbled even them. This city of his dreams proved very pauvre.

They looked inside the thatched house to see a sunken floor overlaid with rushes. Some had natural brick earth floors. In the corner of one, they saw a figure in the gloom working in front of a small oven baking bread. Smoke misted out of holes at the top of these houses. In the back were pens holding pigs, sheep and cattle.

It seemed all inhabitants raised many domestic beasts, mostly for their own consumption; geese, pigs, sheep, goats, cattle, fowl. Besides domestic, they saw carcasses of wild deer, hare, ducks and fish. There was a lot of trading with the surrounding countryside, but little coinage.

Inside London's walls were two Saxon villages spread across two major hills and each had their own markets, called cheeps. Haralde and Riennes plodded along a rough grid of roadways. Everywhere there were muddy streets. There was Ironmonger Street and Poultry Street; a street named for every kind of trade and business. The streets meandered. There was no set pattern. Water, blood and slops ran down an open gutter along Fleshmonger Street. A fat burgher in rich clothing stood before some pens. He scratched his finger in the air, then pointed to his final choice. The two sat their horse for a moment as a butcher strode forward and roughly hoisted a pig out of the pen. As the squealing pig wiggled and twisted in his arms, the butcher took a big knife and sliced it open. The blood and the intestines uncoiled in a pile of offal onto the cobblestones. The two had never seen so much raw meat in one place. Rats dodged and scuttled through the legs of people who came to buy.

The air was rank with the stink of swine, cattle, urine and manure. Slops lay heavy on the streets and human waste looked for a runoff.

A dark foreboding seized Riennes. All of this human garbage was host to some terrible menace he sensed, threatening, if not now, then in a time ahead.

The two stopped to watch and listen to the hawking voices crowing at farmers from shops and even benches. They watched as an ironmonger sold axes to groups of farm families in from the countryside.

Other buildings further on in what appeared to be a wealthier part of London were made of stone pressing close over the street. Now they were in the town proper. They were about to turn west on Cheapside Street when they observed just to the north a huge earthen depression in the ground.

At that moment, a monk in a long brown wool frock to his sandals came shuffling along towards them. Both leaned forward to observe him keenly. This was their first encounter with a Britannic Christian holy man so they took in everything about him. The man was short of stature but fleshy. The frock was stained below his many chins, the mark of a wine imbiber. The dome of his head was bald, the shaved tonsure of a member of the cleric. That left a ring of spike hair sticking out around his head over his ears. A light brown hemp-rope belt cinched not so tight at his ample waist hung down and ended in two huge round rope knots that fibers formed into round monkey-faces. Those faces danced, bounced on each knee as he strode towards them.

They hailed him.

Rolling along, deep in thought, the monk looked up. His first reaction was to angle away from armed horsemen of the king. Yet again, he stopped as he beheld two young men, one with a leg over his saddle and the other with chin in hand appraising him.

One had yellow hair, the other black hair with bright eyes and a smiling face. There was something appealing, something of a presence about both of them that caused the monk to tarry.

The two introduced themselves respectively, not knowing how to address a man of God in this their own home country.

He found them to be amiable. "Ah. Two tall young travelers. I am Monk Petras. How may I be of help?"

When they asked him what the huge depression was, he replied it was a former Roman amphitheatre. He told them, however, Londoners now dumped their garbage and refuse in it.

"Tell us monk. Where is this Westminster Abbey?" asked Haralde. "Is it a small church of some religious import?"

"Nay my sons. It is the holy navel of this country," answered Petras. "There Aedwardi Regis died," he said in Latin, and seeing their confusion, switched to Saxon. "Edward the Confessor, the gentle king. And there was King William crowned and there now is his royal court ensconced in the Great Hall."

"Which way?" asked Riennes in Norman, testing the monk's education.

The monk smiled and acknowledged in Norman French: "Go west along this road then pass out of the city through the western Ludgate. There you will see a road and a causeway passing through a marshy area and over islands. A few miles will take you to Thorney Isle, and your eyes will not mistake the great church of Westminster and its adjacent Great Hall. However, be careful."

He said there were many horsemen and soldiers guarding the area as many lords of the noble houses of Normandy and Britannia now gathered there. "The air about those environs is very volatile I have been told."

"The king then has his royal family in a palace outside the city of his subjects?" asked Haralde.

The monk looked around him, then appraised their looks. "You are obviously not king's men, but foreigners by your speech. No king like William was going to live in a royal manor in the middle of his subjects for fear they revolt against him."

"They are then inclined against him?" Haralde speculated.

"London resisted him in the beginning. It took a promise by William to open these gates. Therefore, the king's court always goes where William goes; Westminster, Gloucester, his exchequer or Winchester, the old Saxon city just south of this city. He likes it there because it is close to Normandy. Just in case, you see, they should rise up again. Therefore, William always has one foot close to London, one close to Normandy. He just does not wear the Britannic clout with a lot of comfort, yet. In fact that is where he is now," the monk answered, looking upwards from half-closed eyes to see if they saw past his politically safe description of the present ruler.

Haralde smiled, and Riennes nodded his understanding.

They thanked him and moved on. They entered narrow and busy ways. Here the buildings were two storeys high and at times the upper floors overhung the street. The two laughed when slops poured out an upper window soaked a group of men below who, with language as filthy as their baptism, scurried for cover.

Then from an open space they saw the largest building in London, St. Paul's Church; a huge wooden barn-like structure with a sharp high peaked roof that dominated the skyline.

Disappointed at first by its rawness, Haralde's evaluation of his city began to change as he rode along and watched his countrymen at their daily drudgery. Raw yes, but he sensed a vibrancy, a vitality. The trading frenzy by craftsmen and merchants of all types began to prick up his interest. The broad river outside, the ships, this brash, noisy, busy walled city essentially by the sea, why put together it was undoubtedly a growing trading centre. He could only guess at the hinterland beyond from where London drew its raw goods.

"Prospect. I see good prospect for us here," Haralde observed, leaning over and smacking his friend's shoulder.

"Amongst all this chaos? Back home there would have been order to this; tradesmen in that quarter, artisans there, and farmers at their outside markets. This, this is falling apart under its own dirt, drowning in its own excrement," lamented Riennes.

"Ah, but what fun putting it back together proper. It would profit one much in the trying," exhorted Haralde. "Look at what we are seeing. The burghers of this town look prosperous, like Muck."

"And like Muck they all need to jump in the river. Is there not water enough in the Thames for a bath by even a few of them? Holy man or not, that monk and his stink needed to be dipped and baptized again," complained Riennes. "No. Mark my words Haralde. A plague stinks here, if not now then yet to come."

After riding a short distance, Riennes continued. "And the women. Small, squat, dark wooly dams with hair coming out of their eyes. If one were to find a passable looker, I bet she would fart in your face if thee were to lie with her."

Haralde chuckled: "Sirrah. I must jump in and defend the fair wenches of my country." He paused as they rode on. "Well, if I could find a fair wench, I would be her champion. . . ."

Two squat, small women dressed in soiled brown woolen dresses brushed along the ground. Wives of fishmongers, they dragged a particular foul bouquet in their wake.

". . . . though I would plead brother," he said as he looked back at the passing fish purveyors, "hold me not to my pledge."

They rode and approached the western wall gate.

"Well, I got thee into your London and so far we have passed unnoticed by the king's outer ring of court taxmen and coarse guardsmen," said Riennes pulling up and stopping. "Now, how do thee get us noticed and afforded royal protection? How do we get recognized as Gher Khan's emissaries by William's inner court officials?"

"Riennes, thee snuck us into London until we could get our bearings," said Haralde. "Now I must find a way to make some noise and get us noticed." Haralde stopped beside him. "What we need now is two long wooden staves."

"Aaaaah, here comes the solution," said Riennes as a farmer pulling a nag carrying a bundle of long wooden poles for fencing entered the city.

Riennes cantered up to the inbound farmer who recoiled at his approach.

"Nay sir. Fear not. I wish to ask the price of your poles. We wish to purchase two."

The farmer set his price.

Haralde shook his head and signaled they should proceed out of the city.

They passed out through the Ludgate western walls past two horse soldiers and a pikemen busy arguing with a peasant family. Before them was a country road and in the distance a causeway passing over some swampy islands of green.

"Why did thee not purchase some poles from him?"

"Because, I thought it better the desert provide," answered Haralde in a low voice, steeling himself for the protest to come.

Riennes chuckled. To 'let the desert provide' was a joke between them. The desert never did provide much. It was and is miserly of life; devoid of water, plants, full of crushing, heat, cold, hopelessness. Yet, they were raised youths in the desert. For them it was always sparse, harsh, tough, lean, cruel. To endure in the desert meant to live lean or do without.

That desert matured a frugal nature in Haralde. For him, to let the desert provide was his way of keeping the purse strings tightly drawn and of following a leaner way.

"Harry! Thee have a purse of substance, yet thee would not buy two cheap wood staves?" asked Riennes. "Surely a bargain was not in our circumstances here."

"Here is a thing," answered Haralde. "We have all this forest wood around us. Why not do what the farmer just did and cut each one for ourselves. Here. Draw your sword and do what I am about to do."

Riennes relented. Never did he object long to Haralde's hesitations over spending money. His brother's instincts over such matters were stronger, always resulting in jingling leather bags of coin.

He heard the song of Haralde's blade as his brother pulled to the side of the road, drew and cut down a 10-foot young sapling. He trimmed off all the small lush branches but left a full green tuft of leaves at the top.

Riennes sighed, followed him to the road's edge and duplicated Haralde's action.

"Here. Tie this to the top under the leaf," directed Haralde, reaching into his saddle pack and pulling out a handful of silk material. Riennes took it from him and shook it out. It fell full away down the side of his black mount and almost touched the dust of the road.

Standing out against the red silk in the top leading corner was the head of a white horse and Turkish script scrawled under it.

"My company standard. Thee did not tell me we were bringing it," said Riennes running his hand over the banner of his command.

His was the flag of 100 white horse. Haralde pulled out a similar red flag and unfurled it. It had a black horse in the upper leading edge with accompanying Turkish script. His was commander of the 100 black.

He tied his just under the leaf tuft and shook his flag out. Placing the butt into the stirrup against the instep of his boot, he bumped his heels into the side of his mount and the animal spun around. Its hooves dug up clots of dirt while it whirled, streaming out the flag behind.

The memories of their past lives flooded over them. Their's were just a few of the silk banners that cracked in the wind behind the vanguard of Gher Khan's army. On the move against his kingdom's enemies, it was a canopy of silk greens, blacks, reds, blues and white accompanied by an army of horses carrying kettledrums.

The beatings of the drums boomed ahead striking fear into the enemy of the Khan's intention to thunder over them. The hooves of a thousand horse were to pound their flesh into a nothingness. His horde was approaching.

Riennes spun his mount around, then urged the black beast into place beside Haralde as they held their staffs of red flags with green leaves above. They started down another of their many roads.

Riennes looked up at the banners as they stiffened in the wind. "I am at this moment not glad I have to ride under this again. Being commander of 100 horse was exciting once. Not now. I do not ever want to ride under the flag of slaughterers of innocent people. What say thee Harry?"

Haralde looked up at the red above their heads, stopped his horse, then leaned over to look fully into Riennes's face. "Ren, yes. We have traveled half the world to get away from them. Our past is behind us. If there is to be a banner we will ride under, it must from now on be our own, of our own making."

"Yes," affirmed Riennes, bowing his head. "Yours will have your personal credo . . . ."

"Honor, duty, service, yes . . . . and thee?"

"I do not know. My mind has not settled on it yet . . . . something like 'heal but harm not." They both kneed their mounts forward. "This one more time, then never again. Let us bury these whether we are successful or not."

Riennes had no more spoken than he felt a hardness that gripped his sword arm and aroused his defensive nature.

"Be warned brother. Something of the air turns against us. Look to us both," cautioned Riennes.

As they rode off a small causeway onto this royal road, Riennes stood up in his stirrup and Haralde followed his example. They saw a grouping of men ahead turn to look at them, three on horse and two pikemen who, squatting on the ground, rose and lowered their sharpness towards them.

The horsemen whirled their heavy mounts around and galloped towards them. Their horses were of heavy hock and hair feathered at their fetlocks. These were brutes of animals bred for smashing into shield lines of men afoot.

Haralde and Riennes judged their own mounts were lighter and quicker of leg. If need be, they could out maneuver the approaching threesome in a horse fight. They tallied up every advantage.

They assessed with warrior interest the weapons and armour of the king's horsemen. All three, bareheaded at first, flipped up a chain mail *coif* attached to their hauberks. The hilt of iron broadswords poked out from scabbards attached to belts. Their sleeves extended to mid-way down the forearms, the wrist covered with cloth, although the leader riding towards them appeared to have leather guards on the wrists. Their woolen leggings were round-wrapped in leather bands and were not protected by *chausses*, chain mail thigh protectors. The two pikemen running behind were not armoured, but wore two Frankish *spangenhelm* helmets, five iron segments attached to copper frames that came to a point at the top. Their halberd spears had sharp wing blades attached behind the spear point. This enabled a spearman to reach over a shield wall to hook an enemy out, thus creating an opening in the line.

"No gloves," whispered Haralde.

"That and look at this fellow coming at us. He has colored ribbons streaming out from the top of his coif. And the rich reins and saddle. A strutting dandy," observed Riennes.

"Defensive only," whispered Haralde again. Riennes nodded.

"HOLD! HOLD YOU RIGHT THERE!" shouted the leader as he pounded up beside Haralde, his destrier throwing up big clots of mud.

The second rider pulled up beside the leader while the third rounded up into a place beside Riennes.

"Who are you? What are you doing here? Do not you know this is a royal road and all are forbidden to ride here," shouted the leader in anger, some spittle ejecting from his mouth. "And what is all this shit?" he asked, waving his hand at the red banner above.

On agreement, Riennes spoke, using the soothing control voice in his Norman pronunciations. "We are foreign emissaries seeking an audience with the king. We bring . . . ."

"You are pig shit staining what looks like good saddles," sneered the leader. His men laughed on both sides of Haralde and Riennes. "Your Norman is false to me. I think you are trying to put one over on us, get by us. Are you assassins, Saxon killers?"

"We are ambassadors representing a . . . ." Haralde was cut short.

"SHUT UP!" shouted the leader right in Haralde's face. "Give me your sword," he ordered pulling out his own broadsword. He then leaned across and yanked out Haralde's shorter broadsword strapped in a scabbard on his saddle.

Haralde heard an attempt at Riennes's kandos.

Haralde spoke softly trying to get command of this hothead's intellect. "We are emissaries and thee must respect our status as. . . ."

"I will have your tongue on this blade if you do not SHUT UP!" shouted the leader. He rapped Haralde's skull with the flat side of his seized broadsword.

Haralde's skull rang with pain; he saw stars; his eyeballs momentarily bulged from their socket.

Riennes heard the iron thud bone. He felt his brother's gorge and red-hot anger rise. He barked his control warning: "HARALDE!" as he saw his brother's muscles bunch.

Haralde heard Riennes's calming even through red haze. He immediately held his anger in check even as he moved. To fight calm was to win.

As the leader leaned over to pull down the red banner, Haralde opened his hand and let the standard flutter down to fall around the man's face. With a swiftness, he drew his hidden kandos, vaulted upwards to stand on his saddle, then stepped upright across onto the rump of the leader's horse.

The dandy struggled with two hands holding two broadswords to free the red cloth shrouding his eyes. Haralde wrapped it tighter around the man's face. His kandos seemed to pass lightly over the struggler's sword hand. It blossomed into a red gash. The man's two swords flew away as he shrieked in pain. Haralde stepped onto the rump of the next horseman who was pulling out his own sword. His kandos also passed over the man's sword hand. Again, an angry spray of red blood and the sword continued to fly away on its own as that horse soldier screamed and grabbed his wrist.

Haralde dropped onto the ground and walked calmly but totally prepared towards the two pikemen rushing him.

As one was slightly ahead of the other, he took him first, spinning to one side putting the first soldier in the way of the slower second. The first pikeman lunged. Haralde's steel kandos rang as he deflected the point. Then he spun again quickly down the length until he was upon the man's grasp of the spear's wooded shaft. He touched the man's hands with his blade and blood spurted over the staff. The second pikeman tried to drive his iron spearhead into Haralde but the screaming first pikeman flailed in his way.

Haralde danced around the screaming man and passed the kandos over the fore hand of the second man struggling to bring his spear to bear. Part of a finger flew away in the struggle and the man dropped to his knees wailing and grabbing at his hand.

Out of the dust kicked up, Riennes appeared from behind the last horse wiping blood from his blade with a rag he kept in his personal bag for these war-like actions. He ran his eyes quickly over his brother to see if he was bleeding anywhere. On seeing no wounds, he next looked him in the eye to see if he was in one of his yellow funks which sometimes overtook his brother if in a fighting frenzy. When Haralde calmly smiled back, Riennes handed his companion in arms his empty bamboo scabbard and they both strapped them on over their shoulders.

"Thee could have warned me. I barely had time to catch up," chided Riennes over Haralde's sudden eruption into action. He slid his kandos into place behind his back.

"Let me look at that," he said as he took Haralde's head in his hand and turned it. He felt his brother flinch in pain but not a sound slipped past tightly compressed lips. "Play not the Mongol stoic with me. If it hurts, I have to know where if I am to heal. Here?"

"Mmmmm," grumbled Haralde."

"Thee are okay. That thick skull saved thee again. But thee will turn purple on this side. And do not be surprised if thee have a bit of a black eye. How thee do it Haralde, I do not know. Thee keep putting yourself in harm's way and keep getting away with it. It is too much thee know." Riennes's warning was a little more serious.

Something moved on the edge of Haralde's senses. "STAY DOWN!" he shouted. They both whirled to see the lout who started the whole mess up on one knee, a sword in his left hand, his sword right hand open and bleeding. The man hesitated, then dropped the broadsword back into the dust. He fell back onto his ass. He groaned in pain with that collapse.

Riennes looked around. Five men, all with bleeding right hands, bowed over to the ground moaning in pain.

"Defensive action thee said." Riennes helped the last pikeman to his feet. Cutting a small piece of leather thong from the pike man's clothing, he tied it around the remaining stub of a finger. "Thee messed up here. This man may never be able to earn his lord's coin while in service again. He is missing a finger."

"Indeed, I did slip up," said Haralde kneeling down. "His friend bumped me as I slid around. I was slightly off balance. I can assure thee, I did try for the palm but his finger got in the way."

When the man moaned: "Please help me. It pains so," Haralde moved to him. "Here fellow, wrapped this tight around your hand. My companion will attend thee in a moment."

Riennes was off checking on the other four. The loud dandy who Haralde put down was sitting whining under his horse. Pain yes, but also from frustration, thought Riennes. He was younger than they were. In his eyes was hatred, yes, but also the hurt look of a child who has just been brought up short by a parent.

Riennes moved the animal to one side and knelt down, only to be greeted by oaths and obscenities.

"You bugger. You have mutilated my hand. I will never ride with sword again. My father will have you for this."

"Your palm has just been opened by something very sharp. The wound is not sour," said Riennes standing. He ignored the curses and went over to his horse where he searched around in his saddle pack and came back with a small apothecary jar. The man struggled and resisted, then acquiesced as Riennes took up his hand with a steel grip on his wrist. "Here. This should help in the healing," soothed Riennes as he smeared an unguent on the open bloody-red smile that creased the hand. "As soon as this is sewn up, thee will start to heal and one day, with care, be able to hold your blade again. Only I fear thee will again use it falsely."

"I will look for you when I do, you . . . !"

"What did thee expect my friend to do when thee struck him oh so harshly in the head. He could have easily taken off this hand. He treated thee justly. Thee treat people badly. When or if thee come for me, I shall not be as kind as he was," warned Riennes, his eyes burning at the man and his hands squeezing the wretch's wrist.

Haralde came over. "Brother. I hear horses coming. A lot of them."

Riennes stood up. "What do thee advise?"

"I do not know. We are very vulnerable. I think I have torn it. This young idiot may still succeed in what he wanted to do; get us in shackles . . . . Thee are quicker than I in things like this. What sayest thee? Do we mount and run?"

"Too late. Here they come. Grab your banner and let us stand together out in front. Let me speak first."

A crowd of riders came around a turn under a canopy of banners high on black lances and spears. They were fighting men on heavy horses and when they saw Haralde and Riennes and the men on the ground around them, a buzz of alarm arose and they urged their mounts at them at a faster gait.

As they approached, some drew swords and kept them at the ready. Haralde and Riennes immediately recognized they were looking at nobles of the king, men of high stature. They wore no armour. Their carriage and rich colorful dress stood out against the dreariness of everything they had experienced of England to date. They wore green, blue and crimson undershirts cinched at the belt with the remainder falling down around their saddles. All clothing was colorfully trimmed. Their leather boots were finely worked. Their saddles were trimmed in brightly polished copper or silver; their saddle blankets were of a velvet-looking crimson material. Strips of red cloth dripped down the flanks and chests of their chargers. The eyes of the most prominent riders flashed not in alarm but with concerned intelligence.

The two watched as armoured and armed soldier outriders formed a van in front of the nobles. Even behind this protective wedge, both took in immediately the larger physical stature of the men behind; obviously the most dangerous element of all the men rushing upon them.

A big hoary guardsman in a black leather fighting vest with red hair sticking out all awry from under a helm with a ring-mail neck guard and nasal protector dismounted in a cloud of dust and gravel. He rushed up to them broadsword in front in the ready taking in his fellow guardsmen bleeding on the ground around these two strangers under their banners.

"Yield you bastards," he shouted, taking no notice of the fact Haralde and Riennes had no weapons in their hands, then veered slightly to one side when he spotted the young leader of the men bleeding on the ground by his horse. "By God it is young Monclair," he shouted to the noblemen pulling up behind him.

Haralde leaned down, lifted up a broadsword from the dirt in front of the sergeant, tripping him as he charged by. The Norman soldier hit the ground, rolled and was up on his feet charging back at Haralde. Haralde stopped him in his tracks by flipping the blade of the offending broadsword onto his hand and presenting the hilt full into the guardsman's face. "We yield," taunted Haralde.

The guardsman cocked his sword back but stopped by a shout from the leading nobleman on a horse moving up on them all.

"KILL THEM," shouted the young hot head behind them who had scrambled off the ground to his feet and was holding his bleeding hand out front in a silent plea for revenge. "Stand down Bec but stand ready," said the tall nobleman in a commanding voice to his sergeant. His horse came up in a tinkle of bells attached to its bridle and nosed the two banners held by Haralde and Riennes.

The rest of the horse warriors crowded around in a cloud of choking dust, a tink of metal harness rings and squeak of much leather. Some of the other mounted guardsmen around the nobles dismounted and kneeled down to talk with the wounded.

"What means this? Are you responsible for these men," The nobleman's voice and demeanor demanded obedience and instant answers. "Young Guy, your injury, is it bad?"

Monclair shook his head no and looked down at the ground, disgraced.

Riennes stepped forward. He knew he must speak quick and clearly. These men looked on the verge of turning on him and Haralde.

"My Lord. My companion and I come as emissaries from a distant king bearing a written greeting of support for William,

King of Britannia and Duke of Normandy. We are bearers of good wishes and gifts from our king to William. Our king is so far distant that he cannot come with his royal entourage, but sends us as his representatives," said Riennes. He watched as his words registered with this one of the king's trusted royal authorities. "We are ambassadors on this road which we understand leads to the royal courts and the king's presence. We seek certification of our status and with respect, an audience before King William."

"By God's eyes!" swore the nobleman in a harsh whisper. He turned in his saddle, looked across the crowd of his companions, and shouted: "Fitz! Attend to me, quickly."

Then, he swung down before Riennes and Haralde, and what he said next were the sweetest words the two had heard in the brief time so far in England.

"Ambassadors. Let me introduce myself. I am William de Poitiers, a vassal of my king. Your Norman is a little stilted but I think I understood everything you just said. I have not the power to recognize your request or to respond to any aspect of your mission here. But one here can and he will be with us but momentarily."

Poitiers glanced nervously back and forth at Riennes and Haralde, then asked: "Pray tell. Did some band of ruffians attack you here? Were my men wounded in defence of your mission?"

Riennes felt Haralde move to answer at his side and jumped in quickly. "Sirrah. I am sorry to say it was your men who attacked us. We attempted to explain our banners and our presence on this road, but that young horseman there seized our weapons, cursed us and struck my companion on the side of the head. It turns an angry color as we speak."

Poitiers looked at the two red banners and then at Haralde, then his face blanched just as another horse warrior pulled his horse up beside him.

"Well?" demanded this tall dark man, who leaned and looked down from his saddle with great impatience. The man locked eyes first with Haralde and then with Riennes. Riennes felt the shock of his character. Danger was written all over his overture. This man, Riennes knew instinctively, was a close confidant of King William.

Haralde too sensed the presence of this horse warrior. A great, dangerous man, hard on friends; someone his enemies always wished were elsewhere. Both would learn in the months to come this, their first brush with this power behind the throne of Britannia, would himself within a year be a monarch in his own right, a Marcher lord, an earl of such power that he would carve out a mini-kingdom in southwest Wales.

Encouraged by William, he and other Marcher lords would wage war on Welsh principalities in their rapacious hunger for more land.

"Ambassadors. Lord William fitzOsbern, chief soldier, administrator and advisor to the royal house. Lord fitzOsbern, these two men claim to be ambassadors who have journeyed here as a special legation from a distant king who wishes to bring greetings to the King of England," said Poitiers, stepping back, glad to dump the problem into the lap of a higher authority.

Riennes and Haralde bowed slightly. FitzOsbern hesitated a moment, glanced at the two banners, then bowed just enough to be respectful but brief enough not commit himself completely. He dismounted, handing the reins of his mount to Bec.

"And I am sorry to tell you these men I set up as the day guards of the abbey road skirmished with these two," admitted Poitiers, physically shrinking from the anger that flared up in fitzOsbern's eyes.

FitzOsbern turned to look at the wounded five who now were all standing but still moaning.

Finally: "I am sorry sirrahs. If this be true, I will attend to it. But pray, on your behalf, did someone else provoke them?"

"Nay Lord fitzOsbern," replied Riennes. "Your young officer struck my fellow here on the side of his head with yon broadsword. We had no recourse but to defend ourselves and our purpose."

"You put five of Poitiers royal guardsmen down yourselves?"

"I am sorry my lord."

FitzOsbern whirled and walked to where the wounded men were attended. He talked roughly with Monclair, then grabbed his hand. He then went to each of the others and grabbed their hands. He turned and came back.

He looked Riennes and Haralde over carefully, glanced at their banners again and then at the hilts of the two kandos behind their backs.

"Montclair again," he comment to Poitiers.

"Hothead," answered Poitiers.

"Empty head," fitzOsbern growled. He turned to Riennes and Haralde. "All five have been cut precisely. Done is such a way as to render them hors de combat, but yet, not seriously hurt. The wounding was precise, deliberate. Not the butchery of broadswords." He nodded at the swords over their backs. "For my own satisfaction, would you show me those?" he asked. "You do not have to ambassadors. It must be just as a favor to me."

Haralde and Riennes looked at each other, then Haralde nodded. FitzOsbern caught that. Who was the leader here, he wondered.

The two kandos sang similar metal as they came out. At the sound, other nobles ahorse turned and drew more swords as they nervously took in the scenario unfolding before their leader.

FitzOsbern crossed his arms in front of him, then one hand came up to purse his chin. He and Poitiers looked down the three-foot curves of silver steel.

"Light little knives. Good for naught but spitting toads," judged fitzOsbern.

Guffaws rippled around his company of young bloods. "Toad spitters!" they joked.

"Foreign," fitzOsbern went on. "No good for heavy work. Yet deadly in close. They serve you well do they not?" It was rhetorical. The two slid their kandos back into bamboo scabbards behind their backs.

FitzOsbern was taken by these two. He liked their bearing, their presence. They held themselves erect, alert. They were also tall. They demanded attention. There was a quality of disciplined ableness and ability about them. And deadliness, he thought, if they could overpower five like that.

He turned to Haralde. "Do you speak Norman ambassador?"

"Alas not well my lord," replied Haralde. "I am still learning."

FitzOsbern was growing impatient with this whole affair on the Westminster road. He was a man pressed by many affairs; all needed attending to with no time to waste. Yet, and Riennes sensed it, the royal house warrior had to address the fact a foreign king was here in support of William's claim to the Britannic throne. God knows, thought fitzOsbern, with rebellion aflame across the land, any foreign recognition of his master's claim over Britannia and Normandy must be encouraged.

"I am uncomfortable ambassadors," said fitzOsbern. "You are foreigners, but from where? Though the incident here is regrettable and we are rushed with our affairs, I would have thought by now you would have introduced yourselves. You have me at a disadvantage."

This King William must hunger for endorsements from others, thought Riennes. It is an opening we must make wider and pass through. He grabbed Haralde by the arms and addressed him in a formal manner.

"My lord, we must step to one side with Lord fitzOsbern here and quickly explain how our king wishes to make alliance with King William. Lord fitzOsbern has many tasks to complete today so let us step beyond the hearing of these other men. Only those at the highest court level must hear our monarch's intent. Do we understand thee are such an official?" asked Riennes as he and Haralde drew the Norman noble some steps away from Poitiers, the mounted noblemen and the guardsmen who were trying to dress the wounds of their fellows.

FitzOsbern obliged by walking away with them. He noted the formal title Riennes used to address his fellow ambassador. He was wondering which ambassador was of the first order and who should he pay most attention to.

Haralde continued fitzOsbern's confusion when he addressed his fellow ambassador with the same formal title. "My lord ambassador will give thee a brief outline of the mission our master has imposed upon us. We have been on a long voyage to reach this time and place. We are both men of position and substance. Forgive me for my bad Norman."

"I understood you," answered the Norman lord.

"We bear gifts for your king . . . ," said Riennes as Haralde fished inside his jerkin, pulled out a small silk wrap, jerked it and a blue emerald dangling on a gold chain dropped before fitzOsbern's eyes. . . . "and his queen if such be his state," continued Riennes. FitzOsbern's eyes widened in disbelief. Avarice soaked his intellect and his hand moved as if to grab it. However, he stopped as caution warned him a king's gift was not to be touched.

"It is called The Blue Eye of the Ocean," said Riennes as Haralde quickly rolled it up in his fingers, wrapped the silk around it and stuffed back into his jerkin. "This ocean stone belongs to your king. The long voyage my lord ambassador was by ship and that vessel now is nearby. Aboard is the property of King William from our master. This is just an example."

And for fitzOsbern, time and his many tasks of this day floated away as he listened in rapture to the tale of these two men from a faraway place.

They told an unbelievable story; of Gher Khan, an emperor master of a desert and mountain kingdom beyond the sands of Jerusalem. They described the Khan's 10 walled cities, of his armies so vast they stretch back over the horizon, of mercenary armies throughout his kingdom made up of Mahamads, Buddhists and Christians, which were his to call upon to join his own army if need be through alliances with neighboring principalities, and of the Khan's wealth of silks, spices, jewels, gold and silver chests, of a value beyond estimate.

"Did you say your king lives out in the deserts beyond Outremer?" FitzOsbern had heard whisperings by ecclesiastics of a desire by Rome for a holy war to free Jerusalem from the Mahamads, the heretics who held the holy city. A king, a Khan who had Christians in his army. *An ally one day?* Such a thought he held to himself, an idea politique only for the ear of William Rex.

"Yes," answered Riennes who had noted in his travels how just the naming of that city held Franks in awe. Was that why he threw that into his discourse? Riennes wondered. He decided not to tell fitzOsbern how too far beyond Jerusalem was the Khan's empire.

"Though it is unlikely the kingdoms of our Khan and the realm of King William and their joint interests would ever likely touch, our Khan has set down strong directions to his servants that any delegation from King William is to be warmly embraced. Our Khan who has heard of William and now to our amazement, Britannia, admires your king. If aid would assist, Gher Khan would respond. What we bear now is an endorsement of that."

FitzOsbern could hardly believe what he was experiencing, right here, right now just a short distance from Westminster Abbey and the king's court. How was he expected to act on this? Too much here.

"My lord, there is a second part to our deputation's mission," interjected Haralde. FitzOsbern turned to Haralde. The two had him going back and forth as this astounding information flowed from them. Was he getting somewhat confused?

"At the completion of our royal presentation, we would ask a boon of thee, and that is, our wish to remain in Britannia," continued Haralde. "My friend will explain."

"Our Khan chose us for this mission because . . . , Riennes glanced at Haralde. Here we go. Take a deep breath brother ". . . . because we are subjects of King William."

FitzOsbern looked one to the other, his intellect trying to grope through this confusion. Then: "This is no jest I know. You must know not to play any impertinence upon me because angered,

I am a man easily riled and quick with the edge of my sword. So you must have explanations, and make them quick. My impatience grows."

Riennes was getting nervous. The explanation that he and Haralde were ambassadors to King William from the Gher was just a ruse. He and Haralde did not know until they arrived in the West that William was now ruler of all Britannia. The two had concocted their mission as ambassadors just to get an audience before the king's royal court so they could plead their case to smoothen the way to Wales. Now, he sensed fitzOsbern might be sniffing out their false credentials.

"My lord. I am Norman born. My fellow is of Saxon and Welsh lineage. We are the Khan's delegation because I was raised a Frankish youth and my fellow ambassador, a Welsh lad, both of high-borne families." Riennes kept going, not giving fitzOsbern pause.

. "Our memories of our homeland, its culture and customs certified in our Khan's mind our qualifications to undertake this voyage home." Riennes took a deep breath. It mattered not that the Khan was on his deathbed at the time and all he did was to grant them after years of petitioning through long service their desire to return home. Cruel he was, but the Khan rewarded loyalty.

He explained how Viking pirates carried them off as youths and sold them and other northerners on an eastern slave market. They in turn were sold into the Khan's service. Rewarded for certain deeds, they became overseers and administrators with their accompanying privileges. .

"My Lord fitzOsbern, may I introduce myself. Haralde, son of Steorm Longshield, Thegn of Neury and Wym who was Housecarl to Edward the Confessor," Haralde bowed.

"My Lord fitzOsbern, may I introduce myself. Riennes de Montford, son of Count Raoul de Montford, a Breton." And he too bowed.

FitzOsbern blinked in utter confusion. He bent over, put his hands on his knees and shook his head. He looked down at the dirt. It was an act of stretching just for its physical relief, as well as an expression of frustration. He had been tied up all day with talks with all the leaders of the various houses of Normandy. King William was going to be delayed in Normandy for a little while longer.

These strong-willed men wanted to get on with their rapacious ambitions of seizing manors here. Things were getting out of control. He sighed. Obligations! He was a man who loved the simple clean satisfaction of action. He found administration encumbered his mind, his own ambitions. *Let someone else do this,* his jumbled mind whispered to him. He raised himself up.

"A Norman and a Saxon. Ambassadors of a foreign king," he cursed, looking at their two banners and as a commander himself recognizing instinctively in any horse company the insignias of host commanders. These two young men carried themselves a certain way. They were not only men of action, but also of substance, of character. *There is something here I must pay close attention to,* he thought.

FitzOsbern walked over and stood close to Haralde and Riennes. "What do you need of me?"

Haralde: "My Lord. We need a paper from thee, an interdict that we may post to protect the king's prize aboard our vessel from unscrupulous tax men."

Riennes bristled over Haralde's demanding tone. Too harsh, too much haste, he thought. He sensed his brother had irritated fitzOsbern. He dropped the timbre in his voice to a soft cajoling tone as he interrupted. "My lord, let us address these things later. Just grant us an appointed time and place for our audience with the king. The transfer of the Khan's bequest to William must be completed quickly," urged Riennes.

Then, the solution for ftizOsbern suddenly presented itself in the scenario of a host of restless horses and their riders who crowded in. They were anxious to complete this affair of wounded guardsmen and their leader talking with two foreign men. They wanted away, to strut themselves, their prowess through the streets of London and the environs. There were women to find, or more likely, to seize.

Haralde, glancing at the press of snorting beasts and dangerous men, spotted a boy, a young squire on a small palfrey holding a lance in his hand. From the lance slapped a small pennon in the wind, a flap of colorful material with an insignia which posted his eyes to it. The pennant was that of a red castle on a green hill, more like a mount.

Before the boy was a tall, dark man big of stature, sitting astride a big fighting horse with such ease, it was obviously a partnership honed through many a campaign. The man was talking to a companion, his head turned away.

"Excuse my intrusion Lord fitzOsbern," interjected Haralde as he stepped forward and gained his brother's attention. In Turkish, he said: "Brother. Look at the staff of that young boy. That pennant." Riennes followed Haralde's direction, then stiffened when he saw the man ahead of it.

He knew him immediately. He held himself in the male profile of the de Montford line. Gilbert. His uncle. And if his uncle, then would his aunt Hilga be near as well?

Riennes turned to fitzOsbern. "My lord, forgive my companion's bad manners for speaking in a foreign tongue. He wants me to apologize for making too many demands. It is obvious we are an obstacle in the way of your many duties. However, may we claim one final boon of thee? It would be but a moment right here."

"I am pressed, but yes, if it would hurry this bloody business."

Riennes knew he could not just walk into the middle of these soldiers and noble commanders of the king. As a commander of men himself, there was a protocol to follow when talking to the hierarchy of any military force. "Would thee introduce us to some of your company? We will have to meet some of them anyway before our audience with the king. I am especially interested in that man with the red castellate pennant."

FitzOsbern was puzzled by that last remark, but he bowed and said curtly: "Follow me then."

The first line of guardsmen opened up at a signal from Bec, their sergeant, who led the way into the company of nobles. "This horseman you have already met, William de Poitiers."

"My lord ambassadors." They bowed slightly to each other. "Roger de Montgomeri." More bows. "And this man you must meet because you will have to sit down and arrange with him the details of your audience and interdict paper, Geoffrey de Mandeville, appointed port-reeve of London by the king." They bowed. "Robert, Count d'Eu . . . . Hugh Mortimer . . . . Eustace de Boulogne . . . . Richard fitzHubert . . . . Lord Gerbod, a baron who led a large Flemish mercenary contingent . . . ."

Haralde walked down the line looking at the houses of Normans who had first smashed down numerous rebel barons, counts and viscomtes and welded for the bastard Duke William the principality of Normandy. Here was the corp, the cabal of fighting leaders who had killed the Saxon King Harold and won for William this island kingdom. It was heady stuff.

They went down the line bowing. Luck had presented Haralde and Riennes with this introduction into Norman power. Being bold, taking the initiative, acting on new experiences and information had always led them to new horizons of opportunity. No, not just luck, thought Haralde. He did not believe luck was a will-of-the-wisp thing. Luck was always the residue of hard work.

He was on edge. All his fighting instincts were heightened. This gang could fall upon them if any sign of falseness on their part became apparent. They were walking down this line because of Riennes, and that amazing sense he possessed. His brother was feeling his way along the currents of circumstance here, so far avoiding counter undertows. It was always thus whenever they got themselves into a tight. It was Riennes who felt the forces, and chose the way avoiding the dangerous ones.

Haralde tried to shrink physically as he followed beside Riennes. Haralde did not want to be noticed. Let all eyes be on my brother, whose intent now was upon the next horseman in line.

FitzOsbern waved his hand up to the tall man with the blue eyes and short cropped black hair. Haralde's own hackles stiffed suddenly on his own neck as he was hit by the physical similarity between the man in the saddle and his brother.

" . . . . and Gilbert de Montford . . . and this is . . . ."

"One moment Lord fitzOsbern if thee will," said Riennes. His uncle. Down through years of the shrinking halls of his memory, he had disciplined his mind constantly as a mental exercise through his dark imprisonment with images of his parents' face and his uncle Gilbert and aunt Hilga. Here was the brother of his father. *In fact, look onto the sharp features, the eyes, the jaw, the shape of the cheekbones to see what? Why, I believe the ghost of my father's countenance. They look so much alike.* thought Riennes.

The noblemen stirred in the saddle and wrinkled his brow, irritated by the impolite scrutiny. His companions began to mumble over this impudence.

"My dear Lord Gilbert, do thee not recognize me?" Riennes asked finally. "Do I not look familiar to thee in any way?"

Lord Gilbert's companions went silent. Gilbert appraised this man at his stirrup, hesitated, then: "Ambassador. What do you mean? Have you and I met before? If so, I have no memory."

"Lord Gilbert. I am your kinsman," said Riennes, pleading for Gilbert to see him truly. As Riennes took the next step, Haralde put his hand on his brother's shoulder. "I am Riennes de Montford, son of Raoul and Matilda de Montford. I am your nephew!"

Gilbert's face reddened. A grumble rumbled through friends in his company who knew Gilbert's family. Riennes felt anger grow in his uncle. "You must mistake me for someone else ambassador. My nephew is dead long ago. How did you get that name?"

"Your wife's name is Hilga. Thee have a daughter Elouisa," said Riennes sensing Gilbert's growing anger.

"Thee had a son Goz who died two years after birth . . . ." Gilbert slowly began to dismount, his mouth a round O. " . . . . One day when I was little, thee, father and I were in your orchard teaching me how to ride. I fell off and bleeding, cried to the point my father gathered up the reins of my mount and said it was alright, I could walk back to your manor, but thee shouted no, grabbed me by the seat of my leggings, hauled me back into the saddle and said no horse shames a de Montford and no de Montford walks, not as long as there is a horse nearby with an empty saddle."

Gilbert walked up staring with eyes blazing into those of Riennes. Then, as sometimes happens when looking at a crowd and a face suddenly jumps out, Gilbert focused on the physical characteristics of Riennes's face. He suddenly found himself looking at the visage of his dead brother.

"There is something in your look that strikes me," whispered Gilbert. "There is a familiarity in your bearing . . . ."

Gilbert seized both Riennes's shoulder. " . . . . By God! Can it be? Riennes? Riennes?" And he shook his nephew.

"Yes uncle. Yes uncle," and tears moistened his eyes. Haralde cast his eyes downward, grateful his brother had found family. After many years of living one life but longing for the dream of another, Riennes had captured his heart's deepest desire. It was materializing rapidly in from of him.

"How can this be!" demanded Gilbert.

Riennes, laughing and almost crying, began to whistle a family tune, one familiar to his uncle. Gilbert's eyes widened. Even within the company of hard men, this intimacy of male memories was too much and he seized Riennes in his arms.

A 'hurrah' went up from his companions. They did not quite understand what was going on but Gilbert, it seemed, was well liked amongst this band of hard men.

Gilbert held Riennes at arm's length. "I do not understand this. You drowned. We found the wreckage of your vessel. We scoured the shoreline for miles even in the face of a terse gale that raged for days," he said.

"We were not aboard," explained Riennes. "We were attacked in the storm by slave-raiding Vikings and carried off . . . ." FitzOsbern stepped into their company. . . . "I will explain everything later uncle."

"Then you do know this man Lord Gilbert?" asked fitzOsbern.

"I find it hard to believe it but it . . . . would . . . . seem so my lord," answered Gilbert hesitantly.

"What is to be done then with this whole affair?" demanded fitzOsbern.

Haralde's quick mind suddenly alerted him. He reacted. "May I make a suggestion my lord?"

FitzOsbern turned and with shrewd eyes appraised Haralde. "Speak."

"If it pleases thee my lord, if thee could appoint Lord de Montford as our sponsor and spokesman, someone responsible for our presentations to court, then we could all get off this road. Thee could attend to your tasks secure in your needs a sponsor will keep the king's interests uppermost in his mind."

FitzOsbern crossed his arms across his chest, one hand stroking his chin. His eyes bored into Haralde, ferreting for any hidden dangers in the ambassador's suggestion.

Finally: "Ambassador. For someone still learning the Norman language, you speak with clarity, and may I add, with some guile. I must remind myself to watch you." He smiled and then nodded: "What are your immediate needs?"

Haralde: "My lord, we have a cargo of gifts for King William. We need a royal interdict against any interference of our vessel's business. We have voyaged a great distance in her to fulfill our emperor's will. That will is sympathetic to that of King William."

Riennes: "We need our freedom of movement not to be interfered with. We need a wagon to move freely between Lord de Montford's abode and our vessel without running into such exuberance as we encountered this morning in the young Monclair who we recognize was only carrying out his duties."

"De Montford!" barked fitzOsbern.

"My lord?"

"Walk with me."

The two walked aside. "Lord Gilbert. In two days, Regent Odo will call all to attend court. He will announce William has been delayed in Normandy, but intends to send our queen, Matilda and family, to disembark onto these shores soon. We will hold this audience at that assembly first. All his premier interests will attend. Then, they will be away to seize their own enterprises and will be beyond immediate control. We will hear the nature and the mind of this foreign king. You will do everything necessary to bring this to fruition. In addition, you will inform me of any information they let slip you determine as important. Understand?"

"Yes my lord. I will need the chief cleric to write out and issue an interdict banning all from boarding their vessel and warrants for their travel. I will take them both under my shield immediately."

"Good. And I will arrange with Odo for their presentation first at court so that we can get this business out of the way quickly," said ftizOsbern. "I want to hear what means this delay to this Island by the king. If he is not arriving in the near future, I do not want to waste my enterprise in London. I will be away early the next morning. I have new responsibilities on the Wales frontiers," he finished as they turned and moved back into earshot of everyone.

As they approached the two ambassadors, fitzOsbern appraised Haralde's character and avarice once again became his ambition. A big man, he thought. There is something of a fighter about him. The other also. For ambassadors bearing gifts, they are shabbily dressed. But if the fair-haired one is bearing a jewel the size of a walnut on his person, I will warrant there is more behind that in their personal baggage. A small stipend for this service I render them must be in order.

As they approached, they observed Riennes with apothecaries go to Montclair, his two horse companions and the two pikemen.

"The damage we have done, I can aid in the curing of your hands," said Riennes.

The five in pain looked one to the other. Then Monclair: "Bugger off."

Riennes shrugged and was about to turn away when one of the Montclair's horse soldiers stepped forward, his damaged hand outstretching. "I cannot do without my good sword hand. Can you?"

Riennes nodded affirmative, took the horseman's hand, and began applying a brown unguent out of his jar across the wound. The others then stepped forward holding out their cuts. Riennes smeared generously, then turned. "Haralde. Could thee . . . .?"

"I have it," said Haralde returning with a small leather wrap from Riennes's horse. Haralde looked around at the faces crowding around them. "Brother. We have got to go. We cannot stand in the road like this."

"I know. But only a moment and I will be finished." He turned to the first injured man. As he opened a leather wrap, the man's eyes opened wide as he saw a row of small curved needles. Riennes took one out and strung it with a piece of horse hair. "I must close your wound so that it will heal. Thee will feel but a pinprick and then thee will see the skin closed. Do thee understand?" Even before the man had a chance to think about it, Riennes began sewing to a small "Aaah!" by the man. The wound closed quickly.

Riennes went from man to man explaining: "Find a medicine man or woman and ask for a plant poultice to be wrapped against the wound. Do not apply animal grease to it. Do not use your hand for any work. Keep it clean. Change the poultice often. If thee do this, the wound will heal. When it looks good, cut the silk gut and pull it out gently. Thee should then be able to work the hand again. Thee sir, keep your cut finger smeared with oil from plants. Keep a poultice over it to draw off any corruption. I will sew it closed now. It will bleed sometimes. That is good. Wash it with warm water. Keep it clean. Then, a new poultice. Repeat this often."

He turned to Monclair who had watched Riennes work over his companion's wounds. Monclair pulled back.

Lord Poitier had watched all in amazement. These two men had cut his guards, put them down, now they were healing them. Use to blood and dismembered limbs and bodies torn open to weep their lives onto the fields of battle was work he had had a part in many times. This, this was a reversal of suffering. The pain had gone out of the face of his men. This young ambassador had not only eased the physical hurt, he had salved the other kind of pain within. It struck him deeply.

Poitiers moved to young Monclair. "Guy. Do not be stupid. Can you not see this man can give your sword back to you? You will be no use to yourself or your father if you cannot wield a sword any more. Your pride will wound you permanently if you do not do this. Swallow it."

Monclair looked at Poitiers, then down at his hand. He pushed it towards Riennes and looked away. Riennes worked quickly. When finished, Monclair growled. "This changes nothing. My father and I will attend you two later."

Riennes smeared some unguent onto the needles, then inserted them into his leather wrap. "Keep the hand elevated and use it not for two months." He turned away, saying under his breath: "Pray then we shall be well away from your like."

As Riennes joined Haralde, he heard his brother whisper: "We hope."

FitzOsbern who had watched this little drama with one arm across his chest and his other hand pursing his chin, came out of his reverie.

He turned and strode towards his horse, a young man holding reins out to him. "Poitiers, post new men on this road. De Montford, attend to these two ambassadors. I will talk to you later of their import."

FitzOsbern vaulted into his saddle, wheeled away and his entourage in a shower of clots of earth and stone thundered after him to London.

Gilbert lifted to his saddle and motioned for the two of them to follow him. "Wrap up your banners. You will be under my pennant now. We will attend first to the script you want although there is not a rider, footman or tax grubber anywhere in London who can read the terms therein. The royal seal, though, should keep them at bay."

Gilbert spurred his mount to beside Riennes just as he and Haralde mounted and were stuffing their red banners into bags. "I am unsure still if my confidence in you, my nephew, is well founded. However, if you are not who you say you are," he said, leaning in close to Riennes's eyes, "you will be found out by your next interrogator."

Riennes held his gaze. "Who?"

"Your aunt Hilga."

Laughter burst from Riennes. "Thee know she and I are close. La, she will shame your doubt."

Gilbert's laughter burst back at him. "Pauvre imposter or prodigal nephew returns? We will see." and he rode away.

Riennes was about to spur his beast after his uncle when Haralde lay a hand on his arm. "Ren, this was a near thing. Does this now allay your fears?"

"But no. Nearer is yet to come Harry."

"And I was supposed to bear this weight from thee. Yet I almost brought us down with my brashness. How sharp thee have been in this."

"Yes. My sharp to your flat," joked Riennes as he pulled away and shouted: "Has it not always been thus."

"Lies. Lies. I poop on your lies," Harry shouted after him. Riennes could be like this. Heavy, depressed one moment, then high, brilliant, quick the next.

Before racing to join after them, he turned and looked back.

Will this road ever end? He wondered. I fear not soon.

Beautiful, beautiful. Fascinating, mused Hilga. *He is so fresh, new, yes, desirable.* She was simply beguiled by her husband's nephew. She twisted in her chair. Her husband sat on a tent stool sipping wine. Across the wavering heat fire of a brazier, she watched the young face of Riennes as he told stories. He no longer was her nephew. He was her husband's nephew. For her, this was a young man who suddenly excited her.

Hours ago, a messenger from Gilbert had summoned her from her place in a London abbey to his field tents west of Winchester. He had burst in, seized her and said there was a man outside, a long lost relative of his family. Would she watch and listen after he brought this man in and tell him later what she thought. Of course my Lord husband, whatever you wish.

In he came, a very tall, black-haired young man with piercing blue eyes. She saw immediately in him her husband's familial male lines. He made no introduction of himself, as Gilbert instructed. He did the cordial greeting, wishing her well and good health. Then he bent Gilbert's rule by telling her a story. Even as he did so, her awareness of something familiar about his character began to excite her as he launched into his tale.

"Your husband and your brother-in-law Lord Raoul tramped into your main hall roaring and drinking great draughts. On the floor they crashed the carcass of a wild boar, one which the men of those two families had spent a week hunting.

"When they were elsewhere's distracted, a young boy came out from behind them. His responsibility had been to keep their hunt camp fire going all day and through the night. Unfortunately, the fire almost went out one night and he had carelessly thrown huge limbs onto the coals to make the fire leap quicker. The coals splashed onto his clothing, they caught fire and his hand was burnt. The boy . . . ."

". . . . asked please Tante Hilga," she picked up the story, "Do not tell anyone. It hurts. Could you help me make the . . . ."

". . . . hurt go away," he resumed. "And Tante Hilga rubbed his hand with . . . ."

"RIENNES!" she shouted and threw her arms around the little affectionate boy who had left her life on a dark stormy night years ago. It had left a second void in her life, one similar to the one that almost devastated her; the death of her baby son two years after his birthing. She and Riennes had been close, sympathetic each to their station in life.

She had squealed when he had picked her up and whirled her around while her husband had laughed and sipped his wine from a Saxon horn goblet at the sight of a piece of his missing family now back with them again.

Now over the fire heat she watched his face and listened to his tale of being kidnapped, of the desert, of fighting, of his Khan, of different peoples, cultures, of learning things, of different experiences, of becoming a trusted overseer in a foreign land. His adventures stimulated in her an exciting creature of life. This was no boy anymore. This was a man, a special man who could read and write, who had travelled widely, who had a different vision of the world, who exhibited a maturity and sense of self seen in few men of greater age. He was excitingly different than any males around her.

When they asked him if he knew about the death of his family and how they died he dropped his head. He showed emotion, reverence and softness. A Norman male would hide everything of that nature behind the stoic male mask. The young man's vulnerability framed his strength. That, she found exciting.

"They are buried in a small church graveyard not far from your family bastion," Gilbert revealed.

He shook his head in understanding, and said he would visit there once he returned to oust the man and his family who had stolen his birthright.

"That should not be long," Gilberts told him. "William is putting down insurrections in his duchy and warding off encroachment onto Norman soil by an ambitious French king. That family stayed neutral when William called for all to join him. He will not long forget such insult. William demands loyalty; rewards it when it is given freely, crushes it when it is withheld. With the aid of all we de Montfords, we should be able to restore that birthright to you in short time."

"If shortly, I cannot attend," answered Riennes.

"You jest of course. Why not?"

"I must fulfill a loyalty of my own and follow my brother," he answered.

Hilga joined in, even though she was expected to sit quiet and not interrupt male talk. "You have no brothers!"

Riennes turned and looked deep into her. She liked his eyes doing that. "How do I explain this? Not by blood but by something deep. Our minds, our souls are joined. Our bodies are deeply bonded. He saved my life, my sanity, my intelligence, hope, health and humanity many times as a boy. He is my life's debt and I bear the weight of it in joy."

He went on. "As men, now we are sand brothers who share the water bond of life in the desert and beyond the desert. I love him. I cannot explain it any other way. Can thee understand what I am saying?"

She flushed. Her husband leaned back, sipped his wine and furrowed his brow. Deep comradeship was a martial strength he could understand. "You are fighting men together, as you both displayed on the road this morning."

Hilga let slip: "No. This is something else. This is intimate, am I right."

Riennes darted a glance at her. A note in her voice sounded a warning. "Intimate, yes, but not like thee think."

Not a boy anymore. Not a nephew. An exciting man. She recounted the hardness of his muscles, his body, his everything when he had picked her up; the harshness of his kidnapping, of his life, his travels, his determination. *I wonder if he would find me attractive?*

"His name is Haralde Longshield. He is Welsh, the son of a royal housecarl who served as King Edward's champion. He too was kidnapped as a boy. We suffered as boys. He traveled with me across Normandy, stood with me in the shadow of my own home as we tried to fight our way in. His blood was upon my blood as we wounded and were wounded. He got me away safely."

Riennes looked at them both to see if they truly understood. Gilbert was somewhat disturbed by the idea of intimacy between men. Hilga's eyes were glazed over, the passion of his tale heating her.

"We are ambassadors. His hope is when we fulfill our obligation to King William, we will set out together to find his family, his lands, his home. I will go with him. The completion of his dream to return is my dream. Then I will return to Normandy and if it pleases the Creator, to sit in the family orchards in peace for years. I have seen too much violence. I seek a cleansing."

"Hmm," Gilbert pondered out loud, then used it to change the subject. "Hilga. Riennes and I must talk about matters. Say goodnight. I shall not be too long to our tent later."

"Yes husband," and she rose, asking: "And Riennes, he will stay and visit for awhile?"

"Yes. He will move into the tent of young squire Robert for a few days until he is presented at court," said Gilbert, struck by the way she looked at her nephew.

"That is wonderful," she curtsied before Riennes, then overwhelmed by her emotions, went up on her tip toes and kissed him full on the mouth, supposedly as a family gesture of welcoming him back. "Good night. I hope to hear more of your times away from us dear Riennes," she said slipping away from them both and out the front of the tent.

Riennes's face reddened as he watched her leave, then turned back and looked to see what his uncle thought of her emotional goodnight. Instead, what he saw in Gilbert's face warned him to prepare not for his uncle but for the king's inquisitor.

Gilbert turned, sat, picked up his wine horn and sipped it. "Ah, Bordeau. The first from our homeland. Been sucking bitter English ale all this month. Found a wine merchant who told me the seas were still too angry for shipments here, but said he had uncovered a little supply. Cost me."

Riennes smiled within but his facial revealed nothing. He thought of Muck.

"Ten years. Your tale, such an adventure. Such relief to be safely home I would imagine." Gilbert peered over his horn.

"I have lain in the dark packed tight beside the bodies of other slaves and I have lain between silken sheets in my own pavilion, and in both I have dreamed of nothing else," answer Riennes.

"You were a slave!"

"I have been many things; slave, thief, camel herder, horse soldier, killer, student, healer, administrator, emissary and overseer, most especially under the service of Gher Khan."

"Tell me about this king of yours."

"Third son of a powerful desert and mountain warlord, a Kara Khitai, a dark Cathayan, who took to wife in a marriage of alliance the Turkish daughter of an invading Seljuk king."

"Was he this Christian king fitzOsbern mentioned to us?"

"No. He was Buddhist and his wife was Mahamad. However, he granted freedom of worship to Nestorian Christians who as *mamelukes* filled some of the ranks of his army and proved by his tolerance to be loyal to him always."

Riennes went on and told a tale of how the father of The Gher conquered many walled cities, but then was beset by other hordes of horse warriors who forged alliances. He was killed in battle. His first son was weak, indecisive, and eventually was killed, some say by poisoning. The second son was somewhat stronger and went to battle his enemies but he was killed in battle. The young Gher Khan disappeared into the Pamir Mountains. He collected loyal fighters around him and waged skirmish war, hitting the supply lines of the alliance which was strung out far from its homelands. Many were the attempts by assassins to kill him, but all failed. Eventually, The Khan grew strong enough and defeated his enemies in open battle. In time he swept the Turks and others out and his kingdom swelled to 10 walled cities containing the fabulous wealth of the Silk Road.

"That sounds like our William," said Gilbert, rising to fill a goblet with more wine, offering some to Riennes who shook no.

"Normandy until recently was torn by barons and viscomtes and any other name they wished to come by after the death of William's father. They went after the boy. Bodyguards fought off assassins even in the young duke's bedrooms and died enabling him to slip away and escape. Eventually, he fought with a growing army of us young chevaliers and powerful supportive magnate families like we de Montfords and he conquered Normandy and welded it into a fighting force that not even the king of Paris dared take on."

Gilbert sat down. "Our king, your king now Riennes, stormed ashore and defeated Harold at Hastings. It was no easy thing. The Saxons were well armed and they fought us almost to a defeat until Harold was struck down. But William's claim to the throne was solid, endowed to him by King Edward before he died. The English denied it and chose Harold to oppose us. Now, this land lies at our feet.

"The wealth of it all is like the lilies to be plucked by us from our horses thundering over these foreign fields of England. The pickings are lush, and can be taken by anyone, you, me, just by the strength of our sword arms. We support William." Gilbert pulled his stool closer and whispered as if to keep the next words away even from the tent walls. "But if he can not keep insurrection down, can not control the country, then we de Montfords plan to seize it ourselves."

Gilbert looked hard at Riennes. "You will keep this to yourself. Do you understand what I'm saying?"

"Royal intrigue is not strange to me."

"You are a de Montford. There is room for you in this, the riches of this land, your Norman holdings and walled keep and tower back home. What I saw out on the road today was fighting prowess although a strange one. You have travelled, have seen many things I cannot even imagine. You will only be a strength to our cause. You will stay here with us now, your family, and become a true Norman again."

Riennes got up from his stool and stood to look down at the coals of the brazier. Then: "I thank thee uncle for your dear considerations toward me. But, yea, I cannot join thee in this."

"I demand you do. Your father would so. You must come home into our embrace. Your status as a young Norman noble demands it of you."

"I wish not."

"How else are you to strike fear into these Saxons. How else are you to be admired and acquire power?"

"I do not wish to be admired," stormed Riennes. "I was a high lord for years. It gainsays nothing. I am quit of that. I wish to heal wounds, not inflict them."

"This is madness. You have been too long away," argued Gilbert.

"Even thus, I cannot. My loyalty now is to my Khan. I will be quit of it after we present his wishes to William's court. Then, I must undertake my brother's journey until his dream, the same we shared through many dark nights, is fulfilled."

Riennes turned and with his command voice reached out and seized control of Gilbert's attention.

"Then and only then will I turn and come back through this way to Normandy and home. I pray and ask thee for your continued good regards towards me."

The tonal strength of Riennes's voice off balanced Gilbert's demands. He found himself accosted by the force of his nephew's character. The revelation he no longer could bend this boy to do his bidding struck him adversely.

"You are a young Frankish chevalier. Your duty is to family and your king."

"In this I am firm," repeated Riennes. "In time I will take up my duties as the son of my father and mother and your nephew. I must risk your goodwill when I say, press me no further on this."

"You must come home. You must return to us, to assume your place, your rank as a Norman noble."

The heat was up in Gilbert. Yea, though not in Riennes. Coolness, discipline, proper instruction and those sometimes fits of deep depression had trained him not to lose control of emotions.

"You are foolish in this nephew. And soft, from what I saw on the road today."

"Pray what means thee uncle?"

"You cut and struck down a chevalier of a powerful family who came at you. Not easy. Then you treated his wound and raised him up again. You helped him only he will see weakness in that and he will come against you again."

"It may be. Or maybe he will think about it. I have seen it time and time again in a caravan of merchants and camels, and in the service of the Khan himself who found thee cannot force friendship or loyalty, but that thee earn it with help and consideration. His kingship was built on this."

Gilbert rose and slammed down his wine. "Your tent and sleeping pallet await you just to the right of this tent. Go there. Your day and travails have been long. Lie down and know you now can rest safely within the heart of your Norman family. We will talk of this in the morn."

"Thee are not happy with me, pray be."

"Tomorrow. Maybe a night's passage will soften the stubbornness of your obligations."

"I will sleep on your words. Thank thee uncle."

Riennes shook hands with Gilbert in the Roman style, grasping forearms under each other's elbows, then passed out through the tent flap.

Gilbert sat down and poured himself the last drop from his wineskin.

Bugger, he thought. I will have to find another way. It is that Welsh dog. Riennes follows him like a pup. I must find a way to get rid of that son of the old thegn. Let us see. Maybe I should whisper ugly into the ear of Rogert Monclair. Did you know a Welsh mongrel mutilated your son? That has possibilities. I will sip awhile and explore this.

Riennes stepped out into the night. There were camp fires everywhere reflecting white off field tents of Gilbert's men and entourage.

Young bloods rode into the camp in a company of noise and laughter, some carrying hawks on their arms; a return from a day's hawking. Others shouted encouragement about the deer hunt on the morrow. These young chevaliers dismounted and demanded in jest drink and women to slake thirst and desires.

Riennes was led to his mount which had been properly fed and watered. He rubbed him down with a rag and generally checked to see the animal was in good shape. No commander of horse would have done less before bedding down himself.

Riennes went to his tent, stripped off his clothes then washed himself down as best he could from the pail of cold water. With a candle burning nearby on a stool, he sat quiet on his pallet, composed himself, regulated his breathing and went through a mental exercise to control his persistent depression. He broke down the day's events into its basic parts, picking off the detail meat from the bones of those elements. In doing so, he digested details that enlightened him as to the dangers on the road ahead.

His last thoughts were of his uncle. *Be alert. Gilbert like my father is a taker. They never learned a giver gets back many fold. He will not give way in his ambitions and my place therein.*

A black apparition then edged into his consciousness. He could not make it out. The shadow of the figure's cowl masked the face. The darkman turned and faced another form. His brother.

Fear grew in him just before he fell asleep. *Haralde.*

Chapter Three

London, as do all cities,
Gratifies a stranger's desires.

It was strange, but as his mount clip clopped through London streets, Riennes felt his spirits lift, freeing him from the net of dread. Just then, his hefty Frisian did himself a little jump and a back kick of high spirits. He guessed he wanted to gallop, to stretch his limbs after so long aboard ship and the tame activity of the last few days.

Riennes smiled. *Why, he thought, it feels like something nice is about to happen today.* He was headed for Ironmonger Street where Haralde's message said to meet him at a certain weapon smith's armory. As he passed the city's residents at toil, he smiled, dug into his saddle bags, pulled out his pipe and began to peal out joyous notes. He practiced until his lips and his heart caught up a melody that welled up but which tried to slip away from him.

The notes rose above the smoky, shouting, banging, blustering citizens at their brutish work. Some men and women straightened and looked around as their ears picked up the slight sweetening of the air. They pointed as he passed. The music brought forth children who ran after him shouting and clapping. Riennes spun around in his saddle and faced backwards, laughed and piped to a grunge of shabby young.

When his horse felt like it was going to stop, he tapped it on with his heels. When he stopped to laugh, children yapped loud and made him get back at it. Mothers and fathers started streaming out of doorways and backyards, grabbing up their brats and cuffing them back to their chores, yelling at Riennes to stop.

Menya, the Saxon mistress of her own two-storey stone shuttered inn with its big log rafters and fire-pit kitchen, heard Riennes long before she saw him. She was outside hacking a hoe at the soil within her stone-walled garden, to prepare it for vegetable seeds. Well, it wasn't really her inn but that of her old husband. However, he had left days ago, headed for Northumbrian port towns to seek out sources of wine, any kind of wine that may have got through canalem storms. London revelers thirsted. The city was bursting with soldiers and king's men and his cellar was dry. He would be away for weeks. So, it was hers to run now.

She hired two local maids from hungry families, made them wash their dirty hands and face and taught them to cook three rudimentary meals for guests. She had cut away their wool dresses to scoop the swell of young breasts. Already, her inn now earned more coinage than her husband had wrung from it. So what if they were frightened by soldiers who managed to get their hands up between their bare legs for a moment. She taught them how to slap their faces, to keep moving so they wouldn't get trapped between the tables and even to make them pay money for such brief liberties. Herself, she sometimes carried a leather quirt cinched to her right wrist. Some men who learned her husband was gone attempted liberties.

They carried red marks across their faces of her reproach. Soldiers, rich burghers, travelers, even strangers promised her great satisfactions within their embraces, far greater than her old man could give.

It was true. Her husband had bought her young with a purse of pence from her desperately impoverished family. His joy was the delirium of lying between his young wife's thighs every night. Only, their nightly nuptials were a ritual of his sighing and voiding his excited seed, sometimes even before he entered her. He was too old for young Menya. He was such an incomplete man. In night and day dreams, she squirmed, a maid unfulfilled. She tried to hide her frustration, but it was a scent she gave off. During ale and food serving times, the Alpha males amongst her customers sensed thus and crowded her.

The playful lilt of a pipe caught her ear and she looked up. The head of a black-haired man popped up behind the brow of the hill on her street leading up from the river. Only the head was bobbing up towards her backwards. It struck her funny. She put a hand over her mouth and giggled. The head bobbed up and down more into view. Then the head of a black horse preceded the head of the man; then bobbing heads of laughing children, then more of the flute music. Then the man and the horse lifted over the hill and she realized it was a young man riding backwards playing a pipe to a crowd of children and agitated adults.

She giggled louder, then stopped and bowed her head to her work as the musical rider came her way. She could hear the big horse breathing, the pounding of heavy hooves, the squeak of leather and the fun in the sweet notes now coming abreast of her.

She looked up to see parents wading into the crowd to pinch their squawking brats on the noses, cheeks and ears and lead them away. The pipe music turned to a squeal, stopped and the black-haired man laughed as his audience disappeared.

She felt his laughter to be as much fun as his music. She looked up, saw him in profile and realized he was a young man, about her age, clean-shaved with a fresh look about him. Not heavy of beard or nose brushes as was the way of London Saxon men. A fair young man, but as well, somewhat foreign. She was always suspicious of foreign.

When he turned to put away his pipe in his bag, his intent got caught up in her hazel eyes and light brown hair, and he was immediately taken by her. Menya had blossomed into a Saxon beauty. She was a jewel who, when outside, glowed her light in the grimness of the dingy streets. It was the shine of her that caught his eye.

She was immediately caught up in his expression and then the singular way he held himself. She turned and hurled herself at her hoeing. He had caught her looking at him and she blushed. The red bloom in her face flushed down into her belly.

Riennes turned round in his saddle and without realizing, slid down quietly to bump upon the earth. The brief flash of this woman's face had captured him. She was beautiful; not only the most attractive in England, but a sexual-touching kind of beautiful. A moist maid nicely muscled, lithe but round in the right places. She was no light wraith of a girl. Her full breasts were a commanding presence. As her arms banged the hoe at the soil, in her bodice her breasts like two piggy's swelled alive and moved against each other, squirming to free themselves from their bower.

He stepped through the open gate, and gently: "Greetings fair maid. God's grace upon thee."

She straightened up over his foreign way of speaking Saxon. Yet, she gave herself instantly to his blue eyes and the mystery within his sun-boned face and his strange way of speaking Saxon. She was quick enough of eye though, to take in his mount, his weapon, his clothing and his bearing. "And God's grace also upon you . . . . sirrah."

He stared at her, then looked up at one of the few large stone inns he had seen in London, his quick mind seeking a topic to prolong conversation. "Could thee tell me the name of the owner of this inn and whether he has any rooms to let?"

"That would be me . . . . my lord." His accent was foreign. And yes, there was a far away look about his eyes. Different yea, but exciting. "And no, I am afraid no rooms are there."

"Ahh," he smiled and bowed to her. "It must be a task to run such a fine lodging in a royal city bursting with as much activity as this."

His voice was so gentle, understanding. "Yes my lord. We are bursting with lodgers. So much so my husband has left for the north to find more drink and victuals. King's men and this city await William and he was expected a week ago. There is no more room anywhere." *Why did I tell him that? He is so tall, and big, she thought. And he reeks not.*

"Then I must press thee no more. It is unfair to impose my unfamiliarity with your London upon the eve of my presentation to William's court." Riennes wrung his hands, then patted his person as if looking for a coin to present for troubling her.

"You are troubled my lord," she sympathized, putting her hand on his wrist as if to comfort. It was not involuntary. A sudden sexual tenseness had reflexed her hand upon him.

She wanted to prolong his stay here. With her. Also, there was the mention of a royal connection. She smelled wealth, power. Raised in poverty, she hungered for the power of wealth. More the power than the wealth. He had of it about him. He was a noble, a foreigner. Would that she could gain some control over him and his station. Could she be partnered with his status? The combination flushed a heat through her. Strange how she wanted him to gain control of her.

He put his hand over her fingers. "Yes. I am an emissary from a far country. I am commissioned before William's court any moment now. I have travelled these many days and am so fatigued, I need a pillow to lay down my head, rest, then leave. I have no place to set down my baggage which contains gifts for the king."

Their fingers were now interlaced. She was aware of that, yet did not want to break the constant of the intimacy. "I cannot help you. I cannot present you a room for days."

He thought of a way to impose further. "Not days, just hours. I must make my presentation in the late court hours of the night, then seek a morning and noon pallet to refresh myself before resuming my travels."

She looked down at his strong hands, then into eyes the color of which sky or which sea she could not even imagine. "The only room I have is my own."

"I would need it for only a few hours sleep, thence I must be off to a far mountain country. I would be gone before your needs regained your room."

More coin, more income, and even more of his company set her mind arush.

"It is not a large room. My bed is but a pallet. It is made smaller by a large wood oak bask in the middle on the floor which is my bathing place." Why, suddenly, did she reveal this?

"I will be most respectful of that." He pursed his chin with his hand, then squeezed her hand with his other. "I would deem it a gift before I left to bathe myself if any hot water would be available. It is the way where I come from, to bathe and keep oneself clean." He turned, went to his horse, pawed around in his saddle bag and then returned. Like a magician, he flourished a vial of delectable oil which when opened, released a bouquet so exotic it overwhelmed her. It hinted of faraway secret places. "Would it be too much if your maidservant would fill that cask with hot water so that a traveler weary might pour in this rare liquid, bath and draw out the tiredness from his bones?"

She stammered: "I cannot do that my lord."

"Such a vial will be left for thee of course," cooed Riennes. "The sweet oil is from the high mountains of Persia. I have a quantity yet that I will make available only to thee."

"I cannot . . . ." Then, she crumbled. "We will see what we can see about that." Confused, she was not sure what she had just said. "I can see it will be. It seems we are of a like, like," soothed Riennes. "Mind you, I would pay for all that."

As the way of a man with a maid, his soft stroking voice with its promise was for her nectar. She rose to his sweetness. She was attracted by his gentleness.

It was the sound of his voice that was the smoothing of her objections. So reassuring, so promising! Even as she hesitated, she lapped up his aura; his robust stature filled the garden.

She smelled the freshness of him. For a moment, she sensed she was yearning to be in another place with him, not anywhere here.

He blew on the smoldering fire of that wish when he unfolded a lovely blue silk kerchief. "Feel it," he whispered. She jumped. "Feel it," he ordered again. She touched it and the smoothness and opulence of it overwhelmed her. In all her life, she had never seen silk before.

"As a favor, it is yours if all can be arranged between us. I will be gone before thee tire from your day's duties," he suggested. "Let us bind ourselves together in this. Here." She heard a tink and felt something warm in her hand. She looked down and beheld a sight never seen by her kind; two Saracen silver coins. "One is yours now. The second on leaving," he whispered taking one back. He sensed her secret; a deep yearning. Yet, he sensed an independent spirit, as one of her own mind. The combination of beauty, longing and awareness of self was so powerful it overwhelmed him. She fired his loins. Wickedness wetted his appetite.

"Yes. The room is yours," she heard herself whisper, joining as if in a kind of conspiracy. "But you must be away before midnight."

"Thee are a very kind person, and a woman of such glorious generosity. And all this set in the jewel of your beauty," he enticed her. He placed the kerchief in her hand, then drew its oiliness through her fingers before it disappeared. "This shall be left err I leave."

She turned her eyes down. "What name shall I tell my maidservants to let past my door?"

"My name is Riennes. I will serve only thee under any conditions thee might impose while I am within your house."

She lost herself in the blue of him. "Until then." She dropped her hoe, turned and made to go into the inn.

"Pray, what is your name?" "Menya." "Yes. It would be such. It is lovely." As she passed, he admired the very roundness of her hips and the form of her body before the sexual image of her disappeared into her inn holding silver and perfume in her hand.

She watched through a shutter as he mounted and cantered down the road. Her eyes stayed on him. Then her heart jumped as he turned and looked, she was sure, directly through those shutters at her, then disappeared around a corner.

Chapter Four

God is faith; religion is politics.

Haralde and Riennes entered the Great Hall beside Westminster Abbey, led in by a Norman court *steiurhdt*. A flat, light, two-wheeled cart pulled by Amont and Raenulf rumbled behind. Under the red and black silk coverings of their battle pennants were the gifts to the king. Amont was dressed in blue silk pants with a black leather vest over his bony chest and with the Blue Eye of the Ocean emerald hanging from his neck while Raenulf, in green silk pants, had a heavy gold chain dangling across his broad bare chest. Riennes and Haralde wore blue and green silk undershirts respectively showing under black leather cuirasses studded with silver metal rings.

Haralde had found Heimr days ago and under the cover of night he, Amont, Raenulf and Jhon Muck had plotted their trade activity if he and Riennes were successful tonight in the Great Hall.

"This is the making of us," Muck had exclaimed when Haralde handed him an interdict with a royal stamp on it forbidding all king's men from interfering with their trading enterprises.

Haralde explained Riennes had acquired the document from his uncle who had petitioned the Port Reeve of London, Geoffrey de Manville, for it.

The Great Hall was a massive wooden building. The high roof was held aloft by a criss-cross of huge beams, renovations made by Edward before his death. Large smoking bronze lamps provided a yellow light, hung as they were from long chains from roof timbers. They passed through two huge doors into the heart of the hall. Riennes leaned into Haralde's ear and commented on the roughness of everything, that is, compared with the stone buildings, marbled floors and silk hangings of the many opulent halls of palaces in the Khan's kingdom. There was no architecture here, only rough timber. Loud noises of a host of people greeted them from both sides. Tapestries hung down on the walls behind trestle tables and benches on both sides of the interior.

They themselves were headed down a central open aisle. At the far end was a raised dais and upon that, a heavy wooden table. On the walls behind hung all around were the battle flags, pennants and pennons of the warrior noble houses of Normandy. Behind it was a barrel of a man, Odo, Bishop of Bayeux and as a half brother of William, Regent of England in William's absence, barking at some of his loyal fellows. He was of some stature, yet he would still be shorter than Haralde and Riennes. Ranging on both sides of him along tables against the wall were loyal earls, barons, counts and viscomtes, members of the fighting families of Normandy. Servants moved behind them and along both side aisles of benches barely keeping up with their masters' thirsts.

As they walked forward, many eyes turned upon them. Riennes and Haralde were oppressed immediately by the stale and heavy air from so many smoking lamps and candles. Worse, the odor of so many unclean bodies soiled the diminishing good air. Some Normans huddles quieted as their foreign entourage rumbled past them.

Others hissed and whispered: "Toad spitters," and then joked as they recognized the two with the long knives on the road. Other belching parties quieted, a salute to the bearing of the four as they walked the central aisle bearing treasure. The young bolds were there to see what they were told would be a strange presentation before the king's court. And immediately the Normans were impressed. Riennes and Haralde were taller than many in the hall, seemingly bigger in ways more than just stature. As the four walked, they could hear ahead the echoes of nobles roistering in the hall, of jokes, of swearing, of challenges to drinking contests, of drinking bowls and goblets hitting wooden table tops. Some young chevaliers on their left burst out laughing when one of them farted, then shouted: "Stand back. Make room for more." Everywhere they could hear Norman French. Yet, when they first entered, there was a buzz of Anglo-Saxon spoken amongst servants, kitchen help, cooks and maids. It was a clash of cultures, the vanquished serving the conquerors, each not understanding the other.

The young chevalier men were cleaned shaved like them. Also, the back of the necks of many were shaved so that the back quarter of the head was bald to the crown. Apparently it was King William's style and the youth in admiration imitated their king. Haralde saw body ornaments and wealth. One burgher with a slim, pale-complexioned woman, wore a mantle over a knee-length tunic and trousers, all beneath a robe trimmed with martin fur. The mantle was fastened by a broach of beautiful workmanship. It was a foreign jewel fastening. The fur was a bit much in the warming spring. His lady had gold and silver finger rings and armlets. Haralde remembered Muck telling him many London merchants could read and write. They were aware of foreign lands from London to Jerusalem and some even beyond.

They were aware somewhat of the Silk Road and the Spice Route and hungered for what goods came over them, over what they considered the land of heathens, a great empty space full of strange animals and monsters and wealth. Of the Norman and

Saxon warriors, no, they knew little beyond their weapons, their horses and their own body functions. Illiterate, the only knowledge acquired was given them by clerics and theologians who told them only what ecclesiastics felt they needed to know. He hoped there was little silk in London. His fortune and that of his brother depended on it. A little, yes. *Enough that they hunger for it.*

He spotted Lord fitzOsbern who had come down from the dais to stand to one side with the other nobles to watch them approach. His vestments were rich for this court but the clothing material was of poor quality, covered with few adornments. Haralde was glad fitzOsbern wore a doublet of blue linen over his dark jerkin. It would set off what he had in mind to present to the Norman.

Haralde reacted on the moment by moving towards the nobleman, but not before Riennes whispered to him to beware of any dark man of danger. Riennes said he would return momentarily and went over to one side to converse for a moment with his uncle and a handsome but pale-faced woman who Haralde judged might be Riennes's aunt.

Haralde stepped back to the cart and whispered to Amont, The captain turned, fished around under the cover on the flat bed and handed a package to Haralde. The roistering subsided as the assembled became aware of the two foreigners standing in the front. As the roistering died, Haralde stepped over and bowed to fitzOsbern.

"My Lord fitzOsbern," opened Haralde. "My resolve weakens before this great company but turns again and feels a little more resolute in seeing a friend such as thee."

"Ambassador. I am glad my presence strengthens your fortitude," fitzOsbern returned the bow. "You have been treated well? I hope that dark eye impedes you not."

"A Norman initiation to welcome me home, I suppose," joked Haralde.

Here, thought Haralde, was an acquaintance of much influence. A count, he was one of the inner circle of tenant-in-chiefs. This man was a house lord and warrior to the king. Haralde resolved to be very amenable and to grant him a small bequest, one he was sure, fitzOsbern had suggested to Riennes's Uncle Gilbert. In short, a little *baksheesh* was called for.

"Lord fitzOsbern. From the moment of your graciousness on the road, everything has gone well and is ready tonight. . . . My lord," and Haralde stepped closer into his company signaling an intimate conversation. FitzOsbern tilted his head towards Haralde.

"Riennes and I wish to make this presentation to thee for your service to our Khan . . . . ," and he opened a kerchief of red silk, one large enough, suggested Haralde, to be fashioned into a large scarlet gorget around fitzOsbern's throat. As he unfolded it, a small gold chain from which hung a large red ruby, flashed intimately between them. Haralde placed all into the noble's hand and folded the hand into a fist so that all anyone nearby might see was a gift of silk.

"This is an expression of our gratitude," whispered Haralde. "Thee who were hard pressed upon your king's business took a moment to hear our plight, to make the proper decisions and to smooth our road to our presentation this evening,"

FitzOsbern's eyes crinkled in the corner as he smiled with the compliment, and with amazement over the value and beauty of the gift. Avarice glinted in those eyes.

"It is little we can offer as we are near impoverishment," went on Haralde, intent on dampening any further thoughts of greed here. "It has cost us privately in the way of many bribes and inducements to get here to preserve the Khan's essential gifts. However, there is somewhat left that thee may, shall we say at a special rate to your household, want to purchase".

FitzOsbern smiled and bowed condescendingly.

"If thee want to send your man to meet with ours later . . . ." and he nodded to Amont and Raenulf . . . . "thee might find your curiousity and maybe that of some of your friends satisfied and your personal household trappings greatly enhanced after tonight."

FitzOsbern glanced over Haralde's shoulder at the ambassador's two retainers by the cart, then, turned and bowed before Haralde. "I understand," he smiled.

Haralde took his leave as he heard Riennes call him to his uncle. As he glanced back, he saw fitzOsbern call over his seneschal, whisper to him and nod towards Amont and Raenulf.

"Ambassador, thee know my uncle," introduced Riennes, "and this is his wife Hilga, both of whom thee know of from me over the years."

Haralde bowed to Gilbert and then to Riennes's aunt. She was a small, sturdy woman, big boned but of pale complexion as if kept indoors all the time. "He may not have told thee yet but our very existence, our very presence here hangs on your names, of the stories and remembrances of thee he held dear as a youth. My lord, my lady, thee kept your nephew alive over the years," revealed Haralde.

"I am glad to hear that," smiled his Tante Hilga who held a bouquet of flowers in both hands. She relished the size of him. Her eyes roamed across his face. "I suspect it was other than Riennes who gave you that dark tattoo over your right eye."

Haralde passed off the reference to his black eye with a smile and moved on. "I hold this moment sacred myself. If my brother had not survived, I would not be here before thee. He saved my life many times. Thus I am deeply indebted to thee both for my own salvation."

Hilga clapped her hands and laughed at his last words. The bouquet swirled around for a moment as she laughed, lending a pleasant fragrance to the air between them. Though his phrasing was foreign, she caught the meaning. The laughter burst sharply out over the din of the hall. It shook loose her graying hair. Riennes and Haralde watched as a flea exited that hair. She wiped at it and converted the insect body into a small red smear on her neck as she laughed.

They are a crusty and sour lot, thought Haralde of their lack of bathing and cleanliness. He wondered if Hilga had brought a bunch of flowers to mask body odours perhaps? Then again, he harkened back to his Saxon father and his own household where water was used naught but for drinking. "I am thirsty, not dirty!" his father used to roar into his cup at the quaffing of his ales.

Gilbert, a severe man whose sensibilities rarely caught such intonations of language, glared at her and she cut short her joyful outburst.

"Anything, anything thee may request of me will be fulfilled instantly. I am alive today because of thee. Riennes talked about his uncle and aunt constantly. The memory of both of thee kept him alive, and thus me also."

Haralde continued and saw Hilga's eyes widen. In their depths was something more intimate than interest. He glanced briefly at Riennes and caught a warning.

"You are most kind to my family," bowed Gilbert. He had been keenly observing Haralde, measuring this companion of his nephew, looking for a weakness, a flaw, something that could be used to bring Haralde down. Instead, he felt a twinge of warning. This Haralde was a stout young man, both across the shoulders, and in his intellect. Gilbert, an ambitious, cruel lout at times, was always cautious around educated people.

"We de Montfords give back our thanks to your safeguarding him. Riennes was groomed to be an important de Montford magnate and we mourned his loss most deeply years ago. We are obligated to you. I will see that you get everything I think you should have."

Riennes and Haralde glanced at each other. They caught his last seemingly strange phrasing of words; as if Gilbert was trying to say something proper but under some confusion bespoke as if a hidden subterfuge of his. His brother had cautioned him about Gilbert with a 'Watch your back with my uncle'.

The din dropped throughout the hall, and everyone turned as an elder steuirhdt of the court holding a high staff strode into the open before the dais, thumped the floor heartily and ordered all to bear witness to the wishes of the king.

While this was going on, Gilbert leaned to his nephew and whispered. "I am glad this is underway without Abbot Lanfranc present. This should go quickly. That prickly inquisitor would make a long dreary night of this," Haralde overheard Gilbert's whisper.

"Lanfranc? Who is he?" inquired Riennes who bent close to his uncle.

"The foreign priest who wormed his way into our king's favor," explained Gilbert. "The rumor is this foreigner will be anointed Archbishop of Canterbury when William returns. I have been told it was he, and not the strength of William's sword arm, that delivered Britannia onto us." Gilbert explained this Lombard churchman was not averse to using disreputable stratagems to gain what he thought was right. The ecclesiastic had turned up in Normandy some 30 years before he was associated with Duke William and the invasion. It was Lanfranc who convinced William his claim to the throne was a little weak, but if he had the backing of the pope, it would be stronger.

Lanfranc then traveled to Rome and secured papal endorsement. The argument was for an invasion of Britannia to reform a less than devout English church. Many great Norman, Flemish and German men of arms flocked to William's flag once they heard his invasion had the pope's blessing.

"They say he is a respected scholar of logic and theology. That kind of shit means nothing to me. All I know he has thwarted de Montford ambitions in the king's counsel many a time. His influence on William is too great. I would like to run a blade up his ass I would."

In the months and years to come, the two young men were to learn Britannia was a rich plum much sought by the Frankland noble houses. For 200 years, It had been loyal, collecting and sending to Rome the offering known as Peter's Pence, and it had always encouraged Saxons, Welsh and Northumbrians to make pilgrimages. Its sin was that it was remote and different. Much of its scholarship and all of its pastoral work were in a confusion of languages, none of them Latin, and it was easy for other churchmen to suspect that schisms and heresies lay hidden behind such a Babel of barbarous tongues.

"And this Lanfranc hates heresies. Like a dark shadow, he swoops down on any smell of perversities of faith."

Riennes eyes widened. "Dark shadow?"

"He dresses in black from head cowl to the floor," answered Gilbert. "One would think as a churchman and a leading theologian he would take on some white. He is a dark fear for the innocent as well as the guilty."

Riennes locked eyes with his brother. "Is he here uncle?" asked Riennes. "No, not that I can see. If he were, he would be standing near watching Odo. The abbot and the bishop distrust each other."

Odo rose. Seated beside him a woman of pale beauty with a garland of flowers around her head followed him with her eyes as he stood and swept his gaze across the might of Normandy.

"Attend all! Attend all," shouted the elder court's man. "Hear Odo, Bishop of Bayeux, and by the grace of King William, Regent of England."

Odo held up his arms. "We hearken to the king's wishes this night. Word has come of his delay to his return. He stays to finish the insurrection of disloyalty on the home earth. All chevaliers and heads of noble houses will gather around me later. The king has set a new date for his arrival. You will be released under new decrees to carry out the consolidation of Norman expansion across our holdings here.

The two watched the business of their home being dispensed. Odo was a round, fleshy man, his voice was heavy with authority, and it carried to the back. His hair was cut in the tonsure to emulate Jesus' crown of thorns. He wore finery this night in his role as regent and not in the woolen robe with the cowl of his order.

Last year he had splashed ashore with other Norman chevaliers and as a fighting churchman, had beside his brother, thrown himself against King Harold's army. Swinging a huge mace from the back of his horse, he had smashed into the Saxon wall of shields and spears. A sword was denied a churchman. Such would shed blood and deal a mortal blow, not compatible with ecclesiastic belief. A mace was a compromise, as a blow from such a weapon would likely only lay an enemy low. On Senlac Hill near Hastings on the southeast coast of England, some thousands of Normans had charged their mounts against the locked shield wall of Harold throughout a long October day. Later that evening, William with Odo and the horde of Franks had opened that wall, killed Harold and vanquished the island's last Saxon king.

"Before we complete that business, let us dispense first with a deputation from what has been told me is a future ally to William. Let the two ambassadors come forward. And blast you no noise. The king's displeasure upon any of you if these two suffer any affront to their dignity."

The senior major domo thumped the ground and motioned for Riennes and Haralde to come to the open space before the regent. The cream of Normandy's occupying leadership now leaned forward.

The din quieted as the two young men stepped into the space before Odo's appraising gaze. They felt his intelligence lock onto them and they knew instantly this man was more than just an austere holy man.

Haralde and Riennes looked at each other with some trepidation. Their hearts were pumping in their mouths. However, they were used to speaking before a royal presence. They resolved themselves to this. Haralde nodded to his brother.

"Bishop Odo of Bayeux, Regent of England, King William's eminence upon his kingdom, I am Riennes de Montford, ambassador of his Grand Presence, the Gher Khan of the 10 walled cities of Kush. But before all this, I am also a Norman."

"Bishop Odo of Bayeaux, Regent for the Duke of Normandy, representative of the Royal House of King William in Britannia, I am Haralde Longshield, confidant of the Gher Khan, the Shield, Helm and Lance of a Thousand Horse and Protector of the Desert People of the High Plains. But foremost, I am Welsh."

A murmur of wonder ran through the hall. These were not the names of foreigners. Disappointment grew in the ranks of they who expected something exciting and exotic to unfold here this night. One lord who had been talking to a companion, turned on Haralde's introduction and his eyes settled intently upon the ambassador.

One of Odo's eyebrows rose as he gazed around the hall and imposed his will upon the restless. At a nod, the major domo thumped his rod on the boards and quieted the hall.

Odo spoke again: "We have been informed these two emissaries are sons of our homelands but from a long time ago. Be still. They have a tale to tell, one of youth, of enslavement, of great travel and of high military achievements. They are skilled in arms. From what I have been told, their bearing, their courage, the strength of their arms, have carried them to high office in great courts in exotic lands we have never even heard of. Listen now. They bring words of alliance from a distant king and they bear gifts to our King William as a token of affection." Odo turned to them both. "Now, start at the beginning, how you left our shores and how it is you now come bearing blessings. . . ."

Haralde bowed, took a step back and gave way to the Norman-fluent Riennes. Riennes gave Haralde a brief 'do not-abandoned-me' glance. Haralde stood one step just behind and gave his brother a reassuring nod.

So Riennes looked at the white faces of all around the hall, then turned to Odo. And he told them their story:

It was of a young son of a Welsh Marcher noble, a thegn of King Edward, snatched by raiding Vikings from a beach near a monastery where the youth was to receive religious instruction. His companion, a young Norman, was sailing homebound from a visit with Flemish relatives along the Lowland coast when his vessel was boarded by Vikings. In the killing of his guardian and of the captain and crew, in the noise and the din and the cries, he was struck down by a raider, carried across the gunnels into the attacking vessel and thrown down a hole where he crashed into the body of this Welsh young boy in chains. Amidst the crying of chained women and children, he and his fellow ambassador here clung to each other. Months of sailing and other raids by the Viking crew brought them into the blue warm waters of the sunny Middle Sea, the Mare Romanus. The slavers told them they would fetch them bags of gold, for here there were Moors, Saracens, pirates, Goths and remnants of still civilized Roman families and estates seeking the status of owning blue-eyed, fair young boys of the Franks as household slaves. However, they were eventually sold as slaves further away, at an Outremer slave market, just east of Jerusalem (the hall murmured at the mention of the holy city). They then were made to walk it seemed for a year across deserts and mountains, made to live like nomads, to thirst, to hunger, to feed and lead camels until they were brought to a major trading and slave center.

Unlocked from the long chain of slaves, he and Haralde were bought by a mean, short, brown man with slanted eyes and licks of long black hair. Hoisted up behind two horsemen, they rode for weeks across a crushing heat and impenetrable loneliness. Taken to a mountain kingdom, their new masters threw them into a compound with other boys, some also with slanted eyes, but others surprisingly like themselves, from the Frankland and the Norse countries, from the Steppes of the Rus and from places even further to the east that to this day they have never seen but learned much about.

In time, Riennes's tale went on, he and his companion here were trained as horse soldiers in the service of the Khan, learned the art of the short bow and sword, grew to became commanders of sections of white and black horse and achieved such victories that they were presented to the Khan in person who came to favor them. They were brought into the royal household and educated in knowledge their Khan wanted them to have. Their king had filled his cities with teachers, astronomers, engineers, mathematicians, medicine healers, poets, philosophers, historians, musicians and monks, priests and holy men of the different religions of the earth. They were able to retain by voice and by writing, the languages of their homeland because in the Khan's kingdom were many slaves from the Roman sea, even from Normandy and Britannia.

It was from them the two learned of great turmoils raging across the Frankland and through the Anglo-Saxon island across the canalem.

"Long had we expressed our homesickness to our Khan. Finally, for our long loyalty, we were awarded our freedom and sent home on a mission with gifts of affection, friendship and a far-off allegiance for William who now is our king both of Britannia and Normandy," ended Riennes.

"Many times through our long voyage, we were stopped, threatened with slavery again, but through the loyalty of such as the two men behind us, we were able to escape with our lives and much of the Khan's prize. What we are about to present is paltry compared to the true expression of the Khan's good feelings for William and his family. Of the Khan's riches that have been taken from us, we have replaced in the way of treasures garnered in our travels. They are wonders of wealth. The Khan cherishes family, loyalty and friendship which we understand William holds dear above all things." Riennes bowed and as he stepped back, added: "Word has been sent back. While the Gher will visit fury upon those he can who stole from us, and he has the power to do that even to the land of Outremer, I am sure many gifts taken from us have been replaced and may be on their way one day to this court."

As Riennes bowed and stepped back, he felt Haralde beside him. "That last bit, thee made up. Why?" As Riennes rose, he whispered low to Haralde: "I do not know. Maybe to secure our place in their good graces over the many days ahead."

Haralde's hiss of amazement over his brother's rashness and intuitiveness was smothered under a round of table banging from the coarser company throughout the hall, overt approval of their story and admiration for their loyalty in coming home.

The nobles in the front trestles turned their heads about, to take in the reaction of their vassal rabble in the lesser benches down the hall.

"My lord, our credentials from the lips of the Khan himself, we will present shortly." Riennes bowed.

Haralde half turned and backed up towards Amont, Raenulf and the hand cart. It was agreed his part was to start the gift presentation.

"Bishop Odo and Lord Regent!" Haralde's voice boomed around the hall "Ambassador de Montford perfectly described the two kings's love of family. Thusly, the Great Khan honors Matilda, the wife of William.

Amont leaned forward, the Blue Eye of the Ocean under his chin in mid air for all to see. While the assembled 'oooohed', Haralde removed the great jewel and moved towards the dais. As he drew nigh, he was intercepted by the major domo who warned Haralde none may approach personally, took the bauble and placed it in the hands of Odo.

The Regent dangled it in the air, his eyes full of wonder. A shaft of yellow light glinted blue off the jewel. Those in the back of the hall 'ooohed' over the sharp, slash of blue.

"Bishop Odo and Lord Regent!" Haralde was back at the handcart, removing a heavy gold chain from the neck of Raenulf. He turned, walked forward in a clink of gold and presented the treasure to the major domo. The crowed 'ooohed' again as they watched the old court official struggled with the weight of it. He crossed and draped it across the arms of the regent. Too heavy, it clunked to the table. "A token of the Khan's regard for William himself."

"Bishop Odo and Lord Regent!" Riennes came from the cart with two cloth bolts, one of blue silk and one of red. "For Matilda and William's household." The major domo scurried back and forth on his skinny legs.

The color of blue and red and the word silk caught the ear of the hall in the land of wool and rough linen. Haralde saw fitzOsbern whisper to a servant and point to the handcart.

"Lord Regent!" Haralde walked forward from the cart with a small wooden keg. "From the Great Khan to William because he knows what cost the peace of a kingdom demands of a ruler." Aided by Raenulf, Haralde swept by the court steward and bumped the heavy keg onto Odo's dais, a clink of coin sounding to the back of the hall. Another murmur moaned through the hall as Odo opened the keg on mid-way hinges and many saw the glint of Byzantium gold piled therein.

"Lord Regent!" Riennes stepped forward with small boxes of pepper, salt, cloves and ginger, all spices bound for the king's household all the way from the storied east. The eyes and interests of the merchants in the hall followed the box offerings to the foot of the dais table. Such rare objects of wealth, only heard of by a few in England, made the hearts of the many traders in the hall thump with envy.

Next, Riennes opened a large bag, pulled out a small brown fruit, and moved forward to offer one to Odo to taste. He was headed off by the major domo again who told Riennes this was forbidden, that food for the regent had to be tasted first. The high court steuirhdt turned, clapped his hands and a taster servant of Odo's was brought forward, his eyes widening apprehensively on the brown fruit.

Assassination by poison was very much a political weapon, even here, and Riennes recognized the move. Tasters were common protections in the Khan's court. A few pitiful royal tasters had met a sudden end to their careers, victims of such attempts. Riennes, not wanting the tempo of the gift offerings to be interrupted, waved the taster aside, popped one of the fruit into his own mouth, and then shouted to his aunt and to all in the hall: "Tante Hilga, will thee join me in this gift to the king?", and offered the small sweet to Hilga.

She looked at the fruit, then at her husband, then without waiting for his permission, stood up, took the date from her Riennes, bit into it and her eyes smiled. Riennes moved towards the dais, shouldered the major domo aside, and offered the same to the slight beauty beside Odo. Taking her lead from Hilga, the lady bit into the fruit, and then a squeak of: "Oh, how wonderful" escaped her.

"It is a date, a fruit of the moist desert oasis, covered in cane sugar. Do thee like it?" asked Riennes. Both women clapped their hands together in enjoyment. Odo stood up, gestured to Riennes for one, popped it into his mouth and then smiled, rolling his eyes towards the crowded hall. "It is sweet!" he shouted, and the hall broke into laughter.

Haralde carried a small wooden box to the dais and set it down. "Sugar!" he revealed, sliding the lid back revealing the brown granules. "For the king's pleasure," he continued. Foods such a stew, chicken, pork, venison, fish, gruel and rough bread went unseasoned amongst the Franks and in England. Merchants leaned way over their tables in the back of the hall to get a glimpse of what they knew were goods worth more than the jewels and the gold. They were aware of these mercantile treasures of the exotic east, so far away that such were unattainable.

And on it went. The court discipline was relaxed as the gifts came forward. From the far East into this austere court of rough adventurers were presented ivory tusk carvings, costly dyes like cinnabar, indigo and henna; exotic medicines like camphor, cubebs and aloes. Riennes presented a string of Indus pearls to Odo's lady and said: "Again for our queen", then came brocades, sandalwood and exotic rugs.

"My lord," said Haralde who brought forth a small wooden box and he too tried to brush aside the court official. Haralde stopped, and asked: "If I may approach?" Odo waved him forward and Haralde stepped up on the dais, turned slightly sideways for the hall's pleasures, slid a top panel aside and there inside on a bed of straw was a set of eight clear glass goblets of a delicacy and quality unseen in this part of the world. With admiration rippling through the noble ranks, he turned and pulled out two glasses, one for Odo and the other for his lady.

"My lord," said Riennes who was handed two earthenware bottles. "We understand our king frowns upon excessive drink. However, if it is his wish to do so on important Crown occasions or serve important men of state, we recommend something new, fresh and exciting for these glasses." He popped a wax bung and started towards Odo but this time the court steward would have none of it. "No, no, no!" the major domo waved. Drink could too easily be doctored by tinctures of poison.

"Aaaghh," growled Riennes in frustration. He turned, looked around, approached his uncle, grabbed Gilbert's drinking bowl and splashed its contents onto the rushes on the board floor. He spilled some of the earthenware light golden liquid into the bowl (a merchant in the back squawked: 'Oh my God' over the color) and drank it. He filled the small bowl again, and handed it to Gilbert. Gilbert looked down into it, then sipped a bit all the while looking at his nephew. Then, his eyes lit up like a small boy: "Oh my God yes. I must have this."

Riennes advanced upon the dais and this time the court senior remained stationary. He poured some into Odo's lady's glass. The color again sparked comments around the hall. She smiled, picked up her glass and drank. "Oh! Oh! It's so sweet, and round, and . . . and yet dry, and not muddy at all. It tastes sweet, like a cherry."

The hall jumped as a barrel was swung out of the cart by the powerful Raenulf and thumped on the board floor. The Viking rumbled it up to the front and set it on its end.

"It is a wine from a sunny place, from the southern shores of the Caliphate de Cordoba in al-Andalusia," described Haralde. "Yes milady, like a cherry. The peasants there under the heel of the Moors who, as Moslems are not supposed to drink wine, but do, grow small vineyards of this. They call it something that sounds like a cherry."

As Haralde spoke, he hoped no one would question why some of the Khan's gifts had to come from pagan Iberia, not far from Normandy to here. Short of gifts, Riennes and he had to find some replacements on their voyage home.

Odo, eyes sparkling, obviously was enjoying the ambassadors' presents and he rose with his glass goblet. "Then I must try some so that I can relate to our king what you have just told us."

"One moment my lord regent," said Riennes as he passed Haralde and went to the cart. Again, he pulled out another earthenware bottle, turned, looked at the frowning court steuirhdt, crossed over to a noble half sitting on his table and asked him for his drinking cup. The noble nodded yes, Riennes poured a splash into it and the man gulped it down. "God that is good! Not course like ours. And strong. Man strong."

"Thee are right sirrah." And Riennes turned and moved swiftly to the dais. He poured a dark, red wine for Odo who bent over his table with glass lowered for the liquid offering. "I recommend not so fast my lord. Sip it," said Riennes who knew of the Norman's penchant for gulping what in this part of the world were coarse wines, to pass the palate quickly for the purpose of inebriation only.

"My, my, my," Odo licked his lips. Laughter erupted around the hall as Odo bent forward and received another glass. He sipped again, then licked again. "You are right. A strong, bracing, satisfying wine, bracing but very refined. Hearty, a man's taste."

"It is a little-known wine again from the Iberian. This time from a small fishing village, Oporto," described Haralde as Raenulf rumbled a barrel past him and onto the floor before the dais.

As Riennes came to stand beside him, Haralde changed the tempo of the presentation. "My Lord Regent, these are gifts from our Khan. However, our Khan wishes now to present something private directly to William. It is a box containing an item that deals with military matters and the safety of his Crown."

There was a stirring behind them. Odo looked over their shoulders to see fitzOsbern, William de Poitier, Robert, Count d'Eau, the Flemish Lord Gerbod, and Geoffrey de Mandeville, all the 'wise men' of the king's inner council, rising as if to move their way around the trestles towards the dais.

"What say you fitz?" asked Odo as he saw concern on their faces.

"We know nothing of their possessing something to do with William's Crown and any threat to him," answered fitzOsbern who had received from Riennes's uncle a full outline on all his nephew had told him about the Khan's gifts and the presentation.

Gilbert had said nothing about this. For sure they did not like the idea of being surprised by these foreigners on matters touching Norman royal interests.

Haralde stepped forward: "My Lord Regent. Let us show thee and thee alone what we wish to present to our good William. If thee feel it is a concern to these good lords of his, then it is your duty to inform them. However, thee might consider them of such import that it be for the king's eyes only. Our Khan wished this to be a secret, a matter of king to king."

Odo held up his hand and halted the advance of the chief nobles. He stood with his hands on his hips, thinking quickly.

Haralde held his breath. Actually, the gift in dispute was less a matter of state and more to gain something from the royal purse. What he wanted was a secret meeting with the king, or at least an intimate moment with Odo. He wanted to talk the crown into a covenant granting him the exclusive right to supply more of what was in the box. Often he had talked the Khan into financing ideas he proposed. Royal charters, he had discovered, were often very lucrative.

Then: "Sit down oh good men of Normandy," Odo judged finally. "I will bow to the ambassadors. Then I will decide if it warrants your concern. Ambassador. You may come forward with this box of yours, and I hope for your sake it offends not me, let alone these good men."

Haralde pulled a small heavy box out from under the cart's cover, walked up to the dais table with the fretting court major domo keeping step with him and wringing his hands. As the box thumped onto the table, Odo dismissed the old man.

"Yes?" asked the bishop as Haralde approached and leaned closer to him. Haralde, ignoring a sour, wine-body odour bouquet about the holy man, pulled open the box. Odo looked down intently into its interior, then frowned perplexed.

"They are arrowheads, a hundred of them," whispered Haralde. "I can see that," the bishop whispered back. " . . . . but what have they to do with royal matters?" he asked.

Haralde picked up a black arrowhead and placed it in Odo's hand. The small cold weaponhead was as long as a man's small finger and just as thick and round. It had no barbs; rather two small flanges ran almost the whole length ending just before its sharp tip.

"It is made of metal called steel. It is the hardest iron ever hammered out of a forge," explained Haralde. "That and its form means it has a narrow entry." The bishop turned it over in his hand, then turned and looked at Haralde, still trying to understand.

Haralde leaned closer and whispered lower. "It will pierce armour. It goes through chain mail easily. If it were to hit plumb, it will go through plate armour. With these, William could defeat armies larger than his own. As it is, there are only a hundred here. Good enough for now to equip those who guard the king."

"Where did you get these?"

"From far away. From a weaponsmith of the Khan's armoury who knows the secret of this steel," whispered Haralde lower.

The bishop bounced it in his hand a few times. Then, he dropped it in the box and said in a voice loud enough for all to hear: "Bah! Archers! A coward's weapon. No reward comes out of this. Arms for only common men of low station and assassins. A good chevalier would break a bow for firewood to warm his backside before he would mount a saddle with one of these . . . . ," and Odo raised the box to show the content to the nobles in the hall and shouted: "Arrowheads. A strange gift from their Khan to our king. A fine gesture, but far from anything that seriously would threaten the state of William's claim to this throne."

The concerned nobles nodded. They made a few comments amongst themselves, sat back down and seemed to relax.

"But my Lord Regent," whispered Haralde. "The chief weapon of all the Khan's vast horse armies is the bow. Such a weapon is a scythe that has toppled great enemies and empires . . . ." but his whisperings were lost, or maybe ignored, under the regent's loud shoutings to the men of rank around the front trestles and under the question William's regent threw at the ambassadors if there was anything more of their presentations before the court.

"Yes," answered Haralde. He stepped back and resigned, left the regent's table. Regretfully, it was obvious the fighting holy man had failed to grasp the importance just handed him in that heavy box. His merchant heart jerked over this loss.

"The cart is almost empty my lord," responded Riennes and with some enthusiasm, he reached for a single object remaining. "However, we have saved the most valuable for the end."

Riennes pulled a huge clay ball suspended from a string inside a half metal arch. The arch was fastened to a round wooden base. As he walked up to the regent's table, the ball, mostly colored blue, but with brown clay masses, spun on its string.

Riennes set it carefully on Odo's table, spun the ball, then stepped back and joined Haralde. Riennes bowed and in a presentation sweep of opening arms, said: "Behold!"

Odo, confounded, gazed upon the turning orb. He watched it a moment, but could not grasp what it was before him. He looked up in question.

"But behold Lord Regent. Thee hold before thee the power of the world. Behold bishop, the world and place where we all live, the firma where all the various empires and kingdoms of the world inhabit, the mighty and the lowly. At this very moment, thee hold a treasure greater than any we have put before our William this night," Riennes tainted his voice with wonder and amazement, hoping to ignite the bishop's intellect.

"See sirrah. We are looking down at the blue seas of the world," exhalted Haralde. "This is the combined knowledge of Christians, Mahamads, Greeks, Phoenicians, Persians, Chinois and who knows who else, sea captains, land travellers, wanderers and traders. Here before thee are the known seas of the known oceans of the known countries of the known peoples. See, your finger sits upon Britannia and your thumb on Normandy, all within the space of your hand. Think of the wonder of that. On the other side of the globe from your hand is the silk land of Chinois, close from whence we came."

"Faith, what worth is a clay toy to a king?" queried Odo, who began to realize what had been placed suddenly before him; the world as a round ball, a heretical belief held to be abhorrent to the church and to God. As a churchman, he released it, and seemed physically to shrink as away from any pagan contamination.

"Knowledge my lord, the greatest gift of all," Haralde urged Odo to grasp. "It is the sum total of many minds and of years of thinking that arrived at this conclusion, that the earth is round. Our Khan killed thousands to capture those with that knowledge. He possesses many of these balls, and he worked with his wise men to fill in the blankness of countries and the voids of the seas. This orb holds the combined knowledge of great men of the world. For peace, it is priceless, for war, it is a power greater than any king's army."

"Sirrah," Riennes joined in to underscore Haralde. "We come from a land where learned men have translated works into Arabic from Greek, Persian, Egyptian, Syriac and Sanskrit. The knowledge from these works has enriched geographers, astronomers, astrologers, mathematicians, philosophers. I myself have seen in great Mahamad cities libraries, bookstores and even hospitals for the people's well being and . . . ."

The air seemed to take a jump, that which they had once experienced just before the first bump of an earthquake. Riennes stopped addressing the regent, fell back a step, then half turned to his right.

And from that direction came a cold, clear, dagger of a voice: "And where, pray tell, in all of this is the works of God, and his son Jesus Christ, exalted?"

Haralde jerked his head round to the crowd on their right and out of that phalanx stepped a monk dressed in black, his eyes shining out of the black shadow of his cowl.

"Haralde!" Riennes warned.

The man of small stature strode towards them, then passed them, made for the dais where he pulled back his cowl, then with one furious swing of his arm swept the globe from the table and sent it crashing into pieces against the floor.

Haralde made to move towards the wreckage but was stopped when the man tred upon the shards. He pointed to both of them.

"Monk!" shouted Haralde. "Thee have wrought terrible damage upon many men's minds."

"Our blessed Saint Boniface once charged an Irish abbot with perverse and sinful beliefs that the world was round. Can I do no less?" Lanfranc's finger pointed an accusation at them. "Are you pagans? Are you giant men from the land of the Mahamads come to pollute King William's power over this land with your gifts?" Lanfranc looked up challenging them.

Riennes reacted first. "Pagans, no my lord abbot. Christians," said Riennes, attempting to place himself in the fore and keep Haralde in the background. "I am Riennes de Montford, son of Raoul de Montford, baptized in our family abbey in our citadel home in Breton.

"Let him speak," ordered Lanfranc pointing to Haralde.

"He is not fluent in Norman French, lord abbot. I would speak for him so that . . . . "

"When I entered the hall, he spoke well enough for the men of Normandy to understand him clearly. Speak!"

Riennes was alarmed. What he foresaw had come to pass. Haralde was alone before this company and the dark of this man. He himself had nothing to fear, a Norman welcomed back into the arms of his family. However, Lanfranc had just now carved Haralde away from him. Haralde now stood alone. Haralde could be banished from here, imprisoned, even assassinated if he was regarded to be foreign and an enemy to the interests of these men. Through Haralde, Riennes thence could be dragged down. Riennes knew immediately his own soothing, persuasive, cunning voice would have little effect upon the power of Lanfranc. All Haralde had now to defend himself was his intelligence, and that innate common sense he possessed that had extricated them both from many a dangerous situation. Haralde's tongue possessed a certain honey quality that had often wooed Riennes and other men into his brother's many enterprises.

Haralde immediately sensed his vulnerability. Riennes was clearly agitated. His brother's body signaled alarm. He stepped forward and knew instantly the danger Lanfranc represented.

Riennes had warned of this moment. The abbot clearly wanted him out onto the centre, there to be pricked, probed, pushed to speak falsely.

"No pagan, abbot. I am Haralde Longshield, son of Stoerm Longshield, a thegn in King Edward's court. Baptized in Saxon Mercia," answered Haralde. *He will have at me. He will be the harrier, I his mouse. I must hide from each of his rushes.*

"Abbot Lanfranc." Bishop Odo spoke from behind his high table. "Of us they may be but be also aware these young lords have credentials. They are emissaries sent from a far king supporting our William."

"You, bishop must deal with these two in the interest of Norman royalty," Lanfranc stated, not wavering in his gaze upon the two. "I come to conduct an inquiry as to whether the integrity of these two men is morally acceptable to even make presentations here."

Odo looked at the abbot, then at the backs of the two young men. He shrugged. "You may have a moment," and sat down.

"I understand ambassadors that you come from a land so very far away that it is even beyond the borders of Outremer," Lanfranc inquired, then continued not waiting for an answer. "This land that you were brought up in is full of perversions, intolerant beliefs, pagan religions, beasts and monsters. Are you from the land of that kind who desecrates Jerusalem today, who daily wipes his vile feet upon Jerusalem's Church of the Holy Sepulcher, the tomb of Christ?"

Haralde stood silent for a moment, then answered cautiously: "We would not know who that would be Abbot Lanfranc."

"I sense you may be Mahamads?" Lanfranc crunched his way over the clay shards and walked around the central space, looking at those gathered in the Great Hall, playing to they who had come for a spectacle promised.

Haralde hesitated, trying to anticipate where Lanfranc was going with this. "No. We are Christians my lord abbot."

"Is this Khan of yours the Mahamad king who seized Jerusalem? Is he the filth that sits upon the throne in the Holy City and who this day is here to present false support of William's claim to this island kingdom which was promised him by the faithful Christian King Edward?"

"Our Khan who does honor to William this day is the royal head of his family and his people who live far beyond Jerusalem, far beyond the great deserts and mountains to the east, far outward from the sphere of Outremer. If we could put together that orb thee just smashed, I could show thee where his kingdom lay on the other side of the world and how great in size it is."

"Do you not believe that mongrel pack of Mahamad worshippers who in turn bow down before their pagan Allah is an abomination?"

Haralde hesitated, then answered: "No, more the most recent affirmation of the Creators promise to us all."

The three could hear Odo's heavy intake of breath. From the hall behind them, there was silence. Riennes knew immediately that those behind the trestles did not understand what was going on.

"Their Allah is a pagan idol!"

"Islam forbids images or idols of any kind. Besides, al-Lah is God," stated Haralde firmly.

"Then why Allah and not God?"

"Different name. Same God. God spreads his many robes to encompass and love many peoples who speak different languages," answered Haralde. "Our God is the God of Abraham and from him the Christians, the Mahamads and the Jews. Before God, was he not known as Yahweh and before that Shaddai?"

Lanfranc broke his tempo for a moment, perturbed by Haralde. *I must be more guarded. This Welsh adventurer sounds educated.*

"For a Christian, you sound very sympathetic towards these pagans."

"I am alive and stand before thee today because Islam honors Christ and the Hebrew prophets and so we were permitted, nay, encouraged to practice our Christian beliefs." Haralde paused to let that circulate around the hall. "Thee call them pagans. They called us infidels, but for our differences we were not persecuted. Through their tolerance, we retain our Christian souls this day. And as for your other questions, Mahamad did not claim divinity, but is Islam's founding prophet. Further, our great Khan is a Hindu, not a Mahamad. A great teacher in our youth was a Buddhist."

Lanfranc said nothing. He glared at Haralde, not frustrated, but impatient over how his own intellect and ability as a debater had yet to sniff out Haralde's vulnerability. Deep down he knew Haralde and Riennes had been polluted, were not of the Latin Church.

"We have seen this," interjected Riennes sending his soothing voice up to Odo. "Other faiths and beliefs in such lands have we seen tolerate each other. . . ."

Enough!" Lanfranc's palm up displaced Riennes's attempt to enter and deflect Haralde's inquisition. The abbot looked around the assembled behind and appeared to be lost in thought. He knew Haralde was trying to distract him with his knowledge from his travels. For the leading churchman of Normandy, theology, logic and a lifetime of ecclesiastic studies would soon expose what he sought. It would not take long now.

He walked a short distance, then with his back to the two young men, he asked in a quiet, soothing, reassuring voice. Riennes prayed Haralde recognized the danger in that tone.

"In your travels, did you see examples of God's presence?"

Haralde stood immobile; then, a furtive glance towards Riennes told him danger was upon him from this quarter.

Then: "Yes, in the things God opened my eyes to learn and the new knowledge he gave me permitted me to understand new things."

"Did he not reveal that some knowledge was evil and men should avoid it?"

"There is no such thing as evil, only ignorance."

"Aah, but it is a fact some ignorant men can be led to evil ways and the church must guard its flock against that. All things that he needs to know have all been given man in God's world. All things are fixed. All God's wisdom and knowledge is centered."

"Nay my Lord Abbot. The latter cannot be true. I see new things every day that we know not of but which later is a wonder to us all. It is that man himself can find truth."

"Man is imperfect and sinful. He finds truth only through God."

"Nay. God's gift to all of us is to discover that knowledge, to question it. It is the one universal gift He has given to all men. Man is capable of discovering the truth on his own, and creating true things that benefit us all."

"Like your false globe? Give me an example?"

"I have seen a blacksmith take different kinds of metals, materials and fire with different kinds of heat and in one night of hard work, changes them from one form into another, new and useful. Such did this smithy transmute one kind of matter into something wholly new and man-made. As long as he has the knowledge to pursue wherever his mind leads him, how can that be evil?"

"It is not that he has knowledge. It is that he uses it to elevate himself, his station above his fellow man, above the church" retorted Lanfranc. "When human ambitions exceed His teachings, that is wrong. Humans cannot use knowledge to elevate themselves above God's wishes. God commands. In the eyes of the church, God's creation does not change."

"Some claim creation was completed by God in a set period of time and now is finished. Yet, it continues," argued Haralde his ire up, knowing that was what Lanfranc wanted.

"It does not!" exhorted the abbot, his voice full of menace. "All knowledge comes from the past. God's work now is history. God was here before. Creation was here before. The struggle with the devil was here, history was here. We must now exalt his works. There is no need to understand anything else beyond that."

"But thee must see all creation continues to change before God's presence?"

"You talk through the mouth of pagans. It does not matter you compare your present world around you based on what you have seen elsewhere in your pagan world. That is just worldliness, pride. God and myself as his servant deal with other worldliness. This more than knowledge is all that you need to understand."

An idea brightened in Haralde's mind over the direction Lanfranc was taking him.

"So . . . ."

"Haralde, no!" hissed Riennes who saw Haralde about to pitch forward into the black hole of Lanfranc's trap. Behind, the assembled grumbled. None of this made any sense to them. Riennes realized the entire Norman assemblage, outside of Lanfranc and Odo, understood none of this. They were uneducated; a rabble who would kill any their ecclesiastic leaders ordered them to fall upon. No poets, no teachers, no scholars, no original thought, nothing enlightened them, his own Norman people. He had come to realize his was a barbarous nation, controlled only by the principles of war under the aegis of a church doctrine, or their own driving lust for land and booty. All was in the extreme. Such now was foreign to his upbringing.

"So," continued Haralde shaking off his brother. "The new knowledge of the earth contained in this globe, is it false because such things come from minds which dared explain what they discovered around them in God's changing world?"

"Who made this abomination?"

"The construct was directed by Mahamad scholars . . . ."

"Thus your heresy was crushed beneath my feet in the eyes of the church!" Lanfranc turned and raised his arms before all in the Great Hall.

" . . . . from information discovered from Greek Christian scholars, incorporated into maps and globes built by the Byzantines, the first to embrace Christianity as the true faith, and thus to be carried into the far eastern pagan lands by . . . ."

"Now is Rome the true church, not Byzantium. What kind of Christians are you?" demand Lanfranc, whirling around, his voice wretched from its soothing calm appraisal to a shocked cold demand.

". . . . by we Nestorian Christians who wandered into the far east and flourished to crusade the word of Christ and to share the new knowledge of the world amongst all as far as Chinois," stated Haralde in a controlled voice that still carried to the back. *Be careful old man, lest this wee beastie bite back.*

Lanfranc had him. A Nestorian. An unorthodox sect, followers of the sinful Nestorius. In 325, Emperor Constantine of the then Church of Byzantium had assembled the leading Christian church leaders from around The Mediteranean and had established Christianity. The Nicene Creed had affirmed amongst other things that there was but one God in a triumvirate state, God, his son Jesus Christ and the Holy Spirit. Nestorius, the Patriarch of Antioch, challenged the Godhead trinity by regarding Christ also as a man. He and his followers were banished from the orthodoxy for refusing to abandon this heresy.

Lanfranc would have named Haralde thus but for Riennes who entered the fray.

Riennes, angry over his own silence, could not take the plight of his brother standing alone, persecuted. *If he goes, I go with him and be damned priest.* He stepped forward and the moment he put his hands on Haralde's shoulder, all fear and depression felt since landing on Britannic shores, lifted. It was gone. He was at ease. Cool and relaxed was he, a state he fought best in.

"Lord Abbot. Yes. We are Nestorians." The words of Riennes carried throughout the hall. "We have borne the cross of Christ's philosophy over pagan deserts and mountains. In the land of disbelievers have we been vilified. We speak what we know to be the truth, yet thee appear not to want to believe us. Thee fail to see the truth of our story. Thee speak not of faith, but as a priest politicking his own power under the mantle of God. Thee fail as a priest. Like us thee are but a man."

"Yes. We hold Christ as the son of man, as a great prophet and the divine will of the Creator as a teacher. We worship him as all of these," Haralde confessed before all.

Lanfranc was about to speak, to crush them both because he heard an underlying subterfuges. *He said son of man. Do they imply Christ was a man only?* He was about to spring his trap, to denounce them unbeliever in Christ's divinity when a din erupted behind him, then rose to a howl he could not ignore.

They all turned, and the sight Lanfranc beheld told him he had lost, that any further argument he might present would not be acceptable to the Great Hall.

For all there, nobles, vassals, young chevaliers, merchants, court officials, were banging on the table, some clapping, many pointing to Haralde and Riennes and nodding their heads up and down with favor in their regard.

Out of the darkness that was England and the Carolingian Empire of the Franks, far off worlds were little known. However, the bravery of the Nestorians they were aware of. The story of a Christian sect rolled up with the image of fighting Christian warriors crossing the far deserts, as false as that was, was gaining audiences. They had heard of a crusading Christian, Prestor John, carrying the sword of Christianity somewhere beyond Jerusalem. The image of Christians marching to free Jerusalem from the Mahamads was heard more and more, fanned by zealot priests. The call for an armed foray of soldiers now grew more audible across Christendom. The image was igniting young, ambitious, poor, landless horse soldiers. Such freebooters saw both salvation and booty blessed by the cross.

In Haralde and Riennes, they saw two who had achieved that, campaigned there and had returned. Stories were circulating of their fighting abilities, of their sword prowess when beset upon the road to Westminster. Tall, exciting, the adornment of adventure and romance now protected them. The spectacle of excitement the hall had been promised had now unfolded. And the assembled elevated the two.

Lanfranc now saw Riennes and Haralde held in growing esteem by the young bloods. He stepped back defeated.

As Haralde and Riennes turned to gaze at all the faces smiling and the mouths yelling at them around the hall, their backs to each other in a fighting defensive stance, still wary in their eyes, a man in the crowd who had been watching the presentations shouldered his way to the fore, the better to appraise Haralde more closely.

A banging of the court elder's staff ended the din.

"It would seem your inquiry has borne fruit my dear abbot," chuckled Odo, amused by Lanfranc's obvious dark look. "Whether bitter or sweet, I guess that goes to your tastes."

Odo's comments, a barb which pricked Lanfranc and which further embittered the bad blood between them, continued. "You do us much favor in bringing a lighter mood to court affairs. I must have you visit here more often in these serious matters of state. You are finished?"

Lanfranc stepped back from the centre. "Yes my Lord Regent. However, I do request a hearing with you over this and other matters later," warned the abbot.

"Yes. I expect so," nodded Odo.

Haralde and Riennes turned to the dais when Odo asked: "Ambassadors. Do you have anything more? The court has other matters."

"One final thing," enjoined a lighter hearted Riennes who went back to the cart and fished a document out from under the covering. He smiled as he handed it to the court elder. For Haralde, it was apparent that his brother's dread, his depression had lifted.

The threat of the darkman had passed, although he and Riennes would be guarded in their actions still.

The chief court official rumbled his throat clear. At a nod from Odo, he crinkled the parchment and read:

'To Royal William, Imperial of all the Normans, Monarch of all the Britains and the future hope of the Holy Roman Empire, I embrace thee as a brother strength who has a vision also of a collective and long peace under your rule. May the fruit of your loins bring thee joy, may the love of your family bring you peace and may they who serve thee fulfill the deepest visions of what thee seek in the years ahead. My viziers, Haralde of the strong hand and heart and Riennes of the eyes that see before, bear greetings and gifts from my throne to thee on high. They are the bearers of my admiration for thee. We are too far apart to be allies in any joint causes that may affect either, but the Deys of my empire are mandated to support any of your interests that may encroach upon my sway, that they are to enrich any ambitions thee undertake in my spheres. My admiration for thee is as a loving brother. Thee gave to me these two administrators who are the spawn of your kingdom. What men of arms thee must have around thee, if these be an example. In all the gifts presented on this occasion, the greatest is the loyalty of these two. They will become the sons of your aspirations. I return them to thee. Bind them to thee with the gift of your love. They will serve thee as a deep loyalty as they have me. Namaste, Grand William. Your humble brother. Gher Khan.'

Odo bothered his chin with a finger. Lanfranc cleared his throat. All assembled sat quiet.

Riennes stepped forward. He was sure the Regent or Lanfranc sensed something odd about the Khan's greetings.

"Regent, I hope the odd wording and strange phrases will not put thee amiss," explained Riennes. "If it strikes thee as somewhat strange, the message was put together by others, advisors, poets, teachers and scholars who applied what knowledge they had of events in this part of the world. Also, the Khan himself dictated it all to scribes and his words are those as through a screen of a foreign reflection. As you perceive, Norman is a language they are unfamiliar with."

More truthfully, Riennes had William's name in the royal greeting in the first part of the opening sentence imprinted in gold filigree by a master of calligraphy in the Caliphate of Cordoba only after they had reached al-Andalusia. It was only then they had heard who was king of Britannia. A small deception. The rest are Gher Khan's. *As Haralde believes, sometimes it takes a wee lie to accomplish a greater truth.*

Riennes caught Haralde grinning sardonically at him as these thoughts passed through his mind.

The court official passed the document up to Odo who glanced at it. "Aah yes, I see." He glanced at Lanfranc. *You dark devil. You caught the Holy Roman Empire reference. I wonder if indeed the shroud of Charlemagne haunts William.* "I shall explain it that way to the king. Your delegation, now is it culminated?"

"Yes Lord Regent," interjected Haralde. "Except for the granting of the request within our Khan's greeting."

"Ah. I think I know. But best you say it in your own words."

Riennes stepped up and stood beside Haralde as his brother said: "We are tired. We have traveled dangerous and hard to reach home and complete our task. We wish to be welcomed into the good grace of our true king. We wish to go home, to be enfolded into the arms of our families. I myself wish to grow old at home. I wish to hold my mother. I wish my heart buried at the feet of my father. Let me rest my soul in the earth of the Welsh highlands of my youth."

"I am assured of home," stepped in Riennes. "Mine is in the heart of Normandy. For this ambassador, my friend, it is different. He is the son of a vanquished Saxon. But I will not leave this emissary with the heart of true courage until he finds his grail. As a de Montford Norman, I stand as sponsor to his dream."

"Hmm." Odo looked at Lanfranc, tapped the Khan's parchment against his cheek and let his gaze wander around the hall. Then he shook his head negative: "This is not a matter I can decide here. It will take some consideration. This has all been rather unusual."

"My Lord Regent!"

All eyes turned to a figure who stepped out in front of the Norman nobility. It was the man Haralde had observed in the Great Hall who had slowly crowded into the corner of his eye during the presentation.

"You wish to speak to this matter?" Odo said, seeing a person of some familiarity. He tried to recall the man's name. The court steuirhdt leaned up over the dais table and whispered into Odo's ear. "Ahh yes. Gerald de Lackland. I have you now. We shared a cup once."

Odo remembered this old Saxon thegn of King Edward's entourage when Edward lived in Normandy as a youth. Edward was more Norman than Saxon before he ascended the Kingdom of the Anglos and the Saxons. This one was one of those old, steadfast royals, loyal to the crown even if he were to lay bleeding on the battlefield or coughing his life away on his deathbed. And now, he supported King William's claim to the Crown because Edward before his death named William as heir.

The man was elderly, short, but powerfully built. His clothing was threadbare but of quality from earlier days. "I have some information that may help you in your deliberations over this brave young man's petition."

"Sirrah, I would like to hear it," prompted Odo.

"This ambassador's story, it has the ring of truth to it. I think I know him," said Gerald. "I was a neighbor of Lord Stoerm Longshield of Neury and Wym and I have a memory of his son, a young fair-haired Welsh youth who was thought to have drowned years ago. Do you recognize me ambassador?"

Haralde's appraisal of the elderly noble was long, but then he shook his head. "Would that I could say yea sirrah, but truthfully, no."

"Ah, thus your tale has more credence as I saw you only from a distance for a good part of your youth," said Gerald who turned to Odo again. "I also will stand as a sponsor of this young man and his petition. His father was a royal thegn, a champion in Edward's court and one of The Confessor's wise men in the kingdom's witan council. Know you that after Edward's death, the witan met and chose Harold Godwinson king. Longshield and I resisted, arguing the king had chosen Duke William as his heir. For that stand, I had to flee. Longshield was eventually seized, and thrown into prison for standing for William."

"And what of my father?" Haralde took a step toward Gerald, the more to look into his eyes.

"I am sorry to say your father died here young Haralde. Some say he died of fever from the bad conditions there. Some say he was poisoned. I know it was poison. And I know who poisoned him. It was a Godwinson agent."

Haralde's head dropped. There was a stirring behind him and the hand of Riennes came to his shoulder to comfort and remained there. "So many years," Haralde voice pined with grief. "So many years taken from me, my father taken from me." His head jerked up. "My mother?"

"She lives still," answered Gerald. "The last I heard, Saran Longshield still holds Neury and Wym up in those mountains. But that was awhile ago. I do not know now."

"Sirrah! Up in what mountains?" asked Odo.

"Wales my lord," answered Gerald. "Up in the March, Britannia's border country and wild frontier. So wild that a Mercian king once built an earthen dyke to wall off the mad, wild Welsh from the rest of this country. They are unpredictable, undaunted, untamed but not without courage. These wild men fight each other in blood feuds. Try to interfere with their turmoils, and they will turn on you with a united army. Even today they threaten all the English earldoms west and east of that dyke."

Odo looked on, pensive. Then: "We shall see for how long."

"Bishop. The Longshields are respected there. I think the Lady Saran still is able to hold on because she is Welsh herself."

"What is it then you wish to say of this ambassador? Or is he one anymore?" queried Odo who looked questioningly at his chief steuirhdt. "Does it end with the completion of his master's presentation here?"

"Return this young man to his lands in the Welsh highlands Bishop Odo. Send this vassal of William's home. His father's loyalties I am sure are his. As a king's man, he will hold his part of the March country to some kind of Royal order if any part of his father is in him.," recommended Gerald who then stepped back and crossed his arms, signaling he had no more to say.

Odo thanked him, stood up and motioned Riennes and Haralde to approach.

"Ambassadors. Of this matter, you two will attend me when I call you. I will think on it and may come to some decision." Odo then waived his hand to dismiss them. "This ends your time before this court."

Odo pointed to his court elder, who again banged the wooded boards with his staff. "Attend me all you men of Normandy! Put down your cups and hear the wishes of your king. All will abide, and his Royal scripts will be carried out swiftly."

Haralde, head down, watched his feet as he walked on the rush-covered floor boards. They were feet that had carried him all this way. What did it matter now? His father gone. No more to see that bearded face, that manly roar, that rough laughter, that good heart. That image had sustained him for so long.

"Haralde. Someone to speak to thee," whispered Riennes who had led him from the hall with the hands of Amont and Raenulf on him also in comfort.

Haralde looked up to see a figure slip through the big doors of the hall as they closed. Gerald made towards them.

"Gerald of Lackland, I thank thee for your support. We were alone in there," Haralde voice almost cracked. He put out his arm and they shook like warriors.

"I do not think so," said the elderly man admiring the cast of men who stood by Haralde. "I wish it had been someone else to tell you of your father. He and I were friends." Gerald examined Haralde's face intimately. "I now believe you are who you say you are. So Haralde, get through your grief, then remember your mother. She is up there still defending the Longshield holdings. I am sure of it. Get there quick and establish yourself." He turned and looked around, "Do not let this robber mob get there before you.

Chapter Five

"Intolerance cuts; love binds."

A mailed soldier walking his duty on the wooden rampart roof of Westminster Abbey looked down from a parapet overlooking a yard upon two figures. The two kneeling ecclesiastics made the sign of the cross, then struggled to their knees. The soldier walked on.

One wore a black robe with the cowl back on his shoulders, a garb dedicated to the spiritual. The other priest wore clothing dedicated to more corporal demands. Both had their hair cut in a monk's tonsure.

Abbot Lanfranc rose to his feet and admonished his struggling fellow. "Bishop Odo, you must pray more. Your knees seemed to have lost their flex for God's company. In your daily priestly duties, you must kneel more to hear the Word of the Lord our God, and less to the demands of our Lord King William."

"Enough abbot. Prick not my soul. My mind is prodded enough by my king," sighed Odo as he heaved up his bulk to his feet and fell into walking beside the most powerful churchman of all the Normans. "When William gets back here and picks up the reins of his power, I will take off the vestments of crown responsibilities and slip on a monk's cloak of piety. I will to my abbey and see to my spiritual duties."

Lanfranc knew better. More likely it will be to sup too much wine and to glutton on your food and women, you wicked monk.

Lanfranc and Odo walked together, a rare occurrence. Both disliked each other. However, today was unavoidable. Lanfranc had a task he needed sanctioned by the bishop before he hastened away to the coast and for Normandy. The word was canalem weather was easing.

Odo wanted to hear what news Lanfranc had of home and to pick his brains as to William's thinking towards he, Odo. Odo had petitioned his half brother heavily for wealthy estates in England, his reward for his service to the king.

They walked back and forth and talked of religious and state matters. Lanfranc's movements through both halls of power were superior to Odo's, and the bishop knew it.

Jealous of William's esteem for Lanfranc, Bishop Odo was always laying trouble for the abbot. However, in one more year the pope would vault Lanfranc over Odo and in two more, the Abbot of St. Etienne in Normandy would become the Archbishop of Canterbury.

On a hail from the yard below, Odo cut the discussion, begged to be excused for one moment, then scuttled down a stair into a yard.

Two mailed soldiers with bows were awaiting a signal from him. Across a clearing, a man was tied to a stake crying and struggling. Odo nodded. One of the bowmen turned, drew back the string of his longbow, and released. Odo saw a line move to the staked man. He heard a hammering body blow and a grunt from the victim. The second lifted a crossbow, loosed, and a black quarrel lined across the clearing and he heard a metal 'crank'

The two bowmen crossed to the dead man. He too was dressed in chain mail and had a piece of thin plate iron across his chest from whence protruded a white goose feather and the quarrel dart. The bowmen examined the man hanging forward over his ropes, then one turned and signaled with his arm to Odo.

Odo crossed himself, turned, puffed back up the stairs and joined Lanfranc who questioned the interlude with raised eyebrows. Odo waived it off with: "Now. Where were we?"

"I want to talk to you about the emissaries," queried the abbot. "Have you reached a decision on them? Will you refuse them?"

"I was going to. Then I changed my mind." Odo was not going to reveal to Lanfranc the latest missive sent him by William. He jealously guarded the intimacy of his brother's secrets.

William, encumbered now by insurrection in his Norman Duchy, was fearful of rebellion in his conquered Britannia. Fearful of losing this ripe plum, he wanted in his absence any smoke of rebellion snuffed out before it puffed to a flame. In addition, the Welsh were forever flaring up, fighting for independence, threatening the stability of Britannia's western frontier.

To that end, large earldoms in the March territory were to be created. Bold, tough, cruel but men loyal to William were to be handed huge tracts of Welsh lands. They were to be granted powers over those holdings greater than any other of William's favorites, as great as the king himself.

Odo had sat up suddenly in the middle of the night with a solution to the appeal of the two ambassadors and that old thegn Gerald of Lackland. William would need as many vassals loyal to him as possible to serve these earls in those lands. Normans and Saxons had already been killed and lost their property in the old border kingdom of Mercia to raiding Welsh armed bands. By luck or good fortune, Haralde Longshield's petition now had fallen within the king's new royal wishes. It suited Odo now to grant that. He was sure his foresight would please the king.

"Longshield is loyal and he is on fire to get up there. I will send young de Montford with him. He has his uncle Gilbert backing him," conspired Odo. "I must be mindful also. They are ambassadors who said their Khan may have sent, and it may be approaching this isle even as we speak, a cargo of further riches for William."

Lanfranc looked at Odo, his estimation of the bishop's intelligence lessening. "Did you not find that document from their king a little . . . . curious?"

Odo looked at Lanfranc directly. "Speak your mind abbot."

"Well, they came from a land so far away I am sure it would take a year to get here."

"Go on."

"When they left, William had to be still in Normandy. His plot to cross the canalem and set war upon the Harold Godwinson family power was still a plot. How could this Khan know of William's final success if it had not even happened?" questioned Lanfranc,

Odo stood quietly and gazed out across the marshes around Westminster. Inwardly he cussed Lanfranc's insight. However, he was not about to budge. "I can only assume the land they came from was closer than you think. And the ambassador was right. If you had not smashed his globe, he could have pointed to the land of his king which was likely closer by."

"I see," smiled Lanfranc. Odo was making sure he, Lanfranc, was going to lose again. "Then I strongly suggest you sanction a request I wish to make, one that will insure the safety of your decision."

Odo smelled the sharp odour of ecclesiastic politics in this. Lanfranc was warning him not to refuse this.

"Yes?"

"I have a young prior monk nearby. He is gifted, a scholar, a dedicated and skilled administrator. His abilities will soon elevate him. However, his priestly experiences have been limited to the cloistered halls of the abbey. I wish to see him more grounded, more infused with a common touch. I want him sent with these two to walk with the common."

"To keep an eye on them?"

"And report back. I sense a danger about these two. They are free thinkers, rebels to church teachings. They seem not to be able to comprehend our Lord God. They also could adversely turn the common folk of that area against the idea of occupation. The prior will teach them on their walk to return to the fold. As well, we need to see a priest up there to convert the many pagans, and some of those Celtic Christians to Latin Catholic disciplines."

"There are churches and many Christians up there," suggested Odo.

"Like a dog to its vomit, those black Celts will go back to lap up the paganism they once had thrown off if we clarks of God do not go there to recur Christian teachings," he reminded Odo. "Only under our Christian William will God finally claim this land to His love."

Sandals scuffed up the stairs and a young priest appeared. He came forward and bowed to the bishop and the abbot.

"Yes Jean?" asked Odo.

"Pater. Guards are below. The two young ambassadors have arrived as you requested."

"I will come down to them in but a moment."

Lanfranc turned to Odo as the young monk moved quickly away. "I must leave quickly now. But first, are we agreed. As a condition of granting them their petition, they must take a young monk with them to be housed, fed and protected in the Longshield holdings?"

"What is his name?"

"Godfroi."

"On a condition of my own. That I see reports he sends to your representatives here so I may keep abreast of the soundness of my decision concerning these two young," countered Odo.

"Agreed. And now lets us go down. We will stroll the grounds for a moment that I may have a parting word with them."

Haralde was examining the upward exterior architecture of Westminster Abbey, the most hallowed Christian site in all of Britannia, and Riennes was talking to one of the royal guards when they heard the approach of the two. Riennes closed with Haralde when they saw Lanfranc. Riennes no longer felt the foreboding about Lanfranc, but none the less, there was something in the air. Not a threat, but something.

Odo led Lanfranc to them. The one guard indicated the swords the two young men wore behind their backs, but Odo shook his head no and waved away the guards. He bowed. "Ambassadors. No, I think it should be young sirrahs now."

"Yes Regent," answered Riennes as he and Haralde bowed back slightly.

Odo regarded Haralde with his slight black eye and somewhat haggard look. "If you have not slept much worrying over this petition of yours, you may now relax. You have convinced me to support it."

Haralde bowed again. "Thee are most kind Regent Odo. I have come a long way to hear just such words. And I shall return your confidence in kind." Riennes came up behind and smacked Haralde on the back. They smiled in relief at each other

"However, there will be some conditions," went on Odo. "As Abbot Lanfranc must be away immediately, we will deal with the first one I will impose. When you leave for these Welsh lands, you will be accompanied by a monk. You will take him into your household, be his benefactor in all things."

Riennes and Haralde exchanged glances. "Why regent?" asked Riennes.

"I want the Welsh to benefit from Christian teaching. I want him to wander through those mountains of yours bringing the word of God. I am sending monks out to many parts. I want a truer version of Christianity than what has occurred here under Saxon rule. I have asked the abbot here to find such a dedicated monk, a priest who will be as one with your people. He has found one. I do not ask you if you agree with this. I'm informing you it has been arranged."

Riennes immediately sensed conspiracy here, plotting. However, there was nothing for it. "What is his name?"

"Godfroi," answered Odo.

"Who will pay for his keep?" asked Haralde.

"You will of course. It is your responsibility to help spread the word of God."

"My lord ambassadors," interjected Lanfranc. "It is good to see you again. Let us all stroll outside for a moment while I explain the need for missionary efforts throughout this land."

The four passed out through a door onto a large green lawn. Lanfranc walked beside Haralde while Odo and Riennes walked behind. "Forgive my rather cold inquiry of you last night. I entreat you to understand my position, that of the moral protector of our William. You are of course aware as a king and a duke, he is a champion of the church and must be shielded."

Haralde nodded his head in understanding but glanced briefly over his shoulder at Riennes.

Lanfranc explained it was important for unschooled, ignorant peasants to have a monk amongst them, to interpret the true meaning of the bible. "We have been ordained to stand between the peasantry and the scriptures so they will be protected."

"Surely not from scriptures?" Haralde commented, perplexed.

"They contain writings with secret codices that we have to use to interpret such things as prophecies," Lanfranc went on. "Some of these prophecies could terrify the common folk. They come to the true church direct from God through the bible. Such knowledge would confuse the minds of the unlearned. They would grow mad if they knew such things were in holy words."

"Go mad from knowledge? Our experience is the reverse," interjected Haralde.

Ignoring him, Lanfranc continued his discourse. "We understand such things because the church prepares us, trains us properly to interpret them."

He turned, stopped their strolling and looked directly at Haralde and Riennes. "It would not do for some uninitiated to turn the word of God in another way and so set men on another course other than what has been pre-ordained by God." He resumed walking. "Men can go mad when they think they know more than the church.'

Haralde smoldered inside. Behind he could feel Riennes urging silence. Muzzle thyself Riennes had warned of this morning's meeting. Haralde turned as if to object to Lanfranc, but the abbot pointed a finger upwards. "No, no. Say nothing. I agree with Regent Odo. A monk of learning in your shires and up in the hilly, mountain country amongst those black tribes will benefit. As the king's subject, accept his will. It is mine also."

He had them. There was naught they could do.

"Now, I must away. I have a long sea travail to make. Then many days on the road." He made the cross before the two young adventurers. "God speed and His love upon both of you."

They kneeled before him as he did. So in the end, they thought, Lanfranc had connived a kind of control over them.

He bid Odo goodbye, spun and swept like a black bird back into the abbey.

"Attend me now," said Odo, resuming the stroll. He started immediately, blunt and to the point. "Are you truly king's men?"

The both nodded affirmative. "Yes Lord Regent."

"Good. Your fathers were. Now you will be. In a few minutes, you will swear allegiance to a noble who will hold sway over your lands. He will impose his own conditions."

Haralde balled his fists. His lips set grim. To remain silent and to accept what befell them had been agreed on by he and Riennes. Both agreed they no longer were the administrators and viziers of high stature of their previous lives.

"The king is to create a number of earldoms in the March. Your lands will be in one of them. The Welsh prick at the king's concerns there. Lord Gerbod the Fleming is to be William's overseer somewhere up in that northern frontier. . . . I think it is near a place called Chester. He will be your overlord. Shortly he will arrive and you will kneel and swear an oath of fealty to him. Yes?"

"How can this be Lord Regent. I inherit the lands of my father. Are they to be taken from me?"

"You sirrah. Even your father did not exactly own his lands," explained Odo. "They were his to enjoy. However, there was a lien upon them, a debt. That debt was armed service. As he was a housecarl, his obligation was directly to Edward and that was in lieu of a moneyed geld to the king each year. Now, King William by right of conquest owns your land. It is to be placed under Gerbod whom you will obligate. Whether you agree to this, matters not to me. It is the king's will. Remember, in all of your obligations, you like your father will continue to enjoy fruits of your holdings."

Haralde nodded. "I so obey." Odo turned to Riennes. "Lord de Montford. You will also swear allegiance to Gerbod."

Riennes face puzzled. "I regent. I do not understand?"

"One of the Longshield estates is to be yours. Which one, settle that between you."

Haralde stepped forward and barked his protest but Riennes stepped forward, held him in check with a hand on his shoulder and objected. "Lord. My holdings are in Normandy. I am here only to support my fellow's petition. Away I must be to reclaim my estates."

The bishop shook his head no. "We recognize and honour Lord Longshield's support for William's claim to the throne. However, there must be for now a Norman presence amongst those unruly Welsh."

"Regent. As a youth I played and hunted with both Welsh and Saxon boys of my own age," argued Haralde. "There was peace there because of my father's influence. Thee must not do this."

"Must! What have I of your musts. I have musts of my own to order and yours are mine. Do you understand sirrah, or do I end this audience now! I have others waiting!"

Riennes's grasp of Haralde's shoulder turned to a grab and he muscled his brother to one side, casting back over his shoulder to the bishop: "One moment my lord."

"Haralde! Tend me," exhorted Riennes. He could see the smoldering in Haralde's eyes. "Brother. Thee must accept these conditions. It is the way now. Accept this as we did the way of the Khan. Do thee agree we have no control here of these things?"

Haralde stood still. He agreed but he growled a frustration. " Aaghh!"

"Do thee trust me?"

That stilled him." With my life."

"Then trust me with part of your lands. Remember. It is much easier to inherit your lands from me when I leave than to have to wait upon Lord Gerbod's pleasure. I can appease Gerbod later. All will be eventually in your hands. Remember what Muck said, that we would find our homeland a place in turmoil. Let not this divide us."

Haralde's head dropped. "As always, thee are right." He nodded yes. "Always have we trusted your instincts. I agree to everything."

"Good." Riennes let go of Haralde's garb and walked him back to Odo who was growing impatient.

Haralde bowed slightly to the bishop. "Forgive my outburst Lord Regent. I am tired. And the road still stretches a long way before me. It is my impatience that I stumble over. Tell me what I must do."

"And youth," grunted Odo. "So green and demanding."

There was a sound of many horses and shouting. Some dust rose on the other side of the grassy area."

"This will be Lord Gerbod and his company. I have asked him to come here so that you may declare yourselves his vassals in a corner of the abbey." He turned to Riennes. "Attend your companion here and explain the ceremony as your overlord is Flemish, speaks Norman but none at all of Saxon."

Odo led the two into the abbey and into a corner. Gerbod came stumping alone up the central aisle of the nave towards them armed and covered in chain mail. His young, armed chevaliers, heavy with weapons, were not allowed to enter the abbey. The whole company seemed primed to get on the road and head for the interior of England after these ceremonies.

The bishop introduced the two to Gerbod.

Odo watched as the three sat down on a bench and talked, Riennes translating from time to time.

Odo witnessed a small outburst, again from Haralde as their lord set out the conditions of their feudal obligations to him. The bishop let his lips slide into a small smile over that. He liked the tall man of the Welsh. In fact he liked what he saw in both large young men from beyond the sea. *Those two have great life in them, great energy.*

Then, Gerbod walked over to Odo. "I accept them as my vassals, as you requested. That fair-haired one was testy over the pouch of 20 silver coins he must pay me annually. However, they are hearty youth and they will serve me well with soldiers they must supply when I call them to my army,"

Odo called a priest who was standing nearby with a holy bible and then motioned Haralde and Riennes forward.

The two kneeled before Gerbod and as the priest read from scriptures and from an oath of fealty, Haralde and Riennes each in turn put their hands together and placed them inside the hands of Gerbod and swore their loyalty: the kneeling before, the overseer leaning over them, the low murmur of acceding to his and the church's demands, all this done to accentuate, to impress upon the vassals their subservient role, to humble them.

As the two former ambassadors then signed a parchment containing the conditions of their service to their master, the bishop walked Gerbod up the central aisle of the church towards the front door where the noble's entourage awaited him.

"Do you know much about these holdings that are now mine. Are they rich? Is the farming good there? I know little of this Welsh land. That young foreigner told me the Longshield holdings were poor, of rough ground, more mountain than farmland. I demanded a pouch of 30 silver but that young pup pleaded the land would be hard pressed to produce 10 of such coin annually. We settled on 20."

Odo chuckled at Haralde's daring. Gerbod was fierce in his greed for coin. The Flemish lord had fine English holdings of lands already, as well as his family estate back in the Low Country. Yet, his greed demanded more. He had pressed the king hard for more.

William had acceded, but warned Gerbod he must live in his holdings in the March for a year or two before he flitted off to visit others of his estates.

"Well, I hear it is an upland area that someone told me grows sheep and good wool. You of all people should know the wool trade is good is it not?"

Gerbod grunted. "What kind of arrangement have you and William got me into with these wild Welsh. Chester? I hear it is a God-forsaken place. Anyway, I must go. I will hold this against you Odo if things do not go well."

Gerbod stalked away, his mail chinking as he trudged out of the great abbey.

Odo signaled Haralde and Riennes to follow him and to resume their stroll across the lawn.

"I hope you did not trick Lord Gerbod out of coin that was his due?" posed Odo to Haralde.

"My lord. I did but explain the poorness of our holdings and bargained for what I thought was fair," answered Haralde. Over his shoulder, Riennes smiled. Odo joined him.

"Well, let us, you and I, bargain. And by the true faith, I will make sure it is fairly done," warned Odo as they all bowed and stepped through a low door into another walled enclosure.

Two armed soldiers were rubbing a dark wax into a staff as tall as they. Then Haralde realized it was an unstrung bow. The other tended a cross bow. He glanced to see if Riennes saw. Riennes nodded slowly. The longbow was the biggest bow either had ever seen.

Riennes's eyes wandered down the grass, then widened as he saw the figure of a man hanging from a stake. Riennes knew immediately the man was dead, bound to the wood by rope. He captured Haralde's attention, then motioned down the grass.

"Ordric. Both?" Odo asked the soldier, who advanced to them and replied. "Both. Through mail and plate iron, my lord regent."

Ordric led them all down the grass and as they approached the dead man, Haralde saw the man wore mail and a dark plate. Feathered shafts were buried into the mail and iron covering.

They stopped six feet away, but Riennes continued up to the body and examined it with clinical interest. The dead man's long hair hung down, his death shroud. Through it, Riennes could see blood still running out of the man's mouth, down his jaw and onto the ground. He had seen battlefields of such dead men. Lung and stomach wounds bled like that. The blood is not yet black. Killed just recently.

"What reason would thee kill a man like this?" asked Riennes, disturbed by the cold-blooded act of a man strapped.

"If you are offended as I am of this man's sudden death, let me tell you of his character," explained Odo. "He is a murderer, sentenced to death by a burghers' hustings council. He robbed a burgher outside of London and killed his wife and child. He confessed before his death it was not his first time. Execution was the burghers' judgment." The bishop bent down to get a better look at the two arrows in his chest.

Haralde turned to Ordric, put out his hand and the soldier handed it. Haralde turned the bow over in his hands. He was intrigued. Never had he seen anything like it. A faint memory from his youth taunted him. He thought the bow huge, cumbersome. Yet?

"The feathers. What kind?" asked Haralde, taken by the size of the bloom at the arrow's end. Bigger than anything he had seen before. "I do not know," answered Odo. "Did someone tell me goose feather . . . . Ordric?"

"You are correct my lord," said the grizzled old guardsman. "I have not seen anything like this in my own fighting. Only a quarrel from a crossbow at close quarters have I known to do this. It went through both mail and plate when aimed straight on."

Odo turned to the two young men. "Do you know what you are looking at?"

"The arrowheads, yes," stated Haralde.

Odo nodded yes. "I thought upon what you told me. I palmed a few of your armour piercing arrowheads. I remembered what our archers did to Harold's Saxon line." He pushed Haralde. "Can you forge these arrowheads of yours here?"

Haralde glowed inside. The seeds of his offering had fallen upon fertile ground. There was money to be made here. "Not entirely lord regent. I worked with the armourer all the time. But he shut me out of his shop during the final steps of these steel arrows. Or so he thought. I watched him through a crack one night. I think I can. It would just take some trial and error steps for awhile. But, yes. Let me set up a smithy and I think I can. But it will take some money."

"I see. And you would charge your king?"

Haralde tapped a finger against the side of his nose. "It would take a bit, say some 30 silver coins?"

Odo looked sharply to Haralde, then shook his head no. "No. You will do it for 20 silver coins"

Haralde's pecuniary nature protested. "My lord regent. My knowledge of such a weaponhead surely is worth more. Any less, and . . . . and it would be like stealing from me."

"Nay. I call it . . . ," Odo paused, then glanced slyly at Haralde . . . " more like good bargaining."

Haralde's face clouded. Then, a big smile captured his ears. He leaned back, hands on hips, and laughed. "Done in, by God. Nay. By a bishop!"

"Nay. By a king. As regent, I stand for William's interests here. You will deliver these steel points to your king in as large a quantity as satisfies him in six months whereupon you will be paid."

"Nay. I will need a year Regent Odo. And money in my hand first for I have not the coin to fire up a kind of hearth, forges and tools needed to create this hardest of iron."

Odo fixed Haralde with hard eyes. This young man's inner boldness at times could be irritating.

The small door to their enclosure opened and the same young priest who alerted Odo earlier hurried over and whispered into his ear.

After he whispered, Odo turned to Riennes. "Affairs seem to ripen around you two. Your uncle has arrived and wants to see you. That yon monk will sponsor you to him in the nave."

Riennes bowed, glanced at his brother, and said: "Be alert . . . ." then moved off quickly to exit through the small enclosure door

The young monk ran with his long bare legs flashing under his woolen robe to keep up with a long-striding Riennes to a door of the abbey.

Just before they entered, another door banged open and a big man in a mail hauberk, his cowl over his head and a metal gorget across his throat, strode out across the grass toward the little gate to the enclosure. He carried a broadsword on his right hip, and on the other hip a lighter, shorter blade.

"Pray tell me, who is that nobleman?" Riennes asked of the young monk.

"Oh sirrah. That is Lord Rogert Monclair. He has been asking of you and the other ambassador. He arrived just now with Gilbert de Montford, who sir told me to tell you he was most anxious for you to attend him in the abbey."

Riennes made to follow the young priest, then an urge made him look back over his shoulder at the armed nobleman. That man was hurrying, his face intent, grim and disturbed. His left hand worried the pommel of the heavy broadsword.

"Sirrah! Where are you going," shouted the young priest. "Your uncle awaits this way."

Wrong! Wrong, wrong! The currents were all wrong, his inner voice shouted. Riennes ran back to follow the stature of the big nobleman ducking and passing through the small gate into the inner enclosure.

He ducked through the little door, stood and beheld a sight he had feared for these last few nights.

Roger Monclair was bearing down on Haralde and Bishop Odo with such deliberateness that Riennes foresaw murder, assassination, killing.

"HARRY! KANDOS!" he shouted.

Haralde jerked up with the warning and a shadow loomed over them. He turned and the hulk of a murderous threat blocked out the sun. A chain-mailed, heavy, tall warrior pulled out a massive iron blade and hauled it one-handed over his head.

"DON'T KILL HIM!" someone shouted.

Haralde's reflexes moved him within the eye of a second. He straight armed Bishop Odo, crashing him aside to the ground to remove the regent from what looked to be an assassination attempt on the cleric's life. With no time to pull his own sword, Haralde stepped into the assailant's rush, turned and slam-spooned his body hard against the tall assassin to come inside the deadly fall of the huge broad sword.

The assassin over swung and the blade struck the ground near Odo, his arm crashing onto and stunning Haralde's left shoulder. Over balanced, the man half fell over Haralde who suddenly stiffened upright and head butted his assailant.

The man's head snapped back and a tooth flew out of his mouth. Haralde had noted the man was left-handed and that he wore a smaller broadsword on his right hip. Haralde fumbled back-handed for it. As the man's head jerked back, he shoved Haralde from him. Haralde came away, the iron of the lighter broadsword in his hand rasping out of the attacker's scabbard.

"MONCLAIR! DO NOT KILL HIM!" shouted Odo rolling up onto one knee.

Haralde turned, spun the hilt comfortably into his right hand and got it up in time to defend himself. A clang rang throughout the enclosure. Haralde managed to jump to one side and deflect the crashing blow meant to cleave him helm to hip.

So he was the intended victim, not Odo. Haralde moved towards the man's left side as Monclair raised his bloody basher. Monclair! The hothead on the road. Guy Monclair's father! Angry retribution flared in Monclair's eyes. He was a big man, mustached, red-faced. He was also quick on his feet. As Haralde shuffled closer to get inside and avoid Monclair extending his arms fully with that mighty hunk of iron, the man shuffled quickly and adjusted to better his swing.

When Monclair raised the sword, Haralde noticed the man's chain coif pull back almost off his forehead, and his sleeve open up to expose the forearm. *His mail ill fits him.* Down came the big blade. To weaken the power of that big plowshare, Haralde moved inside and his blade took the blow closer to his own crossguard. Bang! Still, the strength of this elder warrior staggered him to one knee. *God! This bastard will have me!*

He rose and they bumped. Monclair shoved him away again and hacked. Haralde saw it coming, took the blow on an angle and a squeak of pain passed his lips from the shock of the blow. His weapon too light, he could not last much longer at this.

When next came a horizontal slash, Haralde saw his escape. He went down on one knee, their blades crashed cleanly over his head in iron anger and Haralde released, letting Monclair's strength carry away his lighter sword. The power of the blow carried Monclair himself around.

Up Haralde came, his kandos singing free. The young Welsh fighter passed his blade across Monclair's face and a red smile puckered on the attacker's exposed forehead. Blood erupted. As Monclair drew his blade back and his sleeve opened, Haralde ran his blade up to slice open his attacker's forearm.

Now Haralde was in his element. He had changed the rhythm of battle. Like a dancer, he spun, moved in close and darted under Monclair's left shoulder to get behind him. Monclair two-handed his smasher over his head to deliver the killing blow. His fighting rage up, Monclair did not feel the sudden pain of Haralde cuts. As he swung the blade over his head, his world suddenly turned misty red and his focus lost sight of his victim. His left hand rebelled, flew open from the sudden trauma of Haralde's incision and lost the grip on the sword. The big blade left Monclair and it cartwheeled backwards across the enclosure.

Monclair slashed downward through empty air. The loss of the blade's weight unbalanced him. He fell forward, turned and sought to establish his balance in a red world. Haralde stepped forward, drove a heel into his attacker's stomach and the Norman crashed backward to the ground.

Riennes, Ordric, Odo and others came running as Haralde stood his heel upon Monclair's throat. He touched his sharp keen blade delicately onto one of the Monclair's blood-flooded eye lids and said. "Yield thee murderer." Then: "Why me?"

Odo stepped in and bumped Haralde and his weapon off the down nobleman. "Monclair! You idiot! What have you done? This man is an ambassador to your king. You have attacked an emissary under the protection of William. The king will surely . . . ." the bishop stopped short as he looked down on a face covered by a flowing veil of blood. Blood ran red upon the grass beside the downed nobleman.

Riennes rounded onto the downed man, kneeled down to look at the bloody mess, then stood and looked into his brother's face.

Haralde's eyes were composed. "Your visit with your uncle, was it blessed fruitful? I pray so. I mayhap have done havoc to a man of some import here."

Riennes nodded, and let a slight smile play at the corners. "As thee are wont to do. Are thee hurt?"

"Nay. But the why of the attack I do not understand. It was murder he intended. I do not know this man."

"Eeeee you bastard!" Monclair opened one of the two red maws of his face and spit a red speckle of blood onto one of Haralde's boots. "And I almost had you for the brutality upon my son. I will yet."

"Be quiet Monclair," silenced Odo. "You are shedding much blood."

Riennes bowed down again and examined the wounds. "Yes. Let us do something about this. The head is incidental, not mortal." He looked around, saw the young monk kneeling. He drew a knife, leaned forward, cut some white material off the monk's sash, ignored the protest, closed the slash wound across Monclair's forehead with his fingers and applied the linen with pressure onto the wound.

"Head wound. They always bleed more than normal." He ordered the monk to press down on the bloody cloth. He examined the slash wound on the arm and deemed it more serious.

"Lift him. Take him into the abbey. Get me wine and more linen. Lay him down and quiet him. I shall be there to attend him in one moment," ordered Riennes rising.

Ordric, other guards and the young monk lifted the nobleman and started towards the abbey with Riennes running before them. He was headed toward their horses and his backpacks.

Odo hastened after with Haralde behind. The group ducked and carefully passed the wounded man through the enclosure's small door. As Odo ducked to follow, Haralde caught up the tail of the bishop's cloak and wiped clean the blood off his kandos. Something about a Christian blessing upon his blade for saving the bishop's life this day passed lightly over his mind.

As the party rushed to a small side alcove, Gilbert de Montford came rushing up at all the noise. As he rounded up and looked down at Monclair, Odo heard the wounded Norman whisper through blood bubbles: "I missed him. But I will get him next time Gilbert."

Gilbert jerked up and in a loud voice shouted over what Monclair was saying. "My God man. Who did this? We must get you inside and attend to your wounds."

However, Odo caught what passed between the two. He slowed up and stopped as the party carried Monclair inside. Understanding lit his eyes. *Not a Monclair killing but a de*

Montford assassination? What means this? Longshield and the young de Montford are strong friends.

"What delays thee Lord Regent?" asked Haralde drawing near and not wanting to go inside. He had found a rag piece of material and was cleaning his kandos more thoroughly.

Odo turned. "Nothing. Business of state." He watched Haralde pull the foreign-looking blade with his right hand through two fingers of his left acting as a guide at the mouth of the scabbard behind his back. Haralde then shoved it down and seated his blade.

Odo had known others to wear a sword on their backs. He noted the weapon had only one leading edge and that was very sharp. A foreign characteristic he had never seen before.

"I have never seen a man fight like that. He was fully armed and could have killed you. Yet you prevailed with that, what do they call it, toad spitter?" mused Odo.

"That broadsword was the wrong choice for assassination," answered Haralde. "Too cumbersome."

"You fought foreign."

"I fought inside his reach. A master taught Riennes and I that in the end, it is not the blade but the point that carries the day. Thrust, not slash," he answered, driving both of Monclair's broadswords in the ground in front of Odo.

"You are a surprise to me young man," remarked Odo turning away to go inside.

Inside Riennes ran down an aisle in the abbey. He saw an alter cup, looked inside and saw wine. He grabbed it and ducked into the little alcove where he heard the voices of everyone.

Monclair was laid out bleeding on a bench. More monks were running down aisles towards them with cloth and jugs of clean water.

Riennes pushed his way into the crowd around Monclair and kneeled. He dropped his pack at his feet and grabbed a cloth presented by one of the other arriving monks.

Riennes removed the blood-soaked linen from the Norman's head, dipped the cloth into the cup of wine and washed the gash across the forehead with it.

"That's sacrament wine. You can not use that," protested a monk.

"Good. With God's blessing it will heal quicker," answered Riennes. "Press this down," he ordered the first monk who had attended.

He next pushed back Monclair's sleeve and pressure-closed the wicked wound along the forearm with his thumbs. Surprising everyone, he said: "Wash it."

Opening his pack, he brought out his curving sewing needles and horse hair and for the next little while sewed up the wounds.

Odo joined them. He leaned over, watched Riennes work. The bishop blinked in wonder as Riennes's hands moved across the sliced open wounds and quickly closed them. In his time he had seen monks and leeches and healers attend the wounded and the sick. The skill and the fine instruments used were something he had never seen before. Surprises these two young men had treated him to in a matter of minutes.

"Ambassador. You did not tell us you were a healer," remarked Odo.

"Sometimes. Then sometimes I am not," Riennes said quietly as he worked.

Monclair the assassin finally responded. "You are the one who bound up my son."

"Yes," answer Riennes who finally stood up and wiped his hands. "I tell thee this sirrah. Thee will bear a white scar across your head and up your arm. It may not be bad. Lord Longshield cut thin and clean." He then proceeded to instruct the nobleman on how to dress the wounds in the future and stressed cleanliness, though by the smell of him, Riennes doubted the senior Monclair knew of that practice.

"I must talk to you," his Uncle Gilbert addressed him, grabbed and guided him out of the alcove to the outside.

Odo inside heard them talking, then arguing. He heard Gilbert shout: "Vassal! Not to that lowlander Gerbod. You are a de Montford. You will not go with this Saxon. Your place is here."

The regent heard the nephew's reply. Not his words, but the quiet controlled, commanding words just below his hearing level. Riennes was calm, his tone soothing. More informative to Odo was the quiet strength of that tone. This man was used to command, used to being authoritative. Slowly, he could hear Riennes gaining control over his uncle. He could almost feel himself joining on the side of Riennes. Why not? The young man was right. He, Odo, knew Monclair to be a cur of the Montford house. Any dirty work, any brutal roughing up, any killing, send a Monclair whose position was lesser in the Norman hierarchy. It was not that Monclair was stupid. He was just single-minded. Also, he owed a vassal's loyalty to Gilbert; easily shaped and directed by an influential house to do its dirty work.

The regent heard Gilbert stomp away. Odo stepped outside and sauntered over to a calm but concerned Riennes.

"Well?" he asked.

"I must be away. Haralde awaits me . . . . that is unless thee have some truck with him?"

"Your Khan's emissary acted instinctively. He thought to save my life. I take that as an act of loyalty. But get you away. Things seem to swirl around you. Go, flee, get away, as fast as you can," Odo advised. "Events are hurrying on so quickly here. Fly. Stay with that brother ambassador of yours. I know your course is already dictated, even before your presentation in the Great Hall last night. I be right? And if I may, are you two even ambassadors?"

"No. That part is mostly true. One day I will tell thee a tale about the rest." Riennes dropped his head, smiled and then looked to Haralde across the grass. "Thee are right. My star and his are hooked." He turned and looked at Odo. "And thee probably want to tell me not to trust my uncle, but can not?"

Odo handed him his medical pack and nodded towards Haralde. "Was Lanfranc right? Are you really faithless Nestorians?"

"More questions. Maybe when next we meet, we will both answer the questions between us," ended Riennes who took his pack, bowed to the bishop, turned and walked to Haralde.

Odo watched him walk away. The image of the young de Montford patching up the grizzled assassin Monclair stirred him. His soreness from the blow Haralde dealt him was setting in. The young man's first instinct was to protect he, Odo, as bishop and Regent, from the assassin's first rush. Longshield had acted rightly.

Haralde was indeed a king's man. That confirmed Odo's judgment to release them to their lands in Wales. Riennes, the compassionate healer. Haralde, the warrior compassionate. *There is a nobility about them, more than in most men I know.*

Haralde, tightening saddle straps as Riennes approached, watched in dark apprehension. He glanced at Riennes over his saddle as Riennes began tying his pack on.

Riennes could feel his brother's eyes upon him.

"Are we in trouble over Monclair?" Haralde asked finally.

Riennes set his face sombre, turned and replied in a tone foreboding. "I am not. But trouble may come running at thee across this grass in the form of Odo's personal guards."

Haralde stopped, and glanced at Westminster.

"What must we do?"

"We? My soul is white. Thee! Thee may have to flee out to sea aboard Heimr. Or, thee may whither away in some gaol until, as Odo said, thee learn to control that brashness of yours. Then again, the king might have your head when he returns and hears what thee did to Monclair, or pull the teeth from your mouth to find out where all that money went you filched from all my fellow Normans with your surplus gifts that really belonged to William.

The dark pall hanging upon Haralde lifted. Somehow Riennes's tone was not as foreboding as he feared. S' truth, there seemed a lightness about it, a gibe, a jest, a joke, a Riennes poking at him.

. "Thee know brother," continued Riennes. "Thee are such a weight on everyone's discomfort. Why do I always have to explain your shortcomings to everyone?"

"By the Gher's eyes! Thee make jest of me." Haralde leaned across his saddle and smacked Riennes over the head with his pack.

Riennes ducked away and swung up into the saddle, beaming for the first time in a long time. In fact, he let loose a short bark of laughter. "No. Just enjoying watching thee squirm a little."

Haralde laughed too and joy flooded into him. He loved to see Riennes's face glow when he was happy. It was, after a time of depression and apprehension, the sun come out from behind a cloud. Whatever crisis, it was gone. His brother was happy again.

Haralde let out a whoop, mounted, and directed a rude sound towards Riennes. "Thousay fals. Methinks, really, thee enjoyed it all."

"Where away now?" Riennes asked.

"I must to Muck and finish our business with him. Then say goodbye to Amont and Raenulf and set a rendezvous day whence we meet again. Coming?"

"No. The day is wonderful. I myself must meet with someone wondrous and fresh."

"May she task thee hard," shouted Haralde as his brother thundered away. "I will join thee later."

Menya followed her candle. The bloom of its light drove the gloom before her on the dark wooden stairs. Her tired mind dragged her upwards to her bed, yet strangely her body trembled, anxious, hungry. She lifted onto the landing before her's and her husband's private loft. She cocked an ear to the inn below to insure her day was over. The last drunk was croaking the final stanza of his nonsense song. Other guests curling up on their benches coughed their last. Poor she may have been but now she was mistress of her own. Below, the central fire pit had been banked. The inn was settling down for its night sleep. Had he left with the night as he promised he would? She did not know. She had not seen him enter in the early afternoon but her girls had told her he was in her room. She could not control her trembling. He had paid them a copper each to carry up bundles and to bring hot water to the tub. Bundles! He had promised her more silver and gifts when he left. So busy she was today, she had not seen him.

She stepped out of her rough woolen cloak with its food and wine stains and hung it on the wooden peg by her door. She now was in a light shift that clung only to her shoulders, her legs bare, a state her husband imposed upon her each night before she entered their sleeping loft. He demanded no encumbrances for his wandering hands. Unlike then, she this night experienced an excitement. Her nipples hardened. As she leaned forward to her door, a distant melody brushed her ears. What is that? Music from a pipe? She leaned into her door. Immediately her nose signaled something different was about to happen. She stepped out of the inn odours of food, ale and stale bodies and into a faraway place of ever-so-faint pleasant fragrances. What was that tantalizing bouquet? Never had something so indefinable, so alluring, tempted her. She lifted the latch, squawked open her door and walked into a wonder. Her bedchamber, her normal miserable cell, did not have its miserly single candle piercing the gloom. It did not suffocate her with the stink of her husband's day clothes thrown on the floor. Instead, everywhere candles glowed golden. The air was humid, warm, moistened by her hot water tub in the middle of the room. Here and there little copper cups burned wicks of wispy incense and little burners heated brass pots of liquid perfumes. Her attic no longer resembled her prison, her husband her gaoler. Rather, it teased her with its promise of freedom. She pushed her door open further, and there he stood in the middle of her sleeping chamber, the young lord of her dreams in a floor-length white *djhallba,* his feet bare. He turned, his lips puckering a sultry, tempting wooing from the pipe, warming her desire, her oils, her womb.

"Forgive me," he whispered. He laid down his instrument, turned and advanced quietly towards her, his hands forward to receive her's. She obliged, and felt their warmth and gentleness intermingle. His short black hair and blue eyes beneath captured her. Shaggy, unkempt this young lord was not. His body loomed up over her blocking out the candles and she hungered for the violation of even his shadow. "I should have been away as promised but I could not leave without saying goodbye" His eyes sparked directly upon the flint of her personality. "You were not supposed to be here." "Forgive me for intruding too long. I will leave immediately". "You must." "Before I do, I must honor thee with my promise." "The rest of my money?" This practicality was the final resistance before her submission. "That, and much more I will." He turned, lifted a small red silk kerchief and uncovered two delicate glass goblets filled with a golden liquid. "I bow to your graciousness, your good humour. First, a honey drink brought by me across deserts and seas. Drink this." The richness of the red silk captured her. But the glass goblet, she had never seen a glass goblet in her life. Earthen cups and bowls served all her experiences. She could see right through it, right into the very liquid itself. He placed the stem between her fingers, and then slowly, delicately, tipped it upwards with one of his own until the glass rim kissed her lips. So smooth. She sipped the golden wine and tasted upon her tongue a liquid joy. "Oh! Lovely!" "It is called bhang." "Uummm. What is it?" "The Indus people make it from the leaves of the hemp. Sip again and allow it to slip down slowly. Do thee like it?" "Mmmnmmm. It is so gentle, so soft," Her eyes over the rim of the glass looked to his. Those eyes touched her legs, then moved upwards under her shift, then settled upon the outline of her face. Her breasts flushed, swelled, heated. The liquids, oils and creams of her body began to dew. "It is refreshment from a far away place. I have saved it these many leagues to share together with one as thee." "Then I will, but only with you." And she drank it in a single draught. "Do thee like my robe?" "Yes. It makes you a royal within my house." "I promised thee gifts greater than coin." "You did. May I have some more." He poured more golden liquid. "These goblets are yours." "Mmmmm." "In addition, a gown of silk like mine so both may touch in teasing velvet." He lifted silk to her cheek. He held up a red silk *jhabala*. "Do you like that?" "The silk?" "No. The teasing." "Yes," she giggled. "Let us slip this over your body. But before we do that, look what is yours." He now was all about her. From the wine, his voice was liquid in her ear, on her throat, in her hair, upon her shoulders suddenly made bare by whom, him? She raised her hand to the side of his head and weakly commanded him to desist. She jolted once when her nipples ripened to what she was sure was a brushing by his fingers. "Look! Behold my admiration for thee." A gold chain uncurled before her face and a red ruby dropped into her eyes and more, captured her soul. Wealth like this she had only dreamed of late into the night after her husband's maulings. A soft, cooing, commanding voice wooed her to his bidding. "Look at the swinging jewel that is your heart. Watch it. Listen. Listen to my voice. Only my voice. It is delicious. It is a sweetness. Watch it back and forth. Do thee want to know?" "Yes. Everything!" "It is a gift from me to thee. Do everything I say I want." "Everything!" "Do thee want?" "Everything!" The gold and the red settled around her throat in a chain that warmed her. "Do as I say?" "Yes!" "I wish to adorn thee." "Please!" "I wish to adore thee." "Please, please!" "Now let me slip your silk gown upon thee, but first we must bath and cleanse ourselves to warrant such softness." "Yes." He led her, goblet in hand, ruby chain around her throat and red silk gown flowing through her hands, to her wooden tub. She felt not his hands slip her shift nor saw it settle about her bare feet upon the rough wood boards of the floor. She felt his eyes upon her nakedness as he guided her up over and into the tub of hot water. She took a deep breath to exhibit her abundant breasts, the pride of her body. In that quick passage, his lips brushed hers, her neck, then her nipples. He whispered her name. She shuddered. He whispered his want of her. She whispered back her promise to fulfill him. The goblet once more tipped towards her lips. She felt the soft warmness of his hands travel over her body, washing, soothing, privately visiting her. Everywhere the light of the candles shone golden upon his naked body. He was built long, lithe, muscular. He tipped a small beaker of oil into her water. The bouquet rose to her with a promise of a faraway place. "My gift to thee. My promise. We have ridden wild horses to the high country and through a hidden defile. We are in my mountain pavilion. The winds and snow howl through the passes. We are snowed in. Far below to the hot south, the winds blow over the spice routes across the tropic southern seas. But here, we are left to ourselves. Inside these halls in my mineral baths our bodies must make their own heat." She stretched out, tipped her head back. His mouth visited her throat, then slid up over her lips, sucked her tongue and sipped up the liquor of her mouth. She thrilled to the surprise invasion. She compressed her lips to make it tighter for his tongue. He thrust past them and violated her mouth again. He smothered her breathing, then withdrew. She choked to catch her breath. The momentary struggle to suck air in left her faint with lust. His hands hotted her loins. She jolted, then melted when his fingers touched her hidden femaleness. No man other than her husband had succeeded in seeking and finding her. Where her husband's touch was an intrusion, for her lover it was an open invitation. She trembled under the onslaught of her own young violator. She felt her senses, her touch changing, a gift of the bhang. She no longer felt him upon her. Rather she was sure she was absorbing him.

He lifted her out, dried her, then the silk jhalaba floated down around her body to her feet. He slipped his arms around her, felt her velvet body as he directed her towards their luxurious bed, in reality her floor pallet. He undid certain ties of her jhalaba and the silk gown blossomed open and fell away from her. Now their bodies intertwined, each urging their heaving parts upon the other, breathing heavily even into each other's mouths in long kisses. She was starved for him. She keened for their bodies to join. She wanted to capture him, dominate him. Poor, alone, desperate, fearing any return to her child poverty, her strong way fought to retain any wealth she could accrue. Her rotten husband she was slowly gaining command of. The inn she was gaining control of. Now, here was a rich young lord, a friend of the new king. She wanted his ways. To do that, she needed control of him. In their hotted loving, she unconsciously maneuvered him, to push him down on the bed so that she could mount him, take him into her and set the tempo of their lovemaking. He, sensing her rising domination, prevented it. His strength proved greater than hers. She began to twist in anguish over this. Not wanting to lose what he had gained in their lovemaking, he pushed her slowly downwards. She obeyed his urging, trailing her tongue over his chest, his belly and into his bush. Her lips slid up his cock, then swallowed the hardman of him. By the act of capturing his manhood, she relaxed again, become animated, grunting, mewing. She looked up when she heard him moan. She was pleasuring him deeply. She had found a kind of control. She looked up at him, worshipped him, controlled his pleasure. He was hers now. She was part of him, sharing in his station in life, his privileges, his wealth. She grew excited. The juices of their sex leaked down her thighs. Her lust gorged on him. He brought her up from the floor, kissed her deeply, suddenly swept her up into his arms. He swung and deposited her upon their bed, then fell onto her in a tangle of arms and legs and lips.

I fed on his cock. Now his tongue worships inside me. Oh. He opens me. I am hot beyond disobedience. I will obey. I will offer no less than he will give me more. Oh. Oh. Do not do that. It is dirty. Oh, he whispers dirty to me. Say dirty back. Oh, I am his. I will be the vessel to carry us both. Oh. His fucker is inside me, his fornicator. Lick, love, lash, lust me my lord. Thrust, thrust.

Pump me. Oh, I am his. Be one with him. Meld, melt into him!"

Riennes roared his completion. She cried, she keened, she mewed, she screamed into his mouth. She arched her back, lifted both herself and her lover almost off the bed. Riennes felt her go rigid, then heard her suck air, what the Indus in their Book of Love call the *sitkrita,* the intake of breath signifying the sweet agony of female orgasm. He knew it was her first. So overpowering, she collapsed, unconscious.

Oh, I am awakened. Oh, it is you again. You want for me, for more. Oh. Do not do that. Oh, you are so hungry. Take all you want. So rough. Oh do not make me do that. Yes make me. Take me. Move, match you, catch you. Make me ready for you again. Oh. You are so different, so strange. Your shoulders, so much wider. You are heavier. Crushing me. Can not breathe. I want this again. Oh, you are so violent. Demanding. Music. I hear a pipe playing. Oh. Wanting you my lord, my lover. You are a bull, rutting, ranting, roaring. You split me. Hot. Plowing me rampant. I want my beast. You bellow. Hammer, heat, hard, harder, hurt me. Yes! I am with you. Pleasure me. Pleasure me. Now! Now! I rise.

"Menya! Menya! Wake up!"

Menya groaned awake. Someone was pounding on a door. Her door. She rolled upright. Oh! Her body ached. She was sore. Her eyes widened awake and she looked around. Around her body was entangled a rich, red gown of a material she had never seen or felt before. Silk! Her hair, her body smelt of a sweet dew. Candles drooped in holders all around her. Light through her little window glinted off little brass vessels. Incense was a drug that hung in the air around her room.

"Menya. Hurry!"

"What?" she asked. It was one of her serving girls pounding on the other side of her door. Menya bolted upright as she suddenly remembered. Her hand went to her throat and there was her private gift, her prize, a gold chain with the drop of blood ruby. Across the room her other gifts, the glass goblets, one with a dazzle of gold inside.

"Menya. Hurry. The streeters are inside."

"Who are?"

"Men. Customers. They want food and drink. They have money."

She bolted out of her bed, groaned once at the soreness between her legs, then hurried to clean up. She stuffed her silk robe beneath her pallet, picked up the goblets and brass beakers, pushed them under a bench and threw a blanket over them. She took off her chain, kissed the ruby and hid it in a little chest of her personal things. Scooping the dirty little shift off the floor, she settled it over her head and ran for the door.

"How did they get in?" she asked through it. "The front door was bolted last night."

"Through the side door. But mistress. I myself secured the bar across that last night. I did. Someone else must have lifted it off by mistake."

As she pulled her shift down around her, she saw something on the floor. There, beside her door, were the distinct outlines of muddy boots. Two pairs. Different sizes. She rubbed her soreness. Her nipples hard ached.

"Hurry. There are more outside. They hunger and thirst. They want you."

Menya took in the mud again. Her eyes turned to a daze. A hurt touched them.

Then: "Yes. Do not they all. But for that want, I will see all men pay dearly." She thought then of her bony, aged husband. *Him first.*

"Hurry!"

"Yes. I am coming."

Chapter Six

Not all who wander are lost.
Nor some who stay find home.

"Harry! Wake up!"

Haralde, body curled over in his saddle and asleep, grunted awake and jerked upright with arm rising sleepily up to his kandos.

"Comes our spiritual overseer, our meandering monk?" Riennes posed and nodded to a hunched-over stick figure passing before them on the road below.

The two were temporarily encamped on the side of a hillock overlooking the road and farm field beyond. It gave them a clear view of anyone coming and going. Already, a force of Norman pikemen on foot and soldiers on horse had passed in a racket of dust, obviously in a hurry to get into the hinterland.

Haralde leaned forward yawning. "Ah. Pray not, because he appears a prickly fellow. Look how he scratches at himself."

"He will wear off his very hide if he keeps that up. Vermin do thee think?" suggested Riennes.

The two turned their horses off the high roll of land and dropped down to a lush meadow beside the road upon which their charge would pass by.

In the meadow was a large, four-wheeled sturdy dray. The back of the wagon was covered with a large oiled-cloth spread. Under was all their valuable goods; food, silk, cotton, gifts for home, grains for their horses and small chests of gold and silver secured just behind the front seat. Suits of chain mail and broadswords purchased from a smithy in London covered the chests.

In the meadow a cow also grazed on a short rope pegged to the ground. On her flank, a big bull bawled amourously.

They took up a position beside the road to intercept their charge. "Odo's burden," yawned Haralde.

"Do thee have to do that?"

"I was up most of the night."

Riennes made a denigrating sound over Haralde's crude imagery. "Thee were up? I could not get any sleep, hoarse thee were," accused Riennes. "The trouble with thee Harry is thee do not know how to be subtle with a maid."

They sat ahorse for a little while. Then a quiet: "She liked me best."

"Aaah Harry! How would thee know? She was a lovely young, good for us. Our needs were great I know, but thee could have been more delicate about her. Thee were a horse, snorting vulgar. She being a delicious young woman, thee should not have been so coarse," chided Riennes.

"And of thee?"

"At least I was artful, subtle." Riennes waited a time to see if that got a rise out of him. When none came back, he said softly: "I did not want to tell thee but she whispered to me later she really like me the best."

Haralde snorted. He yawned again and then they sat quiet for some time.

Their impatient horses shifted weight from one side to the other. Saddles creaked. They slobbered. The two sat watching the road. Their minds and loins ruminated through the night's sexual satisfaction. Haralde mumbled.

"You said what?"

"I said I remember the day when our fists were our only lovers."

Riennes snickered. "Mine was more subtle than yours."

Haralde whooped at that, then his ears were first to pick up the slight scuffing approach of someone. Their religious ward?

The monk dressed in a brown woolen capuchin shuffled into view scratching at himself. When he came opposite them, he stopped to wedge out a stone painful twixt foot and sandal.

"Monk!" hissed Haralde. In fright the monk shrunk back at the sight of two horsemen between two bushes at the side of the road. They were huge, the biggest men he had ever seen in his life. He saw the swords on their backs. "Are you robbers? I have no money! I am a poor monk."

"Come this way if thee be Monk Godfroi," signaled Haralde crooking his finger in a signal to get off the road and join them.

The startled monk looked down the road both ways, saw no one coming, then as if surrendering to a fate, walked off the road to them. He had been warned his benefactors were two young giants, very strong and very capable. The security to be found in their formidable sizes comforted him somewhat even within his fears.

Both Riennes and Haralde dismounted. Each appraised the hesitant religioso approaching them. Before them was a thin man, spare of nature, hungry of face and pasty of complexion. A dark robe with cowl hung on his light frame. His face was lean, the hair on his head cut in the tonsure. In the time ahead, both were to suffer this religious man's intellect, one fractured by the prism of religious dogma. Worse, as a man, he was sparse of humor; an anathema for sailors on a tough sea voyage or for fellowship down a long road.

Haralde grumped over the burden of Godfroi. What he saw was a drain of copper pence leaving his purse for an obligation he could not possibly expect a return on.

"Who .... who are you?" asked the aesthetic.

"Are thee monk Godfroi, the same sent by Bishop Odo, who was to meet with us here now some hours ago?" Riennes rebutted.

"No. By my Abbot Lanfranc." Riennes and Haralde darted quick looks at each other over that revelation. "Are you Riennes de Montford and the Welshman, Lord Haralde?"

"Yes monk," answered Haralde as they took him into their company. "We are your benefactors for the way ahead."

"May we ask why thee are two hours late for our acquaintance? Did thee get lost?"

"I was advised to take the west road out of London and that within two hours I would come upon you in the early morning," answered the monk. "However, I am a subprior at St Mary's Abbey near Shepherd's Bush so had prayers to attend during early morning Prime. Are you Christians?"

"Yes," answered Haralde, an irritation growing within.

I must be careful in my narrative thus, thought Godfroi. *Abbot Lanfranc instructed I must try to gain control of them, to guide them down the proper path in my days with them. He said they have heretical tendencies. Rid them of those. I will start with prayer.*

"Then as it is only a short time to morning mass, let us kneel and pray together on the eve of our travels. I will call God's blessings for us all."

Haralde coughed a note of impatience. "Before we do, how many more of these hourly prayer ceremonies do thee adhere to?"

"Well, there is Vespers in the evening, Matin and Lauds through the night."

Riennes stepped up beside Haralde. "Sounds like the muezzin from his minaret calling the faithful to prayer five times a day. This will never do."

"Blasphemy! Theirs is a barbaric heresy, they that bow down to craven images."

"Say naught monk. Thee have no knowledge of what thee speak. The Mahamads condone no images whatsoever in worship, whereas your Latin religion adores a pantheon of them. No, my companion is right," admonished Haralde. "Listen monk. We are your patrons. To maintain harmony with us in the months ahead, thee will suffer our oddities, and that includes our lack of devoutness. Here is what will be done. We will join in prayer to launch our enterprise and our lives together now. Any other prayers thee wish to make, thee will adhere to yourself in the coming hours of daily travel and not halt us in our progress. Do thee understand?"

"No. You must let me guide you in these matters so I insist we . . . ."

"Let us kneel together," Haralde suggested most firmly.

Godfroi, use to gentle firmness in controlling the daily and nightly rituals of his brother monks, bowed his head and stood upright to bring all uncertainties under his control.

"NOW!" A command greater bowled his resolve over. His legs buckled. His knees hit the ground, eyes closed, fingers clasped together. Immediately, he heard a rustle as his benefactors moved. He opened his eyes, and almost gasped as he saw them walk a short distance away from him and from each other, squat down into cross-legged positions and put their hands not together in prayer but open on their knees. Their faces they turned upward to the sky, not down in submission. How disgusting. They are heretics. *Oh God help me. I travel with heathens.*

Godfroi mumbled out an inaudible prayer, not one of calling down
God's blessing for safe travel, but rather, one of safety and protection for himself. Yet, even as he did so, he heard them mumble, each their own prayer just under his. He heard certain words, and became aware the two, each in his own way,

beseeching God for His goodness and His blessing to guide them and to prevent them from wandering off the proper path to home.

Godfroi, confused, blessed the air before them, and rose. They followed him to their feet. *At least they are respectful of I, Church.*

"Forgive us Monk Godfroi, but we cannot spare for prayer. We have a long way and a dangerous path before us. We seek our own kingdom far to the west. We pray thee find your own there also," explained Riennes. "Thee can make up and say as many prayers as thee want once we find our way there."

Haralde stretched and yawned. "Came thee not with horse, even palfrey?"

"Nay my lord. I come only with my robe and cowl to protect me against wet and cold, bread in my pouch against hunger and God's blessing as my armour of protection. Nothing else."

"Hhhmm. Yes, and it seems God also gave thee bugs. Are thee in vermin?" asked Riennes as he watched Godfroi scratch himself again.

"No my lord. It is this wool robe. I am used to softer linen. You see I am a subprior, one who was not to be a hermit amongst the unconverted. I was chosen for higher order. Or, I was until my abbot assigned me this task of traveling with you to convert mountain unbelievers to the true Church. As you see I am not used to coarser raiments."

"Pray it does not become your constant hairshirt," smiled Riennes who had taken the measure of this man and found him to be more than he claimed. This cleric was hiding something, was not altogether truthful about the mission he was undertaking for his church. He sensed another's presence. This monk is no fool. The darkman would not suffer to send such an agent. Riennes felt he already knew this man's hidden intentions. He would impart his feelings to Haralde.

"I see," murmured Haralde. "So if thee cannot ride, do thee plan to walk all the way?"

"God will provide."

"Nay. I wager the Regent told thee we would. So be it. Follow us monk," sighed Haralde, who turned and headed back into the clearing where their cart, wagon, bull and cow awaited them.

He led them to the heavy wagon. "Thee of course know what this is. What I want o know is have thee ever served to guide a beast bull in traces to pull such an engine?"
"No. We had lay monks do such chores in monastery fields."
"Could thee?" "No!" "Thee will!" "I cannot!" "Thee can, or else thee thus must travel back down this road to report to Regent Odo that thee will have no truck with his mission."

Godfroi was stuck. Such would squeeze him between the plotting of Lanfranc and the orders of Odo. He could not reveal anything of this subterfuge. He could do nothing to disturb the surface calm upon the quiet religious and political pond he now swam in.

"What bull?"

"Attend us," suggested Riennes.

Haralde stretched out upon a grassy knoll and stuck a straw stem between his teeth. "That bull." He pointed to the two animals in the meadow. "Are you saying I have to control that bull upon this cart?" "Yes" "Why a bull?" "Why not? He is strong and we need a bull and a cow to bring new blood into the livestock we hope to find in our mountain kingdom. As well, he will plow new fields and help raise new crops. Thee have to understand agriculture is really a very fine and subtle endeavor."

The monk stood stiff, unbending over such a suggestion.

"Godfroi. Thee can walk the long road to the mountains, whereupon thee would be left behind we who will be on horse, or thee can climb up onto the seat and travel in some comfort guiding beast and wagon along with us." Haralde swept his hand before him and waved it to the seat upon the wagon.

Godfroi's fate was sealed, and he knew it. He could not refuse and he could not turn back. He stood unmoved, a moment's resistance.

Then he caved. He climbed onto the seat where Haralde then instructed him on how to handle reins and harnesses to get the bull to pull their cart with its heavy load of supplies.

In the middle of the lessons, Riennes called to them. "Something is unfolding here. Come see this."

Haralde and Godfroi returned to Riennes and sat and stretched out upon the small knoll again. The cow, tied on a short rope, trembled in heated agitation. The bull on a longer rope shook excited. He snorted, then rose up and mounted the cow.

In the middle of the coupling, the bull bellowed. Riennes leaned back and laughed: "He reminds me of thee last night. Not very gentle."

Haralde blinked, looked at the coupling, then slapped Riennes on the back and roared. "Hah! hah, hah! Thee lay a good one on me."

"No!" burst out Riennes. "On her!" Whereas Haralde roared even more. The priest joined their gaze across the meadow, observed what the bull and cow were up to, saw no humor in the doings and looked elsewhere. There was dust, grass kicked up, the heavy sound of two grunting bodies. The bull, finally exhausted, dropped down off the cow. He shuddered and bowed his head, his huge member wilting and pointing earthward. "See," responded Haralde. "She has cowed him," and roared over his own joke.

"Do not mind us Monk Godfroi," grinned Riennes. "We are discussing the subtle points of agriculture," then laughed again at this humorous theme they had now struck. Riennes lay back in the grass and his body shook over his brother's good nature.

"It is about livestock," chuckled Haralde. "He is sticking and stocking more," he bellowed over that delicious crudity.

"You see, we are very carefully planning the new blood lines to introduce into the livestock agriculture of our new lands," Haralde summed up. "We are being very careful, very selective in our animal husbandry. It is almost an art." Godfroi could not understand any of what Haralde spoke.

"Forgive him monk Godfroi," laughed Riennes, wiping away tears from his eyes. "Harry is just trying to be subtle."

Deep in sleep, Godfroi awakened to a shout. The arousal brought shooting pains from his rear to his brain. He was instantly made aware in his nether parts this was the wagon seat's reward for a day of guiding the bouncing cart down the road wrestling with the reins and the bull. It had taken about half the day after leaving the clearing yesterday before he realized the beast needed no reins, that simply letting him find his own way was easier on both of them.

Another shout and he groaned from the sore muscles. Someone, no, two people were arguing. He sat up, the cover dropping from his face in his place under the wagon. He peered through a big wooden wheel and saw Riennes and Haralde arguing with each other, pushing and shoving at each other as they walked away from their sleeping cover.

Suddenly, a ring of steel rang across the clearing as Riennes pulled that wicked short sword from behind his back and hacked, barely missing the other's throat. Out came the other with his sword and retaliated, barely missing an exposed belly as the other pirouetted away.

He heard them grunt, and cry 'aaah!' and 'hah!, as they slashed and moved back and forth against each other.

Dear God. They are going to kill each other. There is going to be murder here. Help me! Godfroi tightened the cord around his robe, crawled out, jumped to his feet and prepared to run away from the wagon and into the woods.

Just as he was about to, his eye caught something of them. There was not violence in their actions, but rather a rhythm. They moved in a kind of deliberation, in and out of what he thought was their coarse and deadly intentions. His legs lost their panic. It was as if he was watching a dance. Their blades flashed in the dawn light, passing it seemed around, through, above, behind their bodies. Yet blood flowed not. He could see the sweat gathering on their faces, their arms, yet they appeared to labor not. Then one smiled, and the other laughed; one lunged, the other let it pass through his body, it seemed. Yea, but no. The blade missed the other, although it did not seem possible. Suddenly one leaped high in the air above the other and cut down. There was a parry and a ring true echoed off the trees, as if of pure silver. Then the first touched down and the two laughed, bowed to each other and replaced blades into scabbards behind their backs.

In all his life he had not seen a Norman chevalier nor a Saxon shield carrier act this way. It was foreign, different, yea, deadly and swift.

Suddenly, one lunged at the other and the two grappled. Their scabbards with swords, jointly fell to the ground. They grunted and locked arms around each other. Shoulders strained against shoulders. They kicked up dust and stones. He saw one go down and the legs of the other cartwheel into the air. They both collapsed.

Godfroi brought his hand to his mouth, to stifle his squeal of dread.

Then, amazement: the two got up, laughed, picked up their scabbards and walked across their encampment towards a nearby stream. They peeled off their clothes as well as their weapons and ran to the stream bank. Their naked bodies were not white like his monks or any other fellows he had seen, but brown, burnished by the sun. They launched themselves into the water.

He quieted his fears and turned his gaze away from them. Why, a game! They play at their combat. A dance. No, an exercise of their skills. They are as brothers. He sat down. What he had witnessed was an expression of joy, of youth, of enthusiasm for life, for each other. What kind of fighting men are these that have such regard for each other, or for that matter, for me?

It was incomprehensible. For reasons he could not understand, the clang of a sword always left him with night dreams of wet dread. At the heart of his fears was a buried memory; screams of his parents slaughtered in a Viking morning raid while he hid a toddler shaking behind a cover of outside stream rushes. Raised by lay brothers in an abbey, even the clang of field implements left him shaking, or at night, with dreams of the dead. The sanctity of his abbey not only saved his life, it saved his sanity. Only there in an island of quiet was he able to live a life peace. There was his intellectual abilities founded.

A light of history gleamed through the fright of his mind. There was something here about these two, something he had never seen or heard before in the violence of fighting men.

His deep ken of life in his Britannic homeland and on the Frankland from his very early days as a youth was of a dark age, of blood, of brutality, of maiming, murder, mayhem, of madness. Traveling monks visiting the abbey recounted the horrors of life outside. He would turn in time away from all that, pursue his love of script and books in the churches, abbeys and monasteries. Here literature and the writings of knowledge were copied and preserved, not that of original thought, but through the mechanical reproductions of some others's intellect. How he had ached to write down his own thoughts.

He gleaned from such old books written hundreds of years before he was born, something of Britannia's fall from peace and good order to the present day anarchy. Once music, art, literature, philosophy, thought, graceful living, manors in pastoral meadows with fountains, rich fields and orchards had flourished across the southern areas of his island kingdom, all maintained by the Pax Romanus and corps of paid soldiers at key garrisons across the island. Then followed the fall, the decay of law, of knowledge and original thought as a hollow Rome withered away from within and withdrew from the most northern of its conquests. The Romans left. Germanic hordes, peoples hungry for lands of their own, broke through the weakening Roman seams holding Gaul together. Vandals, Sueves, Saxons and Alans crossed the Rhine during a winter when it froze over completely and they swept past Roman strongholds manned more by mercenaries of their own kind than regular troops. In a wave of rank furor and anarchy, they slashed their way across Gaul, pillaging, smashing artifacts, burning books and carrying off anything of immediate value. Stopped by the Pyrenees, they turned east and west into the neighboring provinces. Saxons invaders poured across the canalem and hordes fell upon the original Britons and drove them eastward into Wales.

Then came hundreds of years of warring Viking raiders, warriors of blood whose only transactions were through the engines of war; screaming at Saxon, Frank, Pict, Scoti and the monkish brotherhood to kiss the thin lips of their axes, or to redden their spears or spill wound dew upon their broadswords. Although he would not admit this to his superiors, Ireland and the Celtic Christian Church had saved what enclaves of ecclesiastic and private writings had existed on the eve of the barbaric invasion across the Frankland.

For more than 500 years, the continent and Britannia were imprisoned in the Dark Ages of paganism. And heathens were the jailers.

Now it was again overrun, prostrate before the bloody Norman horde. Murder and barbarous slaughter stalked Wessex, Mercia, Cornwall and soon Northumbria; the land in thrall to heavy, ugly men seeking land and loot through the sword. Godfroi would not impart any of these thoughts to the two brash young swordsmen. Lanfranc had emphasized never should he reveal his own thoughts to them, but to relay them directly to the abbot even before Odo. Church discipline was Godfroi's coin. He would not contest any of its usury.

If what he believed about men of arms was so, then what was it about these two young men that lifted his spirits? As he had bumped along in the cart behind them, he listened in, heard snatches of conversation between them. They were so independent of spirit. Their minds engaged in no coarseness. They argued logic, talked of philosophy, medicines, flora, women, books, trade, agriculture, the manure qualities of horse shit, even of the stones in the Roman road they rode on. No Norman or Saxon ahorse talked like this. Those such brutes were unlettered, reacting with swords to slay any resistance to their greed.

But these two armed youth? Brutes they were. Yet, what kind of slayers would talk thus.

"Godfroi!" It was spoken sharp but soft.

His name spoken thusly jerked him out of his deep thoughts.

"Monk. Are thee in prayer? Forgive me if thee are," asked Riennes, standing naked with his clothes bunched up against his chest and one hand holding his deadly scabbard and sword.

"No, I was . . . ." Godfroi looked at the ground when confronted with Riennes physical state. "I. . . . have just awakened."

A sudden strong sense of something wrong washed over Riennes. "Are thee ill?"

"No . . . . no, I am not ill."

Riennes sensed this holy man was afraid, no, frightened. Is it of us? Yes. *NO!* He is afraid of everything. He is frightened by these woods, by his very surroundings. Like a man peering out of the forest dark of night at the light coming from his own house. He wishes to go home. He fears the beyond outside his monastery.

Godfroi looked up and was captured within the eyes of Riennes, eyes that looked into him, touching almost upon his conscience. "Do thee have any favored words that might comfort thee?" asked Riennes.

Godfroi bowed his head, one to hide his surprise and to hide from his interrogator's sensibilities. Like prey within a hawk's strike, Godfroi jerked sideways to slip away from Riennes's scrutiny of his secret. How could this brute know of anything of that? Finally, he spoke: "I rise today, through God's strength to pilot me:

> God's might to uphold me,
> God's wisdom to guide me,
> God's eyes to look before me,
> God's ear to hear me,
> God's word to speak for me,
> God's hand to guard me,
> God's way to lie before me,
> God's shield to protect me,
> God's host to save me,
> From snare of devils,
> From temptations of vices,
> From everyone who shall wish me ill,

Afar and anear,

Alone and in multitude.

"What is that? It is beautiful. Is it of your liturgy?"

"None as a foreigner like you would know," mumbled Godfroi. "It is from St. Patrick's Breastplate, some call it The Deer's Cry. It was thought to resemble the trembling of a deer, to deflect harm from him by anyone seeking him out to do ill. It was his Hibernian Incantation, to protect himself."

"I am foreign. I know him not. Was he important?"

"Yes. He was not Latin Christian. He was of an ancient Britainnic Christian. A hermit monk and bishop."

Riennes considered this. "Would thee be of him, a hermit monk amongst your people?" he finally asked.

Godfroi stirred, uncomfortable before this man's intuition. "It is beyond my ability."

"If my words disrupt thee, please excuse," said Riennes after a moment. "It is just that we have finished our quiet."

Over Riennes's shoulder, Godfroi glimpsed Haralde in the cross-legged squat position gazing upwards. "The mind is refreshed and the belly now demands its refreshment. Can thee cook?"

"Once. But as subprior others now prepare my means."

"There is a bag of meal oats so marked in the wagon. If you would put some in a pot with water over a fire, we will all have some porridge. Alongside it thee will also find some bread and ale. Sparse as it is, with these we break our night's fast."

Godfroi liked the sound of the voice of this young man. It was, however, the wrong tone for Riennes to use. Godfroi interpreted it as submissive to his high position. It allayed his fears, an acknowledgment these two should provide him with his morning meal. Sensing this, Riennes turned away, bemused by the monk's assumptions.

The moons of Riennes's ass muscles shone brown in the morning light. He walked away and began to slip on his clothes. Ahead, Haralde let out a great sigh, shook himself in his nakedness and reached for his clothes and weapon. He arose from his squat, stretched, and an orange stream of steaming piss arched in the chill of the early morning to warm the ground.

It was this, the guiltless, the innocent, the free, the unashamed conduct these two dealt with their nakedness. Godfroi was not shocked, but was somewhat taken aback by their unpretensioness. It was as if their bodies were in liaison with the trees, water, winds and rocks, just another naked adornment of the natural world around them.

That moved Godfroi out of his obstinacy. He went quickly towards the cart to get them out of his view and within the half hour, provided a morning meal for three.

Haralde and Riennes rode out ahead, comfortable on horse for the long day's ride. Home for them was desert days of rocking bare-footed in a saddle with toes clung tight upon the hot circular stirrup, observing the sand brown, the sun bleating down heavily upon their hair, upon the dryness of their mouths, upon the shortness of their water.

Only now, it was the coolness under the trees, scented air upon their faces, upon their interests, upon their curiosity of the flora and fauna so rich that they still amazed themselves this was their home. The trees were giants leaning over them; the leaves gave off fragrances that the mouth tasted. The air like jam was rich-tasting on their tongue. Occasionally, a stream tickled rocks in the woods beside them. As desert dry men, they felt refreshed just by so delicious a sound.

Innocents, however, they were not. They were well armed. Besides their kandos on their backs, there were other weapons readily at hand should they meet bandits, brigands, godins, something they were assured was likely to happen in this up heaved land. Their riding bows were tucked away in a wrap under their saddles, ready to be strung at first alarm. Leather cuirasses wrapped around leather war helmets were stuffed in the cart behind.

Godfroi also heard them talk about weapons. "I never thanked thee for the warning cry back there," said Haralde to

Riennes. "I do so now brother. Regent Odo was much taken with our toad spitters. He remarked he was witness to an impossible sight; a fully armoured Norman chevalier brought down by a man with a long sharp knife and in poor fighting clothing."

"I am glad thee did not mortally wound Monclair Haralde. Thee would never have gotten away from there if thee had."

"I thought as much in a moment. And sure I was he was out to assassinate in that same moment."

Haralde looked at his brother. "He was not to be the murderer of Odo. He was to be mine, am I right?" They rode a short way before Riennes answered. "Yes."

"Because of what I did to his son?"

"Yes, but Haralde , more than that I think. Pray, I will tell thee something now, and I want thee to say naught when I do but will keep thine own counsel on it for awhile. Promise?"

Haralde stared at Riennes, then nodded his agreement. "My dear, if ever we are in the company of my Uncle Gilbert again, stay away from him. Trust him not. Be cautious and wary. He has taken a dislike to thee. And he has power in King William's circle."

They rode awhile, then Haralde: "Did thee take note of the slip from Godfroi's lips? It would seem Godfroi is not Odo's monk pious sent to the March as the religious converter that we thought." suggested Haralde.

"No. It would seem the darkman rides with us still, his emissary sitting astride our own cart." finished Riennes.

Behind, Godfroi was catching snatches of their conversation. He shuddered when they talked about murder and swords and killing. When he heard names like the bishop's and the others, he half stood up from his seat on the dray and leaned forward to hear better. However, the bull chose that moment to bray his treatment at Godfroi's ill use of the reins on him. That was followed by the lowing of the cow towed behind the cart. Haralde half turned to look back at him and the bull. Godfroi sat down and put to memory everything he had heard.

Haralde turned and resumed his conversation about weapons. "What made thee of that bloody big bow the Regent's archer had?"

Riennes shook his head. "Never before have I seen such a thing."

They rode a short distance before Haralde came up with a memory. "It was a big shafted arrow, flight tipped with white goose feathers. It had gone through a piece of plate as well as the chain mail. Ren! That is remarkable!"

"Yea, but most useless for horsemen such as us. Too cumbersome to shoot from a saddle."

"I remember something of such a bow when I was young. My father came bellowing into our hall with such a big stave. I remember seeing a string hanging from one end. He told me about its fighting capabilities and that one day he would show me how to use it. He said he had just seen a Welsh bowman put such an arrow through a thick oak door. He put it in his armoury and told me when I turned 15, it would be mine."

"Not much good against us," remarked Riennes. "I would ride over him with a fast destrier." Haralde said nothing again for a moment, then murmured something that struck Riennes as important. "Not unless he poked a sharp longshaft first through that fancy leather armour of yours well distant from thee."

Riennes urged his mount forward suddenly, then surged ahead. He had spotted an animal bounding across the road. He bore down on it swiftly, leaned out and down and like the superb horseman he was, head smacking into small wildflowers as he passed through them just above ground, made a grab for it . . . . and missed. The animal bounded off the road and into the undergrowth.

Riennes trotted back and standing in his stirrups, shouted back to Godfroi. "Monk Godfroi. Did thee see that? What animal was that?"

"A marten I believe sirrah. God willed that you were to have no truck with him. Worse still would be a badger. He can give a man a nasty bite."

Riennes slid his mount in beside Haralde, then continued with the weapon's theme. "Of arrowheads, thee seemed not too disappointed when the Regent devalued ours below your price?" Haralde smiled, reached back into his horse bag, pulled out a small pouch and jingled it. "Twenty silver coin as agreed." A satisfied look came over his brother's face. "Now we have the exact amount of our annual geld to our Lord Gerbod.

Riennes shook his head over Haralde's dealings. "Yea, but thee have no money now to find a smith, a forge and metal to make more."

Haralde snorted and replied: "In the cart is a small barrel full of them. Thee see. I did not make a gift to the king of all those armour-piercing points." He struck Riennes's shoulder in merriment. "It buys us time. We can pay our lord and make more. And I will bargain the price upwards again, arguing they cost more to make than I thought. That is, if I can remember how it was done."

"Such dealings. Thee turn me confused sometimes. Haralde. One of these days someone is going to run a blade through thee and accuse thee of being a . . . ."

" . . . . a sharp merchant with goods?" and his brother burst out laughing, enjoying a trader's delicious moment.

And so their day went, conversation, the rolling enjoyment and jolting in the saddle by their mounts and the passing forest and fields of their new home. Riennes commented on all the natural wonders around them. Riennes loved all natural observances. Once a black- and white-winged magpie landed on his shoulder and tapped on a silver buckle to try and steal it, then flew off, "Did you see that!" remarked Riennes who then barked out his enjoyment of the raiding thief.

As before in the desert, Riennes began to ponder their course, whether or not they were heading towards where they were bound. However, he had learned always to take his lead from his brother. Deep in Haralde was a direction. In all things. He just seemed to know where. Once Riennes had remarked this to a dried-up rind of a tribal Mongol elder, who answered, that there were always a few who wandered not lost, but with intent for some unknown arrival. Many are lost in life. A few who like to ramble and seek, are not. And then again, the elder said there were those who stayed home but were not satisfied all their lives.

"Do thee know where we are?" Riennes finally asked Haralde. "No." "Do thee know which way we are going?" "Yes. This way." "How do thee know we are not lost?" "I do not." "How is it thee are so sure this is the way?" "I just am."

They rode for a short while. "I think we should turn this way." "No." Haralde's arm went forth, pointing the palm of his hand a rudder vertical to earth and sky. "This is the way." "Thee do not know." "I do not, but I do."

Riennes studied the change in plant life as they moved further west. Then, disconcerted: "Haralde! Thee play with me." "I know!" "Thee have Amont's dolphin with you? That is how thee do it."

"No. Did our captain ever tell thee how he acquired that fish that swims only one way?" "

Yes. The *naukhada* and the Chinois delegate. Is it not amazing to thee how out of the east, not the west, knowledge flows?"

Riennes squinched down in his saddle and let it pass. He didn't want to disturb Haralde's understanding of the east. Some of that came from the west, from Greek and Jewish writings, Greek reason and philosophy.

"I think we should go this way," Riennes finally challenged, taking one more run at Haralde's sense of direction. "No! This way. It goes this way." Haralde was firm.

And so they rode on, through forests, past fields. Once Haralde stopped their caravan when he spotted a peasant farmer and wife working a field. Near them, two rams stood hooked to each other by a six-foot chain.

Haralde sauntered off the road. The peasant farmer and his wife, working behind a rubble wall by the path, looked up, their eyes widening in terror as the armed man of horse came onto their field on a giant black. Neither had seen such a sight. They had seen armed men only afoot.

"Be at calm kind husband, mistress," said Haralde stopping and bowing from his lofty perch. "We are just travelers going home. See, we travel with a monk."

The farmer and his wife looked where Haralde directed and saw Riennes make a small bow from his saddle at the other side of the rock wall. Godfroi stood up holding the traces.

The farmer ceased cowering, made a small bow back. "What wish you of us my Lord?"

"The rams. It perplexes us. Why two on a chain?" Haralde smiled his calming smile. The farmer turned, looked in puzzlement over why something so obvious would stop such grand men on horse and cart.

"My Lords. It is so the two cannot get any distance to rush and to crack at each other in the spring breeding season. Much injury can they do one to the other without it. We do not want that."

"Hmmnn." Haralde threw a leg over his saddle and thought a moment. "Why not separate them? Let them go?"

"Well, then they really would be at each other. Or, they might wander off and we do not want to lose them, especially now their ladies need them, if you ken me my Lord," explained the farmer with a mirthful grin. "Also, this way we can keep an eye on both."

"Hmmmn. Well, still 'tis a strange sight. S'truth. It is a study of constant tension, would thee not agree?"

"My wife and I are glad it pleases you my Lord," agreed the farmer.

Haralde flung his leg back over and asked: "We are in need of feed for our horses. Would thee spare some? Be not concerned if not. We will be on our way and wish you well."

The farmer went to his wife and they put their heads together. He returned and nodded. "I can let you have enough feed for your horses and the bullock for two pence."

"Husband. We are but two worn and poor horse soldiers who have been away for a long time and are just trying to make their way back home," Haralde responded, ignoring a dry clearing of the throat by Riennes behind him. "Is there not something we can trade in lieu?"

The farmer looked back at his wife. She stepped up beside him and then tenderly took his hand. He turned and nodded. "The holy man?"

The farmer's response perplexed Haralde. "The who? The monk thee mean?" He turned in his saddle and looked to Godfroi.

"Yes my Lord. We would gladly trade grain for yon monk's blessing, one that would confirm us as Christians."

Riennes caught it immediately. He turned in his saddle and smiled at Godfroi who was sitting still and confused on the cart bench. "Monk Godfroi. It would seem the mission Bishop Odo sent thee on is about to bear fruit. It seems thee have work to do."

"You see, we are Saxons and celebrate the gods and goddesses of all the Saxon holidays and seasons. But in the last few years, we have followed the gentle teaching of Jesus Christ, stories a Celtic monk in black read to us from a book a few years ago," the farmer explained. "We have found comfort in the words of Christ. We wish to follow Him. Can we?"

Haralde and Riennes stared at Godfroi.

The monk sat frozen. It had been a long time since he had been a common monk working within farming communities, the poor, the sick. Most of his adult life in the monastery had been administering the church's ever-increasing holdings. Yet, this is what he was supposed to be doing now as a holy man.

Haralde and Riennes waited for Godfroi's reaction, both thinking the same thought. *Now what spy?*

Godfroi rose from his bench. "Of course you can, and you must so that you may be forgiven all sins while rewarded for the fruit of all your labour."

He stepped down, ambled through the opening in the stone wall and came towards them. He took the farmer's hand in his, and then his wife's, and bowed slightly. He smiled, his face warm, beauteous. The touch of both their hands in his fired him.

"Do you have any water with you?" he asked.

"Nay Monk Godfroi," answered the farmer. "But we do over there, in our abode across the field."

"Then let us go there so I may consecrate the water and thus baptize you properly."

They moved off, Godfroi's arm across the shoulders of each. They ambled across the plowed field towards a hovel of wattle mud and sticks and rushed around while some sheep grazed and chickens bobbed.

"Let us follow Riennes" urged Haralde, about to prompt his horse to move across the field. "I have never seen heathens become pure before. I wonder, does it hurt?"

"Let us not. Let us remain here Harry," smiled Riennes of Haralde's playfulness.

"Pray let us. We may miss something of import here. It may be he has forgot how to do it."

"Nay. He does. Let us wait for him here. Something tells me to let him alone with those two, that it is a private thing, not only for the husband and his wife, but for our holy man also."

They climbed down from their mounts and sat on the crumbling stone hedge. In the distance they watched as the farmer and his wife kneeled before Godfroi who poured a little stream of water over their heads and blessed with the sign of the cross over them.

Later, Godfroi came shuffling across the field holding a bag in each hand. When he came to them, he gave Haralde a heavy bag and said. "Grain for our animals." The other he handed to Riennes and said: "Two chickens, cleaned and plucked for our supper tonight."

"HAH!" roared Haralde. "The desert will provide."

"No my young lord. God does." And he moved past them to his cart. As he did so, Riennes was moved by the look of peace, nay bliss on Godfroi's face.

That night around their campfire, Haralde ruminated on the day's adventure, most especially on the two horned beasts tugging each other around the field.

He sat reclined, tearing chunks off a hot lick of chicken, the texture which he found tough and the taste, somewhat off. Before the fire he sipped a warm cup of wine. "The chicken. It is strong." The fire crackled. Haralde set upon the day's disturbance of his mind. "The two rams on the chain. The image. It plays upon me. I wonder if I may hazard a truth?"

Riennes was sharpening a small, moon-shaped, thin-bladed disk on a stone, the kind Godfroi had seen both of them scraping their jaws and head to remove hair. Their pursuit of cleanliness was almost obsessive to the point it irritated Godfroi at times.

"What do you mean?" asked Riennes, blowing steel burrs off his hand. He delved into the carcass of the chicken on the spit over the fire. Indeed. It seemed off.

"Do you suppose of the rams, that it is the same with us all? Tugging? Being tugged? Life pushing and pulling?"

Riennes grinned. Haralde was in one of his contemplations; his attempt at wisdom, logic. It usually ended with Riennes chuckling. His brother would miss the mark so.

"Monk Godfroi. Thee are a serious studier. Thee must have read works of logic and understanding. I advise thee to pay close attention for what is to be attempted," chuckled Riennes.

"It reminds me of the pushing and the pulling of East versus West, North versus South," mused Haralde. "Or, evil against good, dark against light."

"How about sharpness against dullness," said Riennes lifting his shaving blade up to the light. "Or faithfulness against infidelity. Atheism versus faith. My Lord Haralde, this has possibilities. Thee rise above yourself. What say thee Godfroi?"

Godfroi sat dark and quiet, intrigued by Haralde's intellectual ruminations. However, he also heard a slight bantering, nay even baiting entering the discussion. He shook his head no.

"I have another one," said Haralde. "How about fingers opposed to thumb?"

"How about evil versus knowledge Godfroi? Or, infidel versus heretic?" suggested Riennes, his eyes directly upon Godfroi to incite his intellect.

"Heretic, infidel, they are the same thing," argued Godfroi.

"Are you sure?" Riennes burrowed in. "Pull that chain shorter. Let us bring them together."

Godfroi dropped his participation to turn and gaze into the fire, then said: "Knowledge is not the opposite of evil. Only God's light is."

"Ah, but evil is ignorance unleashed, as is hatred, would thee not agree?" jumped in Haralde. "And an infidel and a heretic, are they not but put on the same leash to be hated by religious faiths as dangerous?"

The logic, the keenness of their intelligence, impressed Godfroi. His initial judgment of them as dumb, mindless brutes was changing. He must avoid their debate, less he let something slip. Their probings might pry free the lid hiding his true mission. He must divert their fireside ramblings more towards a subject where he might gain control of them.

"Maybe it is not the rams," Haralde rambled on. "Maybe that is too obvious. Maybe the message lies within the chain. We have a companion who is both Muslim and Christian. So does he tug at himself from both ends? Now what do we do with him?"

"What did you mean East versus West?" Godfroi asked quietly.

"It seems from our experience, knowledge, philosophy, religious beliefs flow out of the east," mused Haralde.

"My young lord. Only the West holds the key to all knowledge, of eternal life as we are the repository of His words, His teachings," Godfroi exhorted.

"Hmmm," Haralde mused. "Listen: 'I am the word that is God . . . . I am . . . . Life Immortal that shall not perish: I am the Truth and the Joy forever.' "

"Yes. The Words of Jesus, God Incarnate," understood Godfroi.

"Nay monk. These are the sayings of Krishna. For your ears maybe I can best describe as the Christ of Hinduism, teachings way before Christ was born. Taught to us by a very great teacher. We had to memorize large sections of a religious text called the Song of God. I do believe Christ was aware of these philosophies."

"There are many religions and beliefs in the world, some claiming to be the true faith. We recognize that. Yet, they are but pagan worship, heathen words," Godfroi spoke softly but condescendingly. Even as he said it, it dawned in his ecclesiastic mind that these two were literate, traveled. Not the brutes he wanted them to be, roles he wanted to cast them in his mind. From now on he must treat them as learned men.

"I have been told you both are Nestorians. You do not believe in Christ's divinity the way the church dictates and thus I cast your words out of my mind," Godfroi mumbled. "You play at wisdom. You discuss well, but you are not so wise," Godfroi started in to change the current of thinking. "I have seen you sharpen those stunted swords. I have seen the strange bows you keep in leather sheaths under your saddle. You are fighting men. You have killed. You have murdered, have you not?"

Haralde's cup of wine stopped half way to his lips. He looked at Riennes. Riennes looked down at the dirt between his knees. He made no reply. Godfroi spoke true. Riennes could not balance off the accusation with the number of men whom he had saved through medical ministrations.

"That must come to an end. You are both foreign, newly arrived. You must know the church has imposed two edicts. Men of your proclivity for violence must obey these or face a church indictment, even to excommunication." Godfroi waited for some reaction, and with none, proceeded. "The first of these is The Peace of God first pronounced at a council of bishops in 989 at the abbey of Charroux in Aquitaine. There it was announced universal church sanctions against anyone who plundered a church, struck down a member of the clergy, robbed a peasant or poor man or attacked a merchant. In 1041 followed the Truce of God directed at the nobility and their vassals, the armed men on horse. Both were forbidden to engage in war or strife on Sundays and Holy Days. The nobles and their men of arms came out into a field on a special day thereafter and swore their support and faith in these edicts. In these ways, the church has sought to change the role of plunderer and murderer to protector of the peace and good order."

Honour, duty, service. Haralde saw a kind of role for him in this, one of an honorable horse warrior. He nodded his head in agreement. Godfroi saw that and smiled.

"The nobles and their rabble of armed men swore to uphold these two edicts. And may Christ blind he who plots to pervert these holy contracts," Godfroi further offered.

Riennes, however, sat unmoving, his lips straining tight. Shadow talk. Shaded meanings. Murky words stirred by religious men everywhere.

Riennes finally stirred, and spoke firmly. "Nay Monk Godfroi. You cannot find the soul of men and women through their faith, but in their intellect. And you cannot capture their intellect. Thus, you will fail in this. By this contract, the church now has ennobled murderers as thee call us. The truth be it has elevated the brutes. Your church should not countenance such men within a contract. Their cruelty is a darkness that could violate the light of your church."

Riennes thought a second what he was trying to say, then continued: "It seems to me the church now has a contract with the dark forces. In time, barbarians would pollute thee and the church to their violence. Your church might bed with murder itself if it is not careful."

Godfroi blinked. He was stupefied that Riennes would say such a thing. "Sacrilege! You speak sacrilege! Neither God nor the Latin Church would ever engrace such a thing. You have misunderstood, Lord de Montford," Godfroi was quickly in to correct that misdirect by the young Norman. "It was the church's intent to bring peace by these two interpretations, and you must support that."

Riennes shook his head no. "I did not mean to suggest it was intentional. S'truth, the edicts were passed to bring peace. But it is obvious it will create a whole new chaos. The Creator is inscrutable, immutable, incomprehensible by you and yours. His great clear message to us is of love and peace. Yet by this the church attempts to corrupt His message to its own morality here on earth. Nay. It will gain thee nothing in the end."

"In this, and other things, you must believe," Godfroi went on. "It was to impress upon this rabble a new role, a gentler image, one of a protector of the innocent, champion of the meek." Godfroi pressed his plan to control these two and bring them more in line with his wishes, and those of church leaders such as Lanfranc and the Regent. "We must conduct ourselves in this walk to your shires as the church directs. You must channel any violent behaviour you may harbour within for that of good. You must give your hearts over to Christ, the divine God."

Riennes smiled. "I can see your strength as a subprior, Godfroi. Thee are very convincing, commanding. The Regent must value thee very much."

"Yes, and thusly you will take to heart many more things I will direct you both to follow in the days ahead."

"Nay Godfroi. I sense things may be changing for thee as a high member of the church. I sense of what I just said may lurk as a possibility in your mind, do thee not think?" asked Riennes. "I sense indecisiveness in thee, a want to return home to your monastic life, yet a doubt if there is anything of home left there. Maybe thee should start following thine own heart in the days ahead."

"What do you mean?"

"Let us finish Haralde's imagery of the rams on the chain. Maybe the import is not the two opposite forces, but rather as he says the chain itself. What would thee say about Haralde's imagery if I said a man versus a woman? They are opposites?"

"Nay. There is no tension there. In fact, a fair man and a fair woman can become as one, both in mind and body." Godfroi answered quickly.

"Such as the two thee guided today to a new spiritual union?"

A rush of heat flooded up Godfroi's body and into his face. It was true. Being the spiritual guide and God's vessel for the conversion of the farmer and his wife had settled in Godfroi a deep sense of wonder, of achievement, of completion within him. Nothing in his life or within monastery life had elevated him lately to such bliss. He glowed.

"Take up your new course monk. Thee might find the road ahead leads to your own true home," smiled Riennes as he rose, stretched, and said he would now seek his night pallet.

Haralde joined him. "What was that all about? I lost the thread of what I started," he queried as they rolled into their ground rolls for the night.

"Nay brother. I think your logic has lit a fire inside Godfroi." He chuckled. "I am amazed how your reasoning does hit the mark sometimes."

Godfroi lay curled up under the dray, disturbed. *Is he right? Was I never really home in the abbey? Am I lost to that now? Is the road ahead God's exciting work? Must I wander now? St. Patrick did. Why not I?*

Chapter Seven

The wee fish are God's gift to us,
whose sizes grow by man's imaginations.

Godfroi jerked awake with a headache on a bad nightmare. The singing of steel sharp across the clearing only acerbated the sick feeling in his stomach. He lifted up from his bedroll under the cart and looked through the spokes of the wheel. Riennes and Haralde were dancing at it again in the early dawn.

The grump buried deep within rose up. This part of himself he rarely let out. Only this time it escaped. It came out from his warm bed and stumped across to where the dust rose around the two. At the business with the kandos, he shouted. "ENOUGH!"

Haralde and Riennes reacted not immediately, but seemed to wind down their speed until they slowed to a stop, then stepped back and disengaged. They both turned and looked with some perturbation at the monk. "What disturbs thee?"

"You, both," mumbled Godfroi pressing his hands to his ears. "Those knives, the noise, my sleep."

The two looked at each other, then lifted the kandos over their heads and slid them into their scabbards.

Godfroi rubbed his tummy where it rumbled so audibly even Riennes and Haralde heard it. "I do not feel good. And after our discussions last night about weapons and killing, I would have thought you would leave off this fighting thing."

"I thought it was about agriculture, rams or something," suggested Haralde turning to Riennes with a quizzical, innocent expression.

"We are sorry dear fellow," replied Riennes who turned to Godfroi. "Tis probably last night's chicken. A bit off. Maybe a good bath in yon creek water hole might set thee up. We are about to baptize ourselves. Join us?"

The monk shook his head. "No, no, no. You must listen to me. You both must put away your arms in the cart and we must take a moment to pray for a peaceful day's passing."

"Thee know Riennes may be right," Haralde nodded his head in agreement. "I do not want to insult thee good monk, but there is a rankness about your person, especially when one gets downwind. And those bugs. Do not thee agree?"

Godfroi now had his head in his hands. "NO, no, no!" For the first time in a long time, he heard himself shout. Embarrassed, he looked through the bars of his fingers, and caught a look of guile pass between the two young men. Were those small smiles forming at the corner of their lips?

That angered Godfroi. He dropped his hands and was about to yell at them when Riennes farted.

Haralde giggled.

The monk's anger choked in mid fury. His mouth fell open and he looked aghast.

Riennes chuckled. He pushed Haralde sideways, and at that moment, Haralde farted. And before the monk's eyes, what had been two grown men standing before him, turned into two little boys playing at pranks. Riennes fell to his knees with a face turning red with laughter. When Haralde barked another one, he too bent over and laughed.

The monk had no way of knowing, but what looked like an insult to provoke him, in reality held great meaning for the two big men, tears starting to well up in their eyes.

For farting was a humour the twoplayed as slaves. It was an improvement not only for the body, but also for their souls. It was a silliness that played a large part in their survival, a shield against death and cruelty two little boys were witness to daily. These were two young children locked in iron together. Often at night on the rough food they had been fed, their young developing stomachs churned gaseous when they lay down. It became a game. They would hold sphincter muscles tight for as long as they could.

Through the night, they would hold each other for comfort. When they took turns spooning each other's bodies, that was the time for the inside one to let one go into the belly of the outer, then laugh. The one who exploded with the loudest, the smelliest, the greater was the coup and the deeper the merriment. It lessened the depth of their sadness. "God you are awful," the victim would cry waving metal-shackled hands in front of him while the other tried to muffle laughter under a cupped hand. The shout of "Quiet there. Quiet!" and maybe the lash of an overseer's quirt across their bodies would actually be the joke's ultimate reward.

Godfroi's reserve was on the point of breaking as he took the antics as an insult to his station and his wish for them to obey him.

"LISTEN TO A CHRISTIAN MONK, YOU HERETICS!" he shouted at the top of his voice at the two men mocking him. About to curse them, the worst thing possible happened.

He farted.

Peels of greater laughter greeted his entry into their cult.

Two grown men were laughing in front of him and there was nothing the monk could do. Except he farted again. Then, the gaseous comment brought on a sudden need to vacate itself.

The last Riennes and Haralde saw of Godfroi for the next hour was that of their holy man, bare legs and sandaled feet flying, woolen cloak held up by his hands, bearing for immediate relief in the sanctuary of the deeper forest.

Haralde stood ramrod stiff on his stirrups. Was that a group of armed horsemen moving covertly through the copse ahead on the far hillside? He checked his kandos. It was loose and ready on his shoulder. He pulled out his desert horned bow, placed its end bone knock through the stirrup, bent it across his knee and slipped the hemp string taut over the other knock.

The Frisian whirled, feeling his master's alertness, and completed a full circle kicking up dust around them. Haralde's sharp fighting instinct seemed to warn the beast of a threat ahead.

His hands crept to his saddle pack behind, searching for his leather body armour and helmet. He could not find them. He looked to the dray to locate Riennes. Riennes would know.

Only, Riennes had stopped moments before and stepped into the bush to complete another ablution of his bowels. He had become as loose as Godfroi who had battled his unease earlier in the morning.

Haralde urged the black into the shoulder-level brushes at the side of the path and hid in stillness. He glanced and at that moment, Riennes stepped out onto the path with his black mount just as Godfroi, the bull, the cart and the cow came abreast of him. Riennes tied his horse to the cart, climbed up beside Godfroi and the two chatted as the cart came the one-half mile towards Haralde.

Hide and watch. Haralde sat still and kept a low profile for some time. Then he turned when he thought Riennes was in visual distance and made some low motions with his right hand. Then he raised his left arm and pointed into the forest on his left. Riennes reacted immediately. His brother launched himself onto his mount, pulled off the pathway and disappeared into the forest to the left of the cart.

Haralde watched sharply for awhile, but nothing more. He heard the subdued twittering of a pan pipe deep in the trees to his left. He whistled sharply twice, then remained quiet. Godfroi pulled up beside him and was about to speak when Haralde put his finger to his lips.

Godfroi trembled at the possibility of violence. However, he tenderly tightened the reigns to insure control of the bull if sudden physical action was called for. The holy man was quick. Haralde gave him that.

"Be very still monk. Be like that deer thee told us about," Haralde whispered. "Circle around I must because there may be some threat up ahead. I will whistle for thee if all is well."

Godfroi sat in quiet for 20 minutes while Haralde moved through heavy forest to the right. Then Godfroi saw a horse move on the same far hill Haralde thought he had seen horsemen, and Riennes on his mount stepped out into the sunlight. His arm waved on high. However, Godfroi did not move and stayed where he was told.

Haralde moved through the woods, a bamboo arrow notched in his bowstring while his other hand held reins and two other arrows. His horse huffed upwards towards that hillside. Even as he approached a clearing, he knew he had been spotted. However, at that same moment he heard the soft lowing of a pipe. And Riennes and his black mount stepped out from behind a big oak way up before him.

"There were three or four of them," greeted Riennes as Haralde pulled up to him. "Their tracks show they have moved off in a direction other than ours. I feel they did not see us."

"Let us hope their intentions lie somewhere else," agreed Haralde who turned and waved many times down to the cart on the road below them. "And let us get our charge off this road and into this forest to be sure."

Riennes dismounted. He walked over to a big log, undid his English breeches, pulled them down to his ankles, leaned his ass to the wood and let go. "No more deceitful chicken for awhile, eh brother?" chided Haralde.

"Whah?" queried Riennes.

"The kind that talks behind your back," smiled Haralde.

Riennes grunted a couple of time, then reached for a broad-leafed plant, broke off several, wiped himself and then fastened his clothing back up.

"No chicken, no meal, no bread, nothing for awhile," he growled as he reached Haralde while tucking in undershirt. "There is nothing left."

Haralde looked quizzical at him and asked. "Your meaning sirrah?"

"Haralde. Your desert failed to provide," Riennes sounded gruff. As Haralde's brow puzzled, Riennes admonished him. "Haralde. We are out of food. Godfroi just told me the food box is empty. We looked for another one but it seems to have failed to accompany us. Or, as I suspect, did thee my dear brother draw tight your purse strings to protect the glint of gold against the extra cost of boxes of food for three men and two horses."

Haralde scratched his close-cropped yellow hair. "I must have miscalculated. In times past a box of food would hold any man in pursuit of his desert enemies." It was said in mild sincerity, pleading his failure to provide was an innocent mistake.

"Oh Haralde. In the past I recall all your desert campaigns were waged somewhat on an empty stomach. How many times did we barely get home, sustained only by the milk of our mares," admonished Riennes.

Haralde was about to open his mouth when Riennes cut him off. "And do not tell me how the desert always provides as our last resorts. This is not the desert. These are the forests of your Britannia and just how do thee expect it to feed us."

Haralde scratched himself and then said, as if pleading for some understanding. "Surely there are deer about. Or a farmer must be around to give us some food.'

"A deer. Where? Are they thick as horse fleas? And the last farmer thee begged a meal from, made us shit our breeches. I suspect he foisted his oldest birds on us." Riennes threw his hands and the sound of exasperation up into the air, and walked away. "I will go meet Godfroi and we will camp here for the night. Maybe if we forage around we can come up with something, although I must say my stomach has not yet sat down from its last rebellion." And he trudged off in truculence with horse.

Haralde sat, his thoughts churning. To be chided by his brother always ploughed him deep. Yet, his mind's hurt eased as it always did within minutes of a disagreement between them.

Mortified he became, that he could think ill of his brother. Riennes's criticisms of him were always few but founded. He had indeed miscalculated, and it was deliberate. He had indeed squeezed a pence too hard. It was a failing of his.

"No!" his head jerked up. Not totally. There were times when his mastery of the pecuniary had saved them both. "And I am sure Riennes will acknowledge that to me later, as he has before."

Refreshed, Haralde stirred himself. He looked into the green wood and across the meadow by. He listened to the wind in the oak tops, and to the chuckle of a nearby stream that tumbled down to a river somewhere.

He thought of how rich this land was compared to the barren moan of the desert winds and the dry mountain passes of their young life. "Yea? What is that?" he asked himself as his ears jerked, and picked up a splashing, an interruption of the stream's normal cadence of chuckling.

Curiosity itched at him over the sound of a liquid struggling. He dismounted, led the black behind and went onto a rock ridge where below the normal stream noise and the unnatural struggling drew his interest.

He fell back on this side of the rock. What he had seen excited him. How to get it excited him even more. It challenged his basic nature of out of nothing, something.

He took out his sharp dirk, and his eyes cast around until he saw a stout stick. He started to sharpen it. Then he looked at his horse, and the quirt of rope he knew he had in its saddle pack.

Riennes sat beside Godfroi as the monk 'click, clicked!' the two livestock up onto the hillside and into the clearing under the oaks where Haralde was supposed to be waiting for them. La, and there was a fine fire crackling. The sun was in the last quarter of its sky so there were long shadows growing under the trees.

The dray thudded to a stop beside the fire and Riennes jumped down, asking: "Haralde?"

"Here brother!" answered Haralde walking in with an armful of flat stones and more wood for the fire. Haralde's cuirasse hung on a tree knob dripped water. His kandos blade bare had been wiped clean. Upon Haralde's face was a clarity, a smile that did not disarm Riennes. Riennes had seen this satisfied smugness before. Something was up.

While Godfroi took the bull out of its traces and tied down him and the cow onto a rope between trees with plenty of grass at their feet and water for the horses, Riennes took the saddles of the two blacks, wiped them down carefully and tied a cloth sack with grain to their muzzles.

Then Riennes made his way over to Haralde who laid flat limestone rocks in a ring around the hot coals of the fire. He sat down beside Haralde who was also supping on a cup of wine.

"Brother?" Haralde offered up a cup. Riennes accepted and apologized to Haralde for castigating him earlier.

"I bespoke in haste. I take it back Harry. Thee have always acted to protect our best interests," Riennes repented.

"No. Thee were right Ren," Haralde rebuked himself. "In my desire to protect our riches, I almost jeopardized the success of our travels."

Riennes sipped, snuggled down by the fire, then said: "A strange thing happened when I went back to bring up Godfroi and our goods."

"Oh?"

"I had runs again on the way down. After I attended my problem, I joined Godfroi and we opened the food box in the cart. Yes, it was empty. But the moment I beheld the hollow of the box, my looseness left me. My stomach shrunk, assumed the dimensions of the box and my illness left me. It was as if the realization there was no food anymore made me suddenly hungry. My appetite, it roared back. I was ravenous. Do thee not find that remarkable Harry?" Riennes asked.

"Indeed my brother," smirked Haralde. "The possible duration of your fast, in that I mean, nothing to eat even to the next morning, preyed upon your mind, let alone your stomach.

"Yes! Yes! That was it."

"I too my lord," said Godfroi joining them. "The thought that all we will have to eat this evening is hot water warmed in the pot preyed upon by imagination." Godfroi sat down and addressed

Haralde across the fire. "I must tell you those bags your horses munch on contain the last of our grain. They will have to graze now. As we will because we do not have even oat meal left for porridge."

Haralde looked at the two staring into him over the fire. He knew they wanted to be witness to his shame and guilt. Instead, he chuckled. Then he slapped his knee.

Godfroi's mouth rounded O in amazement. Riennes's eyes went into slits as he tried to scrutinize Haralde's unabashed behavior.

Haralde rose. "I have been accused of being too picky with a pence, squeezing a coin until it cries 'enough'. Well, it is true. But I have always believed one must be resourceful, that finding other ways to get by improves your character." Haralde waggled a finger saucily at them. "And it teaches thee things about life."

"My Lord Haralde. I did not mean to be ungrateful . . . ." Godfroi started but was interrupted by Riennes who said: "Harry. Thee are not contrite. What means this?"

"Ahaa!" and Haralde rose and walked to a bushy tree. There he reached up, pulled on a rope, and a large body crashed down through the leaves and smacked into his arms.

"Behold," he said. "Dinner!"

Riennes was up to him in a flash and looked at the huge body in his brother's arms. It was a big fish. "By the joy of the

Gher himself, a king of fish!" Riennes almost danced around Haralde in disbelief. "Caught by my brother, in a tree no less! How is that possible?" He looked up into the branches, then down at the fish in his brother's arms. Then he noticed the rope tied to a sharpened stick run through the beast's gills.

Behold," grinned Haralde. "See how the desert . . . ." he glanced at Riennes, then started over. "See how the forest provides."

"What is it?" Riennes's eyes shone in disbelief. Instant inquiry always bubbled up in his mind whenever he came across natural occurrences new to him.

"It is a spring-run salmon," admired Godfroi. He explained how this fish had rushed inland from the sea to find its natal stream to reproduce its kind again. Before Riennes could get in another question, he continued: "And by the grace of God, a gift to we three hungry children. Let us pause and give thanks for this blessing He has bestowed up on us," and Godfroi began to kneel and clasp his hands.

However, half way down, Haralde bolted from his presence and shouting in excitement, ran over to some rocks to describe his catch.

"There is a rushing stream on the other side. Hear it rushing? I heard something and when I peered over these rocks, there was this big fish splashing in a pool too small . . . . trying to jump up through a rush of water between two rocks. It was tired I could see. There was nothing for it . . . . in my hunger I fell into the pool, scooped him up in my arms. He wiggled and bucked but I got him onto the earth . . . . cut a stick when he finished with life and hung him up in that tree. Hah! Hah! Thee thought I caught it in a tree. That is good." Haralde wiped the mirth leaking from his eyes. "We eat tonight."

"Indeed we do, and it is as fine an eating fish as you can have," said Godfroi walking over to put his hands on it. "I have had experience cooking such fish. Would you let me?" He looked with permission up into Haralde's eyes.

Haralde looked down at the thin small holy man, then nodded yes. "Here, yes, take him, and let us eat. How long will it take?"

"Oh, about an hour. I have to clean him first, and then wrap him in broad leaves. Build up your fire to get a lot of red hot coals." And he took the weight of the great fish in his thin arms and hurried away.

Riennes beamed at Haralde's joy but shook his head in consternation. "Haralde. Sometimes . . . . How do thee do it? How many times thee have done this. My brother, I will follow thee anywhere. I apologize to my brother."

"Thee should," and Haralde whacked his brother on the back, put his arm around Riennes's shoulder and guided him back to the fire. "But no, no, no! Thee were right. I was wrong. I should have bought more food. I just got lucky this time."

"Maybe. But as our teacher Sena instructed us: 'Opportunity comes to a prepared mind'."

"Such would a *Sufi* say," commented Haralde. "For him, everything is of the mind. Me, the belly comes first."

The two stared into the fire with glazed eyes. The warmth spread though them.

Then Riennes spoke. "I must tell thee something that will not sit well with thee Harry?"

"Then thusly say it quickly. I can stand it."

"Well, Godfroi told me on the ride in the cart that thee are no longer Thegn Haralde of Neury and Wym."

Haralde sat up with that, splashing a little wine onto his breeches. "What say thee?"

"While being instructed by Regent Odo, but I suspect more Lanfranc, Godfroi was told certain things that turn on this very road of yours. It seems there is not a Saxon thegn left in England," explained Riennes. "The whole royal structure is being torn apart. Instead, King William is handing out whole chunks to his favorites; brothers, half brothers, nephews, cousins, bishops, ecclesiastics, his supporters, anyone and everyone loyal to him whom he can trust. The land of your kin is being parceled out. Much will be owned by a few. Many have been driven off their lands. They are without. Some have sold their loyalties to others, some have fled England, some have resorted to robbing. The further from London, more the dangers from desperate men."

"This I have heard. My father was a champion to King Edward. Now it is over. As we have seen in our many years. I gained as much when in the Great Hall Gerald, my father's friend and probably the last thegn of the Saxon kingdom of Mercia, lamented his days were numbered. Remember, he told us later his holdings may not outlast himself, and if that day came, he might ask to repose himself in our holdings. All that I am saying here, I recognize that my father's day and my youth days are over. We must face the new order. Brother! It is nothing new for us!"

Godfroi trudged up to them. He held a body covered and wrapped in big leaves. He puffed as he came up the hill to the fire. Instinctively, Haralde rose and dug away some of the hot coals until a flat limestone rock was exposed. Godfroi laid the beast upon the rock. The holy man shoveled more hot coals upon it, whereupon he laid a flat rock upon that. He sat back to listen to the further discourse of his patrons.

"I heard you mention your father," joined in Godfroi. "He was an armed retainer to our Aedwardi Regis," he said slipping in and out of Latin, "our saintly King Edward?"

When Haralde nodded yes, Godfroi continued. "Was he then a member of the witan?"

"That is Saxon. What is that in Norman?" asked Riennes.

Haralde nodded yes to Godfroi's inquiry.

"Sirrahs. I know naught of war and politics. However, I do know the temperament of the average man, and it is one of individual freedom, of a sense of himself. If I am right, the Saxon, the Welsh Briton man, the men of Wessex and Northumbria will revolt against this imposition by William. There will be revolt.

"The witan was Edward's inner council," explained Godfroi. "Unlike the Norman magnates who hold all in thrall as their vassals, it was an unwritten law here the witan must meet in the name of the people not only to advize but to choose his successor. Unlike you Normans, it was not necessarily the custom to pass on the Crown to the king's heirs through the rules of succession. In England, before William, Britons were freer men, obligated to the king yes, but also reminding the king of their individual state, of the right to have input into the future of this isle. I fear this day has brought an end to this all."

"What do thee feel brother? I fear my countrymen are subjecting yours to this terrible enslavement, this feudalism."

"That we should get home quickly. I feel deeply my mother. She is aching. For why should she continue much longer? She lost her son, then her lover husband. If she is still there, what does she hold herself against, what keeps her to her duty?"

"Godfroi tells me the same," murmured Riennes. "I fear the Britannia thee grew up in has been thrown upon its ear."

"The best of the Saxon loyals died with Harold on that ridge," Godfroi cautioned. "Much the same as thee and I, cast down into the Viking hold," remembered Haralde. "From that moment on, everything changed for us. From then on, the most constancy in our lives was change."

"'S truth. Yet, the best that has happened is that we are vassals to William's loyalty," observed Riennes. "We are underlings, not visible in the king's vision for this isle."

"Yea. So thus it means the land will see much unrest in our time," judged Haralde. "I see brigandry here."

"Those horsemen thee saw up here," pondered Riennes. "I sense something about them."

"Did thee see them?" Haralde's eyes were quick with interest in the firelight.

"No. But the horses they rode were shod, and big. The hoof prints were deep in the sod, as if they carried a heavy man with fighting equipment. These Welsh of yours, are they horsemen?"

"Not likely Ren. Wales is all highlands and mountains, heavy forests and lowland swamps. Not a place for horse fighting. Warfare there is fought on foot. They will come at you as a horde, shouting like banshees, a rage to curdle your blood into fear; painted faces, shields and spears. They have some riders wearing heavy wool on small horse throwing javelins mainly. Unshod. Some bowmen. Why?"

"This moment on I think we should wear cuirasses and keep fighting helmets at the ready," proposed Riennes. "Also those broadswords of ours. I sense some menace about those horsemen. May be they are your brigands."

The three sat around the fire as night settled, Riennes and Haralde discussing their life experiences while Godfroi sat silent, taking in all their words and committing their meanings to his memory so that he would write them down when the opportunity presented itself to be sent in a message back.

Riennes bolted upright, his senses alert. "What is that I smell? It is something wonderful."

Godfroi stirred, then advanced to the fire. "Yes. It is the miracle of the fish. I think we are ready." Godfroi took a limb and sparked the fire and coals aside, exposing the flat rocks.

Riennes and Haralde huddled in close to the fire's heat. Haralde rubbed his hands together in hungry anticipation. Riennes watched the ceremony unfold with wide eyes.

As Godfroi removed the top rock, Haralde momentarily took note of the composition of the flat. It was black shale, the rock of Cymru, Wales. "We are close to home." Then his belly took his attention away.

The monk lifted up the corpse of the great fish and placed it on a piece of bark. The leaves had turned black and they smoked a sweet essence. Godfroi pulled away the leaves with tweezers of small branches, and the dark skin and the pink flesh shone in the firelight.

The sweet smell of food moistened Haralde's mouth. Hunger roiled his stomach and his ass suddenly bugled a ball of gas. His intellect appraised his catch, and it perturbed him.

"It is smaller than what I captured! What has happened to my great fish?"

"Yes," answered Godfroi. "Minus the head and the tail and the offal, all fish diminish in their offering. It is always thus when men catch fish. Always he imagines bigger."

"I could eat the whole of it myself, so great is my hunger," drooled Riennes whose stomach now bossed his mind.

Godfroi smiled. It was a moment he had dreamed of; big, heavy, fighting men always could be turned and controlled by their grossness, their appetites.

"Yes. I know. That is why I said the miracle of the fish. I knew you would be disappointed." Godfroi lifted the steaming salmon across their eyes and placed the bark upon his knee. "Let us pray and bless this great fish."

Haralde and Riennes, Nestorians as they were, still believed deeply in a higher Creator and Jesus Christ. They crowded close to the monk and following Godfroi's example, kneeled.

"You are unbelievers, and do not know this, but what we are tonight is what Christ preached to the multitude," droned Godfroi.

"Monk! We are hungry. Do not preach to us," pleaded Riennes. "We need to eat."

"Yes!" exhorted Godfroi, enthralled with his command over them. "John the Baptist is killed, his enemies present his head to King Herod and Christ flees into the mountains. The multitude, fearful over the death of the Baptist, flee and joins Christ on the height. There, his disciples come to him and say, Lord, there are 5,000 here who hunger. And Christ takes all that they had, five loaves of bread and two fishes, blesses them, and gives the bounty to the multitude that he orders to sit down on the grass and eat. And all feed. And when all eat, there is still fish left over. It is a miracle."

"Yes, yes," urged on Haralde, "and so be it with us."

"Yes. Behold!" preached Godfroi who took a sharp knife from within his cloak, and began to carve. "From this single fish, I will make many more for your hunger." And he began to carve it up in little squares.

Haralde and Riennes with their young stomachs aching, moaned: "Yes! Yes!"

Godfroi gave a chunk to Haralde, saying: "A fish for you!" And another to Riennes. "A fish for you." And he fed a chunk into his mouth. "And a fish for me."

"You said God would provide from the bounty of the forest. Let us give him his portion, and I as God's representative . . . ." Godfroi slipped a second piece of fish into his mouth, "and let us pray as we do."

And Godfroi cut many more pieces, feeding each to Haralde and Riennes and to himself and again to himself.

Haralde and Riennes ate and watched as Godfroi also closed his eyes and ate both his share and God's as His agent on earth.

All slurped and ate and watched each other and the great fish seemed to melt away.

Haralde and Riennes peeked at the fish disappearing into their spiritual spokesman.

Godfroi slipped the last piece into his mouth in the name of God, then smiled in great appeasement.

"Did you eat of the many more fish?" he finally asked, sucking on his fingers.

They answered: "Yes Monk Godfroi."

"Were the number of fishes greater than your expectations?"

Haralde, feeling not quite sufficient, wanted to differ, but Riennes disturbed him sharply in the ribs. "Yes Monk Godfroi."

"As it was then, so it is now," smiled Godfroi.

Haralde and Riennes looked sorrowfully at each other, then upon the bark and the disappeared fish.

Godfroi burped.

"Amen."

Chapter Eight

The Lord of earth who ennobled earls,
From that same earth He cast churls.
(olde English verse)

Riennes and Godfroi, waiting back in the shadows of the trees, cringed as Haralde became more agitated and yelled Saxon curses across the broad river swollen in spring flood. The bargaining with the ferryman on the other side was not going well.

Disgruntled, Haralde turned his horse away and joined them back in the trees.

"Pray brother, something amiss?" asked Riennes. Haralde's face was red and agitated by emotion. The icy green of his eyes looked as if they would melt from the ice fire within.

"That Saxon dog wants a gold coin to take us all across. That is robbery. Ferryman! Bah! More a highwayman," rumbled Haralde. "He would steal the foreskin off my male child's member, if I had one." Haralde turned and yelled in Arabic back across the river, something about camel dung in his sandals.

Godfroi was surprised to hear the strange tongue Haralde spoke. "What is he saying?"

Riennes shook his head. "Best be thee do not ask."

They sat there while Haralde stewed. Riennes studied the scene before them. The river was pregnant and rolling heavy. On their side was a dock with a big wooden wheel and a heavy rope that stretched double back across the river, the arch of their curves bending down almost touching the water surface. Across the river was a wooden cradle full of rocks and beside that was the ferry, a wooden platform flat on floating curraghs, hides stretched tight over wood frames as water hulls.

The ferry had wooden rails all around. On the dock there, the rope looped around another big wheel hooked to a stout tree trunk. The stout hemp also ran through two smaller wooden wheels on the ferry. Dominating the wooden platform was the ferry owner, a big black-bearded man with a woolen cloak to his knees, tightened at the waist by a rope belt. He spread bare muscled legs with feet in leather sandals on the deck. A crumpled *phrygian* cap sat atop his big head. Big muscled bare arms crossed over his chest. Riennes saw a bemused look upon the waterman's mug even from this side of the river.

"He says if we do not like his fare, the nearest ford is 30 miles downstream at this time of the year, and even then it may be a tough crossing," cursed Haralde.

"Hmmnm." Riennes mused out loud. He crossed one leg over the front of his light riding pad. "Methinks it might be our belligerent appearance. Look at us; leather cuirasses, longswords in scabbards hanging from our pads, bow staves lashed under our blankets and kandos on our backs, Mongolian riding boots in stirrups and big horses chomping to run. Maybe there has been trouble in the area and he is discouraging armed men away from his ferry." He sat thinking. His horse, impatient, shifted its weight. The bumping motion burst a bubble of another possibility upon his thoughts. "And then again, maybe it is simply an impasse between two stubborn merchants."

"Brother. Art thee addressing me?" asked Haralde.

"Let me try Haralde," Riennes shifted his leg back and his horse moved forward, leaving the dark of the forest to move out to the light of the sun on the river bank.

Haralde and Godfroi saw Riennes hail the ferry master with an upraised arm. Then there was yelling back and forth. It went on for awhile. After a time, Riennes turned his black around and joined them back in the woods.

"Well?" asked Haralde.

"A quiet word with thee brother," suggested Riennes and they moved off to one side out of Godfroi's hearing. "Methinks we have struck a bargain," he spoke low.

Haralde, picking up on his brother's signal for a quiet consul, whispered: "That be not possible. There is none better at bargaining than myself. I must hear this."

"Yea. Thee two are alike; one trying to best the other. However, I have arbitrated the impasse, and we have a fare to cross," smiled Riennes.

"How much. Bear me brother, I will not let him rob us."

"He says a penny for each horse, a halfpenny for the ox and the cow each, four pence for each man and a sixpence for the dray."

"Hmmm," mused Haralde.

". . . . and a gold coin," finished Riennes.

"Whaaaat! The bugger!" shouted Haralde.

"Ssshh. No. Listen. The pennies are his fare. The gold is to be paid back to us for something he wants, something he needs badly," answered Riennes.

"It is trickery, a sham. A shell game I have played many a time myself," Haralde snorted.

"It would seem, Harry, the value of our holy man there is more than paying your investment in him for your way home," smiled Riennes.

Haralde looked at Godfroi who was leaning towards them trying to hear, then at Riennes, then across the river. "Brother. Confuse me not. Explain this to me"

"It seems that ferryman is in want of our holy man. To get him, he is willing to charge his normal fare, plus he still wants the gold coin. So be it, I told him, but that it would cost him a gold coin to pay for Godfroi's services."

"And that is?"

"There is to be a great joining of the young men and young maids from many nearby villages in a dell in a few nights hence. Some are Christians. Some are of the old religions. He and the elders of this area want a Christian matrimony. There will be much music, dancing, drinking, revelry, swearing, tussling by the young bloods. It is spring, says the ferryman, and there will be no holding back the flesh needs of youth, one for the other, and best it be blessed in formal unions. So they want a monk to sanctify it all," chuckled Riennes. "And he has no gold coin to pay us. So he insists on being paid the coin first."

"Why so?" asked Haralde. "He may not give it back to us. Tell him we will keep it and he can consider Godfroi's service as paid for."

"No. I sense he wants to formalize the agreement, the handing over of the gold coin from his hand to us," smiled

Riennes. "He wants the contract to be properly done, as a certain young lord brother I know likes things done proper."

"At the end of it all, we do get the coin back?"

"Yes. He will us directly when the joining has been completed."

Haralde turned his horse around and went over to the monk to explain the ferryman's condition for the crossing

"Godfroi. Is the request to your liking? Do not let us press thee. If not, we will gladly ride with thee 30 miles down the river and cross at the ford. We will show thee how to hold onto the tail of the cow or oxen and how to swim behind them in the cold . . . ."

"Enough Lord Haralde! It is my duty to fulfill the wishes of these young people to be consecrated in the name of God. As well, Jesus also enjoyed a good wedding. Let us repose within this invitation to do good work, as well as drink and eat and rest."

"Yeeow. We have struck a good bargain." And Haralde thumped his brother on the back. "And thee who mangles the Saxon tongue, how did thee do it? It must be my teachings about trading has finally found fertile ground in thee."

All three drew their company up to the riverside. Riennes yelled his agreement, and the ferryman waved back. A young man appeared from nowhere and jumped onto the ferry. The two hauled on the ropes and made their way across the water to the squeaking of wheels on both shores.

The ferry grounded short of the bank, but the two onboard struck down the end rails and ran out four large planks as a ramp onto their riverbank. The two ferrymen then splashed ashore to confront them.

"I am Mordus, keeper of this ferry and this river," huffed the big burly waterman. "And this is my son Mordic, soon to husband a lovely maid. Her father has two farms, one to be given to Mordic in the joining ceremony in two nights hence." Mordus and Haralde seemed to circle each other, each taking the measure of the other. Mordus was a big Saxon, as big as Haralde and Riennes. He was strong, confidant, sure of himself and he stared into Haralde's eyes directly as he said: "You will pay me now."

Haralde was not offended. He was just cautious, as are all who barter. He liked this big muscled man. There was something of a fighter in him, a daring man. Haralde stared back strongly into eyes of the other, then smiled and nodded, for there was a touch of merriment about the ferryman. Haralde had counted out the fare to the exact amount in a cloth purse and tied it to his belt. Reluctantly he counted out the pences, rubbed the gold coin, and handed it over. The eyes of Mordus widened in joy. He bit it, then smiled. "I have not seen one of these for many a year."

He palmed all the money and it disappeared somewhere within the folds of his cloak. He turned, and walked over to Godfroi, more to appraise than to greet him.

"So, you are the holy monk?"

"Yes. May God bless you and the life waters of your river," Godfroi nodded his benediction.

"You can save your blessings for the young people. And for our wives who have nagged us to find one as you," snorted Mordus. "I am of the old way and will be until they slip me beneath the sod. Not much of you, is there? Never mind. Come along and climb your beasts and cart aboard."

The three of them, plus the two horses, the ox, the cart and the cow thumped their way up the ramp and steadied themselves in the middle while Mordus and his son jammed the rails back into place and began hauling them across the choppy river.

The platform was rough-hewn planks roped together. They lay on a log frame bound together by more ropes at each of its corners. Mordus and his son pulled the ferry back across the water by heaving and walking the rope backwards away from the direction they were going. As they neared the middle, the force of the spring-swollen river pushed the ferry downstream. Everything began to groan. "Do not stand there. Grab a hold! Haul if you do not want a soaking before the far bank," shouted a grinning Mordus.

Riennes and Godfroi leaped to the rope. Haralde did not, but stood firm by his horse, grumbled something about not paying a fare for the privilege of doing most of the work. Mordus laughed but hauled heartily none the less.

The ferry suddenly shuddered and water slopped aboard. The power of the coursing river almost forced the upstream side of the ferry under. The pulley wheels squealed.

Their horses whinnied. Haralde jumped to and joined them on the rope. Mordus and his son laughed, but did not break the rhythm of their hauling.

Finally, on the other side they pulled into a quiet backwater behind a rock outcropping and bumped against the rock cradle dock, a substantially more stable port of entry on this western side of entry.

Haralde, unsure of the monk's ability to disembark the dray and cattle beasts off the flatboat, jumped up onto the cart's seat and urged the oxen forward. The beast bawled and the cow tied to the back complained as the big dray rumbled down and off the ramp. Riennes led the two big Frisians off, followed by Godfroi walking. The monk crossed himself when he stood upon firm ground, thankful to be off the unstable ark he felt would have sunk out there if it had not been for his silent petition for God's protection.

Mordus came around the cart as Haralde jumped down. Haralde looked around at the forests and the countryside, and sensed they had crossed a line, that this was wilder hinterland. He knew he was near the March, the land of Cymru.

Not far was King Offa's dyke, the border between the Saxons and the original Britons whom the Saxons called the Others. Here the Welsh and the Saxons fought and flowed back and forth across the dike, warring at each other, each struggling to lay claim to this beautiful forested, foothill and highland country.

Mordus came up to confront Haralde boldly. However, as he did Haralde sensed a change in Mordus's body posture. Mordus had scrutinized him carefully while all were on the rope. He realized Haralde and Riennes were not common travellers. A brief appraisal and the ferryman knew he had high-borne men aboard.

"I address who?" the plain-speaking ferryman asked directly.

Haralde introduced his company. As he introduced himself, the eyes of Mordus widened.

The ferryman snatched off his crumpled leather cap and ducked his head once. "You are Thegn Longshield then? I thought I heard you dead."

Haralde jumped at the mention of his father. "No Mordus. But I am of that family. Tell me, what do thee know of him, Stoerm Longshield, or any of his family?"

Mordus did not drop his eyes but answered honestly. "Naught, only many of us around here knew of Lord Longshield. His was a good name, a royal overlord up there in the high lands of

Cymru. We heard he died. We have heard naught of the family since then . . . . my lord."

"What of Lady Longshield! Have thee heard anything?" Haralde grabbed Mordus by his arms and shook him lightly. "Nay my lord." Mordus shrugged off Haralde's hands and stepped back. He peered quizzically at Haralde.

"My Lord, I should not have said anything. I speak with great respect, ... but there is something of you that made me say so. I stood once a distance from Thegn Longshield when I served with Earl Godwinson in the winter wars, years ago against the Others up there. Your bearing . . .that big look . . . . there is something of you that . . . . forgive me. That was so long ago. I can say no more."

Riennes and Godfroi joined them around the dray. Riennes sensed a tenseness between Haralde and Mordus, but relaxed when he heard Haralde speak.

"Mordus. I am grateful for what thee have said of my family. Tell me, are there some nearby who might have heard something?"

"That is not for me to say. Yet, you may ask about when you get to our villages," answered Mordus who turned to take in Riennes and Godfroi.

"See this cart path," he pointed to ruts running away from the ferry. "Take it north along the river for many miles. The forest is heavy and deep. Then you will come to open fields and my village. You will see other huts and another village beyond. Ask for Tomas and Wenulf, our elders. Tell him about the monk. Tell him I said to put you up in the barn, your horses in the byre stables and your cattle beasts out on the common. Tell him food and drink for you all."

Riennes mounted up and handed the reins of the other black to Haralde. "Your kindness refreshes us Mordus. Thank thee." Riennes meant what he said.

Godfroi climb to his perch on the dray, turned and said: "God bless you and your family," of which Mordus dismissed with a throat-clearing: "Hrrmm!"

Haralde grunted up into the saddle but before he turned his beast toward the cart ruts under the trees, he said to Mordus: "Remember ferryman, a gold coin to us for the monk's service when this is over."

"I would be most grateful if you were to remind me of that from time to time," grinned Mordus as he turned away. "It would be an awful thing if I were to forget . . . .my lord." He stopped and shouted after them as they disappeared under the trees. "Tell Tomas I will catch up with all at the joining feast. And, oh, watch out for yourselves. There have been horsemen seen in the area. Armed men like you. Unsettled times these be about here."

They ambled down a rough country wagon path. The trees closed over them, shading the light. The cart rumbled down through a tunnel of huge oak and beech. Closer to the river great old willows leaned over and trailed their finger leaves in the current. Past the great massive trunks, they could see more massive trees in clearings beyond. Birds sang, insects buzzed low around them chased by bigger insects. A deer jumped across an opening way away and disappeared just as quickly.

"Did thee see that?" exhorted an excited Riennes. For him, it was a magical place. A great forest full of natural wonders. Haralde grinned at his friend's great enjoyment of his home land. "Look at the spread on that great black hulking monster!"

"That is an oak," volunteered Haralde.

"I know, but just look at the bulk of it. There is enough firewood in it that could have kept our pavilions warm for a year. The forests of your country seem taller, more massive than mine in Normandy."

Riennes leaned back and lay his head on the rolling rump of his charger and looked up at the passing trees overhead. His head lolled back and forth in rhythm with the horse's moving buttocks. Both had stored away their Norman saddles in the cart for simple desert Mongolian pads. They were more comfortable for long-distance traveling.

A dark wing flitted over them. "Godfroi! What was that?"

"A small wood hawk, my lord. After small birds, squirrels, rabbits."

They rode a few more miles in quiet enjoyment of the lush forest.

Riennes felt a growing unease as he looked up into the passing boughs above. Finally, he verbalized a dread: "I wonder Harry."

"What do thee wonder brother?"

"When we come to the end of our long road, I wonder if we are finished. I wonder if we will die."

Haralde did not look at Riennes. Such musings by his brother were not new to him. Haralde had known such dark moments to settle upon Riennes from time to time. He took them seriously. Some had turned prophetic.

Haralde looked around him, into the darkness under the trees, into the dark green of the very thick foliage. All this was very new to them, men of the open plains and deserts. There was an unsettling mood here.

"Yes maybe," he finally addressed his brother's ramblings. "But I think if so, we then go onto another road. No. We never die. We just get out on another."

They both turned and looked at each other. Haralde farted.

They both then roared with laughter.

Godfroi, half asleep on the dray's bench, jerked awake. Ahead, he saw and heard the two laughing, sharing that secret something they always seem to have between them, Godfroi observed. He nodded off again.

It was a little while on with Riennes again stretched out almost asleep on the back of his horse when something niggled at Haralde.

"Do thee suppose the warning by Mordus is our mysterious armed horsemen?"

Riennes blinked once, twice. A foreboding snatched away his reverie. He bolted upright. "Yes. I do!" He leaned forward and slid his longsword up and down to ease it free in its saddle scabbard. He just touched his kandos on his back but knew it was ready. He leaned down, untied some leather thongs and freed his bow stave from under the saddle. He strung one end of his bow, placed the other knock inside the stirrup bar, bent the horn bow over his knee and notched the bowstring. Released, the curved bow was taut, ready, dangerous.

Haralde repeated the same readiness. He plucked at his bowstring. It answered with a deep 'thrumm' sound. "Godfroi. Halt a moment," he ordered, and then guided his black over to the cart. He slipped his hand beneath the cover over the back of the dray, came up with a handful of bamboo arrows, moved away and shared them with Riennes.

"What do thee feel?" Haralde asked his brother.

"Sssshh!" hissed Godfroi, who stood upright on his bench. "I hear something." And the faint sounds he heard agitated him.

"What?" asked Haralde.

"Screaming. Yelling. I hear it faintly," warned Riennes. He cocked his head to one side and said. "There. Down the road ahead of us."

Haralde moved his knees and the mount, feeling his master's urgency, picked up his heavy-hocked feet and gathered speed. The black threw up big earth clods. Riennes wheeled, followed him. Godfroi bumped the reins on the oxen's back and urged it on, fearful of what lie ahead.

The two thundered under the hollow. Ahead, the trees seemed to open and light came through many more clearings. Ahead, they saw a green field, a hedge, a hut, and people running away

They slowed, and through the trees they saw a villein's thatch-roofed house and men and young damsels milling around. Haralde and Riennes screened themselves behind a bush, and peered over. They sat back onto their pad saddles and looked at each other. A wave of anxiety touched their guts, as well as excitement and anticipation. They must fight.

Three armed men were kicking up dust as they struggled to put young screaming maids onto the ground. One wrestled his breeches down off his hips to his knees as he choked a girl downward to the dirt. A second struck another girl with his fist to stop her struggling and screaming. A third soldier was inside the hut but all they could see were his legs and the shoeless feet of a girl struggling under him in the doorway. Under a tree, a young boy with an apple in his teeth controlled four Norman heavy destriers by their reins.

To one side was a man wearing a helmet topped with an iron image of a wild boar. His breeches were a dark green. He wore a wine-tinted hacqueton. A broadsword hung from his belt. His mouth was greasy from tearing pieces of meat from a cooked pork hank while with his other hand he was shoving an old serf away from him.

The last one was the most dangerous of the lot, thought Haralde. He thinks first of his belly before his cock.

Haralde silently hand-signaled Riennes in the way of desert fighters. He pointed to Riennes, put up three fingers, made a motion with his hand from his mouth as if speaking, then stood up in his stirrups stretching back his arms as if a bowman. Then he pointed to himself, drew a finger across his lips to signal his silence, then twiddled his fingers in a walking motion, then finished with a single finger indicating he would engage the chevalier off to one side.

Riennes nodded. They leaned forward and touched each other on the chest, and then Haralde moved off behind the bush towards the leader of the four. Riennes didn't want this. He wanted some time to pass that he might find a different solution other than armed combat. However, there was not time. He waited a moment, notched an arrow, and then nudged his black around the bush and out into the open.

Back behind, Godfroi had pulled up and through an opening in the leaves, what he saw paralyzed his mind. His eyes rounded in horror as the images of yelling, beating, roaring raiders before the serf's hut roused up the childhood nightmare his mind suppressed. He brought his hands to block his ears to shut out the awful thing, only his eyes kept betraying him.

The screaming and the thud of bodies being hit hindered any notice of a horse coming in with a man standing upright in the stirrups with a bow arched and an arrow pointed.

"RUT NO MORE YOU PIGS OR I WILL PUT AN ARROW IN YOU! CEASE SCREAMING GIRLS! CEASE SCREAMING!" Riennes yelled, asserting a commanding and threatening timbre to his voice.

The intended raper with his breeches down around his ankles and his manhood bared turned with a lust-filled anger in his face and stopped what he was doing. His fellow with his breeches half off and one thigh bared, grunted and turned. The third in the doorway kept struggling atop a screaming girl. The young boy at the horses opened his mouth and a piece of the apple dropped out.

"WHAT HELL!" shouted the pig eater whirling around trying to find the source of the interruption. When he saw tall Riennes standing atop a black horse within the arch of a bow, he dropped the meat.

For one moment all sound stopped and all froze. It was a scene of tense expectation.

Then it moved. That man with one bared thigh growled, pulled around reaching for his sword. A line buzzed across the clearing and he looked down at an arrow through his thigh. He screamed and fell over sideways. The ravager with his breeches still down struggled to rise with a knife. Another whisper in the air and a feathered bamboo shaft stitched the fleshy part of his two ass muscles together. Blood squirted out both sides of his white cheeks. He fell back on top of the damsel.

Riennes dropped the reins and the war-trained horse stood still. He dismounted smoothly, ran into the doorway and kicked the raper roistering on top of the young maid.

The helmeted leader drew his sword and made towards Riennes when a voice behind stopped him.

"Thee are going the wrong way, sirrah."

He whirled angrily, then shielded his eyes to look up. Haralde was tall above him, blinding him by the bright sun behind. Haralde pulled out his longword slowly and swung down. He moved away from his horse lest the man were to slash at the black.

The attacker moved in step with him, maintaining the same distance. They stopped in the middle of the farm croft where animals were kept. A baby was crying in the distance. A dog was barking. Young girls were sobbing. A man was shouting insults in Norman at Riennes. There was a body blow. The foul mouth was silenced.

"You bugger. Do you not know what you have done," growled the man. He squeaked a small helm down onto his nose, but Haralde could still make him out.

He was one of those toughed, experienced war fighters of many campaigns one often finds in the rough company of the lower ranks. A noble he was not. He was one of those who longed for a higher station in life, whose ambition drove him clawing upwards. Even now this man affected the garb of a man of means. He was the kind an overlord liked to have in his lower soldier company. A chief who knew of this man's ambitions used his kind to carry out dirty deeds, even murder and mayhem.

Haralde ran his eye over the man's weapon. Swords like this were too valuable for a man of the ranks to possess. This one, a churl seeking higher status, must have picked it up in battle, or killed someone for it. It was an old Viking weapon. The blade was the same width almost to its tip; a hacking weapon. There would be little thrusting in the violence ahead. This killer was going to bludgeon Haralde to death.

"You have attacked the vassals of a Norman baron whose holdings and lands I now claim." The man spat out. "I am his steuirhdt. Now you piece of shit, I am going to put you down. You have injured my men. By my right, they will carve pieces off you after I finish you."

A girl shrieked and ran by them. It goaded the old warrior to attack. Haralde knew immediately this was going to be heavy going. The man was in control of himself. He was in all likelihood a bloody dangerous veteran with the broadsword.

The man feigned a sideswipe at Haralde's legs, then swiftly changed, double-handed the grip and sliced for Haralde's midsection. Haralde jumped to avoid the first move, staggered a bit to pretend loss of balance and to hint at inexperience, then seemingly threw his blade up carelessly to defend himself. The blades met in a ringing clash. The fighter's sword then sliced down to cleave Haralde's head.

The blades met and 'clanged' across the clearing and Haralde staggered back, again suggesting lack of skill. The man over handed and put his weight behind another downward blow. Haralde took it close to the hilt with his blade slightly tilted to deflect some of the force. Even so the clang and the crash hurt his bones and sent a painful shock down into his knees. *My God that hurts. He means to have me early.*

And it began. The blades crashed and crashed and clanged, the man pressing Haralde backwards, staggering him, applying his weapon, his strength, his message that Haralde stood no chance against him. "You bugger! You bastard!" He swore, he spit, he roared foul, howled. On they went, kicking up dust in the clearing. Over, sideways, down, never giving Haralde a chance to retaliate. The man's strength was solid. Sometimes his enemy hit so hard it seemingly spun Haralde around and around again just in time to meet the next blow.

There was no chance to pull his kandos in this kind of combat. He would have to wait for a change in the tempo. Through it all Haralde watched his enemy's eyes, never his blade. The blows came, and Haralde at times absorbed the force of them by pulling his own blade back with the clash. His enemy was experienced, and older.

He was a man of around 40. Haralde staggered and stumbled but always managed to bring his blade up in time. What Haralde lacked in broadsword fighting, he more than made up in guile. That man pressed harder, feeling he outclassed his younger opponent. It would just be a matter of breaking through Haralde's pointed, lighter blade. With every blow and feint and attack,

Haralde started to feel his weapon and to understand his enemy's style. That and Haralde's training would decide the game.

Then, the man's physical movements started slowing up. No. It was more that Haralde was anticipating his actions. The fighter was still attacking strong, but to Haralde, his offensive actions seemed to take longer. Or was it that he, Haralde, was moving faster. Yes. He could feel Tagien's training beginning to master the violence. Rather than move the moment faster to kill, Tagien's dictum not to kill, but to enjoy the moment, to expand it and to move within it quicker and freer, took over Haralde's arms and feet. He waded around inside those moments. His own fatigue waned.

Haralde now started controlling the moments the old man moved in. The man started to pant. Sweat ran down his face under his helmet. The look of confidence in his enemy's eyes turned to confusion. Suddenly, the older man sensed Haralde had been faking, playing with him, laying back. The fight was over. Haralde smiled at the man, and changed the style of the conflict. With every crashing blow, Haralde began to thrust the point of the blade into his enemy's face, close to his eyes. Bang. Defend. Retaliate. Blade point in the face. Fighting tempo changed. The old fighter now found himself backing up, hacking at Haralde's blade to keep it out of his face. Now Haralde picked up the pace. His footwork was faster. He banged the older man on the side of his helmet once. Fear crept into the old fighter's eyes. Terror broke the slashing rhythm of his fighting style. The old weapon used to hack at the shield walls of his enemy was of no use here. Haralde's thrusting and cutting was wearing him down.

Haralde changed his hard stance into a liquid motion. He started to dance, whirl around to throw the old man off balance. Enough! End it! Haralde would not need his kandos for this. When the old fighter brought his blade up to strike, Haralde flowed under and around his arm, turned behind and jabbed the point into his unprotected armpit. The man groaned and turned to follow Haralde around. Blood began to stain his sword arm. Then the end. Haralde struck him a ringing blow against his helmet that staggered the old fighter. Off balance, Haralde flicked the blade into his face, cutting open one nostril and slashing a bloody line across a cheek. Haralde kicked him in the groin; the man grunted and doubled up. Haralde cracked a knee into his face. The head jerked back and the helmet flew off. Sweat showered off his shaggy gray hair in the afternoon sun. He crashed to the ground onto his back.

Haralde sat on him. He lay the point of his blade on the man's chest and reached up and double-handed the grip as if to drive it into the body.

"HARALDE! Do not kill him. He is fitzOsbern's man," shouted Riennes hustling towards them.

Haralde glanced down at his enemy, growled frustrated, turned his blade up and thumped the pommel hard on the bony forehead. The man slumped unconscious. Haralde rolled off him into the dirt to regain his feet, and right through a fresh cow pad. "Aaaah!" he swore in disgust, rolled back on top of the downed man and rolled around until he had wiped all the shit off his cuirasse and all over the man's wine-colored tunic and face.

A girl sat with her back against a tree where she had crawled after struggling out from under her attacker. Another was running away across an open pasture, screaming, putting out a hue and cry. Men and women came pouring out of area villages. She ran to a crowd of people rushing towards her.

She stopped, looked back, then collapsed onto the grass crying and her family and neighbors came gathering around her. The men in the crowd swept by carrying pitchforks and axes and rakes.

Breathing heavily from the fight and sweating under his cuirasse, Haralde wiped his face and looked around him. He still held his blooded longsword.

Two of the Norman soldiers were on the ground, moaning.

Riennes looked at Haralde, nodded to see him well, and then turned to attend to one. The third was unconscious on the ground just outside of the hut doorway where Riennes had put him down. The fourth, the boy with the apple in one hand, still stood holding the reins in the other, stunned by the suddenness of the violence and the change in his fortune.

Back on the trail, Godfroi kneeled on the ground, his head nodding up and down, his hands still clapped over his ears. He was whimpering over the violence, as he had done so long ago as a boy.

Driving the defeated fighter's old broadsword into the ground, Haralde waved a finger to all about him and shouted: "Do not touch it.!" He walked over to Riennes who was attending the man with the arrow in his thigh.

Riennes pushed it through the wound and out the other side to save the arrow. The man yelped in pain. "This one tells me they are vassals of fitzOsben sent ahead to seize the estate, manor and lands of this area and to drive out Saxon lordships and families wherever they want to," explained Riennes. "It would seem our new king has handed fitzOsbern this part of England. What is that shit smell about thee?"

The old man assaulted by the Norman chief limped over, one of the young maids holding him by his arm. He had blood in his mouth. She had a gash across her cheek. Haralde straightened and greeted him.

"I am Kernan. This is my daughter Marta. This is my farm. Thank you for saving mine from these terrible men. They were after our young women and food." The farmer spit blood in trying to get his gratitude out.

Haralde took his arm, more to steady the man, and the girl put her's on Haralde's arm. "Thank you, thank you, thank you kind sir! Are you of Lord Waeltler's family come to protect us?"

"No maid, we are not." Haralde shook his head. "Who is Lord Waeltler?"

"He was our master, until the Northmen killed him at Hastings," mumbled the old man. "His lady and aetheling child were holding to us until yesterday. She fled into the woods from the manor over the other side of yon hill at the approach of these vagabonds. They have taken the wooden manor. Our monk left our parish church a year ago. The church was burned down, we do not know by who. What is happening? Our village has known nothing but misery for the last year."

Haralde turned to the young maid. "Did they hurt thee?"

"Yes, a bit, but naught serious," she demurred him with a smile and her posture turned from hurt to bold. "If you had come but a minute later, I would be a woman spoiled now, and not the damsel that I am still. I thank you for that. The joining holds expectations for me still."

Haralde smiled. "And as for that, I have brought thee a monk. Mordus has sent us here for your joining."

The village crowd rushed into Kernan's yard and surrounded them all with a clash and clatter of wooden implements. The old man held up his arms and quieted the crowd, explaining how Haralde and Riennes had put down these evil men who had attacked them.

"Where is Tomas?" asked Kernan. "We need to gather our men of the council. We need to do something about these vagabonds and provide for our champions here. Mordus has sent them to us with a holy man."

A young boy yelled that he would go and get the elder. A number of senior men gathered around Kernan, stood with caps off, heads bowed and beamed at Riennes and Haralde. The younger ones looked up in awe at the two tall young men. The maids whispered amongst themselves of the bravery of these two in putting down the five men now lying on the ground. The men whispered amongst themselves of the sword and bow and fighting dress of the two and of the bloody size of them.

Godfroi brought the dray rumbling into the settlement. Senior women, wives of these villagers, appeared out of nowhere and went over to him. Men also, with hats still off, bobbing and bowing, talked to him about what had happened.

"Maid Marta, take care of your father. He has been enfeebled by blows to head," urged Haralde, handing the elder over to the daughter.

Haralde gathered up the reins of their horses and walked them through the crowd which parted as he neared Godfroi and the dray. As he passed, he growled at Godfroi: "So much for your God of Peace and Order of Peace. See how it has gentled such ruffians."

Godfroi, who was about to berate Haralde and Riennes for their own brutal blood attack, blinked and was silenced. Shouting in his ears was praise by the villagers over the actions of the two young warriors, men they called their champions.

Haralde made his way towards Riennes. Riennes stood up, wiping his hands on a piece of tunic off the grubby soldier with the arrow-split ass. That man's ass was wrapped in the remainder of his tunic. He groaned as he tried to pull his breeches up. He would have to walk wherever he went in life for the next little while. Senior women of the village handed Riennes white sheepskin. He cut a large piece and wrapped it around the thigh of the man with the arrow wound. Lucky for him it had gone through the fleshy part of his upper leg.

"What say thee Ren? Have thee landed us all in trouble?" asked Haralde, a funny gleam in his eye.

"What means thee Harry?"

"Your trouble brother. 'S truth, thee did bring Godfroi and me here and made us fight against this fitzOsbern's man. For this, fitzOsbern might just garrote thee and rot your remains on yon manor wall."

"Oh, thee call me brother but push me out in front. Thee whine stories behind my back and say he did it, my lord." Riennes wiped the sweat from himself. "Actually Harry, if thee will stop sniveling, I will get us off the sharp sword edge of fitzOsbern's executioner."

Haralde got serious. "Thee can do this? How?"

"It seems the first tale is not true. While I was tending to this one's wound, he told me he came originally from near Breton in Normandy. When he heard my family name, he became fearful and told me Olaf, that's the old sword thee just put down, led them here to claim the manor and lands for himself. He is a soldier of a lesser baron, a vassal of fitzOsbern's. It is likely fitzOsbern knows nothing of this. It goes Olaf is the son of a peasant farmer who ran away and joined a baron's force. Olaf burns to rise above, to become a noble chevalier, a man of land and rank," explained Riennes. "It seems Olaf heard of a Saxon widow here. She was to succumb to his demand she be his wife, become the new lord of these holdings. His company was promised unlimited drink, food, women and warmth around the fire for winters to come, let alone some land of their own."

To grab a moment to think, Haralde wiped the blood from his longsword, walked over to his black and seated the weapon into the saddle scabbard. He sauntered back in thought as villagers followed around him.

"One gold coin and we are amess." Haralde shook his head.

"Hhmmm. I wonder if Godfroi will see it that way," pondered Riennes, who then walked over to the monk to discuss their predicament. After all, Godfroi one day would scribble something about this to a certain abbot whose lips had the king's ear. The crowd of peasant farmers and their wives parted before the young warrior.

Haralde settled his beast under a tree, took off his fighting leather vest, threw it over the rump of his black and tried to cool off by pulling his green silk under tunic off his sweaty skin. He sat down on the spring cool green grass.

He noticed Riennes and Godfroi talking to a knot of senior men. The maidens of the villages were scurrying away, disappearing.

Olaf had awakened. He groaned and sat up. He rubbed his head, then saw blood on his hand from his cut nostril and slashed cheek. Younger village men had brought Olaf's men to sit with him. Leveled rakes, pitchforks and axes surrounded all five. The air was tense, threatening, wild-like.

Haralde did not like what he saw. He wanted no part of this. Rather he wished him and Riennes away. The villagers were pulling them into their local troubles, troubles that belonged more to a local lord.

Riennes and Godfroi brought two elders to Haralde's tree. "Haralde. These men, they are elders of the local council," introduced Godfroi.

Riennes caught Haralde's look of impatience about the whole mess and Haralde knew what his brother was going to say before he said it: "Haralde. These are farmer people of your countryside. They are asking for our help."

His brother was right. These were the very kinds of farmers, peasants, villeins, churls, labourers and slave families who would be on his father and mother's own demesne lands and lands held by these people in common for crops and stocks. It was so long ago for him, but he did have memories of them working hard across his father's manorial holdings.

Haralde's head bowed for a moment. He was caught. They were going to be here awhile, more than just for the great spring joining of the village's young people. It would entail more than just fighting to right a wrong by a ravaging band of raiders and robbers after women and food. He could not turn his back on any of this.

"Yes?" he asked wearily.

Godfroi motioned for the two peasant men to come forward. They shuffled up before him, leather and cloth caps bunched in their worried fingers. They wore hoods pushed back on wool tunics. They wore long stockings that ended below their knees. Their faces were dirty as were their legs. They wore shoes, the uppers of leather and the soles of clog wood. Along with their shabby clothes they came with a farm stink.

Haralde stood and the two men's eyes followed him upwards. "I am Tomas and this is Wenulf. We are elder members of our local council. These men, these barbarians, they are foreigners, killers. You must drive them off. They are not of our kind. Our Lady Waeltler must be protected from them."

"Elder Tomas. Be calm. We have put them down." nodded Haralde.

"But . . . but they have told your monk here they will not leave," stuttered Wenulf. "They say they own us, our lands, our labor, the manor and everything here. They say they are Northmen who have defeated all arms and can take all. They frighten us. We cannot understand them. And when they do, they demand oaths of fealty sworn to them and they will not swear an oath of protection for us."

Haralde stroked his chin, seeking time to work his way through what he knew he didn't understand. He turned to Riennes and asked him in Norman French what should happen here.

"What means this?" the elders asked. "Thee sound foreign. You are Northmen too!" The two men pulled back in fright when they heard Haralde talk in the language of the murderers.

However, Haralde continued, wanting deliberations between the three to be private from the elders.

Finally Riennes spoke: "In a way they do not. My country men have defeated England." Riennes watched Haralde's face to assess his brother's reaction to his bald statement, turned his palms up and shrugged. "S 'truth brother. I hope this does not hurt, but William is the new king, our king. By right of conquest, all Saxons, Northumbrians, Anglos, Britons lie at his feet. That which he wants his chief men to have, he has given permission to take. We cannot interfere with that."

Godfroi listened to the two talk. He stood silent. The language of religion was Latin. The language of the courts was Norman French. As an ecclesiastic, he knew both. As a monk who liked knowledge, he had also applied himself to the present situation his England found itself in. He thought for a moment before entering the fray.

"Saxon, Danes, Irish, Vikings, all have invaded England," the monk recounted. "England has always been weak, always divided, thus always invaded. And yet, when the barbarians settled in, they adopted English laws, right down to the village people. They strengthened their hold by not changing things. And one law persisted through all invasions, that if a peasant gave fealty to his overlord by paying him tithes and taxes, then he demanded one thing in return."

"What was that?" asked Riennes with much interest.

"That his new lord swears an oath to protect him and his family, to keep the peace so that he can work his fields and meet his obligations. In a sense, he maintained his individualism, his freedom to so ask and to so expect."

Riennes shook his head somewhat in amazement. "It has been a while and I have not returned to my Normandy to stay yet, but I do not remember such a thing in my countryside. The poor churls just did what they were told to do. A demand for such an oath would end with the farmer's wife a widow."

"I must tell you," Godfroi continued. "William swore an oath to the citizens of London that he would respect their ways, their property and the right to pass on their wealth to their children. That oath opened the door to the city. Would it not then be the same for all of England under his new rule?"

"Jhon of Muck told me as much," remembered Haralde. "If I can remember, he recounted William saying: 'And I give you to know I grant that you be worthy of all rights of what you were worthy of in King Edward's day. And I grant every child be his father's heir after his father's day and I will not allow any man to do you wrong'. Remarkable. I have heard of no king granting such. It is a granting of rights, of English law. And so far, Muck said, London and the king have been at peace."

"Pray monk thee can not expect these people, both sides, to understand any of this, let alone we three." argued Riennes. "We have nothing here. We must stand aside and let these things take their own course. Haralde?"

"Hmmm." Haralde looked at the two lowly farmers whose eyes darted in fright between the three of them. "Hmmmm. Nothing thee say. Maybe something could . . . ."

"Look out Godfroi," warned Riennes. "When Lord Longshield starts talking about making something out of nothing, comes trouble for thee and me."

"Here is one idea," mused Haralde. And he explained what he would propose to the elders, the villagers and Olaf and his company. In truth, a small bluff might make the Norman raiders move on.

Godfroi turned in puzzlement to Riennes. Riennes shook his head, but took Godfroi by his sleeve and followed as Haralde walked over to the two farmers and assured them they were not Norman invaders, and that the three of them saw a way out of this dilemma.

The eyes of the two peasants widened as they began to understand Riennes and Haralde may not be the champions to defend them as they first hoped.

"No! No! That bastard will not go for it. He said he will swear no oath. No oath, no fealty," cried Tomas.

"For there to be a new lord, there would have to be a *hallmote*," urged Wenulf. "That would mean Lady Waeltler and her steward would have to preside, and she will not."

Haralde and Riennes turned to Godfroi for an explanation.

"It means manor house and mote," explained Godfroi. "It is the lord's manorial court presided over by his reeve to transact mainly villager business, and the lord's business if it touches on his interests. It is where the lord enforces collection of all his fees and taxes and grants *seisin*, that is, legal possession to heirs and receiving fealty from them. The lord and his vassals swear oaths, of protection by the lord, loyalty by the vassals. It may also include a promise by the lord to feed his vassals during the winter if fall crops have failed. Thusly, they are all in this together, one supporting the other."

Riennes, shaking his head slowly, turned to Haralde and said: "This is beyond us."

Haralde said: "No, in fact I think all can be made right, if thee brother will say certain things to your countrymen."

So, Haralde gathered them all around him and plotted how to bring peace to all.

The two elders shook their heads no, that it would not do. Then they acquiesced, said they must present this to their council, and scurried off.

Riennes, Godfroi and Haralde stood and enjoyed the coolness beneath the trees. When across the clearing they got the nod of approval from the council, they stepped out, left the peace of the trees and walked over to where the rogues sat together threatened by a ring of sharp farm implements.

As they approached the huddled Normans, they heard the beating of a human body and the whimpering of a young woman.

Tomas greeted them and grumbled as they walked towards the village crowd. "That is Marta. Too pretty! Too pretty! She attracts men too much. The women of our village say she waved at these Northmen which drew them to her hut, to her sisters and her father Kernan. We have been under some black luck for the last year. We do not need a maid of our people attracting more. This one always causes trouble and it is always men. She is still a virgin, although we as a council have dealt with her transgressions with young men hereabouts. She is on the eve of becoming a man's fresh wife. Poor Kernan, although the wonder of it is she still is a virgin. Now this, just on the eve of the joining."

Godfroi uttered 'nonsense' under his breath as he, Riennes, Haralde and the huge company of the village pressed upon the battered old Norman and his wounded company.

The two elders stepped forward and vocalized loudly so all could hear: "Olaf the Northman. You have assaulted us. A hue and cry went up. All villagers came running to confront this. That is a law of this land and of our common interests."

"Damn your common interests!" shouted Olaf rising from the ground holding a rag to his face and standing grand before them all. "I will have at you all for this attack on me and my men! This kind of shit I do not need. Get thee from here," he shouted. He spotted his sword stuck in the ground and made as if towards it. Just the voice, just the tone of it, just the familiar French of his Norman homeland, stopped him after one step:

"No!"

Olaf turned and took in the tall, dark, blue-eyed bowman with the sword pommel butting over his shoulder.

The old soldier looked him up and down, his carriage, his character, his force. He took in the silk undershirt and the rich leather cuirasse. He glanced down at the Mongolian riding boots, and his brow wrinkled in uncertainty. Visibly, before everyone, Olaf's demeanor changed immediately to a common soldier's compliance.

"You are Norman . . . . my lord?"

"As thee are," answered Riennes.

"May I ask from where?"

Riennes ignored the question. There was something in this man that hungered for higher respectability. "What village were thee born, who did thee foreswear loyalty to as a soldier and how came thee here? . . . . and do not lie, I will know," ordered Riennes.

Olaf stood stubborn momentarily, and then unburdened himself: son of a farmer, a churl who left and joined as a spearman to the noble family Mortemor near Neufchatel-en-Bray, crossed over the canalem and fought at Hastings under a viscomte, a vassal of Lord fitzOsbern.

"Thee are here then on this count's orders?" asked Riennes.

"Uhh . . . . yes," answered Olaf.

"Hhmmm," pondered Riennes who strutted through Olaf's company, examining the eye of each, the wounded standing with a sore ass, the one with the pierced thigh and the youth wide-eyed, fearful, still holding the horses.

He circled past Haralde and Godfroi and whispered quietly: "He is a freebooter, a son kicked off the land, looking for his own. I think he lies about the count. This is a quick grab for his own future and that of his men . . . . and I think by his raw audacity, he could win."

Riennes circle back before Olaf.

"May I know my lord's name?" asked Olaf humbly.

Riennes introduced himself, Haralde and the holy man. Olaf's eyes widened. The powerful de Montford family name was known to him. Yet, he stood his ground. To be a noble himself, he was so close, right now, right here. In fact, he could enlist the help of such a powerful Norman magnate to his own cause. Surely he would understand.

"My lord. You must stand with me against these peasants," Olaf took a step forward. The ring of sharp farm implements closed in on him and he stopped, but closer to his sword.

Riennes stepped between him and the sword and shook his head. "No. Thee must leave."

"This is mine by right of conquest, by my sword."

"No. By your actions and by your very words, thee have shown yourself lacking in the means to be an overlord of these people, to take care of them."

"What do I care about what they need?"

"Thee may be a soldier and a conqueror of this country, but thee lack any understanding of what it means to be a noble holding a manor and villages and people in this Britannia," answered Riennes. "It takes more than a sword to be that."

"I do not understand?"

Godfroi stepped in. "You attacked the very people you wish to rule. A hue and cry went up. In the law here, a hue and cry must be answered. There must be a council gathering to rule on this to see who was in the wrong. And if you are to be a lord in this country and to accept their vow of fealty to you, you must swear to protect them in good and hard times. They may be lowly churls and villeins to you, but here, it is expected by every Saxon and

Anglo that if they pay fees and tithes to you, they get something back in return. In effect, a manor and its villages are in this together."

"Bah. I have to do nothing." Olaf whirled on Riennes. "Is not that my right my lord?"

"No." Riennes admonished the soldier. "The monk is right. Even King William has so sworn. The laws of these lands will continue. And thee are so far away from a Norman stronghold, thee would be wise to abide by these laws. Alone out here" . . . . and Riennes pushed a sharp shovel out of his way as he attempted to face the soldier better . . . . "thee might awaken one night with a pitch fork in your belly. Besides, is it not easier to go into an orchard for an apple and to stand under the tree and have the wind drop it naturally into your hand, rather than shake the tree in anger to try to get the same? Think man."

Olaf put his hands on his hip and fumed.

"To stay, thee must call a council, and thee must make overtures to the lady of this manor who is still the legal owner of these holdings," added Riennes.

Haralde, standing by quietly, stepped into the clearing and into the conversation. "Olaf. There is something here thee may never understand. Thee are a soldier and a soldier knows only of killing. Killing is a way of surviving. Thee take by maiming or killing. After thee have done this often, there is nothing left inside thee but killing. A nobleman understands when the conflict is over, he must set aside his sword and restore order. To become such, he rules, justly as he can. A true noble rises above his desires. To rule, thee must ennoble yourself. These people are commoners of the earth, as thee are, and they understand this. To be a noble man, thee must bring something to them. Something they respect. It is called honour. To do that, thee have a duty to serve not only yourself but also your people. It is the same with them to thee."

Olaf turned away in disgust. "What kind of Norman are you? These are just peasants, dirt." Olaf hawked up sputum and spit on the ground in front of him. "I do not think as you. I will not do as you ask."

Haralde stepped forward, slammed the palms of his hands into Olaf's shoulders, driving him back a few steps. "Then leave," he ordered, then pulled Olaf's old sword out of the ground, flipped it and offered the handle to the old fighter. The village crowd pulled back their implements, then stood in silence to see what was about to happen.

"Take your men, your horses and weapons and walk the river road to the ferry and leave," ordered Riennes. "Lord Haralde and I have holdings nearby. If we hear thee have returned, we will come back and put thee down."

The crowd murmured its approval as Olaf gathered up his men. The women of the village crowded around their horses. They stepped back and hissed as Olaf climbed onto the saddle, his helmet under his arm.

Riennes stepped close to Olaf and looking up at him, whispered: "Or, thee can think, be of the earth as we all are, and accept that. Be the noble that you wish to be. Take the right fork of the road before the river and ride over the hill to the manor and call a council. Take the oath of fealty from these people. Make them your vassals and tenants and give over in return. But thee must ask yourself as thee approach that fork, am I a noble man or just a common like them?"

Olaf shook his head, somewhat negatively, but also somewhat in confusion. The grizzled soldier turned and headed down to the river. His squire and a soldier mounted up and followed behind. His soldiers, their wounds wrapped in rags, did not mount, but limped along on foot trailing their horses behind them.

Haralde, Riennes and Godfroi stood before the village crowd and watched them go. Godfroi noticed something of Olaf's horses. Tied into the long hair of the horses were images, small carved figures, wreaths of vines and roots tied into ugly, tortured faces; a wooden plug with legs but no torso or face. There on another horse's mane was the face but no torso, little leather pouches bulging with something inside, feathers and wooden images, roots and worts and knots of things hideous.

Godfroi leaned over and asked Tomas: "What are those things upon the horses?"

"They are curses holy man," answered Tomas. "To afflict them with ague and pimples and carbuncles and bubbled phlegm, if they so much as come near our homes again. Our women have put charms upon them to deflect their evil. Our women want no more blackness of their devil."

"Pagan worship." Godfroi crossed himself against Tomas's rhyming litany.

Olaf was hunched over in the saddle in obvious deep thought. His wounded men whimpered in walking. Their limping pace slowed. They would not be able to ride for some time. Their wound bindings now were blotted with blood. It was obvious they hurt so much they were not going to make it to the ferry.

The crowd held their breath when this shuffling company reached the road that split off to the right. Olaf stopped, looked down at his wounded companions. He turned in his saddle, looked back at them all, then turned off onto the road that led over the hill.

A moan went up from the villagers. Tomas and Wenulf broke away and rushed up to them. "What means this? He is not leaving?"

Riennes shrugged, turned away and went to look to his horse and weapons. Godfroi looked down at the ground, then turned away and walked over to his dray. The cow and the oxen were bellowing in hunger.

Haralde watched Olaf and company top the hill on their way to the manor house. He looked down at the two elders and also shrugged.

"We tried, but it would seem thee have a new lord," he admitted.

"But we wish not. He is cruel. He will take everything and return naught to us but our labor and pain," whined Wenulf.

"Listen thee men of this village. Britannia is oppressed now. We cannot do more than what we tried. The king who rules this brute rules us. Thee must make the best of it." Haralde watched Olaf top the hill and disappear over it. He smiled. "Buck up. Methinks thee have won your oath from him and he may prove a better master than we judged. There may be more to this brute than we first thought. He may mellow under your good direction."

Haralde turned and went towards his black, the two elders hounding him along the way begging for a reversal of their dark future.

Riennes who was ahorse joined Haralde and the two elders. Godfroi rumbled up to them all in the dray. "Well, we tried the bluff," stated Riennes, who appeared not unhappy with the outcome. "But we could not trick him. Let us hope he makes a thing of it here."

A low chuckle escaped Haralde. "If so, I think the Lady Waeltler may have a new suitor. Either he will go down on bended knee before her or he will kidnap her from her hiding place. I think he will make the reluctant widow his bride."

"What to do?" shouted Tomas and Wenulf.

"Well. All this has made me hungry," Haralde bellowed back at them. "Mordus sent us here. Do thee feed us or not. Do our horses get stabled and get grain or not. And do your daughters and sons get joined by our holy man or not!"

Tomas and Wenulf looked at each other. Then their anxiety capitulated to the needs of their guests. "Come. Mordus has never been wrong with the trade he sends to us from the river. It is a time of holiday, joy and rejoicing," admitted Tomas. "We will attend to our sorrow and our wounds later. Follow us. Let us offer you the hospitality of our villages."

Haralde and Riennes turned their beasts to follow the two elders past Kernan's house and out onto the fields and forests and woodlands. Godfroi bumped along behind, the oxen and cow complaining. They joined the crowd of villagers who headed towards a host of huts and homes beyond ditches, chuckling streams, stones rubble walls and wood wattle fences. Slowly the crowd began to thin as each went to their own holdings.

They skirted a field plowed in many long strips.

"What means those," asked Haralde, his eyes taking in everything agriculture in bright enthusiasm.

Tomas explained: "These three plowings are mine, those three beside, Wenulf works, these two, Kernan's." And Tomas continued to explain how the village held three fields in common; one for spring and summer crops such as oats, wheat, much barley, peas and beans, another field for winter seeding of spring crops and a third held in fallow. Each year each field was rotated to insure they were not exhausted. "Each of us has almost finished plowing and seeding of our own strip cultivations," explained Tomas. "We are well ahead of past spring plowings."

"How is that?" asked Haralde.

Tomas explained that this spring, with their overlord dead, they had been able to get their fields done before they were called to toil on the lord's demesne, the lord's own lands. "Lady Waeltler has put few demands on us this spring. She still pines for her lost lord. The chapel has been burned to the ground. There is no rector to demand the church's food, fees and tithe obligations. We wintered well and no one was sick. It is going to be a very good year for us, if only the curses will stay away."

In the active field with the strips, they passed men behind plows pulled by oxen. Their own oxen and cows bellowed, almost in hunger for the companionship of their own in the traces.

Haralde's eyes and intellect danced. He was stimulated not only with what he saw and liked, but by memories welling up inside. Memories of his youth, buried deep. That which he thought he had lost, now swept up through him. These were his people. The look and smell of everything was familiar. For the first time in landing on English shores, he was beginning to feel less a stranger.

Ahead, a small bee-hive shaped building loomed up behind a hill. "What is that?" asked Riennes.

"A dovecote my lord," smiled Tomas. "Full this year."

"Full of what?" continued Riennes.

"Doves my lord. Captured by the young people and the cotters of our village. Oh. I see. Cotters have no land, no holdings, no livestock," answered the elder. "Their tithe and taxes are paid in the sweat of their brow, from their labours."

Riennes however was more interested in the capture of the birds.

"Have you not had squab my lord? No. Then you will this day. Doves roasted on a spit over a fire are the food of nobles. Delicious! We sell them at market. It puts coin in our pouches to help in our geld payments to the master."

As they rode on, they saw pigs squealing in the nearby marshes, rooting for roots and nuts. Sheep and goats grazed in the woodlands.

They neared a clutch of huts. Smoke poured out of a centre hole in the thatched peaks. The smoke gathered in a fog under the boughs and lay low over some of the pastures.

"Haralde!" And Riennes nodded at the huts, indicating their design.

"They look like desert yurts," blurted out Haralde of the design of nomad tents on the great deserts and foothills in the shadows and canyon entrances of the mountains and the desert steppes.

The huts were decorated with boughs of spring blossoms. Older women came out, shushing young girls behind them, pushing coy daughters back into the smoky entrances of their huts.

Haralde leaned down from his horse and looked through the opening of one into the smoky interior. The floor was dug out so the hut was sunk below ground level. It was covered in rushes. The source of heat and cooking was a central fire burning. The only furniture he could see was a trestle table in the back. Everything was made of wood. All the huts were timber framed with walls of wattle and daub: oak wands daubed with clay. The roofs were thatched still in the way of ancient times, a haven for spiders, mice, hornets and birds. Things hung down from the rafters; a hunk of pork, beef or a plucked chicken.

As they rode on, they passed other homes. The huts had a small toft out front containing some smaller outbuildings. Out back was a larger croft containing the home garden along with chickens and piglets kept inside by a hedge or trench.

Young girls came out from behind trees and huts to beam wide-eyed up at them. Maidens smiled, and looked demurely down at the ground, peeking glances at them.

Haralde felt something touch his leg and he looked down on his right side. Nothing. He leaned over on his left in time to see a young maid walking away from him, a bough of flowers in her hand. She glanced over her shoulder and peeked out from under auburn hair.

Most buildings were small. Another as they approached was large; forty feet long and about 15 feet wide, all of solid wood.

"This is my place," announced Tomas who dashed inside and came out with a mature woman in his arms. "This is my wife Lenni. Lota! Lota! Where are you? My daughter Allota is somewhere about here."

Lenni nodded to the ground. She was a round woman. There was a sense of strength about her. She was the kind of woman who could work all day, come in from the fields and cook all evening, then satisfy her man all night. She stood shy. She would not look up and meet their eyes. However, she giggled a lot. She had mirth in her. "Welcome," was all she said.

Haralde and Riennes dismounted and made a small bow. "We thank thee Wife Lenni for . . . ." The move by two young lords before her poor hovel caught her by surprise. She jumped back, put her hand to her mouth, and then bolted back into the smoke of her home.

Tomas shrugged, and then laughed. "That was kind of you my lords. Nothing like this has ever happened before. My wife will be the envy of women here. You bless my house and my family in your regard for her. You will come back here and eat with us in a moment. But as champions, you will want to attend your horses and livestock first. Come."

Godfroi too was caught by surprise. Not in his life had he seen such an action in the manorial life of a lord. He blinked and looked at Tomas's face. It beamed. He sensed as they departed the two lords had left a residue of good feelings around the longhouse.

The elder led them past other huts in his village to a wooden barn, higher and bigger than any huts. He swung open large doors and stepped down to another earthen floor dug out below ground level. The barn had stables at one end. There were lofts for holding hay and many wooden stalls and different sized wooden boxes. Tomas showed how the boxes were to store grains, food and crops. A few bags of grains, beans and peas were piled in some of the boxes, the remains of a good harvest last year.

He explained crops, food and meats were stored here to be given over to the lord and the parish monk. But not much demand was made on their obligations to the manor this year. "We did not have to slaughter many of our horses and cows at the end of the season, so much grain did we have to over winter. If we just did not have so much cursed blackness fall upon us."

"What blackness?" asked Haralde as he and Riennes went outside and released the ox out of the traces. Godfroi untied the cow. Tomas led them all to a gate in a hedge. He pushed both animals into an empty village common pasture. The ox bellowed his presence. The cow dropped her head to graze immediately.

As they brought their big black horses in, Tomas explained: "Raids, rampages by brigands and thieves. They have carried off some livestock. They have stolen foodstuffs from us. You should be aware there are brigands about. Some say they are a gang of renegade Saxon soldiers who have fled into the forests to hide from the Northmen. They have joined Aelfgar the Wild."

"Aelfgar? Wild?" queried Riennes.

"Yes. He is of them. The Others," answered Tomas. "You know. Those wild ones up in those hills, those mountains, the Wealc. He roams at will, a brigand who takes what he wants. He takes young girls from farms on his campaigns through this part of the country. It is rumored women hereabouts secretly admire him."

Riennes chuckled out loud over that image and rolled his eyes at Haralde. "Your mad Welsh, Haralde." Haralde smiled. It was another step closer to home.

They stripped down their blacks. The two loved horses. As horse warriors, they took very special care of their animals. They wiped them down with straw, ran their hands over legs, and checked their ankles and fetlocks. They murmured quietly to them all the while. Haralde gripped a foreleg and bent it back up between his legs to examine a hoof.

Tomas pursed his lips when he saw hoofs iron shod. He had heard of such things. Never had he ever seen it. These were pampered horses. War horses. Only men of wealth could own such.

"Tomas. This suits us. We will put our gear down and sleep here for the night," said Haralde.

"Very well," agreed the elder. He went to the door and bade them come eat with him and his wife.

The two young men put their horses in stalls and fed them grain. They forked straw into the stalls. They opened the barn door and pulled the dray with all their personal property safe inside. Haralde checked to make sure all their valuables and coin were still locked securely under the dray seat. Then he stretched and looked all around. He critically examined the Saxon barn.

He looked up. Then he walked over and put his hand against a tree trunk. "Look at this brother?" Riennes joined him, put his hand on the trunk and looked up. This tree and others had been cut straight down the middle of their runks. The wooden outside walls were pegged to the cut flat of the trunks. Above, a single bough from each tree had been kept so they arched up and joined to support the roof ridgepole. Such construction afforded a lot of elevation and thus room above for lofts of hay. It was an example of the local carpentry and ingenuity.

Riennes turned to Haralde. "Do these things stir thee of home?" Haralde smiled at his insight. "Yes, some. The smells mostly. We do not have anything like this," he said of the barn's interior. "I am afraid thee might be disappointed with us. We are a rough lot up in the northern hills."

"Yes. I can tell by your stink. We need to bathe."

"Where is Godfroi?"

Riennes went to the barn door open. "He is taking a shit behind yon hedge."

They gathered him up later and walked through the village of smoke, of grass, of mud and animals. The residents stood outside their huts, nodding, smiling, dirt-smudged faces agreeing with their presence amongst them as they passed, knowing they were safe for a while; their own champions to protect them this day.

Tomas greeted them before his house.

"Welcome my lords. You do me honour to come to my insignificant roof and fare."

"Sirrah Tomas," replied Riennes. "Do not humble your hospitality. There is an ancient saying from whence we come: Do not consider any act of kindness insignificant."

They ducked down and entered the abode. It was a substantial long house. He sat them around a trestle table. A single, central, low fire bloomed inside the smoky murk. Doves browned on a spit. His wife Lenni handed earthen bowls of ale to them. While the men murmured men things, Lenni scurried about preparing the food. A young maid appeared from behind a wattled wall at one end of the longhouse, the family's living quarters. She joined her mother in preparations.

Godfroi stood and blessed the house and the food to come.

Haralde and Riennes with eyes tearful by the smoke, grinned in enjoyment of the family atmosphere. It had been 10 years since they had been mothered by a woman's food, by her companionship, within the warm hearth of a family. Tomas murmured talk. Godfroi asked him questions. Haralde and Riennes beamed at each other. For just this moment, they privately warmed their souls in what the years had denied them, a mother's regard.

"Do you not feel that it is time to end this paganism that I sense throughout your village?" asked Godfroi.

Tomas smiled and tried to put his guest at ease. "You may be right holy man. Your chance will come in two days hence when you preside over the joining of such as her," and he pointed to his daughter who seemed to hide in the dark on the far side of the room.

Alotta hid her naming with a bowed head. Yet, an eye sneaked a glance through auburn hair to the firelight dancing upon Haralde's face, and Haralde knew not. Riennes caught it, looked to his brother, then smiled inwardly.

"Please do it well monk. Make it so my child clings to her intended after the night of the joining, before the night creature Aelfgar comes and tries to claim her," prayed Tomas.

Wife Lenni and daughter Alotta came bearing bowls of food to the table. As they were put before them, Haralde and Riennes placed their fisted hand over their hearts and bobbed lightly: "Thank thee for our food, Wife Lenni," said Haralde. "Thank thee for our food kind sirrah," echoed Riennes.

Wife and daughter halted their serving. They looked from the two young men to Tomas. Tomas, food half way to his mouth, stopped, a stunned looked on his face. The blessing, so foreign and strange, caught them by surprise. Tomas looked to Godfroi for some direction, not wanting to insult his guests. Godfroi's eyes flicked from Tomas to the women, registered their bewilderment, sighed, and then began eating. Tomas looked to his women, and then nodded, and they continued the serving.

Soon the room was filled with the sounds of everyone sucking on dove squab, spring salmon and chewing on maslin, a coarse, dark heavy bread that came in four-pound loaves. With it was butter, then cheese washed down by copious amounts of ale. The food was bland, without spices, yet it sweetened their hunger.

Haralde beamed at the plenty. Part of his sufficient satisfaction came from the fact it was all free. "Tell me again of Aelfgar. Thee were telling us about his popularity with the local women?" burped Haralde.

Lenni paused in her serving as did Alotta.

"Yes. It is said he is gentle with women. He calls some young maids from our villages and some have joined him and his kind," mused Tomas.

Godfroi grunted an objection over that. "An end should be brought to this kind of gossip. It would be best Elder Tomas that families here should attend their parish church."

"Yes. It would be best. But the parish church has abandoned us," answered Tomas.

"Was that the doings of this Aelfgar?" posed the monk. "Is this about this blackness you talk about? I was much disappointed with the pagan images I saw women put into the horse's hair today. The actions of your wives disappointed me."

The fire logs crackled for a moment.

"No. Not Aelfgar. Our parish monk was driven away by villagers. He deliberately tricked many into unfair debts and loans. The debts became too much to bear. He was driven away one night by men in hoods. He fled with nothing but the clothes on his back and a woman."

"A woman?"

"Yes. His priest's mare."

Godfroi went silent. He wrapped himself in the cloak of his own sworn celibacy. He looked at his companions around the fire. Haralde and Riennes cracked the small bones of doves and fish. They stayed away from that discussion.

Tomas cleared his throat. "Tomorrow begins two days of the festival of Freya. No one will work. It is the time when boys become men, young girls become women, of flirting, and feelings toward each other. And it gives a time for older men and women to act like young boys and girls and to do with each other what they . . . ." Tomas stopped, and glanced at the young monk, then went on. "The girls will go into the woodlands to bring back spring blossoms. All the villages here will be out. There will be singing and laughing, food and drink. We will all go aganging."

"Who is Freya," asked Godfroi, although he suspected he knew.

"Our goddess of fertility," answered Tomas. He stood up and with his hands rounded out exaggerated bountiful breasts of a large woman. He grabbed his groin and made suggestive copulation motions. His wife Lenni burst out laughing. Alotta giggled. "There will be much joining, but not before you have said the holy words that our women want to hear."

Godfroi was about to object but Riennes headed him off. "Aganging?"

"Yes. It is where we take the young children and show them where the boundaries of each of our lands and that of the lord's demesne are. Young boys are shown the fields of their parents, thrown in the creeks and against hedges, boulders and trees. Young girls are taken to hedges, woodlands and the manor. All is done to show each youngster were the family boundaries are and those of their neighbors. They must know this. There is much squealing and fun. There will be much butchering of fresh meat. It will be a time to forget our troubles, and to bless our children's future."

"Are you not Christians here?" demanded Godfroi who heard nothing of the church's role in these gatherings.

"Some. And with your holy words we will become more in the days and years ahead," answered Tomas solemnly. "It will be a good thing. It might be if you move us, that the parish church will be rebuilt again."

The smoke and the ale and the fire and the good feeling with the family of Tomas went on for awhile longer. Riennes brought out his pipe, and then surprised their host when it made music, music that made them clap and laugh. Riennes played for their supper. Then Haralde, Riennes and Godfroi rose and bade all good night.

They stepped outside. The fresh air made their smoke-filled eyes ache and water for a moment. The sun had set. A Muslim moon hung like a milk-white scythe above the distant black crop of trees.

"Oooo, I ate and drank too much," belched Riennes.

"Thee stink," Haralde jabbed.

Riennes rumbled some more, then brightened. "There is a stream by the barn. I am for it." And he dashed off into the night. Haralde yelled, then chased after. Godfroi, given some weak candles by the Tomas family, headed for the barn and a moment of inside solitude and prayer.

The moon shone upon two naked young men splashing and spraying silver up into the night's light.

A maid peered through auburn hair from a black shadow. She preyed upon the round, brown shanks, ass cheeks and torso of the yellow-haired youth who pushed his fellow first through the barn doors. When he disappeared inside, the eyes closed and the night went black.

Riennes, Haralde and Godfroi rose early and thanked the Wenulf family for the morning ale, cheese and bread they enjoyed around the morning fire outside his home.

Now Haralde sat cross-legged atop a hillock looking down upon the village. He watched their two blacks grazing on the commons amidst other livestock. Their ox and cow munched content in another field.

Riennes was collecting herbs, medicines, poultices, powders of healing and other fawl-dee-dees from the village hags.

Godfroi had answered a call from the manor where Olaf needed to know how to call a hallmote. Later, the monk went to meet with the elders at the ruins of the parish chapel.

Haralde leaned back on his arms. For the first time in years, he was free. No decisions to make. Best of all, it was in his home land. The village this morning had roared at him; dust, din, squealing cart wheels, men shouting at men, women cursing livestock and fowl, babies crying, hogs shrieking, dogs barking, livestock bawling and the clop of a cart and horse.

The smell of it all assailed him. He was nearer home. Yet, all inquiries of the Lady Longshield had gained him nothing.

He spread out his long bare legs and wiggled his bare feet. Not since the desert had he allowed himself such freedom. He wore his silk undershirt. Cinched at his waist, it fell as a skirt almost to his knees. He wore nothing underneath. He spread his legs and allowed a sun breeze to cool his balls. Freedom. Was he getting closer?

He kept the kandos across his knees as he sat up. He had spied some activity in the nearby river that caught his interest. His toes squished moist in the green grass.

Two young men worked hip-deep in the river at an oxbow where the water had flooded upon a tilled field. The two worked long wands, shoved stiff staves into the river and made a fence against a river bank. At times, the force of the current pushed them up against the bank, sometimes under the very water. Their faces would broach. They would blow out a stream of water, and then laugh.

He did not feel her arrive, so engrossed was he. Then, he became aware of breathing, of the smell, of the presence of a person. He whirled around. Alotta, the daughter of Tomas, was immediately behind him. He bowed slightly. Her loose auburn hair fell across her face.

Haralde sat quiet for a moment. She made no move to raise her face.

"Hallo."

She lifted her face slowly. He looked into the appealing pools of her hazel eyes. They glowed with intelligence. She was a large, well-formed young girl. Her face was broad, her forearms full formed. At the same time, she was lithe, quick. He had seen that of her through the smoke last night. He was also to learn she was quizzical, and had a sense of humour.

"Thee are the daughter of Tomas and Lenni. Lota is it not?"

"Alotta," she corrected him. She continued to stare quietly at him, her eyes crawling all over his face.

He returned her examination back. When she said naught, he turned and pointed to the men in the water. One had now crawled up on the bank. He weaved wattle through stakes across a low section of the bank's cultivated field.

"What are they doing?" He turned to her.

She looked past him. His curiosity pleased her. "They are hurdling my lord."

"Yes? But what means that?"

She rose, walked up and kneeled beside him. She wore a drab, dark brown woolen cloak cinched in at the waist. A linen garment was under it. Even through its bagginess, he perceived the curve of her hips, the roundness of thighs and the swell of heavy breasts.

"They are using spillings and faggots to stop the flooding over the bank, my lord. They will build a willowbank."

"Explain please?"

"They have driven live willow stakes into the river out from where the river is flooding. Lengths of live green willow are then woven in between them. That turns the whole bank into a long living hurdle." He wrinkled his brow still, so she went on. "The living willow hurdles will grow, put out shoots. Eventually, it will tighten the whole thing together. Over the years, silt will build in behind and lock the whole thing to the bank. The flooding is stopped."

"Aaah. I understand. From very little to something of worth."

"We will come and trim it year after year. Bugs and caterpillars and insects will come to live in it, and fall into the water at times. Fish will come and eat them, live there. So we go netting fish at hurdles."

He laughed. "That makes sense to me."

A giggle burst out of her, and like her mother, she covered her mouth.

"I make a maid laugh?"

She lowered her eyes. "It is that my lord has interest in simple farming things." She smiled.

He smiled back. "Simple, no. Like all simple things, a lot of thought has gone into that."

Still with eyes lowered, she said so low he barely heard her: "One as beautiful and as strong and as magical as you surely need not think of such things."

Haralde did not know what to make of that, what to say to her. They sat silent for awhile. He continued to watch the hurdlers.

A young maid ran laughing beneath their hill. A young lad ran after and pursued her into the nearby woods. While they were watching the chase, a crow landed beside them, strutted around, cocked his eye at both, and then cawed loudly.

The crow rose into the air and flapped its way to the same woods as the young couple.

"The Others. The Wealc. They believe crows and ravens have magical powers," she lifted her head, and cocked it in a teasing way. "The Others believe the raven is a trickster. We have a rhyme here. It goes: 'If a raven cry just o'er his head, some in the town has lost her maidenhead'."

Haralde burst out laughing. He couldn't help it. She was teasing him, in a way a maid might to make a young suitor blush. He stood up. "I think I will walk your village. There is a lot I wish to see of things happening in preparation for tomorrow."

She rose as he did. "I will go with you my lord. I will explain our ways, as I did with the hurdling."

So they spent the morning and part of the early afternoon going from hut to hut, across fields, through the villages. Young maids went running by with boughs of flowers. Older men in clutches talked, laughed as they ran by. She said they were spring blossoms. They would be used to decorate the homes, even some livestock. There would be bouquets woven in their hair at the joining. They wandered over a hill and she pointed out the manor.

It was a huge wooden building with a two-storey structure rising in the back, as if a guard tower. Smoke poured from a centre hole in the long house structure in front. A wooden wall fortified it. She said the ruffians must have been given food. She could smell venison cooking. Something had been agreed on, she thought.

"Come. I want to tell you a story" she requested. She took his hand and led him down away to a clean, clear-running stream with a gravel bottom of small stones. She sat on a rock. He leaned against a small tree opposite her.

"I have been searching for the road of my life for so long," she began. "It is not a pathway for my body. It is a way for my mind to go, to dare, to adventure ahead. But all around me are barriers, my family, my friends, my village. All urge me to marry to fulfill my role in life as God wills it. I have hated that. God does not will me to hate. There is this wall around my own will. By marrying Aelfric, there is no way out. No direction for me, only his."

Haralde, uncomfortable at what sounded like a silly peasant girl's confession, stirred as if to move.

"Please do not. You are part of this."

That stopped him. He shifted his scabbard with kandos from one hand to the other and stayed to listen, and the more he heard of her story, the more he was drawn into her.

"One day a mysterious man came to our village, like no other we had ever seen. He was very hungry. We fed him. To thank us, he stayed and played music on his funny string box in the village main. His voice was magic. Around a fire that night we all gathered. He played and told us stories of wizards and kings, emperors and beautiful paladins, of magical kingdoms far away, of witches and warlocks, madmen and merlins, of hideous dragons."

"Alotta. Thee should not be telling me your deepest secrets. . . ."

"He told my fortune, as he did many of us maids. He told me to watch for young gods who have ridden mountain peaks and the desert low on black chargers. He said they will bring music and joy to me."

He rose as if to leave, and then sat back.

"It was the vision of the young gods that seized me. Tall, straight, muscled, bare-armed and hard-loined men of beauty and grace showing goodness and kindness to all around us. Not the Welsh nor Northmen brutes who attack our village and rape our sisters. Those tales of his pushed back the darkness of life here."

She glowed, her eyes washing all over him. A dark veil was lifted from her.

"Then you and that dark one playing the pipe appeared. No one had ever heard of you, yet you both mysteriously appeared among us, like light looking down upon us from your black cloud of your horses. The first thing you did to me was to smile. You talked softly and soothed us, a warm breeze. Your faces shone with kindness, a warm sun. I was drawn to you. You looked down when you felt someone touch you. That was me. I fled. But I was there when you dismounted. Your smell wafted over me, a clean male, a touch of leather and the sweet-sour of your horse. To me you were one of those from the tales of the fire. From that moment on, I found my direction. You gave it to me."

"I do not think I do. I am not who thee seek. They are just girl dreams."

"Tomorrow I will marry Aelfric in the mass spring joining of maids in the dell. He is the local miller's son. They live a short distance down the river away from here. He is big. He has some wealth. He has standing. For me, his way is my nightmare. He is a dolt, a dumb brute with an appetite for drink and copulation. He will force his wants, his will, his thirst, his hunger, his desire and demands upon me. For the rest of my life, I will disappear. It is the role I will play in life – wench, wife, mother, cook, servant, whipping woman for all his short comings as a man. He will screw me full of his seed and drink me deep until I am dry. Then one day he will cast me away."

Haralde squirmed. "I . . . ."

"But not now. Not today. I will conceive my own direction and hide it from him. His mind is slow. I will whelp all his children, but before I do, the first will be mine. He or she will be my beautiful secret. That secret will be my strength."

"But thee have just a day before the joining. What do thee intend to do in such a short time? Pray, do not get in your dream to run away with us. That cannot happen. That is not your dream, is it?" Haralde queried sorrowfully.

"Before that happens, I will have inside me mine, a child of a beautiful god."

He looked down upon the maid, who rose and moved to him. She was fair, nay, voluptuous and ripe. She posed in a way that curves and a roundness of youth showed through her woolen cloak. His breath caught, and his shanks heated. "Nay lovely maid," he protested. Or he thought he protested.

She grabbed his hand and pulled him with her, a wily smile teasing him. The ground pitched downward a bit and he stumbled with her onto a stone rubble beachet. Tinkling laughter escaped her lips. She tugged at him, her hand firm around his waist now. She splashed with him across a pool, laughing and promising him secret things about her body. She was quick of action. Before he could protest and stop her, she yanked the kandos from his hand and threw it onto the stream bank towards where they were headed. She cooed and in the pool threw her shapeliness against him. Her woolen cloak floated up around her shoulder. She took his hand, slipped it under her cloak and cupped it around her breast. The wool now smelled dank and odorous. "Take it off," she purred. He did. She was one of those of the strong neck, close, round, heavy breasts with water streaming off them, a flat belly dimpled with her belly button and thighs and legs that enticed him in the forest light. She splashed at him, then pulled him to the other side. They passed between two rocks into a dark alcove of a perfect ring of moss-covered stones higher than their heads. Trees leaned in to hide them. In the secret circle, a large woolen sheep skin was spread over the grass. "Why, thee planned this. Why this lovely spread?"

"To fool that dullard on my joining night. And yes, I have saved myself for you my lord, the young, hard god of my soul," she whispered. She leaned in and kissed him. "Now you!" She signaled his clothes must come off. "You ask a lot maid." "You will get much in return," she laughed as she helped pull his simple shirt off. She pushed him to the ground, then fell upon him. He visited the round velvet of her breasts. She, her lips open in roundness, sighed to the sky as he gently feasted upon her nipples, the moist fruit of her melons. He drank the sweet saliva wine from the cup of her mouth. He muffled the gleeful protest that spilled from her mouth. She talked sweetness and foul to him. It was the full, final pubescent moment of a young girl's life. She smothered her fear of the pain to come and urged him to force fuck her, believing a woman pained in love opens her womb more to the acid of his seed. But he gentled her, nuzzled, stroked until she sighed and opened willingly. He forced his fullness, she moistened it. "Please, no more," she muffled a weak protest that suggested she had changed her mind, then urged him deeper. He snorted and ploughed her juices. She mewled, keened, whimpered; the intimate language of the willing who wants her partner to be more wanton. The smell of mingled sweat, male musk and a woman's juices stunk in the alcove. In the clearing was heard thin keening and coarse grunting; the sweet mingling of love and lust, the jostling of wanting bodies. She drew blood from his back, then coughed out her lust. She rolled over top of him so she could seat her full weight of his maleness deeper in her. He roared and bucked, then stiffened and lifted her with his body. She choked, and her body went warm, warm, warm. A sweet ecstasy flared in her belly. A warm bloom of his male oil creamed in her womb. She whined her victory up to the sky, and collapsed.

She rolled off him, then curled up in his arms. Their heavy breathing slowed. They murmured love words to each other. Then, she started telling him things about her life, her childhood, growing up in the village, the intimate things about being a girl here.

He listened. He wanted to tell her that he was no young god, but just a young man who lived a little further from her in the Welsh uplands, that he was no different from her, except for the clothes he wore, that under certain circumstances, he just could as well be her young man standing beside her in the joining tomorrow night.

Yet, when she came to ask him of his life, he told her what she yearned to hear. He recounted stories of desert caravans, of palaces in the mountains, of great warrior hordes and battles fought, of treasure, of silk, of satin, of beautiful princesses and kings, of exotic animals and terrible creatures in the mountain passes that hunted people down and carried them off to their lairs.

They made love again, curled up, whispered to each other and fell asleep in the cool alcove.

When he awoke, she and the blood spotted sheep bed were gone. He turned slowly, took in the ring of stones surrounding him.

She was never to look upon his eyes again.

The fire of very many piled long logs throbbed with heat and lit up the night black with a gold glow across the dell. Young girls of all ages, hands joined, danced round the fire. Young men in a ring formed around the maids turned slowly in the opposite direction. Husbands and wives also danced gently with hands joined, calling to children and friends. Elders stood with earthen cups, splashing ale over the rims in salutations to friends. The night of the spring joining had begun.

Haralde stood to one side under a tree. Godfroi stood in a circle of young men, going from one couple to the next, blessing them and reading scripture.

Riennes was out by the fire, dancing around, whistling his pipe, trying to pick up the tunes of the many rural songs being sung. Young girls and old women touched him as they whirled past, inviting him to dance with them.

On the other side of the crowd, Olaf stood with a horn of ale in his hand. His nostrils and cheeks had been repaired expertly, thought Haralde. Olaf talked with a group of council elders. His page stepped in ever so often with a large skin and topped up the master's drink. Haralde smiled. He noted how, when he moved towards Olaf, the Norman would move also, keeping the celebrations a barrier between them.

Across the other side of the field was another but smaller fire. He had sauntered over there to discover this was the ancient Saxon ritual way of joining. Under a tree, a large, dark, wooden sculpture reflected mysterious in the light of the fire. It was a woman's torso with huge exaggerated breasts and a pregnant belly. Freya, the goddess of fertility, had no head, but needed none. The message was clear; fecundity and bursting plenty. It was the blessing all farm families craved. The young girls danced before her and exposed their legs and thighs, the young men rubbed their genitals across her heavy dugs. Then entered a crone into their midst who gathered them together and droned a long chant.

He stood now and watched Godfroi move round the inner circle. Alotta was there, the big-boned young miller holding her hand firmly. Haralde had sought her out when he awoke alone. However, he never could find her before this night. He had moved round the circle to catch her attention. She deliberately turned away, stared up into the face of her expected husband, or turned to talk to a sister of this special night.

Someone bumped his arm in familiarity. He turned to stare into the eyes of a man his own stature: Mordus.

"I hope my lord is enjoying himself."

"By God, surely I am, now that thee are here. Is your son down there before the monk?"

"Yes. He is the one with the black-haired beauty on his arm, there, see. He's not my son." Haralde laughed and gave his felicitations to the big ferryman. "Are things well for thee?"

"As always, with great expectation of profit, and goodwill. My lord! I seem to have forgotten something. I think it has to do with gold. Would my lord know what that is that bothers me so? Never mind. I hope Lord Longshield is enjoying himself. I must be off to find my wife and family."

Godfroi stopped. He held the bible high above the circle and in a sharp, clear voice blessed the couples and told them to go forth and multiply under God's magnificence. There was a whoop, a shriek and the high, expected cry of excited young men.

Godfroi jumped back in surprise as the young crowd broke around him. Couples streamed past him into the dark of the fields, of the woodlands and of the night. Many a young man had planned ahead and there were secret places all through the forests and fields where they would spend the night, not to be seen for days.

Haralde walked through the village, farm couples laughing and glowing and meeting with the families of their newly-wed children. There would be much drinking and even coupling of the seniors themselves.

He stretched out on the bedroll of his hay bower and set his kandos at arm's reach. The moon drifted past cracks in the boards. He was almost asleep when Godfroi came in.

He heard the crackle of straw and the grumbling of a holy man over a community's audacity to practice its pagan ways in the presence of a Christian holy man.

In the pre-dawn, Riennes crawled into his own bedroll. He awakened his brother.

"Pray, I hope thee were subtle with her," Haralde whispered sleepily.

Riennes turned in his saddle to take in Haralde who was below him, shouting goodbye to Mordus at the ferry dock. He heard the two exchange insults, the kind new friends will exchange over an emerging friendship.

"The bugger," complained Haralde as he joined his brother on the road to the mountains both could see above the tree line. "He says he no longer has anything to do with my gold coin. He told me to remind him of it, remember before we left."

Riennes nodded. "Hmmm. I remember that. We had just left to go to his village. What was it he said?"

"He said . . . ." Haralde stopped, his eyes went to slits and with his voice, accused: "Wait. Thee were a part of this. It was something thee two arranged between thee. What trickery is upon me?"

Riennes laughed, and flipped a gold coin in the air. "I should tell thee, your friend Mordus is an honourable man. He has paid Godfroi for his holy services."

Haralde's merchant mind went up one side and down the other of the agreed transaction. "Thee mean the agreement has been fulfilled?"

"Yes Haralde. Thee have done it again," Riennes congratulated as he turned to wheel away and start up the road ahead.

Haralde sat back in his saddle, smug in the comfort of his accomplished dealings. He sat ahorse. Then, he looked down into his empty hand. "Wait. Where is my gold? Who has my coin?"

Riennes laughed as he thundered up to the top of the hill, stopped, and flipped the gold coin in the air, then slipped down the other side out of sight.

Haralde shouted, then spurred his black to catch up with his brother and his disappearing wealth.

Chapter Nine

God gives not the answers to all His mysteries.
Yea though if you seek, He will give you the questions.

Now the roads of ease were over. Now upwards, upwards rode the wanderers into higher hills. At times, they grunted and huffed themselves and their animals up into the rolling uplands. They rode the rounded hillocks and the lows of this high country, more up and down than level. No other way could they go forward towards Haralde's dream.

The river bottoms denied them, flooded with jammed logs as they were. The lowlands were wet barriers, soaked with quagmires and marshlands. It was spring, and water was backed up everywhere. The thick forests covering hills forced them to follow old hunting trails and peasant trails up and over.

Bluebells lent a distinct blue haze across the upper meadows. Riding the highlines, they glimpsed a snow-crowned mountain through distant haze. Black magpies with white-tipped wings fluttered through the trees while a song thrush piped melodic airs from a topmost branch. They watched otters humping along flooded riverbanks. Blood coursed through Haralde's body, not altogether from the effort of going up and up. The look and feel of the country stirred the well of his soul. Suppressed memories of his boyhood bubbled up. Somewhere near was home.

He wanted to hurry, to leave behind the dark of their last many years away; of hunger, starvation and thirst; of fighting, slaughter, war and massacres of whole cities, and of the responsibilities of administering a mighty king's vast herds and wealth of animals.

Yes, he wanted to hurry, to use knowledge he now possessed to do things in the peace and quiet within the safe memory of his childhood home. No more would he wander or leave these hills, forests and mountains.

All this ran through him in the numbing, steady motion of the muscled, big black beast under him. So lost in it was he that Riennes's discourse on the types of local herbs and plants to use as medicines if prepared a certain way was slow to bring him out of his reverie. He heard his enthusiastic brother ramble on about herb Robert, mouse ear, orpine, polypody, plantain and yarrow.

"Did thee hear feverfew is good for headaches," Riennes droned away, happy over jars and earthen bowls he now possessed jammed full of these local medicines, dried leaves and roots and powders old wives and hags and healers of the village had showed him how to prepare. The real import, said Riennes, was the where of where to look for them and the how of how to use each, dried or powdered.

They were huffing their way up a narrow road towards a hilltop. Godfroi was up ahead, sweating his oxen upward, almost crossing into his forbidden country of oaths. Haralde was bringing up the rear, his eye keen on the holy drover and his inexperience with this kind of wagonry. In front of the monk, Riennes rode backwards on his horse, the better to engage Haralde's attention on his recitation over medicines and the experience he had in the village of Mordus.

"If you make hot wild tea and stir in sage and honey, it will ease a sore throat, or smear it on a cut, it will heal the wound. Did thee know that? I now have a supply of all that . . . . thee are not at all with me in this, are thee?" Riennes admonished him.

"In this? I am with thee in all my heart and do share with thee the joy of your discoveries. It pleaseth thee no end, I know, and thus it pleaseth me," nodded Haralde, his words truly heartfelt as he snapped out of it. "More so, that it involves medicine, and therefore the well being of us all through your very important natural philosophy am I also excited."

Riennes was not totally fooled by the feigned exuberance, but he settled for it. "Thee should be. Now I have local apothecaries to heal the cuts from your physical misadventures, or to soothe the victims wounded by your carelessness. There is much here. Your land is rich in natural healing plants. The desert could not hope to offer such plenty for good health."

They had been talking all day about their stay at the village. Haralde had told him of Alotta, of her dreams, of the circle of stones he found himself within when he awoke. "They were old, moss covered, the distance between each measured the same. There is something here . . . ."

Riennes replied he was beneath a night tree. "This Freya, this wooden figure that youth paraded their fertility before, I have seen this in so many places in time. A woman, frustrated with her husband and who loved my pipe, became my Freya in a hidden bower. She was in the moonlight a carving in pure fecundity."

"Is that how you saw it? Must you be blind also," grumbled Godfroi. "It was a godless object, a maiden of the devil. I saw how the young people fled to worship at its base after I joined them with God's blessing. The wood insult pulled them to its paganism."

"Hmmm." considered Riennes. "Or more, it spoke to them of some truth. Might it be we each see something in different ways?"

"It is obvious. I saw a wooden statue carved to seduce a boy and a girl to embrace and rut," chuckled Haralde.

"Yes, and maybe more than that, to go forth after their coupling and to be fruitful and fertile in all their efforts. I understand she is a goddess of fertility, one of a pantheon of Saxon Viking gods and goddesses. I have seen such figures in all my travels. It is a way to explain things, such deep emotions. It is an attempt to understand the natural world around us."

"Oh holy man. Hold tight to thy Christianity. When Riennes gets into this of the natural world, he gets into his true religion," warned Haralde in amusement.

"Thusly, this woman was much affected by her goddess. She took me through the night to an old crumbled foundation from whence came a spill of water from cultivated rock into a pool under the moon. She bowed before it and offered herself to me. . . .

"Thee can stop that brother!" admonished Riennes of his brother's chortling. "Haralde! I think we came upon this village at a magical time, or something like a maid's time of the moon. These people believe in the rhythm of time, in myths, in magic, in mystical things, of an age, old. There are strong legends and beliefs here. This homeland of yours is as old, maybe older than many places we have embraced through our youth."

Riennes said he had never known such excitement, not in the desert, not in the mountains, not even in the orchard lands of his own Normandy. The plants, the trees, the leaves, trunks, rhizomes, in all their profusion, were beyond anything he had ever known. The senior women, the elderly, the hags, preached dark and light, legends and truths, secrets and lies, poetry and sagas of life in these hills. "They are much affected by tales and old beliefs they hold as truths. And they told me the more we go west into these hills, beware. Beware of tales of bold warriors, of little people, of ancient trails and followers of those forest paths that lead to dragon's lairs."

They talked on about their experiences in the village.

"I noticed Olaf's rough looks had been stitched up and it seemed to put humor in him. Forgive me, but did I see your hand in this?" asked Haralde.

"It was a request by the Lady Waelthler."

"Aaah! And pray tell how did she enter in all this?"

"It seems Olaf's concern for the health of his injured men softened her heart, and she came out of her recluse. She asked the ladies of Mordus to help. They came to me. They gave me horse hairs dipped in honey and we repaired the damage caused to ass and thighs of those amorous soldiers we had discord with. When I left, the lady and Olaf were in negotiations," explained Riennes.

Riennes was glad Haralde had paid the villagers for all the food and grain and drink they now carried. Haralde replied it was cheap and fair, for the amount of pence they had paid. Riennes had flipped him his gold coin a morning's ride from the ferry, admitting: "Again, thee struck a sharp and fair bargain."

"Tell me. Who was that young boy holding the horses?" asked Haralde. "He was not belligerent like the others. It seemed his task was to chase after his master Olaf."

Riennes nodded. "He was Olaf's *pedites*." Seeing Haralde's non-comprehension of the Norman term, he explained. "It means literally, those on foot. He runs before and after taking care of all his master's needs. It is a thing all chevaliers now seek to have. I saw many about my uncle's camp. It has become the fashion to have this pageboy look out for all his master's equipment, to serve him. In return, such a squire who enters a horseman's service hopes to learn the fighting trade and rise to be a chevalier himself."

"Paahh! That must be expensive."

"It is. Of course, it is expensive to own a sword and a hauberk. Chevaliers need many horses. That is why men of Olaf's ilk go adventuring, must find new sources of money to sustain their new status. My uncle says it is a thing that is growing in Normandy and the Franklands around Paris. It is a growing part of the Norman fighting man, a sort of noble thing to be. He says it will be part of England in . . . ."

A hail from Godfroi above cut him short. They butted the blacks with their heels and surged up to the monk.

"Look!" shouted an excited Godfroi who pointed down to a meadow in front of them. Riennes looked as did Haralde, who let out an excited 'whoop'!"

Riennes shook his head in surprise. Below them a rounded, high berm of ground and grass stretched like a giant earth worm squirming across their path from one horizon to another. It seemed to slither over the hill in the distance and reappear over another hill further away.

"What construction be this?" pondered Riennes.

"We are near my brother Riennes! We are near home!" shouted Haralde. "It is the dyke! The dyke!"

"What dyke?" wondered Riennes out loud. "It holds back no water."

Haralde paid no mind, but rather butted his black in the ribs and they both surged forward. Haralde rode swiftly down the slope to the berm earth works, yelling the whole way. He rode down to it, then up onto it. He whirled his black around, stood straight up in his stirrups, spread his arms out and yelled: "Behold Ren! On this side, Cymru, on this other side, Saxon Britannia. I was once here as boy with my father.!"

Riennes smiled, then laughed over his brother's infectious joy. He surged forward on his black and thundered down the turf to come to a halt below his brother. "Harry! I rejoice with thee," he yelled up. "It has been a long road."

Haralde spun his horse around on the spot, and laughed and laughed. "My father once brought me here, but I was too young. I do not remember it. But I remember him telling me about it. To the west, my mother's people, to the east, my father's. Ren! We are in the March. We are in the frontier of my youth!"

Godfroi rolled up with the oxen and cow and cart. "I know of this. It is Offa's Dyke. I have heard of this."

"But monk, no water!"

"No, but it was built by old King Offa to keep the flood of the mad, raiding Welsh from flowing into his old kingdom of Mercia. It runs north to south. It could be hundreds of miles long. It demarcates the Welsh Britons from the Saxons. It was built, they say, along old Druid lay lines of energy. Pure paganism. It means nothing of the sort, of course. The Welsh, the Others, they are a dark and insular people, full of superstition and magic. Yet, they are known as Christians. Bah! Black Christians maybe."

"I think thee have at times regarded us in the same light, pray tell?" Riennes dismounted and walked to the base of the dyke. He kicked up a turd of earth and grass. "Is it a dyke, or is it a ditch? This would keep out nothing. It is just an earth bump rolling across the land."

"'S truth. It is no Hadrian's Wall," enjoined Godfroi.

"Come!" shouted Haralde. "Let us ride this dyke north. I may from its height see something of my land."

"I do not think I can get this dray up there my Lord Longshield!" Godfroi shouted back.

"Yes, well come ride with me Riennes. Godfroi follow us below. I think we may find a low spot in this wall to get thee and the beasts up here."

Godfroi waved his hand and turned his cart northward as Riennes ran up to the top pulling his black behind him. He mounted, joined Haralde and together he and his brother talked and walked. Haralde gestured with his arms towards things he seemed to remember. A vision rose upon the horizon of his expectations, of a round mountain with a wooden palisade half way up and inside a stone house, a keep with a wooden tower looming over it all.

In time, they did find a low saddle, Godfroi joined them and they moved north, sometimes going around a tree growing out the top of the dyke.

As the afternoon waned, they followed the dyke until it climbed skyward up through the woods towards the summit of an old rounded mountain.

The three came down off the dyke and headed westward along a narrow road that also cut upwards into another old mountain hideout that dominated the surrounding countryside. Godfroi moved ahead and the two followed.

Haralde's face was filled with joy. The face of Riennes reflected his brother's good feelings. Whenever Haralde was good,

Riennes's disposition was better. They both chattered away about many things.

"There is something about your wild March countryside that excites me," remarked Riennes. "The old ones back there told me about this . . . ."

Haralde cut him short and motioned him to an immediate problem above. The ox was squealing and the cow was bawling.

The two quickly surged past a struggling Godfroi, grabbed the reins and harness of the ox and pulled all over a step of interfering black shale and brought all free onto the height of this hill.

"My lord," exclaimed the hooded monk, "I am exhausted. I can go no further with these beasts!"

The day was almost finished. Haralde looked around, found they were in a pleasant meadow surrounded by evenly spaced huge oaks. The oaks leaned over a fire pit. They saw signs of others who used the clearing. Small stems of young trees evenly spaced, as if planted deliberately, formed a hallway leading up to the mountain height above them. It was a good place to encamp for night. He looked around to talk to his brother about the monk's finality, and found him on the other side of this upland meadow on his knees rooting at plants.

He instructed Godfroi to stand down, hobble the beasts and to start a fire. "We settle here for the night."

No sooner said than he heard a yelp from Riennes. Haralde urged his black swiftly across the clearing, dismounted and kneeled before his brother who was quietly examining his hand.

"I am on fire," Riennes stated calmly. "Look! My fingers are swelling. Haralde! Count slowly from zero to whatever count I say. I need to time this. And make note of everything I say . . . .ooooh, this stings!"

Haralde was alarmed. Had Riennes been bitten by some beast or stung by some poisonous serpent. "Where does it hurt?"

"Count! Look!" instructed Riennes. Haralde looked but could see nothing. There were no puncture holes from that of a beast. Counting, he already noted Riennes's hand looked enflamed. Riennes described it as a spreading fire, a potion or poison alien to the area affected. "I remember getting burnt once by a light liquid while working with Sena. It feels like that, only under the skin." He continued describing its effects.

Haralde held his brother's hand and at the same time, examined the ground Riennes had been plant plundering. A memory surged up. A smile crossed his face. "My Lord de Montford. Do not touch these plants again. Thee have been stung as I was stung as a boy – nettles!"

Riennes struggled to his feet. "Is it that a plant bit me?"

"Yes! And if my memory serves me, my mother once told me it was good to stir those with faltering hearts, or loosen anger of the leg and finger joints."

"Keep counting! Now that is interesting. I must get gather of these."

"Nay brother. Thee will come with me and sit by the fire. Within an hour, it will subside. However, through the night it may make you restless from the irritant in it. I must admit, it can deliver a biting sting."

Haralde settled his brother by a fire started by Godfroi. He stripped Riennes's horse and his own and fed them, wiped them down and hobbled them in the meadow, then attended to the livestock while Godfroi bustled around food.

Within the minutes of their chores, Riennes sensed something of a shadow, no, a wraith passing over their camp.

He jumped up. "Who was that?"

All stopped when they heard ravens cackling. Riennes, nursing his hand, murmured: "Look!"

Three black ravens dove on a flying heron with a fish in its mouth. The heron desperately turned over their camp. It swirled and whirled, its silver underlings flashing in evasion. It squawked and cackled, an old man protesting against a bothersome bunch of young beggars. When its mouth opened to protest, the fish fell, was snapped up by one of the black birds, then all flew away in a joined direction to feed as thieves upon their crime.

All three men stood in contemplation. Then Riennes said: "A young maid told me stories of the ravens and crows, of their magic in the border country here."

"I was told the same," Haralde whispered.

They watched from their hilltop and spoke of the events of the day. They took a moment to pray. Godfroi kneeled and gave thanks to God for the blessings of the day.

The two young men crossed their legs and sat in meditation, murmuring to certain parts of the monk's prayer.

The sun, a red coin, was halved by a slit in the clouds. It slowly deposited itself into the pocket of the night. The black vault of the sky shrouded over them.

After blessings of the food and the meal, the two men attended to their weapons and chain mail and Godfroi to his nightly prayer rituals. The central fire threw a pleasant orange glow through which their shadows passed.

Haralde arose, drew his kandos out and whirled it before him. He insulted Riennes, and warned children of Saxon-Celtic warriors preferred Norman horsemen to wipe their wastes upon.

Riennes chuckled, said that was very good Haralde, but begged off the ritual discipline this night, saying his hand seemed not to have the grasp of the blade's fine balance.

Haralde kneeled before his brother. "Thee be fine or ill by this?"

"Nay. It hurts naught, though it leaves a blush of fading embers," reconciled Riennes. "I am much taken with the potency of this plant. It will be with your help into one of my earthen jars before we leave here on the morrow's first light."

Godfroi, who had gone to complete his evening's ablutions, came hurrying out of the dark. "We must leave here. It is accursed!"

The two young men jumped up. "What alarms thee monk?" asked Haralde.

"Up there, through the trees, there is a place of black worship." Godfroi jammed his fingers in the direction of the line of young trees. Dimly in the firelight, they could see a raised place above their campsite.

Haralde and Riennes moved towards the direction the agitated finger pointed. They passed up between the line of trees and stepped up onto a flat plateau.

The ground was bare. They stepped upon a floor of exposed flat black shale. Two upright slabs of rock with a bare slab laid across the top loomed out of the night. They passed under it and came into an amphitheatre surrounded by more upright slabs of rock in a perfect circle. The moon was risen, shinning through the opening they had just passed through, casting silver upon the black shale.

At the far end, two smaller upright slabs were set in the ground with a rock table before them. Godfroi came up to them, hunched over, shaking his head negative.

"This bodes evil. This is what holy church has preached against. These hidden places must be pulled down," he exhorted. "This is the evil of The Others."

"Haralde. To me!" Riennes murmured in the dark.

Haralde came over to find his brother staring at something looming blacker out of the black night. He moved sideways to throw the light of the moon upon it. The moon shone black and silver upon a rock. It was high. Upon it, a contorted face looked down on them.

"See! Another graven image. It hates us. It glares at us. It is abhorrence," spat out Godfroi. "It is another heathen image in a pagan place of worship. It is a place of the old Druids. The Others come here in the night." He whirled and looked at the table slab at the back of the circle. "What thing is sacrificed there one can only imagine."

Haralde studied the twisted face, the long curved nose, the smooth lips puckered to one side in a sardonic smile, it seemed to him. "No. I think it mocks us. I think the rock is amused. It is enjoying some kind of a jest. Maybe over we humans. That is all I have to say on the matter," and Haralde turned and walked away.

As he passed his brother, Riennes mused out loud: "Again, we each see things we want to see, but which are not there. What thee both see in the rock is but the face within yourself. In truth, it is but a rock carved by wind and rain and sun. A jest yes, but of nature."

Godfroi came and stood beside Riennes to throw more moonlight onto the rock and maybe to reappraise. But: "No! No! It is pagan. Yea, without a doubt."

They stood there in the moonlight looking up. Haralde continued to walk away.

Something in the set of this whole scene in the clearing rose up like a gorge inside Riennes. He whirled around and pulled Godfroi roughly behind him.

The moon shone silver on Haralde's back as he walked away. Then it went black as a shadow passing between, then silver again.

"HARALDE!" Riennes shouted and his kandos rang in the night as it came into his hand.

Haralde turned on the shout and the sound of a kandos loosed. His blade came out as fast.

"Something passed between us! Watch to your right!"

Crouched, each turned slightly to peer into the night, each with both hands on their blades. There was no wind. The silver light of the moon bathed the clearing but showed nothing. The hair on the back of Riennes's neck stood up.

As if cut in stone like the rock face, they stood unmoving. Then both turned their heads slightly from one side to another to see if anything moved in their peripheral vision. Nothing. Godfroi had fallen to one knee behind Riennes, unnerved by the unsheathing of sharp steel.

As if on a signal, both men stood up. Riennes lifted Godfroi up by the scruff of his cowl and pulling him along, moved towards Haralde who in turn advanced towards them, his eyes still casting from side to side.

They met in the middle. "What was it?" "I do not know. Thee disappeared behind a black shroud for a moment. It moved." Riennes turned to Godfroi. "Did see thee anything?" "No. I have no eyes for such things. Did I not tell thee this place is all wrong?"

"Hmnnn." Haralde cast his eyes around within the circle as did Riennes. Then they carefully moved off, found the hallway of young trees and descended in bright moonlight to their camp. Only then did they sheath their bright steel.

For awhile, they sat and stared into the fire. The slim frame of Godfroi relaxed, then nodded forward and dozed. The two nudged him awake and directed him to his bedding beneath the dray, saying they would sit up and keep watch over him.

Once, Riennes shot upright and stared into the night. Haralde half raised his hand to the pommel of his kandos. "Anything?" Riennes, a finger to his lips, signaled silence. They listened.

"Nothing," he said finally. Riennes and he murmured for awhile. Riennes said. "There is nothing here. There was nothing up top . . . . yet? Haralde! Are there djinni here in your country?"

Haralde thought of the desert tricksters, the spirits of the sand, some dangerous. "No. At least I do not remember. No. My mother is Welsh. If there were such a thing, she would have told me. By the eyes of the Gher I swear, she told me of every other thing to scare me into behaving; merlins, dragons, warlocks, witches, Vikings, yes but not djinni."

Riennes stretched out and relaxed, as a sand leopard would be satisfied after a kill, thought Haralde, who knew that long, lithe, muscled form so well. "I am not sure yet. I feel a definite energy here, but elusive. I just can not grasp it."

The wind came up. The gusts blew sharply, the kind that drags in a sudden change in the weather behind it for a few hours before moving on, leaving all as it had been in its wake. The wind pushed against the great oaks. They groaned from the sudden pressure.

A tree moan awoke Godfroi, already sleep disturbed. He swiveled in his bedding and looked out onto the clearing. The clicking parchment leaves of the oaks were a thousand spiders' bones rattling in the wind's violence.

Godfroi looked at the lumps of the two young sleeping men who tossed his mind so much every time he tried to set them to his thinking. They seemed Christian, but when he applied Rome to them, they challenged him, nay they ignored him. And their challenge, foreign indeed, confounded his comfort.

Set that aside, he was grateful for their kindness, protection, and fair regard for his holy order. Most young men today crudely brushed him aside whenever he admonished their shortcomings.

Suddenly, one of the lumps rose, a white ghost in the dark night. Slowly the white night cover slid down to reveal Riennes's face. He shook off his covering, stood, and lifted his arms. He began to walk around the clearing. Haralde jumped up, threw off his night wrap and made as if to assist his friend.

Godfroi sat up, and immediately was struck by the blankness on Riennes's face. Then, the monk beheld the vacant eyes staring all around.

"Brother! What ails thee?" implored Haralde.

Riennes turned within the circle of great oaks, his arms stretched out as if to touch the very air between them. "I sense now something here. We are visited." His voice was flat, unemotional. "I feel spirits here. There are little things, big things. Look! A wraith, a spirit there!" And Riennes pointed, his finger moving at something in the upper limbs of the trees. "Embodiments!"

Haralde walked out of the night and stood by his brother, his best friend. "Can thee see them Ren? Do they have form?"

"Unseen. Like wandering souls. Yet, I feel them. . . . They move between these trees." Riennes moved towards one of the big oaks. His outstretched arms enfolded one. "There is a thing inside this tree." He stepped back, looked up, then walked and stretched his arm around another: "and inside here . . . ."

Haralde came and stood beside Riennes. He put his hand on his brother's shoulder, as if a connect might feel what his dear brother was feeling. Nothing. "Is it something evil or contrary to man?" asked Haralde.

Riennes let go and stepped back. He stood for a moment, as if listening to something. "No. It is something more of a wonder, magic. . . . a suggestion of something unimaginally small that is also the size of heaven . . . . the Creator!"

Godfroi heard these words. *Holy blessed Jesus! This man is possessed.* The monk rolled out from under the dray. He had heard these kinds of words before. Tree worshipping was a thing of witches; something he knew practiced on dark nights in the villages around his monastery. He strode quickly down, stepped out of the gloom and into the clearing and through the sparks streaming out from the low fire.

He strode up to Riennes, made the sign of the cross on the young man's chest and said: "Oh mighty God, hear thy servant. Protect this young honest man of standing. He has touched a pagan thing and it attempts to contaminate him."

Haralde stepped in and pushed Godfroi away. "Holy monk! Hold thy prayers. This is a thing not of the devil, I am sure of it. I have seen my brother do this before in the desert, but only not as deep and complete a thing."

The monk was not to be deterred, and attempted to step back to reclaim what he felt deeply was an innocent youth, but stopped as Riennes spoke. This time, it was in a voice clear.

Both Haralde and Godfroi saw Riennes's eyes, and they were blue and sharp again. "Harry. This is not a place of pagans or blackness or evil. This is where people came a long time ago and planted these ancient oaks, and young people not too long ago who planted that hallway of young oaks leading to the circle of stones up there. This must be a sacred place for some reason. I think these oaks are acknowledging us."

Godfroi, disturbed, bowed his head. Never in life did he think he would be anywhere near such tree worshipping as he now was.

"My son, you must not talk. You must not hold such ideas. The church decries such pagan ideas." Godfroi entreated Riennes with his hands, making the sign of the cross several times again.

Riennes smiled. "Be at peace holy man. Trees are a blessing to us from your God. Do thee know they are very much alive, and they may be a creature greater than men."

Godfroi: "You cannot believe such a thing!"

"Holy man. Look about thee. We cut them down, we burn them, we use their bodies to our own end, and they repulse us not. We take them down in great numbers, and yet they endure. God blessed them. They grow again in large numbers over the earth. They have made peace with a higher force, God if thee will. They are just God's finest example of plants, the basis of all life for man."

"God gave us dominion over them. They cannot be but we want them to be," admonished Godfroi. "They are not like us. They cannot walk, or talk or . . . ."

" . . . . ah but they can run," interrupted Riennes. "Harry! Remember the tumbling weeds of the desert. They roll along across the sand faster than a man can run, dropping their seeds along the way."

"By the Khan's beard, that is right," Haralde exclaimed, brightening and feeling wonderful in the glow of Riennes's intellect in full bloom again.

"Did thee know that plants can swim?"

"My Lord de Montford. Thee must be serious about these things. They go against church . . . . How do plants swim?"

"They do as small drifting plants in a pond or river. I have been told they swim in infinitely small forms as great hosts under the sea. Do thee know that plants can fly?"

Godfroi was going to ask how again, and then turned silent. He looked at Riennes and Haralde, believing they had done this purposefully, that they were pulling him along in one of their many jests again, at his expense as they had done before. And secretly he was glad of it. At least it had nothing to do with this worshipping of trees.

Riennes, however, continued in all seriousness. "Have thee not gone out into your own fields, split open the pod of a certain plant, waved it around in the wind and watched seeds with little feathers fly away to distant fields?"

"Yes. Indeed I have."

"And did thee know there are plants, some of them trees, which so spread their seeds in such a fashion, and that such seeds drift across sea worlds to land on far flung shores?"

All Godfroi could do was nod his head no.

"And thee call admiration for such a place as this inhabited by creatures such as these, pagan and evil," admonished Riennes. "No holy man. This is a place of the Creator. Remember, all things depend on plants. Without plants, man perishes. So, I urge thee to take up the study of trees and things. The stimulation of the great outdoor natural world would a better heritage be to find truth, than your monastic cell," smiled Riennes.

He turned and put his hand on his brother's shoulder. "The wind has eased, and I also am at ease. They visited and now are gone. Calm has replaced my anxiety over this place. I am instead touched and pleasantly challenged by all. I will think on this a moment." and he yawned. "And now I am for sleep." And he went over to the fire, threw a log in, sat down under one of the oaks, curled his legs before him and put his hands on his thighs. He closed his eyes, seemed to hang there under the tree, commiserating, communing, unaware of the current, and eddies of perplexity he left behind in the mind of the thin man in black.

Godfroi shook his head. He looked at Haralde, whose face was bright and beaming. So taken was Haralde by this wild and inexplicable streak that was an intimate part of his brother's very soul.

"I never complain and I never criticize, but I must ask you, Lord Longshield, if you have ever had doubts about Lord de Montford's state of mind.

Haralde was silent for a moment. Then: "Thee must understand holy man. My brother seeks the why of the deeper truths the Creator has put on his people, rather than the little truths thee are satisfied with in your quiet life."

"What does he mean by the Creator? All of God's truths are obvious. They come fully complete."

"That only meant our days in the light of His truth then have just begun," murmured Haralde lowly.

Godfroi wrinkled his brow and demanded: "I do not understand?"

"We do not know the mysterious of what is the natural world about us. Some of us want to know, thus they must go and find the why of it, 'Seek and Ye Shall Find' the reason for it," answered Haralde, echoing a philosophy Riennes felt deeply about. "Riennes seeks another God, the Creator. His Creator is not a moral God."

"It is not for us to challenge His reason for creating mankind," Godfroi stated adamantly.

"Yes it is! He challenges us to do so. He demands we ask the questions about the mysteries he has presented us. Find the correct question, and the answer will follow. Or at least that is what Riennes claims."

"There is no such thing. Only through church teachings do we . . . ."

"Here!" Haralde almost shouted as he leaned over and thudded on Godfroi's cranium with an iron stiff finger. "Here is His gift given to us all. Your brain. Your independent right to think. The Creator of all gave one to each, and demanded we use it. By use it, I mean think of things solely for yourself or what interests thee. It is a sin to let stupid men think for thee, or for thee to grow lazy and echo the urgings of others." Haralde leaned over and said full into the face of the thin holy man. "And that is what happened here tonight. Riennes has discovered something here of import. He has not grasped it all, and maybe in a year or two he will work it out and tell thee or me. Is he of sound mind, thee ask? Sounder than yours and mine holy man. Now, with your blessing, I will sleep."

The wind came up. The gusts blew sharply, the kind that drags in a sudden change in the weather behind it for a few hours before moving on, leaving all as it had been in its wake. The wind again pushed against the great oaks. They groaned from the sudden disturbance.

Godfroi lay in his bedding under the dray, his sleep disturbed. He listened to the great beasts moan.

What is the Truth!? That which I garner myself and own comfortably, or that which others trouble me with?

Chapter Ten

.... but the greatest sin of all is stupidity.

"My lord brother! Wait for us," pleaded Riennes jokingly. He pulled abreast of Haralde. Both horses were huffing up an incline. "Thee hasten on so, that we keep falling behind thee. Look. Godfroi and his animals labour to catch up with thee."

Haralde glanced over his shoulder and sure enough, the dray was a way back. He glanced at his brother. "I hasten so brother because over the next hill must be home. I feel we are near. Ren! I want to break into a canter."

"Ho! Hold brother! We will get there soon enough," Riennes also glanced back. "Let us rest a moment and let Godfroi catch up. Not a word has he said to me this day. Is he morose?"

Haralde pulled up and looked back. "Not a word between us either this day. No. I think he is meditating. See how his head is down and bobs with the motion of the dray."

"Or, deep in sleep he may be. What did thee say to him last night?"

Haralde shook his head. "Nothing of import. . . . though I told him to use his brain, to think for himself."

"Hah!" Riennes chuckled. "An ecclesiastic and thee told him to think independent? Hah!" He watched Godfroi get closer. "He must be thinking. Look. It must tax him so. It may have exhausted him. T'is unfair. I should not say thus."

Haralde chuckled, turned and resumed their travels as Godfroi finally caught up to them.

Godfroi's face was hidden under his cowl. Haralde and Riennes also wore their short woolen capuchins with hoods and their faces were somewhat hidden therein. All three looked as monks. They wore their cloaks to keep warm. It had turned cold last night after the storm and they waited for the day to warm.

The sun was still struggling upwards to its noon mount. They had risen early, dropped down from the old rounded mountain of worship and were headed upwards into vast stands of trees interspersed with meadows. They were following four wagon ruts in the ground, two going towards the trees, and two coming back from them. They felt they were on a road going to a nearby village.

Riennes and Haralde talked as they entered the trees. Some way into the forest, they fell silent and rode quiet.

Haralde felt Riennes must be commiserating with the trees again. What that was last night, Riennes said nothing more. However, Haralde knew one day he would. Haralde was unsettled still by his brother's intensity, his mysticism in the oaks. Haralde had seen Riennes do these things before. Only, he had seen his brother go very deep this time, be very absorbed in it. It was as if he had stepped outside himself.

"Haralde!"

Haralde pulled up. "What say thee?"

Riennes pulled up beside him. He was looking all around, again with that intensity. It was dark under the trees. "Harry. Think thee we should arm ourselves?"

"If thee think we should?" Riennes sat still, as if listening to the shaking leaves. "Aye. I think we should."

They waited until Godfroi pulled up behind them. They turned their blacks around and passed by Godfroi to come to a halt on each side of the dray. "What is it my lords?" asked Godfroi, seemingly coming awake for the first time this day.

"It is warming up and the chill has left us holy man," mentioned Riennes. "We dress now for the day, and any unexpected happenstance."

Even Godfroi was getting use to these sudden changes in Riennes. He was witness to Haralde who took very serious these uncommon changes in Riennes.

The two young men stripped off their cloaks, folded them and slipped them under the dray's back cover.

Haralde watched Riennes, followed his lead.

Riennes pulled on his leather cuirasse. He next pulled out a small Mongol leather helmet and stuffed it in his saddle bag. They already wore their Mongol riding boots. Out came a handful of arrows. He checked the belt across his chest holding his kandos behind. He looked at Haralde and Haralde did the same.

They set out in the lead again. Haralde leaned forward a bit and slid the longsword up and down in his knee scabbard. "Yes?" was all he asked and Riennes turned his palms upwards and shrugged. "Maybe something."

They rode through the morning, eyes all alert. They broke out of the woods and entered a meadow with wooded ridges on both sides of them.

Haralde felt an unease, as he always did when the landscape changed so that it lent itself to an ambuscade. His hair suddenly bristled. He saw movement behind low-lying bushes high up on one ridge.

Riennes pulled up beside, stopped, yawned and stretched his arms as if relieving tired muscles. "See them?" he asked nonchalantly.

Haralde nodded his head, as if talking casually with his partner. "I saw movement up ahead . . . . to our left?"

"Yes. Glance around while I signal Godfroi."

Haralde scratched himself.

Riennes turned in his saddle and loudly urged Godfroi to hurry up, that he was nothing but an old monk holding up their travels.

Haralde passed his eyes briefly across the top of the ridge, then looked down. "I make five of them. They are all on horse."

"Yes. I make the middle man, the taller one, the leader." Haralde glanced again. "The one standing up now and leaning out of his saddle towards him is estimating their chances of taking us."

Godfroi caught up with them and stopped. "Why are we stopping? Is it time to break our fast? I have eaten nothing this day."

"Do thee think . . . . ?"

"Yes. Brigands, bandits," Haralde whispered back.

He slid his hand across his chest and tightened up his cuirasse. Riennes bent down as if to check a strap on his saddle.

As he did so, he turned his head and whispered back at Godfroi. "Monk! There are horsemen in the bushes above. These men are going to tumble down upon us. Do not look up! They mean to rob us."

Godfroi's mouth stiffened in fear. Again, violence was about them. All he could think of then was the sanctuary of his cell.

"And they intend serious harm, monk," whispered Haralde. "When they fall upon us, we will stand firm," Haralde murmured to Godfroi. "When they charge us, we will stand quiet for a moment, then charge them sudden. When we do, thee move those beasts and charge with us. Stay as close behind us as thee can."

"I am a priest. They will not harm me, surely?"

"If they come down, then they are cut bandits. It is a priest they will surely want to rob. They will steal everything. They will take your life, the coin from your belt pouch to the tonsure on your head," whispered Riennes as he dismounted.

Riennes lifted the front leg of his horse and examined the hoof. Then he moved to check the back one, sliding as he did so his horn bow from a case under his saddle. He stuck one end onto a rock, grunted and leaned on it until it curved, then nocked a bowstring. As he stood up, the string went taut. Still behind his horse and hidden from the view of the men on the ridge, he took out a similar one from under Haralde's leg and repeated the action. He handed the taut bow up to Haralde.

He mounted and they sat there, two fighting Mongolian horse bows across their knees.

The riders began dropping down in a file off the ridge, making their way down through the bushes and trees, breaking out on the run into the clearing ahead of them.

Haralde leaned, pulled out the riding helmet and clapped it on his head. Riennes did the same. They cinched up leather chin straps. Then they both leaned briefly inward and touched each other on the shoulder.

The brigands were dressed in an assortment of vests, some with chain mail sewn into them. Some had no protection at all, but just patched worn surcoats. The leader rode with a round wooden shield on one shoulder. He drew a broadsword. His companion behind leveled a spear. Strung out behind were two with bows, and the last an axe.

They were a loose, ragged band with no discipline apparent. Three of the horses they lumbered along on were small farm beasts.

They started shouting, to scare Haralde and Riennes from the monk and the dray.

Haralde turned and growled at Godfroi: "Monk! We go now. When we hit them, turn to one side and find a bush to hide behind."

In any horse clash where one is outnumbered, engage the nearest enemy horse and put the riders down quickly to discourage the rest. But Haralde saw an immediate greater danger. He yelled at Riennes: "The two bowmen!" Archers represented the real threat in all their fighting experience,

Riennes nodded his understanding. Haralde jumped his black forward with a "HAH!"

Godfroi yelled to his bull, and cracked a whip over the beast's ear. The dray's harness snapped taut as the bull lunged forward. The cow bawled as it was hauled forward.

The brigands had failed to join together, but came at them still in a single line with the leader and his companion slightly ahead of the others.

Charging full forward, Riennes yelled and both stood up in their saddles. Each loosed three arrows within a moment's hope. The arrows passed over the two leading bandits and fell upon the two with the bows behind. The arrival of their arrows surprised the two robbers who had theirs arrows notched in bows held beside their legs. The two middle riders slumped. One groaned, his horse came to a halt and he tumbled.

Haralde and Riennes crashed into the first two bandits in a free-wheeling sort of a way, dreading death again but thrilled by the physical action of the fight. Their short kandos went in and clanged and rang in the clearing in one sharp, short, smashing entanglement.

The charge carried the first two bandits through. Both bowed over, hurt, bleeding. They swung clumsily away and fled. A third rider followed, slumped over, a bamboo arrow's feather jerking in his body. The fifth brigand failed to close with Haralde and Riennes, but pulled up short, then snorted his horse into some bushes and disappeared.

The two brothers pursued the three riders who fled up to the top of one ridge and down the other side. Shortly, they pulled up, not wanting to chase in strange country. The brigands disappeared into the forests ahead. The blood trail was easy to follow, but the two pulled up short.

"One is down with my arrow and my blade carries the blood of the leader!" shouted Haralde.

Riennes stopped, wiped his short sword clean, then sheathed it in his bamboo scabbard. "One carries my arrowhead in his neck! The other I cut deep! I fear he will die before nightfall! Would that I could follow, bind him, stem his death."

"Nay! One may be this bandit leader we heard about, what do they call him, Aelfgar the Wild? Best we stay away from him or others he rides to."

Godfroi clicked the bull, dray and cow across the clearing where the fighting had taken place. He was afraid of the bandits, of the violence that had erupted so suddenly. He had not hustled his charges off to one side to hide behind some bush as he was instructed. That which he feared, that which wracked him out emotionally, also drew him in, as a flutterby to a flame.

He passed by the place of violence, by a horse standing still, a body in the grass: a feathered shaft buried in a body on the ground fluttered in the wind; an arm rose up in the grass.

"Help me! Help me father!"

Godfroi hurried by, looked down. As he passed the horse, he saw an arrow in the bandit's neck and blood on his face. Seized by a paroxysm of fear and loathing for the bandit, he urged his cart forward and fled the scene. He pulled all up in another glen, bowed his head, and vomited over the side. He could not help it. Violence sickened him.

He sat there, his back to the clearing of the fight, to the arm that sometimes raised itself in pleading. Godfroi knew he should do something, but couldn't settle on the one thing he knew should be done.

Haralde and Riennes returned.

Godfroi watched Riennes pull up his horse, dismount and walk to the bandit with the arrow in his throat. He kneeled and examined the man in the grass.

Godfroi watched as they talked. Then Haralde rose, swung up on his black, and then urged the horse towards the monk.

"Are thee clear of harm?" asked Haralde as he thundered up in a jingle of metal and the squeak of leather. He dismounted, untied the thong and swept the helmet off his head.

"Yes. I am well," answered Godfroi. "What are you looking for? Can I be of help?" he asked as Haralde slipped his hands and rattled around under the stiff waterproof covering over the dray.

"Riennes needs his medicine bundle," he answered. He pulled it out.

"You willingly go back there? His fellows might return and kill you. I saw him," said the monk. "He has blood all over him. He was going to kill you."

"Yes." Haralde regarded the monk in some consternation. "But he is injured, thee see. We did that to him," he said as he walked up, reined his still spirited horse around and quieted it down with soothing words. He stared at the priest. "Did he ask thee for help?"

"Yes. But I just kept going. I did not want to go near him," he answered.

"I see."

Godfroi nodded.

Haralde mounted and his horse effortlessly turned and thundered back to the clearing where Riennes knelt.

Godfroi watched Haralde hand Riennes his bundle, then knelt with Riennes. They were that way for awhile, talking, nodding, Riennes busy with his hands.

Godfroi, unsettled, knelt and prayed. He brought his agitation under control, soothed his mind and settled into a quietude for a short while. Then he stood, looked back across the clearing, and immediately fell back into alarm. Haralde was standing, waving him to come to them.

When Godfroi failed to move, he saw Haralde put his hands to his mouth and shout. Oh Lord! He wants me and the dray to come to them. Godfroi froze, then turned to go in one direction, stopped, turned back in confusion, then stepped up onto the dray seat. He stared at the back of the ox whose head was down munching on grass. Oh my Lord!

He pulled the beast's head up, 'clucked' him forward and they headed back into and across the clearing. His heart beat as he approached the two young men. As he approached, he heard them talking.

"Do thee think thee can do this?" asked Haralde.

"I saw it once done. I stood with Sena one day when a wounded horse soldier with an arrow in his neck was brought in. Teacher Sena described what he was doing and told me to attend closely, that it was an opportunity for me to learn," answered Riennes. "It has to be done now, here."

Haralde stood upright and sighed. "Then, it must be done," he agreed.

Haralde walked over to Godfroi. "We need to get the arrow out right now. We need your help." Haralde realized he was looking into frightened eyes. "We need to cut him. He is seriously wounded. He is young. He can recover, but only if we do this well. Gather wood and make a fire. On Riennes's instructions, we will need two bundles of wood made into torches. We will fire them. Thee will hold one, I the other. Riennes needs as much light as we can give him."

"STOP! This forbidden! You can not cut into this holy creation of God. It is forbidden by the church. It is endowed by the holy spirit. Either we die, or live but are not to interfere what is fated. I . . . .!"

"Do it and do it quickly," ordered Haralde who knew it was best to make the monk busy. "If we gave him a potion that made him better, would it not be the same?"

"No. It is the cutting and opening up of the body's sanctity that corrupts God's creation of us. I see! You learned this you heretic from the Mahamads!"

"No. We learned this from a very great physician." Haralde did not want to tell him Mahamads also forbid surgery on humans, that Sena had learned about the internal workings of the body at night in secret places.

Haralde did not force Godfroi, but rather scrambled around, gathered wood, made a fire and bound up sticks of wood with burnable material wrapped into them at one end. Then, Haralde did herd Godfroi quickly over to Riennes and the downed figure.

Riennes, who had experienced this ignorance before, assured Godfroi: "You are right. But the hurt to this young body was committed by us, not God. We people must correct our wrong doings. So help. I cannot delay any longer."

Godfroi was on the verge of turning away, when he saw the supine body of a youth. The arrow stuck up from his throat. There was a bubble, a leak of red blood dribbling along the neck. Godfroi looked at Riennes, and saw in his eyes something wondrous, tender, competent.

"I think the arrow point is just touching or has punctured lightly the main blood line that runs up his neck to his head, here!" Godfroi looked with interest. "I am going to cut into the neck on the side of the arrowhead opposite that blood tube and gently pull it away from the leaking blood line and into the space we create. Hopefully we then can staunch any bleeding in the wound the point of the arrow caused. If the wound is too ruinous of the tube, the blood loss will be too great and we will lose him anyway. Thee do not need to know this monk, but it might ease your mind if thee know why thee hold this torch for me. Look away if you wish."

Mother of God. He is going to open up this boy's body. I have been told Eastern physicians do this. Godfroi looked into the face of the wounded young man. His eyes were closed. The monk felt sudden compassion quiet his fears.

Godfroi saw Riennes unfold a roll of leather to reveal little pockets with small instruments in each: little curved and straight sewing needles; one of his half-mooned, thin steel blades, the kind he used each morning to shave his facial hairs; scissors, little thin wires and little metal thin knives. They all looked keen and sharp. Riennes pulled out a little thin knife that fit in the palm of his hand but stuck out so that it appeared as an extension of his index finger. There was no time now for protest. "I will pray for him, and you if you do this vile thing," Godroi added.

They waited on the fire Haralde had going for a while. Then, Haralde came over and lit the torches. Godfroi was directed to hold his close.

He did so, and then turned his face away. Out of the corner of his eye, he saw Riennes's hand pass both the half-moon and the thin blade through the fire of his torch. He followed Riennes's hands down to the neck of the unconscious boy, and for the next few minutes, watched in awe, yet surprisingly with academic interest. Riennes seemed to point down the young man's neck. A red line appeared, then the red maw of a wound opened up beside the arrow buried in the flesh. It was done quickly, intentionally, no hesitation. It seemed only a moment and the arrow and head came away.

Godfroi could see a pin-sized wound pumping a thin bubble of blood from the throbbing blood tube the arrowhead had been pressing against. His gorge almost rose again to a vomit at such a sight. *My Lord. He has violated this boy, opened and exposed his soul and the body sacred to the world.*

Riennes handed the shaft and broadhead to Haralde, who in turn handed him a little wire made white hot from the nearby fire. In a smell of burning flesh, Riennes cauterized the little pumping wound. It ceased squirting. Riennes closed the wound, sewed it swiftly, wrapped the neck of the youth in linen, then in his special white sheep vellum wraps.

"Did you do it?" asked Godfroi in open amazement.

"Yes. I think we did. I cauterized and the bleeding stopped. Thankfully, the puncture was but a knick. Thank thee both. Thee did well." Godfroi looked into shinning eyes. The monk knew instantly that this murderer, this young man who nearly killed this boy was also a healer, a man sympathetic of his fellow beings.

They waited a moment to see if the wrappings would soak in blood, indicating the puncture had not been sealed.

Haralde passed the two blades through the fires again, then put out the torches and stamped out the fire. When the vellum stayed clear and white, they slipped a blanket under the young man, lifted him gently and placed him into the back of the dray.

The youth groaned as they packed things around him and wedged him in tight.

"We must get him to a nearby village. He needs to rest quiet," said Riennes who tied his Frisian beside the cow at the back. He bounded up onto the seat of the dray and signaled Godfroi to join him. "Go as easy as thee can. Stay out of the holes," he urged the monk.

Haralde headed out on the road, signaled them the direction they should take, then thundered away down a wheel-rutted pathway. They followed.

As they rumbled gently down the road, Godfroi kept glancing at Riennes beside him. The young man seemed in a trance. He didn't even look around at the trees, at the passing landscape, as he always did. Sitting close, hip bumping into hip, he realized Riennes was a boy-man; equipped with a boy's young fresh body but with a man's mature realization of the world around him. Godfroi wanted to know how that could be.

"Why did thee pass the blades through the fire?"

Riennes didn't respond at first. Then he shook his head. "I do not know. Such was always done by a very great healer who taught me the same. He did not know why either. He just told me he had learned of that way also, that no flux and infections followed after that action."

"Who is this Sena?"

"Yaqub ibn Sena. A very great and compassionate man. He is an Egyptian, a court physician to our Khan. He is renowned throughout the world in the East. He has written a text, Doctrines of Medicine, which lists hundreds of ailments, medicines to heal them and different ways in the cutting into the body that result in cures. I have studied and memorized that text. Even today, even Christian kings and lords who are sick seek out a Moor to attend them, those who have have heard of Sena." Riennes looked at Godfroi, then smiled, then pricked at him, jested: "He is a Muslim, a heretic."

Godfroi's face went dark. "I did not mean to belittle."

"I am sorry holy monk. Thee are right. Thee did well back there. Thee were interested."

Godfroi nodded, turned to his companion and smiled. "I was. I truly was. Because I saw something great, something blessed happening. I was not offended when thee opened up the body. Thee made it seem that it was right to do. Yea, though, how can that be? We are God's creatures. These bodies are in His image. Sacred. Beyond man's jurisdiction. If we are ill, it is His will that we either recover or die. I was taught we must nurse and give comfort but not interfere with that will. "

Riennes smiled at Godfroi. He leaned over and tapped the monk's skull. "Monk. Thee are starting to think. The Creator has the answers to all things. He has given us the gift of seeking the questions. It is by His will that we find the questions and follow them to the answers, as thee just did. When we seek, the answers will be made known to us. One day, when the last question is answered, He will reveal himself to us. The Creator is pure light, pure reason." Riennes tapped the monk's head again. "This is its gift to us all. To not use it offends it. The only sin in the Creator's eyes is stupidity in an intelligent man or woman."

They rode silently on. Godfroi was disturbed by these words. The books of others he spent his life copying contained information that disturbed him the same way.

Haralde returned and in a quick pivot, hooves kicked up mud and stones. "The road ends in a small valley and I can see a number of villages and pastures and plowed fields. It is but a moment to the first one. I will go on, prepare help."

Riennes nodded his head yes. Haralde swung and plunged down the road. Riennes instructed: "Follow him!" He dropped off the dray, let it pass, then swung up behind to kneel beside the wounded youth. He stayed with the injured one until they bumped into the village. Smoke curled up out of the holes atop many wattled huts.

Women came out those hovels and moved forward and around behind the dray. In the fields beyond, they saw men come running, their implements still in their hands.

One of the women suddenly cried out a name and directed the first men to arrive to quickly carry the boy to her hovel nearby. Riennes followed with his medicine bundle.

"She recognizes him," said Haralde as he arrived and dismounted. "I think he is of her family."

Haralde stepped down right beside Godfroi. As with Riennes, he was very close physically to Godfroi. Godfroi peeked upwards out the corner of his eye. My, but the young man was tall and big. Haralde appeared tired, weary to him. It was in his face; strained, lined, drawn. The two had come a long way, the monk understood. The weariness might also be anticipation weighing him down. Close, but still a short way to go. That short must seem interminably long. Haralde's clothing was travel worn.

Godfroi looked at some of the rips and tears in the dress of both. His whole appearance was that of a poor man-at-arms. Mind you, like himself, everything had been sewn and mended by Haralde's own hand. The monk looked at some of the sewing patterns. He had seen the same in the patched clothing of sea-going men. If Haralde was tired, he was also agitated, the monk observed.

"Will he be alright? Godfroi made conversation.

"Methinks yes. Riennes seemed satisfied when he went into that hut." Haralde held up a bamboo arrow tufted with brown feathers. "It was his arrow that struck the lad down thus. I wish strongly to see him recover."

Godfroi stood quiet a moment, then said: "Do you feel badly? You should not. You have helped him."

Haralde turned on Godfroi and used the full force of his personality to upbraid the monk. Godfroi almost shrunk from the intensity of those green eyes put upon him.

"It might have helped him, and yourself, if thee had stopped where he was injured and implored thee to ease his pains"

"Yes, but he is an outlaw. The hazards of that profession befell him."

"A man lies injured at the side of the road, asks for help and thee pass on. What were thee thinking monk?"

Godfroi stared at Haralde, his face reddening. Haralde's description had a familiar ring to it. An injured man at the side of the road.

"Monk? What is the most important law in all of Christendom?"

Godfroi answered immediately. "Thou shalt not murder. Thou shalt not rob."

When he saw it was not what Haralde wanted to hear, he fell back onto more sacred ground. "Thou shalt have no other God before thee. Obey God, Jesus Christ and the Church."

"NO! That is your church doggerel. The greatest law is to help one another. The responsibility upon thee is greater if one asks thee for help. It is even greater still if one cannot ask but is injured and thee know he is in need of immediate help. I am just a lowly soldier, a murderer if thee will. Thee are a holy monk. Thee know this to be truer than other men."

Godfroi retaliated. "You attacked him! You injured him! You violated the same law!"

"This was a matter of defending ourselves. They fell upon us. Blood and coin only would settle their minds. One must prevent this if one can."

Godfroi was struck by Haralde's simple sense. How could he argue against it?

"Do thee know what the greatest sin thee can commit against yourself and God?"

Godfroi nodded his head slowly yes. Thou salt not kill jumped into his mind but somehow he knew this was not it.

"Stupidity!" Haralde whispered softly. "When thee know the truth God gave us but continue to repeat the falsehood by word or deed. Especially since God has given us the gift of reason and yet we should repeat our stupidity. I am a poor Nestorian but I do remember something in the Bible about . . . ."

" . . . . the Good Samaritan. Do not preach your heresies here. You are a foreigner and undoubtedly a pagan. Thee know nothing of the scriptures."

"Yes. I am just a man trying to find his way back home. And yes, I have sinned so many times, in the killing of men, women and children, repeatedly, that I could stand it no more. I have dedicated my life to confronting my sins, my stupidities."

Haralde turned, walked away, turned and came back to the monk. "Thee and I have much to learn, thee beyond the walls of your priory and archbishop and I beyond my Khan and now my king. Here among my people, thee will learn about the true path of life, about your beliefs and about your much-vaunted church. If thee and I do not, then damnation awaits us when we put down our final load."

He started away and over his shoulder flung back his final words. "We have been taught the Qur'an and the Torah. We have memorized from great teachers original Greek parchments telling the story of Christ and his apostles."

"You have memorized the original four gospels of our Saviour!" Godfroi choked over this revelation."

"Nay monk. Not four. Many original Greek gospels. They relate not the story of a divine Messiah but of a prophet, a man who chose to walk and teach amongst the lowly, the weak, the sick and the helpless."

"There cannot be writings which say thus. It is blasphemy! To say this means you are not Christians," berated Godfroi.

"One need not believe in Christ's divinity to be a Christian," answered Haralde. He walked away, leading his black through a crowd of people, who parted as a wave pushed ahead by a boat. Men gathered behind Haralde, then followed in his wake.

The actions of these local common people were more than a crowd gathering to witness something new from the dull drudgery of their labour. They followed as if it were their duty.

Haralde gathered up the reins of Riennes's black from the dray and turned to lead both war horses towards the hut. He was in hurry, anxious to be on his way. A large crowd had gathered before him. He came out of his reverie when he looked into a wall of white faces.

Haralde pushed his way back through and as he neared the hut, the wattled door was pushed open and Riennes stepped outside.

"What of the young lad?" asked Haralde.

"I have such things to tell thee, brother." In such an expression of enthusiasm, Riennes led Haralde to one side.

"What about the boy?" Haralde again asked.

"He is recovering Haralde. He awoke for a moment, looked at me with clear eyes, nodded, and then fell asleep. It appears he is the son of the man and woman of this hovel."

"That pleaseth me muchly," smiled Haralde into the face of his brother.

"Here is the oddity of this young man's attack on us. The brigands are part of this Aelfgar the Wild's band. It seems Aelfgar forced this youth to join his band. If not, his mother and father would be killed. It seems Mordus's village has been fooled into believing men and women join this Aelfgar willingly. He robs, rapes, kills and murders and threatens all hereabouts. It seems your March has been laid waste by incessant wars and now is fertile ground for thieves and murderers such as he."

"Tell me not this. We left the Khan for the peace of home. And now what you say is nothing has changed," Haralde lamented.

"Attend me. Here now is what thee really need to know. Harry! Thee are home! This is Wym! This is one of our villages." beamed Riennes. Haralde heard the words, but they did not register.

"What is more important, your mother lives!"

Haralde jumped, seized his brother's shoulder as if to shake him.

"What they tell me is she is hold up in your Longshield stockade against this Aelfgar."

"Is she well? Is she unhurt?" Haralde shook his brother once.

"They do not know. All here say she is secure behind your walls and they themselves are hiding in the woods whenever this rebel Aelfgar comes near their villages. Everyone is terrified."

Haralde walked over and leaned against his horse.

Riennes approached and clapped him on the back. "These are your people Harry. This is your home with your mama. You have completed your long walk home. I give you joy."

When Riennes clapped him on the shoulder, it hit home and Haralde half staggered against his horse. He leaned there, his head on the warm roundness of the beast. The days behind washed over him: a stinking hand over his mouth as he was hauled into a Viking dragon ship; sleeping on the smell of iron around his wrist amidst the cries of other slaves; the cough of camels; the cries of battle, crimson blood on golden sand under a red desert sun and the sleeping on the cold of a marble floor to be ready at hand lest their Khan awake and demand something in the night.

Riennes felt his pain, joined him momentarily in the memories that were his also.

Haralde turned and touched his brother. "And thee have walked with me the whole way. Thee have been true to me, to us."

"I had to Haralde. *Inshallah*. Al-lah put thee in my way."

"*Inshallah* Riennes. God put thee in my way for all time."

Chapter Eleven

A man is Free by right, not by favour.

"My lords. I am having trouble with the wagon and the beasts," yelled Godfroi some distance behind them. The monk was struggling through young brush and juvenile trees beneath a heavy canopy of oak and beech.

Haralde and Riennes turned ahorse and looked back at their religious instructor and necessary wagoneer. The trail had petered out. The forest now closed in tight, an impediment, and an encroachment upon any semblance of a path or trail.

They were in the Welsh uplands. Here was a high country, sometimes highland meadows where farming carried out was little, except by those in little stone huts who tended sheep. They had seen, from time to time, white fluff balls on distant mountain meadows. To the west was a backdrop of a sharp ridge of mountains tipped lightly with snow.

"Look there," shouted Riennes pointing to a wall of oak, beech and ash forest before them where no dray nor beast would be allowed in. "Any further into there and one would get so lost, he would not be able to follow himself out."

Haralde pulled up on his horse beside Riennes. "What say thee? Once more please."

"I spoke plain enough," replied Riennes, a little petulant that Haralde did not understand him. It was somewhat jumbled and wasn't exactly what he meant to say, but he stood by it.

If Riennes was reluctant, then Haralde was resolved. "Brother, thee are right. Thee could find me in there only if thee did not look for where I had not been."

They both looked at each other, blinked their non-understanding, then laughed at their own gibberish.

"What was that?' Riennes chuckled.

"I do not know! Thee started it," Haralde laughed back.

Godfroi pulled puffing up beside them. "My lords, I cannot go further. There may be a crack in one of our wheels. I think I bumped heavily over a tree root back there."

Haralde rubbed his clean-shaven jaw, turned in his saddle and looked around. He held up his hand, palm like a rudder vertical to the earth, turned and pointed it around. "Methinks we have come too far north. We must drop back and turn east. Neury is east of here. I do believe we are in wild Brekin."

"Brekin. Is that another country? Thee never mentioned Brekin before," questioned Riennes.

"No. I never did. Forgive me brother. I never thought Brekin would be in your future," answered Haralde. "Brekin is a wild land. It is an adjunct to Neury. It lies between the ford of Neury. My father brought me here hunting many times. No farming. Only a few sheep men. It is wild, wonderful, and full of mystery. There are no *hides* here."

"Hides?"

"A hide is a basic field measure upon which one pays tithe or tax to the king. My father once told me Brekin was a royal hunting area, part of the king's demesne, so was unvisited by the king's taxman."

"Thee told me we are in Wales here. How can a king of the Saxons have ownership of land in Wales?"

Haralde shrugged and put his hands palm up. "It is not in my ken. In my times, ownership of the March passed back and forth between the Welsh and the Saxons. He never put any value on it so never paid any geld on it. It is a place of waterfalls, wild deer, boar, maybe even merlins and magic. Purely for my father's pleasure."

'Stop it. Let not wild imaginations capture your intelligence," admonished Riennes.

"It is true. My mother told me tales of smoke and fire at night up in those mountains. Once, my father and I were hunting up there and got snowed in. Around a blazing log fire we huddled one night and watched fires play up in those rocks. She claimed the last of the ancients still worship up there. Course, she is Welsh. The Welsh still raid through here, claim it as theirs. My father fought long and hard to keep them from claiming it. He told me tales of campaigning through here. Old King Edward granted father Brekin. He kept it a hunting reserve for our family only. Now, let me look at this. I think we should turn back, then east to Neury. I have missed a cut somewhere."

"My lords," whispered Godfroi. "Look at that beautiful creature!"

Haralde and Riennes followed the monk's pointing finger.

A deer stepped out from brush and into the sun down clearing from them. It stood, ears erect, and then dipped its head to graze. It stepped out more into the opening, it grazed, its head shot up, its ears twisted around. It was nervous. It stood rock still, and then turned as if to slip back into the forest.

Godfroi was not aware of it, but the warrior ears of the two young men picked up a sudden slight disturbance in the air. The deer's head jerked up, it jumped, and met with a large arrow in mid-jump. A second line crossed to the deer and struck it before it fell to ground. A third arrow passed over it. Struck down, the doe kicked up dirt as it tried to regain its feet. It did so. Ran a few steps, fell and could not rise again. It lie there, struggling. Two wood stems with brown flowers seemly grew from its chest. It struggled, hemorrhaging internally all the while.

Riennes and Haralde slid quickly from their horses and creeped to a screen of brush on a ridge. Haralde put a foot on a rock, leaned on a knee and watched the deer expire. Riennes turned briefly and signalled to Godfroi to be silent. The two peered through the leaves to see who the hunter was.

The two looked all over the immediate clearing. Nothing. They murmured to themselves. Then, movement. Not where they expected to see a hunter, that is, within a bow range, but much further away. Downwind yes, but too far for any hunter to attempt this.

"It could not have been he. Too far," mused Haralde.

"There must be another of his fellow close by," suggested Riennes.

"Poachers," guessed Haralde, disgruntled.

The two peered and peered all about the foliage of the clearing. All the time, the fellow kept coming up towards the deer.

"I see no other," concluded Riennes. "Thee do not suppose . . . ?" The two rose, and Haralde put his finger to his lips at Godfroi.

They stepped out into the opening. The man down meadow from them stopped, stood still for a moment, and then unslung a bow.

Haralde hailed the man in Welsh: "*Henffych cyfaillt! Beth am dyn ydych chi?* Hail fellow. What man are thee?"

The man stood unmoving. Then he shouted back: "Wealc!"

Haralde waved him up and went and sat on a fallen tree trunk, his body language non-threatening. Riennes went over and put a foot on the deer and stood there examining it all the while the man advanced, still a distance away though.

The man in the clearing came forward slowly, moving along the wall of trees and brush on one side as he did so. Haralde noticed this movement made the man hard to discern. His clothing seemed as if with the forest.

Behind, Riennes whispered: "Did thee see that?"

Haralde lowly whispered: "Aye."

A wild was in the hunter's eyes and in his deportment. That was what struck Haralde first of the man walking towards him. He was Welsh, just by his wild stature. His clothing was rough but neatly repaired. He wore a woolen undergarment. His woolen leggings to his knees were of a terra cotta color. He walked with feet bare. He wore a leather green blouse cinched at his hips by a leather belt and over this, a fur vest. On his head he wore a brown cloth Phrygian cap. A knife for dressing wild game hung from the belt. He held a notched bow with a taut string. It was of the kind shown them in London. This one seemed stouter, bigger.

Haralde and Riennes as archers, appraised it as the bowman drew nearer.

Like his bow, this was a stout fellow. His hair was black, as were his eyes which like two black balls, took the measure of them. His face was gaunt and intelligent. There would be humour in that face when he smiled, Haralde was sure. This was a solitary man, independent. Haralde liked what he saw.

Riennes stepped up beside him, and whispered in Norman. "Watch this one. He is a thinker."

The man stopped. For one brief moment, it seemed to Haralde the indecisive forester was about to slip into the green and escape when his eyes met those of Riennes. The hunter calmed. Something about the Frankish warrior challenged him. He stopped quite a distance from them.

"Hail fellow," greeted Haralde calmly. "My companion here has been admiring some hunter's shot. It seems well done."

The man ran his eyes up and down them both, widening at the unusual swords at their backs. Then in Welsh, he demanded: "You there. You spoke in the Frankish way. You are a Norman?

"I am sorry sirrah," answered Riennes shouting back in Welsh, smiling at the man's shortness. "My Welsh is not good.

Can thee speak Saxon, and yes, I am a Norman. And how did thee hear me from so far away?"

The forester turned his attention to Haralde and shouted in Saxon. "And are you a Norman too? And if you are, you will have to leave too."

Riennes almost wanted to laugh and whisper to Haralde, 'a bit snotty are we not' but declined, sensing this was a proud man and he didn't want to be impolite, and the man did switch to Saxon. Haralde picked up on that when Riennes nudged him.

"Ho! A bit abrupt are we? No. I am both Saxon and Wealc. This is my brother."

"Ho, ho yourself," smiled the forester. "A Norman and Saxon walking together on my land. Very strange. This interests me. Well, you can stay then, at least for the moment."

Haralde chuckled at that. "Your land? Sirrah, let me introduce ourselves. This is Riennes de Montford, a Norman lord, and now overlord of Wym. And I am Haralde Longshield, soon to be Thegn of Neury and of Brekin. I own the very ground thee stand on."

The man answered quickly: "I am Rhys, Wealc, free among men and no man can own the land. By own, I meant own it to feed and clothe oneself, no more." The man cocked his head to one side. "And who you are, how can that be? Thegn Longshield died some years ago."

"I am Haralde, his son." *A free Welshman. Rhys the Fremen, eh?*

"Aha. I have caught you out fellow. I have been told his son drowned many a year ago also?"

"Nay. I am he. I was wrongly carried away as a boy," answered Haralde. "I have returned and am making my way home as we speak. My fellow, could we stop shouting and would thee join us?" Haralde made the suggestion because he had grown nervous. He saw the man had a small sheaf of arrows in the hand clutching the bow, and he just knew that hunter could use them quickly.

Here they were, he and Riennes, standing out in the open. He felt very vulnerable. That man, and maybe his partner poacher nearby, could put him and Riennes down, standing as they were in the open.

"I intend to. That is my deer," shouted Rhys.

"The second one, he who made this kill must be close nearby," whispered Riennes, forgetting Rhys's acute hunter hearing.

"Nay Frank. It was me," shouted Rhys who then moved his bow deliberate and slow. He raised his arms with the bow skyward, the string above his head, and the four fingers of his right hand pulling back the string. Huffing, he slowly pushed the bow away from him and downward at the same time. He brought it down until his chest was framed between the string and the bow. He pulled the tension of the bow until the arrow touched its full compass. Captured within the arc, Rhys the Fremen breathed the joy of the moment, and then loosed the string which sang the sharp arrow into the air.

Riennes and Haralde could actually see the line of the arrow come the impossible distance up the clearing towards them. They dove for cover and ducked as the arrow past nearby. It passed over the downed deer and they heard the loud hammering impact of a heavy arrow into the tree just past the animal. The two were to learn from other bowmen later this action was called 'shooting in a longbow'.

They turned to challenge Rhys, but he had disappeared.

"By the Khan's beard, I would never have believed it!" exclaimed Riennes who hustled over to the tree, tugged hard and pulled the arrow out, examined it, went over to the deer, pulled out an arrow and walked all over to Haralde. "Look!"

Haralde examined both.

They were tipped with a hunter's arrowhead. Both were tufted with white goose feathers, except two strands of each had been dyed brown. All bore the workmanship of one man.

"They are the same." Haralde turned around and measured the distance again. "An impossible long shot."

"I grant you it was a good reach." Haralde and Riennes whirled at that voice and there was the fellow sitting on the same fallen tree Haralde had sat on moments ago. He was swinging one bare foot and leaning on his big bow like a crutch. "It was a desperate shot, but thus I had to make at the last moment. You two were noisy. I shot early for fear of losing my dinner."

Haralde and Riennes walked over to take stock of his character.

As they drew close, Rhys dropped onto the ground, an arrow lightly notched in his bow. He said: "I see you spoke untrue to me. Now up close, I see you are a Norman and a Saxon, but definitely not brothers."

"Not in blood, but in soul. No. We spoke the truth," answered Riennes, nervous as they stood near each other. "It is a long story, but we are who we say we are."

"Aah. And why then would Norman and Saxon soldiers with two large war horses in the woods be traveling with a monk who sits trembling in his hood astride a wagon with two field bovines?" mused the bowman.

Riennes called to Godfroi who came out momentarily. "Yes Lord Riennes, Lord Haralde?" Then Godfroi started when he saw the Welsh bowman.

"Aaah," exclaimed Rhys, still not easing up on the notched arrow. "Then you appear to be who you say you are. You are all very interesting, lost as you are up here in these wild uplands." Rhys made a small bob of his head. "Thus, I greet you Haralde of Neury and Riennes of Wym. Welcome home. I suspect you have quite a story to tell of your travels."

The man's tone told Riennes the Welshman was toying with them, still not convinced of their story.

"Who are you?" asked Godfroi.

"I am Rhys of Gwent, holy man. A longbow man who has fought the likes of you two all my life, who left his home because of it and who has come here to live in this borderland. I hid in the wild seams between Wales and the old Saxon kingdoms, and all I ask is to be left alone."

"That weapon of yours, such is a longbow?" asked Haralde showing genuine interest.

"Not a weapon, but my livelihood, but aye, Haralde of Neury." Rhys hefted his bow. "It is a longbow of a kind." He held it against him. It started at his knee and stretched to his head. "You are archers as I see by the bows under your saddle pads so I will explain. This is a hunting bow. It has about 50- to 60-pound draw weight. However, I have a war bow also, if one is to live here. Mine, which is hidden down the road behind you with my pack, has a 120-to 160-pound draw weight. With it I could put a heavy ash arrow through both of you."

Haralde and Riennes, trained as fighting men and military commanders, commented their amazement. Godfroi was not interested. However, he stood witness to the tone used by men like these. He watched as the three men talked of weapon things. The three looked down to the ground sometimes, stirred dirt and sticks around with their toes, took the measure of each other.

"I have shown some men hereabouts how to make such bows. They too are skilled now in their use," said Rhys. "I disclose nothing in telling you, others are joining us. You will find that soon."

Haralde liked the man, his honesty and his forthrightness. This was a man he would like to call a friend, a man he could talk to about his holdings, about the news hereabouts.

Haralde asked: "Can I look over your bow?"

Rhys's eyes widened at that audacity. Then: "Yes, if I can look over that sword you carry."

Haralde rarely released his kandos to any man, other than Riennes. He considered the request, and then intuitively, he agreed.

Riennes stood straight up in surprise. Haralde had never done this before. He held his breath. *Harry. What means this brother?* He thought for a moment, and then remained quiet. Haralde always followed his gut instincts in moments such as this. Most times, it served him well.

Haralde's hand went up and the kandos sang clear. Rhys's eyes widened at that sound. He watched as Haralde reversed and presented the pommel to him. "Be careful. It is sharp," he warned. Rhys handed his bow over. "Be careful. The bowstring can cut." They both looked up at each other sharply, then chuckled.

Riennes smiled. This man felt right. Haralde was right.

Haralde hefted the bow, ran his hands over the round wood, felt a kind of oil rubbed into it. Rhys held the pommel in his hand, felt its light weight, and looked down a curved blade. He had only ever seen blades that were straight and long. He tested the sharpness of the cutting edge. Something told him it was not iron.

"My lord Ren, I cannot pull this bow." Haralde huffed and drew on the taut bowstring and managed only slight movement. "By the Khan's eyes thee could never use this ahorse."

Rhys thumped Haralde's chest. "You are big of chest and arms. You will one day. There is a trick to this, as there is for everything."

Rhys made cutting motions slowly through the air with the kandos. "No sword man am I, but I know enough to say I have seen naught like this in my lifetime. This would do terrible things in close fighting."

They returned sword and bow each back to the other.

Rhys slung his bow across his chest and said: "Enjoyable be your company, but now I must take my deer and away."

Haralde seemed to saunter over into his path.

Rhys understood the move immediately. "Haralde of Neury. I hope you are not standing between me and my deer?"

Godfroi felt a tension settling between them. He looked to Riennes. Riennes watched both intently. There was something here, more than it seemed.

"My good fellow, but is this really your deer?" pondered Haralde, looking down at the carcass.

"As you have seen, it was I who struck him down. Now I must go. I have hungry mouths to feed."

"Aye, but thee took this deer on my land, did thee not? Now how do thee pay a tax or a tithe for such a right. It seems to me thee owe me something. No, the more truth of the matter is this land is royal demesne, so this is a king's deer," suggested Haralde.

"I pay no tax or tithe to any man. I am a free man, not a farmer nor a ploughman," answered Rhys, wary now, glancing at Riennes.

"A man such as thee must know, we all have to pay a tax or tithe eventually in life. I am obligated to pay a geld to my overlord, either in kind, coin or in a warrior's service to his king in times of strife."

"Tis because you are not a free man," Rhys chose his words carefully. "To be a lord is to be a slave of your manor, your obligation to your people, to the favor owed thee to your overlord."

"And thee see this as your right?" asked Riennes, much interested in Rhys's argument. "It is not by favour, nor obligation. Yes. It is mine by right," answered Rhys.

"Hmmm," considered Haralde. "Then thee will pay me nothing on any deer thee take from these lands?"

"I will walk away from it if I must, and seek my food in other places," answered Rhys, his eyes darting between the Norman and the Saxon. Haralde considered this

"Who are these mouths to feed? Are they children. Do thee have children Fremen?" asked Godfroi.

Rhys looked about him, at Riennes, at Haralde, then realizing the holy man was here, answered unafraid: "Yes. Two. A young boy and an older girl."

"Where are they now?" "Hidden. Like wolf cubs. Where neither you nor anyone can find them."

"Then I will give thee this deer, as a favour to thee and your family," Haralde conceded. The Fremen shifted from one foot to the other, then said:

"Nay Haralde of Neury. I would not wish to rob the king of his sport. My children can do without until I hunt down another free from favour."

Haralde stood for a moment thinking. Then, decided never again to pursue this with Rhys. The Fremen was a man he wanted to know was about, at least for now.

"Take your deer, Fremen," Haralde answered finally, walking back to stand with Riennes. "Take deer thee need for thee and yours. Thee and your children have the greater right to them."

Rhys visibly relaxed. Like his bow, the tension went out of his frame. The notched arrow was eased, then left the bowstring. Mirth returned to his features. "I take my deer then, with no obligations."

"One thing I ask."

"Yes."

"If perchance one day your hunt is so successful thee find yourself with an extra one, I would take it as a kindness if the hearth of Riennes and I may have it. Fresh meat is always needed."

That struck a deep sense of rightness in Rhys. It went to his maness. He walked past them both towards his deer, then stopped, turned and leaned on his bow like a staff.

"My Lord Haralde. I was not sure before. Now I know you are truly the son of Stoerm Longshield," revealed Rhys.

Haralde was caught by surprise. "How do thee know?"

"I came here some years ago with my family to escape the unjustness of the wars raging through these borderlands. I did so because I heard of a firm, tough but just thegn who maintained a peace in these hills. That was your father. I never met him. I think now I just did." What Rhys next said made Haralde jump physically. "I have one other mouth to feed. Your mother Saran.

She stands alone today, as she did a week ago when under the night I brought her household a deer. She is hard pressed, as she has been for years. Her hard, unbending Welsh heart has been her stronghold. Now Aelfgar the Wild presses her. He wants her, Neury and Wym. If he can not have her, he will kill her, take your fiefs by terror and force any way. There is murder and rapine in your land. I could not believe when I walked up this clearing in your words. I thought you might be of Aelfgar. Lord Haralde! Move in haste now! You are needed by your mother! Let me show you how to get to Neury."

Haralde shot across the clearing, grabbed Rhys by his shoulders and shook him. "My mother! Thee know of her! How is she?"

"Better, now that you are here." Rhys shook his hands off. "Come. You must go." Rhys took Haralde by the arm to the dray. "Turn around and go down. Steer for that high old mountain peak there to the east. Down there within hours you will cut an old Roman road."

"I know that road. I know my way from there. It is to the ford on the River Clee at Neury and from there to home up in the hills."

"You have it. I must stay, bleed and dress out my deer while it is still fresh. Stay clear of any band of men. God be with you Lord Haralde. I will watch for you."

"Come. Hurry!" shouted Haralde to everyone. He gathered up Riennes and they hastened away, one to the horses, the other to turn their dray.

They were busy in their exertions when Riennes called out lowly: "Haralde!"

Haralde stopped, then his eyes went to where Riennes nodded.

Rhys kneeled before Godfroi, the Fremen's hand on the upright staff of his bow. Certain words passed between Godfroi and the Fremen. Then the monk made the sign of the cross before him, leaned over and helped the bowman up.

Haralde got beasts sorted out and the dray turned around. Riennes came up beside him on the bench and handed him his horse's reins. When Godfroi hurried across, Haralde dropped to the ground and gave him a lift to his loft on the dray.

"Thee have found work to do here monk," Riennes jested lightly.

"A most amazing child of God," Godfroi nodded back.

Haralde mounted, spun around to wave goodbye to the Fremen, but he was gone. Haralde's black leaped forward and they all headed back and down.

It was 'hurry! hurry!' all the way down.

However, at one point they slowed when Haralde heard Riennes mumble something to himself.

"What say thee brother? I did not hear. Were thee talking to me?"

"Freedom!" shouted Riennes across to Haralde. "He believes in the freedom of each man."

Haralde shouted back over. "He can be as free as he wants, but only after he pays me my favour. Without it, such would be chaos. He is but a dreamer."

They rode on so Haralde did not hear Riennes mutter: "A dreamer. Interesting dream."

Chapter Twelve

Never space nor time nor death separates child from mother.

Riennes squirmed around, the leather of his saddle squeaked as he did. He was uncomfortable, ill at ease. A moment of supreme joy just minutes ago now had slipped away from his brother. Puzzlement and dark disappointment now clouded Haralde's face.

Stronghold Longshield, the *caput* of Neury and Wym, loomed higher up before them. They had hauled Godfroi and beasts up a forest road, broke into a large meadow cleared of timber long ago and Haralde had stood in his stirrups, raised his arms and shouted in joy.

There it was, Haralde's wooden-walled manor. More than ten years of homesickness, hardships, hopes, of holding so tightly onto a dream that it comforted him through nights of loneliness. Going home was their talisman through all the years of their exile, the one hard bright reality small boys could hold onto through what was at times a nightmare.

No sooner had Haralde yelped in joy, than the partially open gate of the wooden palisade closed amidst shouting. Smoke climbed voluminously to the sky behind it and defenders appeared on the walls armed with spears. Pennants appeared on flag staffs, obviously a signal to all inside.

Now something was amiss. Was the disappointment made greater because the reality was not as perfect as the dream, Riennes wondered? He was disappointed at what he saw of Haralde's birthright. Even though Haralde had described it to him many times, he was not quite prepared for the harshness, the crudeness of this wooden redoubt. It seemed a primitive, frontier fortress, all of wood, rough boards and beams. It was just like those of his Viking ancestors who waded ashore in inland bays and rivers to raid in the lands of the Franks west of Paris. These North Men stayed and became Normans. They erected such wooden fortresses. However in the lands where Roman influence was stronger and things were more permanent, they quickly changed and built stone *donjohns*, and walls, and moats, and bridges, and towers, architecture that lent itself to security against strong enemies who wanted to evict these strong north people.

Here in England, a land still ravaged by bloody times, the motte and bailey wooden fortress construction still prevailed. The motte was the huge earthern mound upon which was built the keep and the bailey. Inside, the yard was filled with squalid huts and hovels of the serfs and slaves who served the manor.

It matched his impression of frontier Neury. Just over an hour ago, they had found the Roman road, no more than a wide laneway through the woods. At times, they had to help Godfroi guide the dray around trees growing out of this so-called road.

They thundered through the village of Neury, a clutch of village hovels by a wide river. One surprise, was the single, two-storey stone house with a crude stone outbuilding behind. It was all deserted, although he thought he saw someone standing in the shadow of the doorway.

The ford was shallow although Haralde claimed a bridge should have been there. With the dray's high wheels, they bumped over what were obviously once the bridge's underwater stone footings. Men just upstream working weirs built to trap spring-running fish, splashed their way out of the river and scattered into the woods.

And now this primitive home. No one had dug bulwarks or revetments in the field before the walls to impede or slow invaders laying siege. It was large, Riennes gave it that much. The walls encompassed the bailey village of farm families serving directly the mistress overlord. There would be crafts people, butchers, a smith, a carpenter or two, maybe a tanner, miller, ale makers, slave servants for the main house, and family members, cousins, uncles, any clan affections, and of course soldiers. How many, that would depend on the character of Lady Saran, if she was still in good health in there. The walls marched up the hill, and surprise again, a stone *donjon* standing inside the wood. Only instead of being high, it was long, like the house at the ford. It did reach up, but one could see its upper floors had been added later, a bastardization of the original structure. Riennes's eyes narrowed, and he recognized the familiar base architecture of it: Roman. It was a former Roman building. The whole keep sat high and long, on a *burh* or mound of earthworks, maybe thrown up by a forgotten former Roman garrison here to quell the Wealc of long ago. The donjon at one time had a wooden tower, but not now. Riennes could see it collapsed on the ground behind. The donjohn would have a panoramic view of the whole valley before it.

Riennes's disappointment changed somewhat. Primitive it may be, but someone had an eye for pulling together elements that made it sounder and stronger than it looked. Obviously, he was looking at the hand of Steorm Longshield.

And there, look at that, thought Riennes, as his eye snagged on another Roman contrivance. An aqueduct! A small Roman aqueduct! A stone aqueduct came down the mountain to obviously feed the stronghold fresh clear water.

If Lady Saran was alive and vigorous inside, it was because she was protected by the ghost of her husband. Without good siege engines, this would be a hard stournmount to sack, thought Riennes. Of this I see Stoerm in Haralde. The fortress is father of the boy.

"I do not understand." Haralde was disconcerted, disconsolate. "They have closed my home against me. What is wrong?"

Riennes kicked his horse forward. He whispered to Godfroi: "Hold fast," as he passed the monk. He slid in beside Haralde. "Brother! Look at us. We put on our cuirasses. Swords are sticking up everywhere and we are riding war horses. Thee are not Haralde. Remember what the Fremen said. Thee now are Aelfgar the Wild."

"Aaah yes! And that would be like my mother, ready," smiled Haralde, relieved.

He jumped down off his black, released the belt of his kandos and gave it to Riennes, then tore off his leather cuirasse and placed it carefully under the dray covering.

He ruffled his yellow hair, now a little longer from the trek to Cymru. Haralde said to Riennes and Godfroi: "Stay here. Better they see one man."

Riennes nodded and Haralde walked across the clearing towards the wooden wall, to the dangerous men who manned it, and he prayed hard as he walked, to the only human woman he loved dearly. *Pray, God, the one who made me, let she be there!*

Lady Saran heard someone shout her name and rose from her bed in her chamber in the keep. It was cool here, comforting. To hide, to rest was why she always came here. Tired she was, so tired, but habit and consistency lifted her.

She picked up the small sword her husband had given her. She clapped her family Welsh leather helmet on her head, a gift from her father so long ago, and headed out to the stairs outside her chamber. She no longer wore a small chain hauberk given her by Stoerm. Her fortitude was weakening. She no longer cared if she looked to her own people like a warrior woman, a lady overlord in command. She had been called to the wall so many times over the years, that she thought the helmet and sword was enough to intimidate those on the ground below the walls.

She floated down, her sword held irresolute beside her. When she burst out into the sunlit court yard, she was met by Tyne, her Irish soldier commander. He was also her lover.

"There is one man walking towards the front gate," warned Tyne. "He was armed when we first saw him. But he is not now. We also saw him with some others back in the trees. They seemed to be armed."

"Do you think Aelfgar tries something new here?" she asked as she walked with Tyne down a path to the front walls and they both hurried up a staircase. She peered carefully over the wall lest a bowman assassin lurked out there. Over the years, marauders and ambitious men had tried to woo her or carry her off if they could or kill her if it came to that. The Longshield romance and legacy, and the love of her local people, made her too big for anyone to ignore her hold over Neury and Wym just because she was a woman. They would have to capture her to take these holdings.

There he was, a tall young man walking across the clearing, the sun turning his hair flower yellow.

She liked fair hair on a man. She herself was once a black-haired beauty. Time and care had robbed her of some of that. Touches of grey now streaked her once shiny mane. Yet, Tyne did arouse the young girl in her at times.

"Bold is he not," commented Tyne. Tyne was a hairy, short, powerful man with bandy legs. When excited or aroused, his red hair seemed to bristle outwards from his composure like a wild boar. It did now and the ends of the hair and those of his short beard glowed ochre in the sun. He barely matched her in height. He stepped up and peered over the sharp stakes of the wooden wall. In his hand was a sword, one that belonged to her husband.

"I think he is doing this deliberately to hold our attention," judged Tyne. He turned to the handful of soldiers bunched up with them on the front wall. He called to a subordinate. "Spread your men out along the side walls. It may be Aelfgar is trying to slip in behind us while their fellow here holds our attention."

Saran smiled weakly. Tyne had been her right hand now for two years. He had quickly assumed the male role, the military strength of the stronghold. He thought of things she never could, defensive things, fighting ideas, strengthening weaknesses. He also warmed her bed at night, heard her fears, and wiped away her tears sometimes. It would not be too much longer now before she gave in to his desire to be her husband, to replace Stoerm in her heart and let him be the new lord of this land

The young man now walked up the road and approached the front gate. A soldier remarked on his size.

"Should I put an arrow through him Saran," asked Tyne who signaled a farmer archer standing nearby to get ready.

"No. Wait a moment. He wants to talk to us." She watched this tall, unafraid young man stride up to the front gate. It was his boldness that made her hold back. They stood back out of sight.

"HO! THE WALL! I COME UNARMED!"

They did not respond, but stood with heads down. Then Saran nodded.

"WHO ARE YOU? A MAN OF AELFGAR'S?" Tyne shouted back through the timbers.

"NAY SIRRAH! I AM A TRAVELLER FROM LONDON! I COME WITH TIDINGS!"

Tyne looked at Saran. She nodded and indicated the wall with her finger.

Tyne moved to the wall. He was accompanied by the archer with an arrow notched loosely. They both appeared above the wall and looked down.

"Yes. Speak!" he ordered, not having to shout now they faced each other.

"First, is the ladyheart of Neury and Wym there with thee? Is the Lady Longshield well?"

"Who needs to know this?"

"Gerald of Lackland!"

Saran blinked. The name was of a distant friend from her long ago. Yet, before that, what did he just say? The phrasing of those other words: ladyheart! Ladyheart! Stoerm's word of endearment. Her breath caught on that. She leaned forward and pushed on Tyne, indicating to let him continue.

"Go on."

"Ask her if the honour of Neury and Wym still hangs on the back wall of her great hall. Ask her if the blade of the big, two-handed claymore still hangs bright without rust."

Saran's hand came up to her neck. The claymore was a giant sword, an ancient Viking fighting scythe passed down by the grand men of Stoerm's family through the years. It hung on iron hooks on the wall now. Cut formally in the rock beneath was one word: Honour. And it was always the charge of her son to keep the rust off with a . . . . Her face turned red. A flush, the kind she experienced sometimes with woman's troubles, flooded hot upwards.

She jumped to the wall and leaned over. "HOW DO YOU KNOW THIS?"

She looked into the face of a beautiful young man. The young man stared up at her, mouth open. In that instant, time and space compressed. They just stared. Anticipation locked them together.

Haralde bent over, put his face in his hands. He rocked back and forth and silently wept. Then he stood straight and beheld her face again.

"OH MAMA! DO THEE NOT KNOW ME?" he answered intimately.

She stood dumfounded, shocked, stooped over the sharp-pointed timbers. Slowly she shook her head no.

"YES! Look at me. I am Haralde, your son. . . . YOUR SON!"

One of the points of timber started pushing sharply into a breast. It began to hurt, yet she flinched not. She just could not put all of it together. She could not comprehend a thing at that moment. She was looking into the face of her husband, Stoerm, yet that recognition would not yet pierce the fortress of her solitude. She shook her head slowly disbelieving. Then her inner strength collapsed. Her face went white.

Haralde broke into a song, a song a mother would sing to a baby. Then he changed it over to a whistle, a hunting whistle his father taught him.

"YOU BUGGER! WHAT THE HELL ARE YOU ABOUT!" Tyne was leaning over the wall, shaking a fist at him as he saw the reaction on Saran's face.

"Mother! Remember this?" And Haralde moved toward the wall. The archer pulled back the bow string and followed him with his arrowhead.

"I had gone fishing and father did not want me to. It was night when I got back and father had ordered the gate closed. He wished to teach me a lesson as I was not supposed to go out. But I was a climber, and had my secret way in. And I did THIS! And you caught me!"

Haralde explored along the wall with his hands. He moved sideways, praying the spot was still there after these many years. He was wearing his Mongol riding boots in hopes it would help in his climb. There it was. He stopped. Two poles lashed together were not as soundly close seated together as the rest. Each was warped. They wowed in places, leaving many slight openings and closings as they went upwards. He knew this would hurt. This climb was meant for a boy's mischief, not a full-grown man's feet. His hands found an opening between the timber, he lifted a foot, shoved it sideways through the opening, then turned it and wedged it tight, tight enough to hold his weight. Up he went a stride. Another grab on something, then a foot up, a twist, a lift with some pain, then repeated. Suddenly, memory found hand holds, and he started to scuttle adroitly upwards, gathering speed.

Now he was a boy scaling walls that needed to be scaled by mischeviousness. How many times had he done this? Then a mother's scream of concern. Then at the top, a mother's embrace, and tears of fear. Then an ass warming by his father. Then to bed. Then the next day, scaling the wall again when no one was looking.

Saran, bent over more and more to follow his progress, and to hallucinate another vision, another personage.

Haralde reached the top, grabbed at the two spiked peaks, got his foot up between them, hauled himself up, then vaulted over and onto the catwalk.

She fell away from the wall, her hand on her mouth. He took a step towards her, and then stopped. They stared deep into each other, moist green eyes worshipping moist black ones.

Tyne lifted his sword as if to ready a strike, but then just froze.

"Mama! I ache to hold thee!" Her startled face saw and heard his cry, widened in shock. She drifted towards this tall man, seizing his face roughly in her hands. She ate his green eyes out. A cry wretched itself up from a deep emptiness within her. Gently, oh so gently they embraced, as if each afraid the other might fade away again. The men around felt the deep power of that joining, turned away or glanced downward, to not be part of that intimacy. Tyne felt a sudden foreboding and looked at those men around him.

"Haralde!" she cried as the embrace tightened. "My Harry! My son, my child. MY BABY LOST!" A flood of love rushed in and flowed to fill a barren womb bound by pain. First her son taken from her, then her husband murdered. All that remained was a duty, to fight and save her memories, to defend the family property.

Men. So many men had at her, battered at the wall of her grief, at the stronghold doors of her refuge, to become the man of her holdings. She had fought them all off.

For what? To protect the void within? Now, a long lost love rushed in to take its proper place, to flush out the empty dryness of her soul. Now she could give it over. Now she could give it up.

Within the embrace of her beloved son, her own living flesh, she fainted, the helmet falling off her head.

Chapter Thirteen

-Report of a Welsh lord's homecoming written years later through the eyes of a monk found within notes of Abbot Lanfranc's leather portfolio lost on his road to Rome.-

Abbot. I did not see him carry her down from the wall, son carrying mother. I heard after Haralde just came down and left soldiers standing astounded on the wall. Villagers poured out of their huts and work places, afeared some told me. They thought a moment Aelfgar had scaled the wall, had her and others right behind, to doom them all. They told me leader Tyne stood, surprised, sword hanging down.

They say Haralde parted the crowd with Lord Saran in his arms. Halfway to the Lordship Saran's great stone bastion, she stirred. Lordship, yes, they called her that. She has been their leader, their rock for all these years. A boy said he saw her eyes open. She stared. Then an arm raised, turned her son's head to look down at her. Then she pulled him to her face, then kissed him gently. He almost stumbled as he went up the stairs and into the great hall. It was after the noon. They remained inside for hours.

A servant girl ran out; whispered into Tyne's ear. That is when Riennes and I first saw Tyne. The great wooden door opened. He waved, hurried us in. Riennes led us in pulling their big horses, me, dray and beasts. When we entered, people parted afraid before the great black horses and the tall, foreign-looking Lord de Montford. They crowded behind me and took the head traces of the ox beast in their hands, called to me, 'let go'. When the wheels stopped, I swung down. Told Lord de Montford never again would I steer that engine. Riennes smiled at me over that as he swung down. Told me I was probably wrong because I was the best dray driver he had ever seen. Tyne approached and we met the curt fortress commander. The same servant girl came running with others carrying gourds, gave us water, cold, fresh, sweet from the mountains. The crowd pleaded with the girl to tell them what was happening. Tyne signalled for us to come to a fire stirred to life in the courtyard before the donjon. I followed Tyne and sat down. Bread and ale were presented me. I hungered for such fare, blessed it, started in. Riennes called to Tyne to bring him some. He had climbed onto my dray bench. He sat with a cup of water, Haralde's weapon on his knees. Tyne brought him ale and meat. Riennes offered Tyne to eat a bit with him. The commander hesitated, then chewed some off. It was only then, Lord de Montford smiled, and ate. He became very amiable. Children gathered round and stared at him. I ate, heard laughter and saw the little ones jumping around the dray, him laughing, feeding them pieces of his meat. We remained like that for hours. Riennes would not leave the dray.

Darkness closed all about and we drew close to the fire. These people, they comforted us, told us of their imprisonment. Aelfgar's band of rebels outside, beating the walls to break in. Yet they were resolved. Always, they said, Lord Saran had outwitted raiders. Riennes sat immobile, trying out the Welsh names of some of the children. Wary he was of Tyne who hovered nearby. Many came to me asking for meat for the children, words of comfort.

Music. Lord de Montford was leaning against the dray. He played his pipe. He picked up our spirits. The children danced with laughter. The darkness did not frighten us. The door of the stone main house squeaked open. A square of light shone on faces. A shadow came out of that light. She stood in a white robe. Haralde stopped behind her.

She came down the stairs. Her eyes stared across a silent courtyard. The night wind stopped. After we swore the fire ceased crackling. She walked, her eyes fixed only on one object in her universe. No one moved. Everyone parted for her. Riennes stopped playing his pipe. His eyes met hers. She walked straight bearing down on him. He stood away from the dray. She came up to him and into his arms. She framed his face in her hands. She kissed him, full on the mouth. Tyne moved somewhere. She tipped his head down, kissed each of his eyes. She lowered his head, kissed his hair. She then drew his head to her breast, broke down and cried and cried, and cried. Riennes's pipe fell to the dust. She leaned down, picked it up but did not rise but bowed low to him. She wrapped her arms around his legs and we all heard her declare, although the versions I found later changed depending on whom I talked to: "Blood of my blood, family of my family, brother of my son, son of my soul. Forever, you will be a part of me. Thank you! THANK YOU FOR MY SON! No man. No woman. No family walks here who is not your kin." The people cheered. With fire brands they crowded around the two standing in the middle of the courtyard. Many wept.

I awoke. There was a noise. I heard for a moment Tyne and his soldiers coming through the open great gate of the fortress. They closed it. I peered past the wattle doors of my hovel. Tyne strolled by with a deer carcass over his shoulder. They talked about the man Rhys who came some nights like this and left deer hanging from the front gate in the middle of the night, as of before, they said casually.

They carried me to this pallet from last night's homecoming. Many came to me asking for my blessing well nigh into the lateness of the moon but I no longer could keep my eyes open. Forgive me pater, but the weakness of the flesh overcame me. I must report some of these people are still Christians of the Irish Church.

They know not the Latin liturgy, the prayers, and the rituals of our church. They pray and sing songs in Celtic, Gaelic, Wealc, Irish, Saxon, I know not what. And they are not correct. Some of their prayers include pagan images. There are pagan artifacts all around me. Some have little pagan images on small family alters. The family I stay with has a sheaf of plants over the front door, to keep away the evil, they told me. There is a carved beast's head outside on the great gate of the fortress. You were cognizant of the failures here. Until all hear the Roman Latin, I fear many different tongues will fail to hear the proper message of salvation from our Latin Church.

A babble of different tongues. We must unite them to us. The salvation of their souls is my charge. I will work hard. Already I have been about, listening to the fears, hopes, wants of these Welsh people. Pray God blesses me in time with their tongue that I might understand them. I will endeavor to turn them to ours. They are a good people.

I passed by the door of the stone fortress. Inside, I saw Lady Saran, her son Haralde, Riennes, and Tyne seated around the open fire pit. The men were arguing. I walked on. I am called back by Lady Saran to come in and mediate. I say Lady Saran because overnight, Haralde has established his lordship over us all. Tyne chafes at this. As a peace keeper, I listened to the differences. Tyne argued he has been loyal to Lady Saran these many years, a comfort to her, both in her bed and in the defence of her fiefs. Haralde roared at this and threatened to strike him over his affront to his mother. She calmed him. I am called upon by Riennes to calm him, to evoke the authority of London, Westminster and his overlord Gerbod. Haralde must know things have changed, that changes are all about him. Tyne did not accept this. He stalked outside. He threatened to leave. The argument ended. Haralde sits inside his inheritance. He is the natural thegn of the fiefs of Neury and Wym. Tyne fails to accept this. He had designs on this lordship himself. Lady Saran prowled behind, beseeching Tyne. The two disappeared into the gloom of the bailey.

I awoke the second night. Screams. Smoke. Men yelled. People ran about shouting. Pigs screamed. Dogs barked. I heard Tyne yell warnings from the wall by the aqueduct. Horses chuffed below outside the wall. Haralde arrived at his side. A ladder had been pushed against the wall on the outside. Brigandry poured over the wall. I saw Tyne and Haralde back to back, flailing with fearful weapons. Riennes half naked ran up the stairs to the catwalk to join them. I was sick with fear. Two bodies fell from the catwalk above and struck the ground in a cloud of dust. Young men dashed out of their family hovels with axes and harvest forks, and struck the bodies. Fathers came out and pulled them away. I threw up, I am ashamed to say. I saw Haralde and Tyne push the ladder away. There was quiet again. Haralde punched Tyne manfully on his shoulder. Tyne stood there panting and grinning. Then they walked away. Unbeknownst to my understanding, some sort of peace has settled in between them since then. I am not asked to be a mediator again at the family fireside discussions.

A relief has fallen upon the Neury bastion. The godins were hard hit by the night's resistance. They seemed to have gone away. The soldiers reported they did not see the brigands prowling around in the trees any more, watching the fortress. The besieged now go about their work with smiles. They have seen Lord Haralde, Lord Riennes and Tyne walking together, animated, hands waving around. They were not angry. They were discussing defense things, the children told me later. Haralde has made a point of talking to each of Tyne's five soldiers on the wall. He knows their names. He appeared particularly interested in the fighting farmer with the longbow. The farmer, pleased with the attention, showed off his skill with the weapon, shooting arrows long distances across the grounds.

Haralde clapped his hands in glee. Lady Saran led Haralde over to greet her uncle, an old man. Haralde shook Gwengarth's hand warmly. Then she introduced him to three distant male cousins. He shook hands with them. The youths told me later Haralde checked out the soundness of their forearms as he did so, and declared to all how strong these three boys were. Next day, he had the three young men practicing with the farmer's longbow. They brought out longbows of their own. The whole village heard Lord Haralde whoop his delight. Now all practice with their bows at a regular time every afternoon. He sits with them at night and tells them they all may have to fight in the days ahead.

Tyne and Lady Saran continue to live in sin. Sometimes I see Tyne and Saran walking the field outside the battlements, talking. Haralde now grudgingly has accepted this. Lady Saran came to me, wanted to unburden herself of her sins, and asked for my blessing. I urged Lady Saran to embrace God's wishes for a man and a woman to be joined within the blessings of the church. She told me before she could not accept him as a husband, not while she defended her people and fiefs. Now, with a mischievous smile, she told me tender feelings for him are growing. Lady Saran is a woman in her late '30's. She is robust, and she has a need for Tyne in her life. She has asked me to influence her son, to persuade him to accept Tyne. I have started gathering allies to my campaign; Saran, her uncle, her people. I approached Riennes. He would not commit, but smiled. His head did, I think, nod up and down.

Haralde has felt in this my wishes as friends press him. He stomps around grumbling.

Lord de Montford has caused a stir. He now is popular. He is pressed by lines of women. I feared their admiring gaze of his near nakedness the night of the brigand attack had turned their attentions away from their husbands. But nay, it seems he has accomplished a healing miracle. The uncle of Lady Saran is ill, can only work for a few hours, then chest pains force him to stop. Lord de Montford went and sat with him one day and they talked for hours. The next day he returned with one of his apothecary medicines. The uncle drank a tea with powder from a local plant, those nettles I think. Now, he can work lightly all day and the pains do not come as often. They now petition him over their aches and pains. He has helped many, especially the children. Some of the men grumbled about him, that he possessed dark powers that turn women's heads. Had I not seen his healing abilities, I might have thought the same. The women shushed their men. I talked to the men. Now, the young nobleman has picked up all their spirits. They feel with their strong leaders and a healer amongst them, they can truly survive attacks by the brigands.

Pater, you were right to send me. These two men have turned these people to them. The two young lords do things no one has ever seen before, talk of things no one has ever considered before, suggests things to them that has turned their minds, and maybe one day their souls, to believe things you and I would protect them against. I will work hard dear abbot to negate, to purge from such simple people some of these beliefs they have taken up. It would be dangerous indeed for other simple people if such things I have seen and heard spread out beyond these walls into the countryside.

Chapter Fourteen

Duty and service is owed
To all who are loyal.

"By the Khan's anger, I would know how many men Aelfgar has against us out there if we are to do anything," growled Haralde, kneeling and peering out through a chink in two timbers of the fortress wall. "Are we facing 10, 20, 50? We must know."

Riennes and Haralde were on the wooden walk peeking through timbers of the wall looking for enemy activity. Both hid, not wanting those outside to know two new fresh fighting men were inside.

As if reading his thoughts, Riennes said: "Aye. And doth Aelfgar question the loss of two good fighting men the other night? We recovered two spears and a sword from them. Such are hard to come by out here. Haralde, he must be wondering what happened."

Haralde agreed. "Something of the aqueduct interests Aelfgar. Tyne thinks Aelfgar is suspicious mama has managed to hold out so this long because she is somehow getting fresh water from it, even though it is broken and does not reach our walls."

Both continued to observe from their knee. Lady Saran, faced with a water shortage during an attack by an earlier raider, had taken the problem to her carpenter.

He solved it by taking two long rough boards, hinging them together lengthways with leather and wood-nailing it into the shape of a V. They shoved it out from the wall at night with the support of long poles, and settled it into the broken end of the aqueduct. Water flowed across into the fortress. It gave them more than enough fresh water. Barrels of it were stored as a reserve. Riennes, Haralde and Tyne contrived to have barrels of it on the parapet of the stockade in case Aelfgar were to resort to torching the wooden walls.

Haralde smiled and shook his head in amazement.

"What?" asked Riennes.

"Mama. How I like the sound of that. Is she not something?"

Riennes nodded in agreement but lowered his head.

Haralde felt his sadness, reached out and put a hand on his shoulder. "Forgive me Riennes. I forget your family grief."

Riennes lifted his head and smiled. "It is eased by the presence of Lady Saran. She says I must regard her now as my mama."

"Yes, and well and good, though I notice now, as brothers, she likes thee better." They both chuckled.

Haralde beheld his best friend deeply. "I know thee have good feelings for Godfroi. Do thee talk to the monk about this, your family, or is it a thing just between us."

"Our monk is gone."

"What did thee say?" asked Haralde softly, his eyes again scanning the open field beyond.

Haralde's eyes finally came around and looked down into the village enclosure when Riennes nodded that way.

Godfroi sat on a stool under a thatched hut overhang, a white goose feather wiggling away on a white vellum parchment cloth.

"Methinks thee are weary. He is right there," indicated Haralde.

"Nay. That is not our monk. That is our spy, our judge. He writes to tell Lanfranc about us and your people. He found my sketching charcoal, made ink and now scratches out his report. He asked me when he can send this to the Bishop at the Hereford Cathedral. I think I have that right.

"That be a wee distance south of us and much to the east, if I remember right. Ah, tell him send it we will when we dislodge this renegade chief who stands in all our way."

Mischief returned to Riennes's face. "When he does, I think thee are in trouble."

"Me?"

"Methinks he is writing the abbot about your strange beliefs. And then there was the Ten Commandments, and thee tapping him on the head telling him he was wrong."

"Hmmnm. When he comes back to us, am I right he has found much favour here?"

"Yes. Your people are glad he is here," said Riennes. "I think he, also. He says nothing, but I think this is what he was made for."

They both sat silent awhile, peering out; watchers watching the watchers. Haralde was sure some came and went, that Aelfgar was not here all the time. If thus be true, was Aelfgar out there pressing more men to his cause? Was he out there trying to build some kind of siege engine, anything to get him over these walls?

His mama had told him they had never attempted a frontal attack. These rebels had few ladders, so no way to top the walls.

Haralde moved closer to Riennes and peeked through another opening. "I think I see movement over there." "There are six." "How do thee know that?" "The trees." "The trees?" "Yes. The trees tell me."

Haralde carefully glanced sideways at Riennes, not sure his brother was serious or if mischief was coming. Riennes had never given him an explanation of the strange night haunting of the trees. Maybe, Haralde thought, he now had a special relationship with them. He didn't know what to think. His brother at times was a strange man.

Then: "Nay. Trees can not tell thee anything." "They do. Haralde, thee must learn to trust the trees." "But I do not see as thee do." "Sure thee do. To the left of that small ash. See, there are six horses tied to its branches."

Haralde looked where directed, snorted and bumped a grinning Riennes away from his peep hole.

They watched the horses but the distance was too great to make out any details. Haralde peeked over the top for a moment to get a better perspective, then turned, slid down the wall and sat with his knees drawn up almost to his chest.

He adjusted his kandos belt to be more comfortable. "Ren?" "Yes?" "Do thee remember what thee said after we crossed on the ferry, about dying when we reached the end of our road?" "Aye, I do." "Do thee still feel that way?"

Riennes thought about it a moment, then: "No Harry, I do not. Do thee know why?" "Yes. It is because we have not come to the end yet, have we? In fact, this feels like the beginning. I thought when we got home, all would be settled: home, family, hunting, farming, a roaring fire at the end of the day, spilling maybe too much wine over the brim, laughter, peace."

"Aye, when we arrived at my manor at Montford and we had to fight our way out, it laid me low. It was as if we were of the Khan's host again, fighting his enemies." "Aye. Nothing has changed." "Harry, one thing has." "What?" "The enemy now is ours. Now it is personal. If we want what is ours, put them down Harry."

"Then all will be settled?"

Riennes lowered his head for a moment, then: "Let us go down that road and find out."

They sat there a moment, and then Riennes added: "Harry, we may have another enemy."

Haralde sat up. "Where?"

"Here, within our own walls." Riennes turned around and looked at the people working around their hovels and outside fires. For him, the images foreshadowed something grim.

"It goes not well for us shut up behind these timbers. There is some sickness here. The children, they are wan, of need of better food. Our own horses and bovines, they need to be in the field out there, grazing. We cannot stay this way much longer. I wish to do some things."

Haralde nodded. "Go on."

"Their night slops, and that of our animals, they throw them anywhere between the huts. Let us stop this. Throw all over the wall each morning."

"Yes. At the aqueduct. What a surprise for Aelfgar and his men when their boots get stuck at our shit. That will make them shout and curse." Haralde barked out laughter. "I would like that."

"The fresh water sustains us. But, let all clean up; rake the ground in the common and around the huts. Let us slip out at night and bring in fresh meadow grass and seeds for the animals, roots, berries, anything for the rest of us. They will know where to look. And Harry?"

"What?"

Riennes moved around to the other side of Haralde and squatted again. "Stay downwind of me from now on. Thee are become sour."

Haralde grunted. "Kind I was not to say the same of thee. Now thee insult me, your favorite brother. I do not know what our mama sees in thee. I know, I know. We need to bathe. Everyone needs to bathe"

He barked out laughter again. "What would they think if we ordered all to strip off their rags and do so? Do thee know some here are suspicious of one who bathes? Superstition makes them believe it steals something away."

They sat quiet for a moment watching the villagers. Then Riennes said: "Get us out of here Harry. Find a way."

Haralde dropped his head, and nodded slowly. Riennes said what he said because he knew it preyed on Haralde, and because he knew Haralde was a schemer. His brother would find a way.

"How many? How many against us? We can do nothing without knowing that," mused Haralde.

Riennes thought a moment, then said: "Remember I said thee must trust the trees?" "Riennes, not now." "Aye Haralde. Now. Let the forest provide thee with the answer." Haralde shook his head. "How?" "Thee have a friend in the forest here." "Who?" "Rhys. He can tell thee how many are out there."

Haralde jumped up. "And he brings gifts of venison almost every other night." Haralde slammed a hand into a fist. "Now, if we just had more horse fighters than thee and I. What I could do with six more armed men ahorse, five more archers. Why, we could surprise them with such a force."

A thought welled up in Riennes. He turned and looked along the wall. He looked down and saw Tyne sitting on a big log, digging with his sword in the ground of the village common, looking up at them in agitation.

"Haralde!" He nodded at Tyne's five soldiers keeping watch at different points on the wall. Then he looked down at Tyne.

"Six!" burst out Haralde, who added, "But horses have we none." Haralde looked at Riennes whose face slowly brightened into a smile, and the realization lit up Haralde's intellect. And they both shouted in unison: "LET THE FOREST PROVIDE!"

Haralde whirled and peered through the timber at the six horses still tied to the ash branch. "How to get them! How to get them! . . . ." Haralde mumbled as he plotted. Riennes observed Haralde's eyes blink as each piece of a plan fell into place.

Stand back, mused Riennes.

Yet it was still naught. Haralde suddenly stomped away, down a ladder, through the village and up and through the great door of his family's keep.

Haralde stood before the wall in the family hall, looking at the long, heavy, two-handed scythe of a sword. His grandfather had served with the old Viking King Canute. He had brought it out of Northumbria to the nearby kingdom of Mercia where his father was born.

Beneath, carved expertly by some mason was one word: HONOUR. He touched it, remembered it. It was the first word of his own code. He smiled. Of course, it would be. It was one of the memories he had held deep and close. A wrinkle disturbed his brow. He looked up at the claymore, then the wall.

He stepped back and looked to see how the great sword was centered. It was. He then looked at the carved word. Strange. It is not. The word was just under the beginning of the long blade, just forward the hilt. I never noticed that as a lad. Was it because I hated the duty of always cleaning the rust off, because it was a chore? Why, it needs more words. Did my father forget to finish it? Or Stoerm Longshield, did thee do this directly?

Haralde stepped back to the wall and ran his hand along the blank stone past the word. He smiled. *This thee did deliberate. Thee left a message here. For me?*

Deep in thought, Haralde still registered the swish of a gown entering the room. Never would he forget the rhythm of that stride, lose the cadence even of her breathing, not be aware of her presence anywhere near him. Still half in thought, he looked over his shoulder.

She swept up behind him, put her arms around to his chest and lay her head on his back. She kissed the very clothing on his back. Then, she felt the iron in his posture, the firmness of his thoughts; the irresolution of a problem that held him engrossed. *As it was when I hugged Stoerm. The same . . . .but different.*

He swiveled around as she loosened her embrace. She was about to step back but he held her in one of his arms.

"If it does not please my son that I do this, that I should not hug you so much, I will gladly . . . ." "Heed me mama. Never stop. Fill me with them. There is a deep well within that needs filling. So, so long have we been apart." They squeezed each other, then turned and looked at what Haralde had been perusing.

"What is it my son?"

"The family code, HONOUR, it is not centered. It likely means nothing. Yet . . . ."

She stared at it for awhile, shook her head, not comprehending, then she brightened, stepped forward, and touched the chiseled letters. "I remember. One night. A year after you were lost to us. He was here. I came in. He was doing what you were doing, touching the spaces after. He said only one thing, 'For the one who was to come after us'. Your father did not cry easily. He cried then. I thought it was just words he was saying, to release more of his grief."

"Aaah! Thus I was right. Stoerm Longshield left this for his son to complete. Now more than ever, it is a message left to me. The son to complete the father."

Tears dewed both her cheeks.

They stood, mother and son in embrace, remembering.

Finally, she stood away. She wiped her cheeks, and then looked seriously at him.

"I must address you now as Thegn of Neury and Wym. More than just your mother. It is of Tyne. Haralde, you must resolve yourself to this man who has kept order in your lands. He has sustained me in my troubles."

She expected him to protest, to stomp away, as he had done every time the subject came up. As he did not move this time, she held onto her initiative and plowed ahead. She argued well, about the honour the man had afforded her, her holdings, and thus now that he was alive, her son as well.

"This man is not Steorm, your father. He never can be. This man is Tyne, a man of his own right, who in his own way has been loyal to us, to our people and their holdings. He completes me now. I need him. And now, thank God do you, I can relinquish everything, and be his woman. To be a woman again is what I want, I need."

Haralde turned away, walked in a slow circle, looked down at coals glowing orange in the big, common fire pit, at the walls and the stairways leading up to the family rooms, then turned and looked at the claymore.

"You have a duty now. You must serve even he, my man. You owe him words of support, nay, loyalty," she finished.

As she said it, his resistance collapsed, and as its companion, a chess piece moved in his mind to the final solution of his own martial problem.

Honour, Duty, Service. She had him.

He turned and looked at his mother. The years had taken some away from her beauty. He remembered his beautiful mother, always there, always protecting him even when his father's angry demands for more discipline for his son seemed to her a threat to him. Somewhat of that beauty shone through today, Maybe it was that she was protecting someone she loved again.

He walked up to her, hung his head and pantomimed a sad face. "Thee have just chastised me. To all here, I am the lord of these lands, but to thee, I am still a little boy who needs chastising." He looked up. "I can do naught but what my mama says." And he beamed a big smile.

She gave a little squeak, did a little dance with her feet, clapped her hands and came in, hugged him, and said: "If a little boy you be, then you be a handsome one, made more handsome when you smile." She wagged a finger at him. "Do it more often. Know you that a smile is a curve given by God to set something straight."

His laughter ripped through the emptiness of the family hall. He indeed was her son for she heard echoes of her boisterous, love-of-life husband in the timbre of Haralde's laughing tone.

She delighted in making him laugh, as she had Steorm.

Tyne sat on a bench, tapping his sword on the ground, confused, impatient, even angry. From time to time he looked up at the wall, where Haralde had stood a short time ago before leaving, then back to his sword tapping.

Two years ago he had come with his men to seek their fortunes. His chieftain in Cumraugh had been defeated and killed in clan fighting in Hibernia Ireland. He had to flee. He was landless, without prospects. They had come over from Hibernia with a small army of Dublin Vikings to raid along the shores of the Dee Estuary off Chester.

It was there he heard stories of Lady Saran and her dead husband. He had hurried here to take her land holdings, by force if necessary.

Tyne was a wild man; in a fight a berserker, smashing out left and right at any man with a weapon. Any foot soldier close to him was at risk, even his own men. They had seen him strike down one of his own in his heated fury, so they tended to fight in places on the line other than with Tyne. The profile of Tyne at the exhaustion of battle was famous. Tyne, the wild man of Cumraugh, standing alone, unmoving in the field amidst the carnage, huffing and wheezing for half an hour to let the bloodlust cool. He was called Tyne Crowfeeder. Crows picked out the eyes of enemies he left dead in the field.

When he came here, all that changed. Changed because of Saran. The Welsh widow gentled the mad Hibernian warrior, even just by standing before him. She pulled him into her, a man deeply in love. He knew it helped she was a widow, held in esteem by her people, heir to land, taxes and tithes. The bonding between them was immediate. Yet, there was always something, a hesitation, a holding back of part of herself. It was an obstruction to his ambition to become lord here.

Now this. Now Haralde, her son, the legal heir of the manorial holdings, lands he wanted for himself. Now, his own avarice for land and wealth, doused as water on fire by this young man's arrival. What to do?

I could run him through in the darkness of some night. Tyne imagined all kinds of scenarios. Maybe in the heat of battle, an opportunity would present itself. But no, there was Saran. Kill her only son? Could he live with that? And then there was that other, that Riennes. Always present with Haralde, inseparable. They walked through a day as if with the same heartbeat. And those eyes. He looks into me with those eyes and knows what I am thinking. He is suspicious of me. Then, there were those vicious things they carried on their backs. Riennes would not let me draw another breath if I put Haralde down.

And on top of all, Saran now confused him more. With Haralde here, she had softened to him. The wall was gone. She had turned tender, girlish. Their lovemaking had turned voracious, delicious.

Tyne sat and fumed and plotted through the morning, and just grew more frustrated. He could find no answer, no release from his former ambitions

A shadow came over him. A voice jerked him out of his dark thoughts.

"Tyne. I would speak with thee. Come walk with me." Tyne looked up into the broad face of Haralde. It was strong, commanding. He stood up and followed. He never thought not to.

Haralde did not make Tyne follow, but waited until he was abreast of him, so the two walked together through the smoke of small fires. People stopped working and watched the two, assessed their demeanor towards each other, their voice levels, their looks one to the other; friendly or friction.

"We are in serious trouble here, thee know that." Haralde's statement was a simple fact.

"Aye, yes. I ken that," answered Tyne, suspicious of where this was all going. Haralde was taller than he, so the Irishman watched him carefully, girded himself against any Saxon or Welsh trickery.

"We cannot stay bottled up in here much longer, lest we starve, fall sick and our animals die for want of proper food. I have been told we are already late in plantings of our spring oats, barley, peas, beans. We face serious hunger this winter if we do not do so soon."

"Aye."

"Also know thee and I and the rest of our fighting men will not be spared the sword if he breaks in."

Tyne noted Haralde's inclusive use of 'our'. Yet, Tyne had not thought the rest through as Haralde had and he pursed his bearded chin in realization of his personal danger. "Aye. You be right lad. He will not."

"Now, thee and your men could slip out a night when we are all asleep and make a run for it. But who is to say how many are out there, who thee might bump into in the dark and whether they put arrows into thee or slit your throats." Haralde looked sideways at Tyne to see the effects of his words.

They came to the stone verandah leading up to the great wooden door of the keep and Haralde stopped and sat on a stair. Tyne joined him, reluctant and wary.

"Tyne. We are about to defeat Aelfgar. Indeed, I intend to kill the beast. I have a plan."

For the next while, Haralde outlined it. The villagers below watched them, silent, holding their breath, awaiting the outcome of this meeting between the two antagonists. He used his voice of command, to show he was a leader, his ideas held authority and had merit.

Tyne sat, listened and made no comment, although Haralde caught him nodding almost imperceptibly in agreement on some points.

Then Haralde switched his approach, drew Tyne into the plan, and asked him his opinion. Within a short time, Tyne warmed to some of Haralde's ideas, made suggestions. In no time, they were talking enthusiastically, fighting men discussing fighting points, weaknesses and strengths, heads nodding, heads shaking no.

Slowly, through soldier talk, they began to establish a comaraderie, as they did in one slashing moment in the dark on the parapet fighting their enemies.

They paused. Haralde saw his opening and cut into the discontent between them.

"We cannot succeed in this without thee. Thee know Aelfgar. Thee know how he fights, how he stalks our lands. Tyne of Cumraugh, I wish thee to stay, thee good and true Irish man. I want thee as commander of fighters of Neury and Wym. There will be times I may have to go away and need thee as my overseer. If thee stay, thee will be a vassal of mine. Thee will swear an oath of fealty. In return, I will swear an oath of protection to you. It will come with land of your own, a large estate running down to the River Clee. From it I will ask no tax, no tithes, but only a geld of military service. Will thee do this?"

Tyne looked deeply into the face of the boy-man who had robbed him of his ambition, but who now tempted him with another.

"I cannot answer," whispered Tyne. "I must think on this."

Haralde leaned forward and in a quieter voice: "Do so. Know also I ask a boon of thee." Not wanting to be too familiar with this rough man, but to be insistent, he put his hand gently on Tyne's shoulder. "Join our family. Ask the Lady Saran to marry thee. I can think of no finer man I would want as her consort. My mother wants thee. I want thee."

The offer jolted Tyne to his feet. A moment ago he was plotting how to kill this interloper of his dreams for a higher station. For days this son of Saran has railed against the notion of his mother marrying. Now this. Confusion reigned across the kingdom of his face.

"Thee have but a short time to do that. Shortly, I will assemble all in a hallmote."

"What is that? I do not understand," Tyne asked, still confused.

"They tell me it is a manor house and mote meeting. Normally of and for the villagers, I will make it a meeting of vassalage to me. All must know who is lord here, who commands. If we are to break out of this, total obedience is necessary. Sirrah, if thee are with us, I expect thee to be there with Lady Saran, Lord Riennes and myself."

Tyne nodded, hesitated, and then turned away.

"Tyne. Whatever your decision, bring my father's blade to the meeting."

Tyne looked back over this shoulder, nodded, and walked away.

The afternoon was waning, and there was much to do here.

Haralde, Riennes and Lady Saran stood on the stone verandah of the donjon, looking down. Below, some 32 villagers from Neury and Wym were gathered. All chatted with each other, asking what was happening. Skilled tradesmen, farmers who also worked the Lord's *desmesne,* their families, loyal relatives and the five soldiers of Tyne on the walls, all looked to the three-some. Why had they been called to the open area before the keep.

All lived within Fortress Longshield. All defended theeir interests of safety and protection. And most were afeared those interests could not stand the siege strain much longer.

Godfroi stood within the crowd, curious as to the proceedings about to unfold. Bored children ran around chasing each other. Parents shuffled, and grew restless. It was time.

Haralde and Riennes moved to go down the stairs to the people when Saran asked if it would not be best they speak to the crowd from the high stone verandah. Haralde nodded no, Riennes grinned assurance up to her, and the two continued to the ground.

Haralde moved into the gathering. Riennes followed. It was a leader's device. As commanders of 100 horse of the Khan's mounted, they had used such many times. By moving amongst their men, describing their tactics for the battle the next day, they soothed their fears. It was as if their commander was talking to each personally. It drew all intimately together.

The two stopped in the middle and the people gathered round them.

Haralde and Riennes were wearing their leather cuirasses, but no helmets. They bristled with arms; kandos behind them, pointed swords at their side and a dirk in their belts. They stood, heads bare. Haralde put his hands on his hips, and began:

"People of Neury and Wym. Know us, thee do not. Thee have only recently come to know us as the sons of Lady Saran, newly arrived. Yet, thee have heard we are to be lordships of your lands and your properties. Let us thus begin to know each other. I am Haralde Longshield, the only son of Thegn Stoerm Longshield, and this is my brother, Lord Riennes de Montford, now of Wym.

"We are both king's men. My father was a king's man and we be king's men. The new king of Britannia is from across the water. This Norman duke claims Britannia by right of conquest and as legal heir named by our dead King Edward. So be it. From him, through a king's chief man of arms, my right and the right of Lord de Montford to hold my ancestral land has been affirmed. My brother has been instructed to hold Wym. We will obey the king's will. Now, from this moment, thee will obey ours. Everyone, KNEEL!"

The sharp command buckled the knees of the men around him, their women followed. Children were pulled down to their knees, or cuffed down.

"Hear me. Thee will swear an oath of loyalty, of vassalage to me and Lord de Montford. When thee are finished, Lord de Montford and I will swear as men of honour a pledge to thee, that we, as your overlords, will protect every citizen of Neury and Wym. To all owners of land and chattel, we swear to protect thee, your family members and your property, and your right to pass on property to your children, or any of your heirs any part of your property. And when we complete this, I will ask and thee will answer: 'we so swear my lords'. And by this, know thee if thee violate your oath as our vassals, we withdraw our protection and your rights and thee will feel the wrath of we, your overlords, even to death. If thee honour your oath, know yee that it will be our duty to honour your place within our manorial holdings, that no man can usurp your place in our good will."

Haralde looked around, hoping to see Tyne amongst them, but he was not here

So, he recited a simple oath of fealty to all, had them all recite it, and in turn both Haralde and Riennes bespoke individually their oath of duty to protect them and to work with them in good spirit.

"DO YOU SO SWEAR?"

"WE SO SWEAR, MY LORDS!" they thundered back.

"Good." Haralde walked over to the nearest man, Munch the farmer with a big longbow in his hand, and lifted him up. He smacked him on the back and asked: "What say thee Munch? How feel thee about this?"

Munch, flushing at all the eyes upon him, looked around embarrassed at all the attention, then turned back to Haralde. "Well, my Lord Haralde, good!"

Haralde smacked him again. "How can that be Munch, when thee are so bothered by bugs that thee have to scratch at yourself all the time."

"Bugs my lord? They do not bother me."

The crowd laughed at that.

"Sure they do." Haralde strolled around, smiled at the families, winked, and then turned back to Munch. "They are called Aelfgar fleas. They bother thee and me all the time, and we are going to get rid of them. What say thee now?"

"Aye my lord. Those kinds of fleas. Sure. You scratch yours and I'll scratch mine harder."

The crowd roared. Haralde joined in, and Munch looked all about, laughing.

"Good!" shouted Haralde. "Because we will put thee outside the gate tomorrow and thee can scratch the first flea with your big limb of a bow."

Munch stopped grinning, fear choking off his laughter. Peels of laughter followed his reaction.

Then the laughter died quickly as a man walked across the clearing and entered the crowd. It was Tyne and he carried Stoerm's old sword two-handed in front of him. He walked up to Haralde and Riennes, drove the sword into the dirt, dropped to his knees, and shouted: "I SO SWEAR MY LORDS!"

From the walls for the fortress, Tyne's five soldiers also swore. The crowd's roar filled the Longshield fortress. Upon the verandah, Lady Saran cried out her joy, bunched her fists to her mouth and bit her white knuckles.

"Stand then Master Tyne, kiss the sword and accept your burden as commander of Neury and Wym," exhorted Haralde.

Tyne did so. Haralde took the sword from him and slid it into the Irish man's scabbard. Riennes stepped forward, clasped Tyne's arm in his, and the two shook the warrior's way.

"We are together," shouted Haralde.

Chapter Fifteen

In the moon of the night,
Things die in the dark of that light.

The besieged bumped into each other as they scurried about under their lord's orders. Tasks were pushed onto them as the result of a council of war by Haralde and Riennes with Saran and Tyne. That meeting had contrived a night battle plan.

Tyne had gone up to the wall and gathered from his soldiers all their spears. The five patrolled the wall now carrying sharpened sticks with pennon flags attached to appear to anyone outside that nothing had changed. Tyne took the spears to Riennes who was waiting for him with two carpenters.

Riennes had also instructed the fortress smith to fire up his forge. The smith removed the spear heads from the six-foot wooden shafts and re-fastened them to longer shafts.

Tyne shook his head when Haralde described another change. The smith placed bars of iron in his forge, heated them to white hot, then hammered out cross pieces that were to be cooled and handed to the carpenters. They were designed so the carpenter could fix the short cross pieces called lugs onto the shaft immediately behind the iron spear heads.

Also, a tanner wound tight wraps of leather thongs around the other end of each shaft. He was told to wrap in such a way that each soldier could couch the butt ends under their arm pits.

"But my Lord Haralde, all this, too cumbersome. Our men cannot throw these at our tormentors!" anguished Tyne.

Whereupon Haralde answered in a beguiling tone: "I do not want our men to throw them." Tyne, scratching his head, walked away carrying the lances to the waiting soldiers.

Riennes and Haralde gathered up Munch and the three farm boys and all dug pot holes, six in total at the far end of the common. They then slid six stout poles with crosses into the holes. The crosses were set upright about the height of a man above ground.

His mother sat in a circle with farmers' wives in front of huts, directing the stuffing of dried grass into old worn woolen clothes on wooden frames, plumping them so as to make them look full figured men.

The bustle of many hands working helped everyone control their near terror. Haralde and Riennes saw the fear on all the faces within the palisade when they first came through the gate. For the men, it was the fear of fighting, of killing; something the corp of serf farmers had no experience at whatsoever. For the women, it was the specter of seeing their men cut down, bleeding, and of themselves being raped or stabbed by sharp iron.

Though the work did not alleviate their fear, it set it aside briefly. They were taken aback by the uncommon sight of their two lords digging holes side by side with their husbands and sons. Their new masters were hard working like them.

Also, they had a plan; a way to lift the siege, something these two large, impressive young men had swore an oath to do. Their lords would protect them now.

Riennes came up and sat beside him, wiping a rag across his face. "Done!"

Tyne strode in right behind him, obviously perplexed over the changes. The Irishman shook his head in confusion over the six crosses now on the common, turned to Haralde and Riennes, and opened his arms wide questioningly.

Haralde grinned. Their Irish commander needed an explanation. He glanced at Riennes who nodded and stood to explain.

"Thee and the soldiers will not throw but will lower your new spears and charge," he explained to the Irishman.

"Against who?" demanded Tyne.

"Them." Riennes pointed to the crosses.

"Nay, no man can run that far with these longer heavy spears," protested Tyne.

"Sirrah. You can not, but your horses can!" revealed Haralde.

"Horses! What horses?"

Haralde and Riennes leaned their heads close to Tyne and the full plan was laid out. At one point, Tyne looked up at them in disbelief and protested that he and his men knew naught of horses, of holding lances, that they always fought on foot throwing spears at their enemies.

"If what we hope happens tonight, thee all will have fresh horses charging with these new lances of yours," chuckled Riennes. "Thee will charge again and again at six of our enemies who now stand right there. I know to thee they look like crosses, but they really are brigands."

Haralde outlined everything, his strategy on how they would surprise Aelfgar, charge suddenly at him. He also described another surprise they would throw at the brigands.

Tyne barked his disbelief. He just could not see it working. "These are farmers. Some will get hurt."

"Yes. Probably thee, foot soldier. Do thee know how your ass will hurt after just a few hours practicing on a horse?" quipped Riennes.

Tyne laughed, swearing such a sight Riennes would never see.

Haralde was enjoying the man talk when he glanced past Riennes and saw something that disturbed him.

Munch had Saran's three young male cousins practising with their longbows. Under Haralde's instructions to Munch, the farmer had them all shooting a fair distance across the commons at the crosses and he and two of the boys were beginning to hit the wood.

Haralde's eye caught upon the third. The youth stood well within the arch of the bow and released the tension perfectly. Yet did his arrows pass over his wooden cross consistently.

It was deliberate. Haralde rose, asked Riennes to explain to Tyne the why of the lug bars behind the spear points and walked out onto the open space.

As he approached, he took note of the shooting accuracy of the two youths. Also, they were loosing arrow after arrow in short order. They were very much improved under Munch's instruction.

He came up and stood behind the third. Loosing arrow after arrow, the youth's rate of fire was as good. The mark, he was overshooting and he was making no adjustments.

Haralde knew he was named Owain. Just beyond, the youth's mother Anline, sat in the circle of women with his own mother stuffing dried grass in clothing.

"Lower your left elbow just the thickness of a grass blade," Haralde ordered coldly. "Hit the stock."

Owain looked over his shoulder, saw who it was, became agitated, loosed and the arrow buried into the dirt just short of the pole.

"Owain. Jab two arrows in the dirt beside you. Ready the third. Take a deep breath. Do it again. This time put three into the stock."

Owain steadied himself, obeyed Haralde, notched the third, drew taut, then let all crumble in his arms. He dropped his head and shook it. "I can not kill."

Haralde crowded in, turned him and hung over him. "Thee have to. And not once but many times. Or, die yourself within these walls with Aelfgar's sword in your belly. It will hurt so bad, thee will scream, want to fight back, but your limbs will not obey thee."

The bang of activity had stopped. Everyone stood silent, watching Haralde and the youth. He turned the youth around to face the cross pole again. Owain stood there staring at it.

No fear, no fire could Haralde ignite in him.

Haralde glanced around, saw his mother Anline standing with her knuckles in her mouth, fearing for her son.

Haralde strode away towards her. The women saw the look on Lord Longshield's face and pulled back. He kicked benches out of the way. Women fled. Saran stood, shocked.

Haralde grabbed Anline and she squeaked. Behind, Haralde heard her boy shout: MAMA!"

Haralde dragged her into the open and before her son, before everyone, his kandos rang clear and he stabbed at her.

Riennes jumped up, taking in everything. He saw Haralde's blade pass through to the other side of her, was running, fearful of what his brother had just done.

"MAMA!" screamed Owain, dropped his bow and ran towards her and Haralde.

Haralde dropped her to the ground, strode out and intercepted Owain, grabbing him up in his arms.

Owain screamed again, then choked off. Over Haralde's shoulder he saw his mother roll over on the ground, then stand up. A drop of blood ran from her nose. She wiped it and it smeared red.

Riennes stopped running. The pass by Haralde's kandos had been cleverly done. It seemed even to him his brother had run her through.

"Thee see Owain, thus will happen to your mother in a few days," explained Haralde, a little more softly into the youth's ear. "They will pour over these walls and cut your mother. Blood will flow."

Owain relaxed, slid down. Haralde released his grip on him.

"I know it is an abhorrence to thee. But thee must," urged Haralde. "Thee must put away the boy and be the hard son. Protect your own. Be hard on yourself. Be hard with the bow. Strike the arrow now."

Owain made to move to his mother but Haralde hissed at him.

Thus, Owain turned, stepped back up to the line, took up the bow and took a deep breath. He stood frozen, unmoving.

Haralde waited. Nothing. He cursed and strode back to the women's circle. His mama put her arms around Anline but Haralde surged past the scattering women, grabbed up the stuffed form of a man, stomped out to Owain's pole and tied the dummy there, arms out along the cross pieces. It seemed now a man was pinned to the cross.

He stomped back to Owain and shouted: "There! THE ENEMY IS WITHIN OUR WALLS! KILL HIM!"

Owain pulled taut his bow. He loosed in quick succession and struck at the cross' centre, twice out of three into the stuffed man's chest. The fourth he hammered into its head.

Haralde nodded. "Do it again!"

"My lords." The words spoken softly signaled the end of sleep for Haralde and Riennes. Riennes rolled over to look into the face of Tyne hovering over them. He looked at Haralde who was not responding. He gave his brother a gentle kick. Haralde grunted awake.

They had eaten a quick supper, and then fallen asleep under a rigged canopy in the shadow of the wall near the gate. It was dark. They had work to do this night.

"Haralde!" hissed Riennes.

"I hear thee," mumbled Haralde. "Do we have to?"

"My lords. It is time to go," informed Tyne. "Rhys came. He is outside but wishes to be away."

Haralde nodded his understanding, rolled out of his bedding on the straw and the three ran across and bounded up a ladder to the walkway at the top of the wall.

"No venison this time," puffed Tyne as they reached the walk and hit the top of the palisade's sharpened poles.

They leaned over and looked down. The moon was half but enough light glowed on Rhys's milk-white face looking up.

"Good evening my lords de Montford and Longshield," smiled Rhys bemused, hands on his hips and foot on a bag at his feet. "What are stout men such as you doing prisoners behind your own walls? Come out! Come out! Join a free one like me."

"Aaah! Our Fremen," Riennes grinned back. "Nay woodsman. Why, we like it in here. Food, drink, warmth, women. Come on in. We will drink a cup of ale together."

"Oh. I think the ale be bitter gall and the food, ah, you must be down to gruel by now." Rhys spread his arms wide. "Come join me. This hunter's moon will give up fresh game. And we will drink a sweet cup of cold spring water.

Haralde and Tyne chuckled. "And leave all this?" Haralde joked back.

"Aaah! But of course. You be not free men. I hear you have obligations."

"We will miss your venison," observed Tyne.

"Aye. My bow has misbehaved this day, but . . . ." Rhys leaned over, reached into his pack and brought out a stringer of big fish. " . . . . I just caught these. Fresh from a rushing stream. And the bag is full of them."

"Good. And for your generosity, I will not tax thee for all the deer and fish you have caught and brought us," assured Haralde.

There was a short bark of laughter from below.

"We thank thee our good Fremen," Haralde said seriously. "For all that thee have done for our people."

"I may need you to do the same for me one day." Then Rhys also spoke serious. "Thank not me, but the Lady Saran."

Haralde, curious, asked: "Why is that?"

The Fremen, however, did not answer but gathered up his bow. "I must away."

"Rhys. Join us," suggested Haralde.

"I cannot. My children are hidden nearby asleep."

Haralde turned to the seriousness of their position. "Rhys. How many men does Aelfgar bring against us?"

"Thirty, maybe more. I do not know my lord. He is about trying to recruit more."

"Are there just six with horses watching us?" asked Riennes.

Rhys paused and grinned up at them. "Someone up there has eyes. Yes. And so sure are they that all are asleep."

"Good. We intend a visit with them in a moment," said Haralde.

"They have a fire going behind that hill there. Swing around and come in from the west downwind. My lords, take care. I think two are there against their will. They could be of us."

"Aye. We have thee," nodded Riennes.

The moon went briefly behind a cloud. And Rhys disappeared with it.

The three pushed off from the wall and clattered down the ladder.

Saran was waiting for them with torches. A group of men stood with pitchforks, sharp axes and clubs. Women held bovines and their two horses in assembly.

The huge gate creaked open a crack. Tyne slipped out and returned with the bag of fish which he handed to the men and women.

"Make sure the children get a good serving of those," advised Riennes as he took off a leather vest.

Haralde and Riennes stripped down to their silk undershirts. They made sure they had no metal of any kind that might tink. They wore wool breeches with leather wrappings and recently tanned leather shoes so their clothing would not whisper as they moved through the underbrush. They did not take their kandos for fear they would catch on bushes. Night stalking they had done many times.

No one, Haralde said, was to go outside until they returned. Then all the animals were to be put out for grazing hobbled for the night, and to be brought back in before first light. Foraging would be allowed in the nearby woods. Then, all must be back inside and the gate secured before sunup. The crowd murmured their understanding.

Then, the front gate creaked open again and with a warrior's wish for good hunting from Tyne, the two slipped out and just glanced up at the pagan god's ugly visage on the gate as they went into the dark of the night.

The half moon was their ally, shining just enough light to show them a way over the open ground but not enough to reveal any real form, their's included.

In an hour, it was as Rhys described, five men asleep wrapped up for the night around a low fire. A sixth, the watchman, was sitting but bent over asleep. With hand signals, they indicated to each other that two of those asleep were boys.

As they could not take prisoners back to a stronghold scarce with food, the killer business began. For his carelessness, Haralde dispatched the watchman first. Riennes, an expert on the human anatomy, efficiently used his knife and put two to death. When the fourth awoke to a noise and attempted to rush Riennes, Haralde was upon him out of the night and put him down.

They moved, quick shadows towards the last two. When they kicked them, two youths rolled over rubbing their eyes. When they saw two shapes standing over them with blades bare, they yelled.

"NO NO! PLEASE DON'T KILL US. We are your subjects," cried one.

The other cried: "We are of Neury! We are of Neury! We are not of these!" His hands went up to cover his face to hide from the death blow.

Haralde and Riennes stood before two cowering youths. Haralde put the blade tip under the chin of the youth in front of him and lifted his face.

"Who are you? Quickly!" demanded Haralde.

"Tud ap Bleddyn."

"Fletch ap Dafydd," sobbed the other boy before Riennes. "The godins made us do this, to fight our own Lord Saran. They would kill our fathers and mothers and sisters if we did not."

Haralde and Riennes slowly straightened, their killing blood cooling.

"When did this happen to thee?" asked Riennes

"Two days ago master. Two of these horses are ours. Aelfgar said we were to become like his men, to fight in a few days." He pointed to a straight wooden stave beside his bedroll, a hunting bow when strung.

"We do not want to! We do not want to!" sobbed the youth Tud, Haralde's blade still tipping his face up.

"Tud. Why do you call her Lord Saran?" demanded Haralde.

"We call her Lord Saran after our real lord died."

"Who was that?"

"Lord Stoerm Longshield!"

Haralde darted a look at Riennes who nodded slowly. It was obvious, the two were Haralde's own vassals.

Haralde walked over to Riennes. "Now what?" he whispered.

"Well, I guess besides six horses, thee have two more for your army," suggested Riennes.

Haralde turned to the two shaking youths and ordered to gather up the weapons of the dead men.

"Who are you?"

"There is no time, except to say we are of Lady Saran, and we go to her right now. Gather up your things. Go bring the horses here now. We must be away quickly."

They scrambled, gathered up their things, then ran to the horses, casting a quick glance of disbelief at the dead bodies crumpled around the campsite.

Haralde and Riennes worked to erase all signs of a campsite here. They wanted it to appear as if the four brigands had disappeared, taken their horses and equipment and deserted Aelfgar. Haralde would send a party back later to pack the bodies out and to bury them elsewhere.

The two youths walked back into the now darkened campsite leading the six horses. Riennes and Haralde mounted and turned away, leading horses each. The two youths followed.

As they went into the night, Haralde leaned over and whispered to Riennes.

"Your forest needs stop providing like this. Going against Aelfgar with a bunch of scared boys is not my idea of how to win a fight."

Chapter Sixteen

Fight or flee. Kill or die.

Riennes grunted in his sleep; disturbed by illusions. He bolted upright. Immediately he felt a dampness on his cheeks. He knew what it was. Fog. He had been dreaming he was at sea, steering into fog. Had the dream awakened him in this, one of the Longshield family rooms? Or, was it again that feeling of unwanted expectation. He could not get back to sleep.

He rolled out of his straw pallet, slid on his clothes to warm himself against the dampness. He slung and tightened his leather cuirasse around his chest, clipped his scabbard with broadsword onto his baldric and his kandos onto his back. He slipped downstairs across the family hall where slave servants lay curled, sleeping beside a dying pit fire. One small girl, curled up beside her mother, was shaking in her sleep from the chill. These stone walls gave off a damp coldness that went to the bone. Riennes swore they emanated sickness.

He placed two big chunks of wood on the fire, side by each as the Welsh here said, laid a wrap over the wee one then exited quickly outside.

It was dark, but dawn lay just over the rim. Sure enough, fog lay heavy on the commons. Fires glowed dimly through the mist over the village below, adding a smoke pall upon the fortress.

He walked down to the walls near the gate. The soldier who was to be walking the catwalk on guard was curled up asleep, wrapped in a robe against the cold. Such carelessness should have prompted him to kick the man upright.

Yet he hesitated, and then realized it was not quiet. Was it this that woke him? It was knocking on the wooden wall outside. He leaped to the ladder, scrambled upwards.

He peeped over, and a figure seen dimly through the fog hissed up at him. It was Rhys.

"Who is that there?" Rhys asked.

"It is Riennes, Rhys," he answered.

"Aah, my Norman. Quickly. They are come against you. They were encamped some miles away. They move here now."

"How many?"

"I count 35." Then he disappeared.

The guard who had been asleep kneeled down beside Riennes, his face contrite over his failure to stay awake.

"Quietly, go wake Tyne and Lord Longshield. Tell them men of arms are come." The guard nodded and rose to run. "And tell your lord to bring my bow, and his as well."

Riennes walked up and down the wall, peering over, checking the wall from one corner to the other. He heard the fortress come awake behind him. He dropped to the ground and ran over to the wall in the area of the aqueduct. He went up and looked over. All was clear. He judged that no advanced party had arrived yet, a very real possibility in the coming hours.

Haralde and Tyne ran out of the fog to him.

Haralde handed Riennes a wrap. Riennes pulled out his recurved bow. "Here," said Harade fishing inside his clothing and handing over two dry bowstrings. Riennes described what had happened. He did not string his bow yet, protecting all against the chilly wetness of the fog.

Deftly, all of Fortress Longshield swirled out of the fog and gathered to them. All the soldiers stood beside their horses with Tyne, lances upright and ready. Munch stepped out of the mist accompanied by five distraught young archers holding unstrung bows, all their faces buried under black woolen hoods.

Lady Saran appeared with the two Frisians and monk Godfroi led the ox with dray behind. There they were all gathered; the frightened, the farmers, the fighters, and the foolish who pinned so much hope in the hasty, thrown-together plan they had all practiced over and over. Munch and the now five youths hammering arrows into the poles; the foot soldiers tumbling from the strange roosts called horses, charging the crosses and burying their lances into the stuffed man figures, and the farmers and their wives with sharpened field tools.

"How did thee know?" asked Haralde as he fished around in the dray behind Godfroi.

"My bed was wet," answered Riennes as Haralde pulled out heavy oilskins from the bed of the cart which clinked as he manhandled them. "The fog. I thought we were aboard."

Riennes loosened and took off his cuirasse as Haralde opened the oiled material and held up a chain-link hauberk, the one wrought by a London smithy. After wiggling into it with his brother's help, Riennes retied the cuirasse over the mail, then helped Haralde do the same.

They donned two Mongolian fighting helmets, mostly hard leather with silver –hammered frameworks. The two cinched tight the helmets over their chain cowls. With swords in place, their amour was complete.

The people, eyes wide, murmured their admiration. None had ever seen anything like this. Their two lords now appeared before them as fighting men, competent, fierce. It comforted them. Their fighting vestments were a physical statement of the oaths of protection the two lords swore.

Haralde took something out of the dray, tied it to a spare lance and handed it to Riennes. Down fell the red silk with the white horse in the upper corner; the standard of a long-ago Riennes.

Haralde did the same, with the black horse in the red silk's upper corner coming into full view. The families stood there, mouths open, peering up at the priceless flags. None had any idea of silk, but was awed by the images on the material's sheen.

"I thought we were finished with these. We agreed, never again," Riennes admonished Haralde.

"That road we thought we had left. It is here again, only it is our fight this time," answered Haralde. "So did thee say."

Riennes looked at this standard, and then nodded his understanding. As comrade in arms as well as in life, they leaned and embraced each other. Saran wrung her hands and stifled a cry.

Tyne nodded, smiled over the rightness of it all.

Haralde turned and looked at everyone. "Yes. It has come now. We know what we have to do."

Haralde turned to Munch and reviewed the fighting plan. The big farmer and the boys were to leave immediately and make for pits they had dug into the side of a hill and covered each in wattles covered with rocks and dirt. Tyne had observed how in the past other armed men as well as Aelfgar and his host came around that mount of earth and took up positions facing the fortress, presenting their backs to that hill.

"We are agreed. When thee hear us charge out the gate, thee will come out and shoot swiftly," instructed Haralde.

"Aye!" they all said in unison. Haralde walked over to the boys and putting one hand on Owain's shoulder, said to all: "I know thee be afraid. Lord de Montford and I also. Shoot only at the backs of these brigands. Think not of their eyes or their souls or their bodies. Shoot at only those who stand and fight. Those that break and run, let them go. Think of nothing else but their asses. Shoot just above," he finished looking into Owain's eyes.

Riennes nodded to Godfroi who stepped into the inner circle of fighting men. He raised his hand and began to pray. Those who were Christians dropped to their knees Haralde and Riennes dropped to one knee and bowed their heads. Men and women back in the dark dropped to their knees.

"God be with you and protect you, the innocent in this matter," finished Godfroi, justifying his blessing upon all who were to commit violence.

They rose. Haralde said: "Go now quickly. Listen to Munch," he finished, smacking the big farmer on the back.

The gate creaked open and Munch and his flock of chicks ran into the fog.

Riennes was talking to Tyne and the five soldiers. "When we go out, we go together. Keep your lance high. When you get near enough to the brigands, lower as taught you. Strike at only those with shields and those who stand and resist. Run the nearest one through. The bar behind the blade will prevent thee from burying it too deep and tearing it from your grip. It will pull away easy. Go for another. Of all things, listen to Tyne. If all goes well, they will scatter. Pursue. Then it is of thee for yourselves. If one shouts he is from Neury or Wym, let him go. He is one of us. Do this, and it will be exhilarating, a terrible success. Thee will tell your children of this day."

They all raised their lances, a foreign weapon to them, and saluted, "HAH!" to Riennes and Haralde.

They were foot soldiers. Here in western England and in Ireland, they were trained to get off their horses. If they rode to a battle, they always got off and fought on foot. Fighting from a horse, well, it could all be a disaster, the two lords thought.

Tyne led them and all the horses back into the fog and towards the gate.

Lady Saran walked up. The two knelt and she tied two ribbons around their throats. Then she kissed them and whispered: "Godfroi and I will pray for God to return my sons and my terrible Irish to my bosom."

The armed band came against them not in force, but in a scuttling of skulkers, sappers.

The two lords were standing by their black Frisians when Saran's uncle, Gwengarth, standing guard, tapped a pitchfork on the catwalk above, and signaled them to come up. They did hurriedly in a chinking of chain mail.

Peeping over, they saw two figures dimly through the fog, piling brush and tinder against the wooden wall. They splashed an oil on the heap for burning. Someone planned to set fire to the wooden wall. Gwengarth beside them was about to shout alarm when Riennes put a hand over his mouth.

Haralde nodded his understanding. Haralde then strung his bow, as did his brother. Leaning over, they pulled their bows into a tight D configuration, and loosed. In the dark below, the two infiltrators coughed 'ooomphh' as if they had bumped into something. Then quiet.

Haralde and Riennes knelt down. "That is two fewer against us."

"Yes, and we took out six the other night." figured Riennes. "Now if he will just send in more to fire the brush, poof! Aelfgar would find himself standing alone out there."

They waited. The fog began to tear apart. They heard a horse cough out there. Someone dropped something metallic on the field. The sun broke through

"Oh my God. There they are!" exclaimed Gwengarth shrinking back in fear.

Haralde and Riennes peeked through chinks in the logs. Before them stood armed rows of men. Barely through the dissipating mist, they saw a bearded man ahorse, wearing chain mail, arms wrapped in leather guards and a Viking helmet with a nasal guard. His body was protected in a Saxon *byrnie,* a chain mail dress that fell to his knees. Below that, his legs were bare but ended in leather wrappings around his calves above leather boots. He had a sword and he carried a spear held aloft.

Haralde shouted down into the stronghold and Tyne came bouncing up the ladder. He settled beside his lord and peered out.

"Thankfully, it is no *teulu,*" Tyne grunted in relief.

"Teulu?"

"Aye. A Welsh lord, his household army and with his goodmen. It would not be well for us," the Irishman answered.

"What say thee?" demanded Haralde.

"Deadly, if it were a teulu. We small few would be tatters in a few hours. No. It is Aelfgar. It is the brigand with his army."

He was the commanding presence out there. His people had told Haralde they thought Aelfgar had lost all his lands. He had in anger turned to outlawry.

Beside him, his second wore a leather vest, a metal helmet and other fighting protections. He sat behind a shield on his horse, a spear also held aloft. Dangling down his side was a big axe.

Two ranks of men stretched out behind them, most with helmets, spears, axes and other odd sharpened metal things. The line was stretched wide on two wings. Some had faces painted in blue and red. Three had bows slung around them. They all stood barefooted.

Haralde and Riennes looked at each other.

"I make 34."

"Yea but six of them have no shields, no armour and only sticks with iron on the ends. Two have but slings only. Notice they are just on the end of the line there," calculated Riennes.

"I make them ours, from Neury and Wym," judged Haralde.

"Yes. They will run at the first conflict."

Haralde thought a moment, their 10 years of experience in the Khan's wars going through his mind. "Methinks if luck is not with us this day, they will fall upon us out there and chop us up."

"Buck up brother. We have worked hard. Everyone is in place. This is a weak force. I think luck and surprise will fortune our day."

"Yea by the Khan's anger. Even from here, I see gaping holes. He is a man reaching high with his bluff," agreed Haralde.

"LADY SARAN!" Aelfgar's voice rang strong in the clear morning air.

As they agreed, Saran mounted the ladder with Tyne's assistance. She stepped up to the wall and showed herself to her tormentor.

"Saran," said Aelfgar more softly. "Come out now my love and join with me. If you do, all will be allowed to follow you out and I give your people safe passage to go to their homes."

"And if I do not agree?"

"If you resist, I still will protect you." Everyone could see the fire in the brigand leader's eyes. He stood, shook his fist as he added: "All others will be put to the sword. TYNE OF CUMRAUGH. RUN OUT THE BACK AND FLEE. IF I MUST COME AGAINST YOU, I WILL CUT OFF YOUR HEAD AND STICK IT OVER THAT GATE. RUN NOW. RUN NOW. I WILL WAIT UNTIL YOU AND YOUR SOLDIERS ARE GONE."

The line of soldiers behind began to howl, and gesture, and beat their weapons upon their shields. They began to chant, a deep, rhythmic 'Uuhhh! Uuhhh!'.

Haralde, Riennes and Tyne mounted up. "It is called a rage," Tyne explained to a frightened farmer's wife assigned to hold his horse until he mounted. He told her to be not afraid. "They shout and carouse to frighten us. They who have nothing use this empty weapon of fear. He is but a ball of snot."

Haralde urged his black to step forward. "We will bring him in and present him to thee, to beg your forgiveness." The woman gave a wan smile, and nodded her thanks to her lord for his comforting words.

"Go away brigand. I declare you all bandits, and I urge my people and those of my neighbors to turn against you, to fall upon you and slay all here today," warned Lady Saran. "Already I have received messages that many are coming to my aid. Best you flee before they arrive."

"My beauty," answered Aelfgar. "Let us join our beds together, and as one we will greet your guests as a warm, loving couple."

"You revolt me and all here, Aelfgar," shouted Saran.

Aelfgar nodded, and then turned to a bowman beside him. A flame flared and a fire arrow was loosed. It arched up into the air and plunged into the pile of brush his men had put up against the wall in the night. There was a 'wump' of wood daubed with animal fat, and the brush ignited. Another bowman shot another fire arrow into another pile stacked against the gate. It caught fire.

Tyne had anticipated such. Barrels of water placed on the catwalk were burst open, tipped over the wall and the cascade poured down to extinguish Aelfgar's only siege tactic.

With all attackers' eyes on the hoped for fire to catch onto the wall and the gate, Haralde choose that moment.

Haralde leaned over and touched Riennes on the shoulder and his brother returned the salute.

Haralde turned and shouted to the two men at the gate: "NOW!"

The great gate pushed the fire pile before it. The ugly pagan face turned outward to the spectacle of death that was about to unfold.

The black Frisians leaped for the opening. Tyne roared his battle cry behind them, then surged forward with his five, newly-formed horse warriors.

They swept out in a host. As they passed under the palisade over the gate, Haralde and Riennes lifted their silk standards and they unfurled blood red in the bright day light.

The bang of the gate slamming open drew all eyes of the attackers from the fire. Suddenly, a host of armoured warriors with standards and lances and war horses broke through the smoke of the gate fire and bore down on them. They had never seen such a fighting force here before. It was as Lady Saran warned.

The lances came down and were leveled. It was the surprise more than anything that made Aelfgar and his second in command shout, and turn and gallop back to the their thin line of men.

The sudden startled fall back of their leaders seemed to signal a retreat. The one wing of six young men turned and ran. The main line wavered, then some of the bare-footed brigands pitched forward with arrows in their backs. A warrior cried out in pain, his shield falling to the ground. He fell onto his shield, an arrow through his throat choking him.

Aelfgar saw holes in the hill behind his men open to disgorge archers. A buzz of arrows came at him and his men. All in the line did not know yet where the arrows were coming from. More fell onto their knees, then their faces pitched forward into the grass and dirt.

The brigand leader yelled to rally his men, attempted to yank his horse around, saw the leveled lances about to reach him, turned his horse back and fled.

Haralde and Riennes saw the brigand and his fellow ride through their own men. The line buckled, men turned, saw the youths on their right wing already fleeing, threw down their cumbersome shields and they ran.

Haralde and Riennes charged into them, drove their lances through some still standing to fight, withdrew their lances with the now blood-soaked standards, and threw them away. They slowed up, pulled out their compound horn bows, strung them, then loosed a volley of bamboo arrows at the final few still standing. Five brigands locked their shields together to form an impenetrable wall.

Tyne and his men crashed into them, banged lances straight through the remaining shields and broke the wall.

Haralde and Riennes kept going, pursuing the rebel leader and his chief. They rode through their own archers and yelled at them in a whoop of glee. But the farmer youths were too busy to return the yell. They were too absorbed in pursing the fleeing remnants of the brigand force, stopping to loose one, two and three arrows into the backs of many of them.

The two brigand leaders rode hard, trying to distance themselves from the bloody rout. Haralde and Riennes followed. Riennes slung his bows over his back, stuffed a remaining arrow into a quiver under his riding pallet and settled down to a hard riding pursuit.

The joy of riding again in a wide plain overtook them. The wind, and the 'huff, huff' of the horses, the leather squeaking and the horses' sweat spitting back up into their faces, sent a jolt of exhilaration through them. They shouted at one another. Riennes stood up and signaled to Haralde he would follow Aelfgar's chief. Haralde stood up and patted the top of his head, then pointed to the fleeing Aelfgar.

Riennes whooped and bent low over his horse, diverging from Haralde. They rode as if they wore no armour at all.

Haralde closed with the flying Aelfgar who tore off his helmet and pitched it away. Haralde stood up in his stirrup, cocked his bow and let loose a ranging shot. It struck.

Aelfgar's horse screamed and tried to turn his head to bite the arrow now sticking out of its rump. The horse's speed dropped, and his pace floundered. Aelfgar's chief slowed down to support him. They turned and headed up a hill, then stopped on the edge of a thick wood.

Haralde and Riennes saw Aelfgar drop off his horse, followed by his chief. They ran into the forest.

The brothers pulled up beside the horses. The one horse struggled round and round trying to bite the arrow. Riennes made a motion with his hand to ride into the forest to his left and Haralde nodded yes, indicating he would go right.

Haralde 'clicked, clicked' his mount into the heavy brush, soothing it to go slower. The Frisian made with heavy breathing, trying to restore the demand on its lungs. From the back of the beast, Haralde could see a good way ahead.

There was nothing artful about the ambush. Haralde sensed it coming even before it happened. Aelfgar rushed out of a bush and threw his spear at Haralde. However, Haralde had already slipped from his mount. The spear flew over the Frisian. The horse spun around, putting itself between Haralde and his attacker.

Aelfgar pushed the beast aside, and came at Haralde with his broadsword waving in circles over this head. Haralde unbuckled his baldric to get rid of his own longsword. He didn't want it tangled in his legs.

Out rang the kandos and now, Haralde was comfortable. Fighting one to one with very little space for his attacker to move around was exactly what he wanted. He would hound the brigand, corner him, take away the very air from him.

The leader cleaved with a wide, hard downward swing at Haralde's shoulder. Haralde's move sideways was too quick for Aelfgar. As the brigand's blade fell, Haralde deflected it with a slight 'ting' and the heavier blade smashed into the earth.

Aelfgar swung hard at him again. The two blades clanged in the clearing. Again and again they made the noise of fighting men. Haralde's blood now was up. His fighting ire was mounting to a berserker madness. He wanted a hard fight, a mad fight.

It was that strength, or weakness Riennes would claim, that clouded his judgment.

As he moved round to deliver a body-opening cut, Haralde felt his foot step on something. Like a forest trap, his discarded longsword scabbard levered up and entangled him.

He felt himself fall backwards. The blade of Aelfgar's broadsword swished an air's breath by his face. It was intended as a skull crasher. Haralde hit the ground, and continued rolling to get away from the next attack.

He rolled around too late and saw Aelfgar raise his sword to smash him. Haralde could not free his kandos and arm from under his body fast enough.

Two wooden stems tipped with white-goose feathers flowered from Aelfgar's chest with a 'thump, thump' sound.

Aelfgar took one, two steps backwards and grunted 'uh,uh', his hand coming up to pluck at the wood rooted in his chest. He sat down on a big fallen tree trunk and looked down, his face contorted in surprise and disappointment at what was impairing his breathing.

Haralde was upon him. Not in a slicing move, but in a push, pull action, the hardest, sharpest steeled sword in the world scythed down onto the back of the brigands's neck cutting through skin, muscle, sinew, backbone and cleanly through.

The head leaned forward, tumbled down the chest, hit the ground and started to roll away down an incline. The torso stood up, hands out as if to follow and retrieve its errant part, took a step forward, then crashed to the ground, great geysers of blood pumping out and splashing onto the greenery bush.

Haralde whirled about, kandos leveled, and peered through a yellow veil, looking to fight more. He took a step forward, pirouetted, then leveled his blade at a figure coming towards him.

"Haralde!"

For a moment, Haralde's blood was still up, and he would attack.

"Mama wants us to go home now," said Riennes as he walked calmly over and looked at the body on the ground.

The yellow funk flowed out of Haralde. He stopped, stood erect and looked at Riennes.

"Ren?" asked Haralde.

"Look at this Haralde. Two arrows. Do thee recognize them?" Riennes asked calmly.

Haralde passed his sword hand and kandos across his face. He wiped his brow. Then looked down at the blood on his hand.

He shook his head no.

Riennes pointed to the two white goose feathers, each with two strands dyed brown.

His brother stood up. "It seems our Fremen joined thee in your struggle. Where is he?" asked Riennes looking round, but out the corner of his eye carefully appraising the state of Haralde's awareness.

He walked over and touched Haralde on the shoulder.

Haralde looked about him. "Your man?"

"Dead. We have broken them all Haralde." Riennes answered. "What say thee to me."

Haralde looked around. Finally: "I am complete now. It was a near thing." He whirled around. "Is Rhys here?"

"Not here. He has gone my lord," answered someone from behind a tree.

A man, nay, five men with longbows and quivers of arrows hanging from their hips, stepped out of the green forest. All in a knot they stood before Haralde and Riennes. They were dressed in green and brown woolen tunics with hoods hanging behind. Some wore rumpled Phrygian cloth hats, belts and leggings wrapped in leather. Daggers for skinning animals hung from leather belts. They stood bare-footed.

"Who are thee?" asked Haralde taken slightly aback by their sudden appearance, kandos up again. In the same moment he knew these were not poachers, not men of the forest as Rhys. They stunk of urine, manure, farm beasts and grass. These were serfs, men of farms.

"Your vassals my lord," said the first man.

Riennes stepped forward and looked over their bows. "Serfs. Yet these are sturdy. Thee hunt with these?"

"Aye my lord. Rhys showed us how to make them. He is also a hard task master. He also demands we practice in their use . . . ." he looked around at his companions, who grinned when he went on . . . . "constantly."

"Forgive us my lord," the man went on. "I am Bleddyn. This is my friend Daffyd." He went on to introduce the other three who were neighbors of his.

Haralde came up, shook off his funk, and brightened. "Wait. Thee have a son, Tud. And thee . . . ?"

"Fletch my lord. You saved my son. I had come this day with the rest here to fight against the brigands. We arrived just in time to join our sons in putting goose feathers into their backsides. We saw you pursue Aelfgar and his man. They have been a plague upon us, upon Neury and Wym. We did not know at the time who you were. Our sons told us. We ran here as quickly as possible. Rhys led us."

"Where is he. Here?" asked Riennes looking about.

"Gone my lords. As always."

Riennes looked them over, and then he went and started cleaning his blooded sword on some plants. He pulled a rag out from his clothing and finished. Then he went and handed the cloth to Haralde, looking him over carefully as he did. Haralde also finished cleaning up. Both slid their kandos into their back scabbards.

The five men watched it all, their eyes wide. They looked to the headless carcass, blinked, and their eyes went back to the two tall lords.

"What would you of this?" Bleddyn asked of Aelfgar's body.

Haralde looked at the body for a moment, then said: "Go back and bring a dray and men from our fortress. Take the head of this one to the border of Wym and the body the other way to the edge of Neury."

He turned to Riennes and asked in a gesture, and Riennes jabbed a thumb over his shoulder. "There is another dead brigand back there. Take them and hang all from trees. Pin a sign on them with one word, 'Brigands'. Let it be a warning to others."

A bush parted and a sixth serf bowman stepped out leading the Frisians.

All the men stood around as Haralde and Riennes gathered their things. They were about to mount, but hesitated when the knot of men continued to stare at them. There was about them an air of expectancy.

Haralde looked at Riennes expecting an answer, but seeing his brother as perplexed, turned and asked: "Thee wish of us?"

"Aye. We did not believe Rhys when he told us. We have looked upon you, and indeed you are your father's son. How, we do not know," remarked Dafydd.

Then, all the men dropped to their knees and in the green forest clearing, swore vassalage to Haralde.

An effusion of joy flooded over Haralde. He was home. These were his people, and they acknowledged his sway over them. He smiled, and then lifted his hand up, that they should rise.

They did so, but only after saying: "Our sons told us of your oath to protect us all of Neury and Wym," they answered.

Haralde, now alive to the forces flowing to and from him of his holdings, gently chided them.

"As thee have seen, we have done so this day."

They rode out of the woods with their subjects trailing.

Riennes hummed a little tune. "First their sons and now the fathers. If the forest keeps providing, we are going to have quite an army to protect all of Neury and Wym."

He glanced at his brother and saw a man physically weary, but happy in his soul. Now at last his brother had arrived in his heartland with his people drawn around him.

And Riennes thought that would be just fine with him too.

-end-

Glossary

baksheesh – graft, bribe.

caput – the lord's main residence, stronghold.

chausses – chain mail thigh protectors.

curragh – a small round boat made of leather, usually seal skin.

demesne – a lord's agricultural and forest holdings.

donjon – keep.

fey – a prescient, one subject to future happenings.

hide – roughly 80 acres.

Heimr – old Norse for home.

hacquetons – padded vests as protection against the cold and sword attack.

inshallah – as God wills.

jhalaba – a floor length eastern rob.

jongleur – a troubadour, singer, story teller.

kandos – a short, curved Manchurian sword of the hardest known steel.

keffieh – an Arab headdress.

naukhada – a captain of an Arab dhow.

phrygian – a cap of common cloth or leather.

quarrel – crossbow arrow or bolt.

rasa – an Indus aesthetic mood captured by a melody.

sitkitra – the held breath of a woman in orgasm.

steuirhdt – a steward, court official.

sufi – an Arab mystic.

Bibliography

The Adventure of English. Bragg, Melvyn. Hodden and Stroughton Publishers. (2003). Brisih Library. ISBN: 0-340-82991-5.

Anglo-Saxon Thegn AD 449-1066. Harrison, Mark. Osprey Publishing (1993). ISBN: 1-85532- 349-4.

The Archaelology of Medieval London. Christopher, Thomas. Sutton Publishing Ltd. (2002). ISBN: 0-7509-2718-6.

The Beginning of English Society. Whitelock, Dorothy. Penguin Books. (1952).

Circle of Stones. Waldo, Anna Lee. St. Martin's Press. (1999). ISBN: 0-312-19843-4.

Encyclopedia of Medical Plants. First Published by Dorling Kindersley in Great Britain. (1996). ISBN: 0-7513-1209 – 6.

English and Norman Government and Lordship in the Welsh Borders, 1039-1087. Abstract of D. Phil. thesis submitted by Lewis, C. P. Merton College. Oxford 1985.

A History of God. The 4,000 Year Quest of Judaism, Christianity and Islam. Armstrong, Karen. Random House Inc. (1993). ISBN:) 0-345-38456.3

Lanfranc of Bec. Gibson, Margaret. Oxford University Press (1978). ISBN 0-19-822462-1.

Life in a Medieval Village. Geis, Frances and Joseph. Harper Collins, New York (1990)
ISBN: 0 06 016215 5

London. Rutherford, Edward. The Ballantine Publishing Group. (1997). ISBN: 0-449-00263-2.

Longbow a Social and Military History. Hardy, Robert. Haynes Publishing, Great Britain, (1976). ISBN: 1-85260-412 3.

The Middle Sea. Norwich, John Julius. Chatto and Windus, Random House, London. (2006). ISBN: 0-7011-7608-3.

The Norman Conquest. Higham, N. J. Sutton Publishing Ltd. (1998). ISBN: 0-7509-1953-1.

Paradise. Eberhart, Dikkon. Stemmer House Inc. (1983). ISBN: 0-916144-52-6.

Saxon and Norman London. Clark, John. Board of Governors of the Museum of London. (1989). ISBN: 0-11-290458-0.

Spices. A History of a Temptation. Turner, Jack. Harper Collins, London (2005). ISBN 0.00 655173 . 4.

Timeline. Crichton, Michael. Ballantine Publishing (1999). ISBN: 0-345-4176-3

When Was Wales. Williams, Gwyn A. Penguin Books. (1985).

Vikings. Magnusson, Magnus. British Broadcasting Corp. (1980). ISBN: 0-370—30272-9.

1066. The Year of the Conquest. Howarth, David. Barnes and Noble Inc. (1993). ISBN: 0-88029-014-5.

1066. The Year of the Three Battles. McLynn, Frank. Pimlico Publishers (1999). ISBN: 0-7126-6672-9.

Biography

When John Wright retired as a reporter and columnist of 25 years experience, he knew nothing about fiction writing. He knew nothing about the soft skill of creating something out of nothing. Then he met two magi from out of the East on a bridge in Wales. They tempted him to try. Thus, The Healer.

Born in Owen Sound, Ontario, Canada, John has been writing all his adult life. A graduate of Ryerson's College journalism program, he has been a reporter, editor, columnist, magazine, travel and outdoor writer. He has won seven Ontario provincial awards and one national Canadian award. He finished his career as an outdoor writer with a focus on environmental issues.

An outdoorsman, hiker, camper, sailor and cruising skipper of his own 35-footsailer, he has rolled many of those outdoor experiences into his journal writings. When the first tracings of the plot for The Healer began to excite his mind, he hiked and traveled through The March, the border country between Wales and England, and found rich medieval history in a Shrewsbury library in an account of Norman invasion and Welsh resistance. The Healer and Knight Haralde were born, followed by a completed manuscript, The Welsh Lords. To come, the final outline of the fourth to be titled. Today, he lives with his wife Elaine on Canada's Bruce Peninsula on the shores of Lake Huron.

Manufactured by Amazon.ca
Bolton, ON